ETHIOPIA

— AND —

ERITREA

ETHIOPIA
— AND —
ERITREA

INSIGHTS INTO THE
PEACE NEXUS

Belete Belachew Yihun, Editor

TSEHAI
Publishers & Distributors

TSEHAI
Publishers & Distributors

ISBN: 978-1-59-907231-9 (Paperback), 978-1-59-907232-6 (Hardcover),
and 978-1-59-907233-3 (eBook)

Tsehai books may be purchased for educational, business, or sales promotional use. For more information, please contact our special sales department.

TSEHAI Publishers
Loyola Marymount University
1 LMU Drive, UH 3000, Los Angeles, CA 90045

www.tsehaipublishers.com
info@tsehaipublishers.com

First Edition

Publisher: Elias Wondimu
Layout and Typesetting: Befikadu Teka
Cover Design: Sara Martinez
Cover Photography: Aron Simeneh

A catalog record data for this book is available from:
Wemezekir Ethiopian National Library, Addis Ababa, Ethiopia
U.S. Library of Congress, Washington, DC, USA
British Library, London, UK

10 9 8 7 6 5 4 3 2 1

Printed in the United States of America

Los Angeles | Addis Ababa | Oxford

CONTENTS

Acronym	*ix*
Editor's Note	*1*
Foreword by Bahru Zewde	*4*

1 THORNY FAULT LINES IN THE ETHIOPIA-ERITREA
RELATIONSHIP: THE WAY FORWARD
   Belete Belachew Yihun

Introduction	9
Major Fault Lines	14
Political/Strategic Underpinnings	15
Security/Defense Considerations	21
Economic Imperatives	24
The Way Forward	31

2 GOOD PROSPECTS FOR PEACE BETWEEN ERITREA
AND ETHIOPIA
   Tekeste Negash

Background	39
Prelude to Badme, 1991–1998	42
Legacies of Colonialism	48
Eritrea as the Industrial Center of the Ethiopian Empire, and Addis Ababa Spoke Tigrinya by Night, 1952–74	51
The Fall of Haile Selassie and the Steady Decline of Eritrea and Eritreans in Ethiopian Affairs, 1974–1991	57
Ethiopia and Eritrea: Unequal Partners, 1991–2018	64
Encouraging Prospects for New Relations	70

3 PROSPECTS FOR MAINTAINING THE NEW ERITREA-
ETHIOPIA PEACE: LESSONS FROM THE PAST.
   Senai W. Andemariam

The Sinuous Eritrea-Ethiopia Relationship: Pre-1991	85
The 1890–1941 Period	85
The Fate of Eritrea Decided: 1945–1950	86
The Federation and Its Dissolution: 1952–1962	87
Struggle for Eritrean Independence: 1961–1991	88

Contents

The Sinuosity Continues Post-1991 and Ends with a
    Ruinous War: 1991–2000   90
Algiers Crafts the Peace Formula: June and December 2000   93
The Algiers Agreements of 2000   95
The "No Peace-No War" Years   98
The Pandora's Box of Good Tidings: The Rapprochement
    of 2018 and the Asmara/Jeddah Agreements   99
Look into the Future, Not the Past   101
Conclusion   106

4 THE ETHIOPIA-ERITREA RELATIONSHIP: REFLECTIONS ON PENDING LEGAL DISPUTES
Wondemagegn Tadesse

Introduction   113
The Boundary Dispute, the EEBC, and the
    Current State of the Dispute   114
Claims, the EECC, and the Current State   128
Other Legal Issues of Concern   142

5 EXAMINING THE ROLE OF STATE AND NON-STATE ACTORS FOR SUSTAINABLE PEACE BETWEEN ETHIOPIA AND ERITREA
Wegahta K. Sereke And Daniel R. Mekonnen

Introduction   145
The Overall Political Situation in Ethiopia and Eritrea   148
The Absence of Major State Institutions in Eritrea   150
The Role of Non-State Actors   153
Other Issues of Concern   157
Concluding Remarks   160

6 ERITREA-ETHIOPIA RAPPROCHEMENT AND ITS IMPACT ON FOREIGN POLICY.
Patrick Gilkes

Ethiopia and Eritrea Agreement and Joint Declaration   165
Djibouti   170
Somalia   176
Ethiopian Diplomacy   179

Contents

Kenya-Somalia   182
Somalia, Qatar, and the UAE   187
Red Sea Security   190
Sudan   193
IGAD and the Red Sea   197
Medemer   199
Eritrean Diplomacy   205
Integration   210

7 MAKING SENSE OF THE "DEAL"
Medhane Tadesse

Introduction: Imagining a Peace Deal on the Edge
    of Global and Local Politics.   217
The Precursor   221
The Ethiopian Agency   232
The Deal and Its Failure to Bring Peace.   237
By Way of Conclusion: Crisis of Intention or Implementation   245

Milestones: Ethiopia-Eritrea Relations in the Post-1991 Period   *249*

Contributors   *263*

Appendices

A. Agreement of Friendship and co-operation between the
    Transitional Government of Ethiopia and the Government
    of the State of Eritrea   229
B. Agreement Between The Government of the State of
    Eritrea and the Transitional Government of Ethiopia on the
    Establishment of the Joint High Ministerial Commission   233
C. Algiers Agreement between Ethiopia and Eritrea   239
D. Joint Declaration of Peace and Friendship between Eritrea
    and Ethiopia   247
E. Agreement on Peace, Friendship and Comprehensive
    Cooperation between the Federal Democratic Republic of
    Ethiopia and the State of Eritrea   249

Index   *251*

Acronym

AARSGA	Arab and African Coastal States of the Red Sea and the Gulf of Aden
AfDB	Africa Development Bank
AMISOM	African Union Mission in Somalia
ARSIWA	Articles on the Responsibility of States for Internationally Wrongful Acts
AU	African Union
AUHIP	Africa Union High-Level Implementation Panel
AUPSC	Africa Union Peace and Security Council
CSO	Civil Society Organization
EAC	East African Community
EEBC	Eritrea-Ethiopia Boundary Commission
EECC	Eritrea-Ethiopia Claims Commission
EEFORT	Endowment Fund for Tigray
ELA	Ethiopian Lawyers' Association
ELF	Eritrean Liberation Front
ELM	Eritrean Liberation Movement
ELS	Eritrean Law Society
EPLF	Eritrean People Liberation Front
EPRDF	Ethiopian Peoples' Revolutionary Democratic Front.
ERSTAS	Eritrean Shipping and Transit Agency Services
EU	European Union
FFC	Forces of Freedom and Change (Sudan)
FOCAC	Forum on China-Africa Cooperation
FRUD	Front for the Restoration of Unity and Democracy (Djibouti opposition group)

FTA	Free Trade Area
GERD	Great Ethiopian Renaissance Dam
ICC	International Criminal Court
ICJ	International Court of Justice
IGAD	Inter Governmental Authority for Development
KSA	Kingdom of Saudi Arabia
MoFA	Ministry of Foreign Affairs
OAU	Organization of Africa Unity
OPDO	Oromo Peoples' Democratic Organization
PFDJ	Peoples Front for Democracy and Justice
PTA	Preferential Trade Area
SITC	Standard International Trade Classification
SSG	Security Sector Governance
SSR	Security Sector Reform
TPLF	Tigray Peoples Liberation Front
UAE	United Arab Emirates
UN	United Nations
UNAMID	United Nations-Africa Mission in Darfur
UNCOI	United Nations Commission of Inquiry
UNGA	United Nations General Assembly
UNMEE	United Nations Mission in Eritrea and Ethiopia
UNMISS	United Nations Mission in South Sudan
UNSC	United Nations Security Council

Editor's Note

Belete Belachew Yihun

This project was conceived soon after the commencement of the Ethiopia-Eritrea rapprochement in July 2018. The emotional rollercoaster at full display and the resultant anticipations associated with the peace process, characterized by a series of incidents afterwards, lend a sense of urgency to the initiative. Soon an earnest discussion ensued among colleagues on how best to manage the unfolding thaw, with the keen purpose of informing the process of realizing meaningful and lasting peace, cooperation and integration between the two countries as well as the sub-region.

A group of Ethiopians, Eritreans and few expatriates readily committed to the task of producing chapters in their respective areas of specialization. Altogether, nine scholars partake in the project, and seven made it to the finish line. Here I would like to especially appreciate the encouragement and support of Tekeste Negash; and the dedications of all the contributors – Patrick Gilkes, Medhane Tadesse, Senai Woldeab, Weghata Sereke, Daniel Mekonnen and Wondemagegn Tadesse. I would also like to convey special gratitude to Prof. Bahru Zewde for writing the forward section.

Ethiopia and Eritrea share a contested and tumultuous past, replete with an equally wide range of polarized interpretations and perspectives. Observers and pundits often amplify politically sensitized viewpoints readily tailored to reflect leading sentiments of the time. As far as Ethiopia and Eritrea are concerned, historical accounts as well as policy orientations more or less have fixated on these unnatural characterizations, their interactions swinging the extremes just in accordance with the dominant sentiments and perceptions. Self reflection, critical appraisal and sober assessment of developments have been visibly missing, or intentionally misconstrued, in the overall discourse analysis.

As a result, not only historical accounts and policy prerogatives, but also the very existence of the two people and countries as well as the well being of others in the sub-region have been affected. The disastrous thirty-year civil war (1961-1991) was replicated soon after Eritrea's independence, this time lasting two decades (1998-2018), in the process taxing involved parties heavily. All the altercations in the peace-conflict dynamics were perplexing in their intensity as they were unprincipled and whimsical in nature. More specifically, events of the post-1991 period have yet to be properly analyzed and understood.

Closer assessment of developments in the post-1991 period reveals some striking parallels in the overall matrix defining the Ethiopia-Eritrea relationship. These realities manifest in their local, bilateral and regional interactions. Irrespective of the peace-conflict situation, both remain heavily invested in the affair of the other and endeavor to dictate the course of events unilaterally. Deep rooted psycho-social attachments have apparently forced them to bypass and disregard norm references dictating inter-state relations. Whether the agenda is peace, cooperation or regional integration, securing immediate interests at the expense of the other for long has determined the outcome, often with unintended consequences for both countries and the region.

Now that Ethiopia and Eritrea have decided to mend fences, attention is being fixed on analyzing and understanding the whole issue in its entirety. In a region besieged by layers of local, bilateral and multilateral complexities, and diverse group of spoilers actively feuding to alter proceedings in their favor, achieving this might not be an easy task. Asymmetrical interests and viewpoints from multiple actors on the ground have constantly influenced the way the two countries handle bilateral and regional affairs. No wonder, a vicious circle of peace and conflict have dotted their interactions in the recent past. Therefore, this time around, attention should be categorically focused on making this process deliver meaningful and lasting results. This in turn requires cascading priorities and unpacking the complex realities surrounding the process.

This project was launched with the objective to positively inform the rapprochement between the two countries. Peace, cooperation and integration should not be the sole prerogatives of the political elite. The euphoric tendencies and political sensitizations, as manifested at the beginning of the accord in July 2018, unnerved keen observers of the situation. The emotional rollercoaster and the disastrous consequences of the mismanaged affairs of the past three decades simply would not merit the same approach in taking the two countries forward. Ethiopia and Eritrea, specifically the people, can't afford to squander this opportunity.

The political elites obviously have their designs and plans. But their schemes, if not grounded on practical realities, are fallible to the slightest of challenges. Apparently, far complex factors are at play, each potentially determining the progression of events. Unless otherwise all the critical elements in the equation are carefully appraised and accommodated, then, it would be tantamount to squandering a rare opportunity. Immediate political considerations of those driving the process aside, for the current Ethiopia-Eritrea rapprochement to yield the desired result, a number of crucial issues require careful consideration. These range from understanding the overall post-1991 dynamics to critical appraisal of local political realities in the two countries, objective assessment of the technical and legal hurdles and scrutiny of the geo-strategic underpinnings informing the whole process. The very resilience of the process, with direct impacts on peace, cooperation and integration in the sub-region, basically depends on crafting a comprehensive package addressing these diverse factors. Rather, all depends on the effective management of the peace process, with all the elements skillfully integrated and addressed. These salient issues consistently manifest throughout the volume.

Engaging Eritrean and Ethiopian scholars in a project designed to assess mechanisms ensuring the sensitive issue of peace and cooperation obviously requires craft and caution. In this vein, a deliberate and conscious decision to circumvent extended discussion of historic events, specifically those before the 1991 period, while forcing the contributors to focus only on their areas of expertise, is applied in earnest. All participants have approached their topics with commendable self-restraint and academic rigor, focusing on points potentially impeding the ongoing peace process, and aiming at the assigned task on how best to inform policy decision makers in both countries.

It has been worthwhile stating here my sincere gratitude and appreciation to all the contributors. They have readily accepted the invitation to participate in the project merely out of sheer sense of duty; and irrespective of their busy schedules have managed to produce excellent chapters. Eritrean and Ethiopian scholars, together with an equally concerned expatriate, brainstorming on how best to bring lasting peace and cooperation in the two countries and the region at large is indeed a rare treat. Let's hope our effort contributes to the realization of meaningful peace, cooperation and development between Ethiopia and Eritrea!

Foreword

Bahru Zewde

In the summer of 2018, the Horn of Africa was yet again the focus of global attention—only this time for the right reasons. A daring move by the newly elected prime minister of Ethiopia, Dr. Abiy Ahmed, brought to a dramatic end the nearly two decades of frozen relations between Eritrea and Ethiopia. Following the costly 1998–2000 war, the border between the two countries had been sealed in a Horn of Africa edition of the Iron Curtain. This, as Sereke and Mekonnen have noted in this volume, was arguably the longest period of total cessation of cross-border relations in the history of the region. The public euphoria that attended the reciprocal state visits of the two leaders told its own story of the enduring bonds of the two peoples. The opening of both terrestrial and air links reunited long-separated families. The emotions exhibited during those family reunions were stark reminders, if any were needed, of the inhumanity of war.

President Isaias Afwerki of Eritrea took this euphoric mood one step further when he boldly stated (as quoted by Tekeste in this volume), "From now onwards, anyone who says that the Eritreans and Ethiopians are two people has not understood the truth. Eritreans and Ethiopians are one people in two countries." But then, he said more or less the same thing in 1991 in the wake of Eritrea's de facto independence, and the whole world knows what happened seven years later. The EPLF-TPLF/EPRDF honeymoon that attended the simultaneous seizure of state power—the former in Asmara and the latter in Addis Ababa—was rudely interrupted by a war more ferocious than the one that had raged for thirty years. The agreements that were signed between the two countries following Eritrea's formal independence in 1993, and the series of ministerial meetings alternately held in Asmara and Addis Ababa, could not give the camaraderie that had emanated from the joint struggle and victory the institutional basis it needed.

That experience is quite sobering when one contemplates the unfolding of future relations between the two countries. As Belete emphasizes in this collection, one should learn from the mistakes or failures of the post-1991 honeymoon in order not to repeat them. Already the initial euphoria has subsided. The borders have been shut once again. Abiy was awarded the 2019 Nobel Peace Prize in recognition of his peace initiatives not only in Eritrea but also in the Horn of Africa as a whole. But President Isaias seems to be sulking at his exclusion from the honors, shirking even the elementary courtesy of sending a congratulatory message to his partner in peace. Abiy has promised to celebrate the honor together with Isaias in Asmara. It remains to be seen whether that is going to materialize.

Even more disturbing for Eritreans is the fact that the dawn of peace has not been attended by any political liberalization in their country. The constitution remains suspended. Political prisoners and journalists remain in detention. Civil society organizations are practically nonexistent. The national military service that has inflicted so much misery and hardship on Eritrean youth and their families still remains in force; nay, its silver jubilee was celebrated with much fanfare a year after the thawing of relations. The only beneficiary of the peace accord seems to be President Isaias himself, who has come out from the diplomatic cold and begun to exercise the role of regional peace broker. The expeditious lifting of the sanctions that had been imposed since 2009 was of more benefit to the Eritrean leadership, which was the main target of the sanctions, than the Eritrean people.

The euphoria that Eritreans exhibited during Abiy's visit to Asmara emanated as much from the anticipation of such domestic reforms as from joy over reunions with their kith and kin across the border. The juxtaposition of a democratizing Ethiopia and an incorrigibly autocratic Eritrea cannot bode well for the sustainability of the peace process. In fact, Isaias's closing of the border has been attributed to fears of an exodus of Eritreans to the more convivial atmosphere in Ethiopia, as well as apprehension of the destabilization of his own regime in Asmara, particularly from the marginalized TPLF and/or its agents.

The TPLF remains a complicating factor in the new rapprochement. Since its loss of power in Addis Ababa, it has effectively barricaded itself in its ancestral stronghold and shows no inclination to bow to the inevitable and adjust itself to the democratization process. Isaias has not concealed his glee at this dramatic turn of events—from his now famous "game over" statement to his flying over the region to commune with leaders of the Amhara region in Bahir Dar. Viewed from this angle, the concerted struggle of the TPLF and EPRDF against the Derg regime in the second half of the

1980s looks like an isolated episode in a history otherwise characterized by estrangement and mutual suspicion. Isaias has apparently neither forgotten nor forgiven the TPLF for the escalation of the 1998 border clash into a national mobilization that inflicted a heavy defeat on his forces. Yet the sustainability of peace between the two countries partly hangs on the resolution of the TPLF problem. At the end of the day, Tigray is the region that is closest to Eritrea both territorially and linguistically.

The global and regional dimension of the peace process is also something that is worthy of consideration, as discussed extensively by both Medhane and Gilkes in this volume. The United States and the European Union have both had their share of influence in bringing about the rapprochement. Above all, the Gulf States (notably Saudi Arabia and the UAE) have played a pivotal role in bringing the two leaders together. Indeed, while the first peace accord (the Joint Declaration of Peace and Friendship) was signed in Asmara on July 9, 2018, the second (the Agreement on Peace, Friendship and Comprehensive Cooperation) was signed in Jidda on September 16, 2018. The latter was attended by the award of the highest Saudi medals to the two signatories.

It is an axiom of diplomatic history that no power, be it global or regional, takes initiatives for altruistic reasons. While the strategic interests of the global powers are all too well known, more novel is the assertiveness of the Gulf States, who have been flexing their muscles in the Red Sea area in recent years. The Saudis have even gone to the extent of establishing an exclusive club known as the Arab and African Coastal States of the Red Sea and the Gulf of Aden (AARSGA). The restriction of this club to the littoral states effectively shuts off other stakeholders in the region, particularly Ethiopia, which has demonstrated its intention to rebuild its navy and is taking concrete steps to that end.

Abiy's peace initiative has not been confined to Eritrea. He followed it up with a series of diplomatic démarches with varying degrees of success. He tried to reconcile Somalia with Kenya and Djibouti with Eritrea. Perhaps the most successful initiative has been the tripartite accord that he initiated between Eritrea, Ethiopia, and Somalia. He also succeeded in bringing the two belligerent parties in South Sudan to conclude their nth agreement. More significantly, he has brokered with the African Union what appears to be a durable transitional arrangement between the military government and the civilian opposition in Sudan. All these initiatives are indicative of a broader agenda of regional integration, possibly culminating in a confederation of Horn of Africa states. Idealistic as that may appear under the circumstances, it is an ultimate objective that more than one observer has suggested as the final solution to the thorny problems of the subregion. Here again, the challenge is to transform what have so far been personal initiatives into an institutional one, possibly through the agency of a revitalized IGAD, although the broader scope of that organization (including as it does the East African states) might pose a problem.

The Eritrean-Ethiopian rapprochement has been predicated on acceptance of the 2000 Algiers Agreement, yet the decisions of the commissions that have emanated from that agreement still remain in abeyance. It is in that context that Senai and Wondemagegn argue in thier contributions that one cannot advance into the future by forgetting the past. Whether those decisions can be enforced in toto under the current circumstances remains problematic. It is worth noting that both agreements signed in 2018 refer only to the boundary decisions, with implementation of the two other decisions apparently untenable. Abiy's rhetoric is all about building bridges rather than borders.

In the longer *durée*, though, one might ask whether it would not be better to forget the past. For history—and historiography—has been a battleground in relations between the two countries. The thirty-year war was fought as much in the history books as on the battlefield. Two irreconcilable interpretations of the history of the two countries (or one country) have dominated the discourse. For one side, Eritrea and Ethiopia have existed as independent entities from time immemorial. For the other, Eritrea (at least the highland part) was part and parcel of Ethiopia until the advent of Italian colonialism. For one side, federation was a formula imposed by the US-led imperialist forces. For the other, it was a solution adopted to accommodate the strong unionist feeling that prevailed in Eritrea. Now that Eritrea has won its independence, fought yet another bitter war with its erstwhile annexer, or motherland, languished in two decades of cold war, and opened what hopefully will be a new chapter of peaceful coexistence, all those historical arguments sound irrelevant. What are needed are pragmatic solutions to address the longstanding problems of governance and development both countries face. This volume hopefully contributes to a better understanding of the contemporary challenges as well as possible ways of overcoming them.

1

THORNY FAULT LINES IN THE ETHIOPIA-ERITREA RELATIONSHIP
the way forward

Belete Belachew Yihun

Introduction

Now that Ethiopia and Eritrea have decided to usher in a period of mutual cooperation and friendship, creating mechanisms guaranteeing resilient and durable arrangements remains a priority. An assortment of complex hurdles can potentially frustrate practical execution of the process, all the more underlining the need for the careful handling of flashpoints and fault lines. As was the case elsewhere, imperfections abound within their interactions. Unique sets of association the two have sustained, some traceable to the pre-1991 period, continuously have informed their socio-cultural, economic, and political life, often resulting in indecipherable altercations. As a result, the union-separation, love-hate, cooperation-conflict dichotomy permeates the entire discourse.

Understanding these subtleties, designing a mutually beneficial line of engagement and finding a middle ground long eluded the two, ultimately spoiling opportunities for coexistence and their becoming positive forces of change in the region. Coming out of a twenty-year slumber, Ethiopia and Eritrea awoke to new realities and dispensations. Current economic, political, and demographic realities set both countries wide apart, rendering the prewar dynamics inapplicable to current situations. Yet points of discord that basically infused the violent conflict two decades ago still remain relevant. If left unattended and not properly addressed, these issues are bound to impinge on ongoing attempts at rapprochement between Ethiopia and Eritrea. An attempt is made here to unpack the thorny issues at the very center of the costly discord and suggest possible ways out of the impasse.

The post-1991 period simply fits the narrative where opportunities were squandered over political and economic trifles, and untoward sacrifices were required to justify hegemonic perceptions. Viewed in retrospect, all attempts at political posturing, incessant wars, human suffering, and economic deprivations were considered nonissues in the face of missed opportunities that could have immensely transformed the entire region. As long as it fits their immediate political designs, those at the helm of power on both sides of the divide jump on the bandwagon of policy frameworks without due consideration of associated side effects.[1]

Often times, as actions witnessed over the past twenty-eight years corroborate, respective rulers easily disregard the fact, specifically in the post-1991 setting, that Ethiopia and Eritrea are two autonomous states with distinct policy, strategic, and ideological orientations. Rather, gross violation of the basic tenets governing interstate relations were in rampant display, easily justified through abstract notions of socio-cultural ties, euphoric representation of developments, and selected application of past anecdotes.[2] Within this context, agreements were easily inked, affairs of state were left to whimsical and emotional explanations, and the love-hate, cooperation-conflict matrix was justified. Norm references governing their relationships start and end with the political elite, and their justifications are expected to be beyond reproach or scrutiny.

More problematic, in this regard, has been the tendency in times of conviviality to take good relations for granted and let proceedings dictate the course. Agreements were reached, and various ministerial and technical commissions and advisory groups were left to wither away unattended. If any follow-up meetings and consultations occur, they happen on the sidelines of other functions. This was the case in the post-1993 period. The Joint High Ministerial Commission (JHMC) only met four times between 1993 and 1998. Even then, confusion and indecisiveness had reined in the

---

1   Dr. Tekeda Alemu's assessment in the January 2019 CDRC Digest remains the most valid and comprehensive take in this regard. Tekeda, "Conundrum of Present Ethiopian Foreign Policy," 5–11.

2   Reid, "Caught in the Headlights of History,"467–88; Iyob, "Ethiopian-Eritrean Conflict," 659–82.

handling of delicate issues. One can't escape feeling *déjà vu* all over again with the ongoing rapprochement initiative, for formal consultations and follow-ups are clearly missing.[3]

Not only Ethiopia and Eritrea but also the region bore the brunt of these vagaries in the relationship. The flagrant display of conviviality in the immediate post-1991 period was as confusing to others in the region as had their intense animosity proved destabilizing. Probably indicative of common socio-cultural and historic roots, the two have demonstrated a knack for blowing developments out of proportion and riding the torrents' currents. Confusion reigns in the region as well during periods of accord. The Ethiopia-Eritrea relationship, as is the case elsewhere where the unconventional abounds, has remained an enigma yet to be properly analyzed and understood.[4]

Still, one can't escape the premonition that the very absence of resilience in these endeavors bespeaks to the lack of depth and integrity in the entire approach. Blatantly put, the post-1991 dynamics involving Ethiopia and Eritrea has fallen short of feeding into the broader regional picture. Rather, the way the whole matter has unfolded gives the distinct impression that the remaining states in the region have been relegated to secondary consideration, picked or dismissed at whims per the exigencies of the two countries.[5] Now it has become absolutely essential to remedy the situation and devise an approach that addresses bilateral and regional misgivings in their totality.

A distinct characteristic, standing in stark contrast to the normal conduct of interstate affairs, has been the party domination of Ethiopia-Eritrea relationships in the post-1991 period. Negotiations, agreements, and even conflicts manifest ideological orientations and tactical/strategic imperatives of the ruling elements, easily projected so as to assume a national agenda.[6] Unabashed displays of intimacy in times of cordiality match intense animosities observed during periods of open conflict. Popular sentiments, propaganda campaigns, and even scholarly output all readily align with the whims of those dictating proceedings from the top. Perceptions and justifications easily alternate between the extremes, lest a culprit is assigned by simple consensus. Unfortunately, the rules governing succcssion of states and interstate relations have been time and again

---

3   Belete, "Recent Ethiopia-Eritrea Diplomatic Thaw," 36–40.

4   Reid, "Ghosts of the Mesafint," 189–211; Taddia, "Post-Twentieth-Century Eritrea," 7–29; Alemseged, "Not with Them, Not without Them," 459–91.

5   Belete, Conduct of Ethiopia's Foreign Policy.

6   Reid, "Old Problems in New Conflicts,"369–401.

disregarded.[7] Procuring immediate advantages from the process has for long remained *modus operandi*, with respective governments in Addis Ababa and Asmara keen to apply them in earnest.[8]

One also has to factor in the personality traits, expertise, and governance styles of respective leaders to best understand long-existing interactions between Ethiopia and Eritrea in the post-1991 period. Competing and at times contradicting approaches pursued in the post-1991 period, characterized by the personalities of Isaias and Meles, the *modus operandi* of the TPLF and EPLF/PFDJ, as well as the ideologies and governance styles of Ethiopia and Eritrea, are considered central to the previous discord. Latent feuds and attempts at the unilateral manipulation of proceedings have been rampant, and no one ascertains that this will not be the case going forward with the current rapprochement. Existing perceptions within the respective ruling groups are still claimed to have been instrumental in shaping events.[9]

In this regard, dismissing the probability that each side would scheme to maneuver the course in ways guaranteeing short-term advantages is tantamount to a total disregard of realities on the ground. In the absence of recognized reference points facilitating discussions, the side capable of marshaling the best expertise and acumen is bound to reap the most benefits. Obviously, the government of President Isaias possesses the comparative advantage now, viewed from the perspective of the caliber of current leadership circles in the two countries. But the situation equally poses challenges to Asmara in particular and the peace process in general.[10] Unless Asmara reforms soon, at long ran the process may prove detrimental to the overall socio-economic and political life of the people and the country. Of course, this comes at the expense of further jeopardizing the initiative for peace, security, and cooperation.

---

7   Kohen. "State Succession in Matters of International Responsibility" (Provisional Report).

8   Belete, "Recent Ethiopia-Eritrea Diplomatic Thaw"; "Conduct of Ethiopia's Foreign Policy.

9   Some scholars stretch the argument even further, attesting that the TPLF's ploy to unilaterally countervail Eritrea's economic and political imminence of the early 1990s, shrouding it as Ethiopian policy, contributed to the impasse, and even associating the whole dynamic with deep-rooted conflicts of interest between the TPLF and EPLF. Tekeste and Tronvoll, Brothers at War, 12–18; Tekie, Shattered Illusions, Broken Promises, 272; Plaut, Understanding Eritrea, 30–32; Wrong, I Didn't Do It for You, 366.

10 Woldemikael, "Promise and Pitfalls," 16–19.

Given historical precedents, it would come as no surprise if the ongoing peace initiatives between Ethiopia and Eritrea relapse to the bad old days of mutual suspicion or cyclic bickering. There are enough spoilers from within the region and afar that can easily stir the process to the negative. Any change in the status quo will induce dramatic altercations on geostrategic alignments, in the process offsetting the equation on how any peace process is being handled. Never has Ethiopia-Eritrea affairs been solely determined by the two; and it will not be the case in the foreseeable future.[11] Viewed in this context, therefore, it remains incumbent on the negotiating parties to comprehensively address their basic fault lines and points of disagreement. Failures to do so have taxed the two countries and people enormously over the last two decades, and not resolving the problem now will come at an even greater risk of wasting a rare opportunity altogether.

No one can doubt or diminish the value of peace, nor can anyone with a right mind relish the previous dispensation that for decades has kept the two countries and their people apart. Such an approach, in turn, has effectively deprived the entire region of the prospect for peaceful coexistence and mutual development. However, peace comes at a cost, more so in a volatile and complex region like the Horn of Africa.[12] Objective realities on the ground as well as a practical application of proceedings demand careful handling. Abstract notions like peace and economic integration are often associated with varying interpretations, with each party affixing specific qualifiers to the process.

There exists ample historical precedent refuting the notion of "peace" as an all-encompassing end in this volatile and dynamic region. In this regard, Ethiopia and Eritrea might approach practical negotiations with irreconcilable denominators, in the process trampling upon delicate geostrategic alignments in the sub-region. The integrity and resilience of the ongoing peace initiative between Ethiopia and Eritrea, therefore, depends on how the process appraises and accommodates the concerns, interests, and expectations of respective citizens as well as key actors in the region and beyond.[13] Below, issues associated with politics, security, and economy

---

11 Shumet, Unionists and Separatists; Tekeste, "Italy and Its Relations," 417–52; Zewde Retta, Ya Ertera Guday; Lionel Cliffe, "Regional Dimensions of Conflict," 89–111.

12 Muller, "Back to Square One," 22–25; Wrong, "When Peace is a Problem"; Plaut, "Eritrea and Ethiopia Have Made Peace,12–14.

13 Mengisteab and Okbazghi, Anatomy of an African Tragedy, 283; Bereket, While Waiting or Working for Change, 9–25; Mosley, "Eritrea-Ethiopia Rapprochement," 7–11; Woldemariam, "Eritrea-Ethiopia Thaw."

as primary drivers of Ethiopia-Eritrea relations in the post-1991 period will be assessed.

Major Fault Lines

The post-1991 reality poses a critical departure in Ethiopia-Eritrea relations. Preexisting historical and cultural ties simply haven't prepared the two sides for the daunting task of properly managing bilateral affairs as distinct sovereign nation-states.[14] Rather, there emerged the tendency to disregard internationally sanctioned norm-references guiding interstate relations, with the focus on emotional and whimsical considerations. It is these considerations that somehow muddled the operating field and contributed to the creation and sustenance of multiple fault lines.

Not only the newly ordained state of Eritrea but the traditionally bureaucratic Ethiopia as well easily disregarded the cardinal rule of succession of states. Interactions have been mostly restricted to rhetorical and emotional aspects, applied fairly easily in accordance with the degree and level of the apprehension of involved parties. Foremost a factor contributing to the status quo has been this disregard to a principled and institutional approach by respective governments in Addis Ababa and Asmara. Developments in the past two and a half decades have amply demonstrated the tendency on both sides to resort to the unconventional, thereby jeopardizing the resilience and comprehensiveness of their relationship.

The recent past has witnessed numerous conflict-cooperation matrices in the relationship between Ethiopia-and Eritrea, with potential ripple effects on the wider region. Akin to the unconventional character of their interactions, the two countries have displayed a unique tendency to tread uncharted territory, rushing into unsolicited accords and headlong confrontations. Controversial and inconclusive agreements were signed in July 1993 and July/September 2018.

More daunting a prospect in these deals has been the inclination to stretch the conventional limits in interstate relations, with the introduction of provisions not usually applied elsewhere. The proclivity to yield and compromise in times of accord has easily matched the intensity displayed during periods of conflict. Fraternal feelings then give way in an irrational manner to enmity, forcing the two countries into an open display of animosity and headlong confrontation. In particular, the current agreement falls far below basic standards, with most of the articles in the Asmara and Jidda accords too generic to be applied to any other given state. In this case,

---

14   Tekeste, *Eritrea and Ethiopia: The Federal Experience.*

Eritrea saw it fit to insert a clause directly related to a speedy resolution of the border problem, while the other signatory failed to make the process binding to its immediate interests.

Fault lines in Ethiopia-Eritrea relations manifest on various levels, encompassing the political/strategic, security/defense, and economic imperatives. None of these dynamics have been properly addressed, with the potential to muddle bilateral affairs in the foreseeable future. Each of these factors has unilaterally and collectively contributed to the state of affairs between the two countries. Viewed in hindsight, no serious effort was made to approach these matters in their totality. More significantly, if not properly handled, irrespective of local, regional, and global realities simultaneously driving the accord, the two countries stand the high risk of jeopardizing the current delicate peace process, which has yet to stabilize and yield the desired result.

Political/Strategic Underpinnings

Both the July 1993[15] and July/September 2018 deals[16]presupposed peace, friendship, and cooperation, and both underlined cultural, historic, and strategic ties as core values guiding interactions between the two countries. Each instance was antedated by political upheavals in Ethiopia, which somehow overlap with the broader Eritrean interests. Either by coincidence or design, Eritrea almost always has featured in Ethiopia's political life, often generating controversies and marking the overall process in un-delineable terms. Short of apportioning blames, though, the whole dynamic begs

15 The Agreement of Friendship and Cooperation, Addis Ababa, 30 July 1993 and the subsequent twenty-eight protocols signed in Asmara in September the same year include specific provisions on economic, social, monetary and finance, technical and scientific, cultural, transport and communication, trade and energy, natural resources and environment, foreign policy, security and defense, and immigration and boundary issues.

16 The five pillars deal signed in Asmara on 9 July 2018, the Joint Declaration of Peace and Friendship, stipulates a) the state of war that existed between the two countries has come to an end, and a new era of peace and friendship has been ushered in; b) both countries will work to promote close cooperation in political, economic, social, cultural, and security areas; c) transport, trade, and telecommunication ties will be resumed and diplomatic ties and activities renewed; d) border decisions will be implemented; and e) both countries will work together to guarantee regional peace, development, and cooperation. The Jeddah Agreement of 16 September 2018 basically copied the Asmara deal, adding two articles: one on defense, trade, and investment, and another providing for the establishment of a high-level joint committee to guide and oversee the implementation of the agreement.

existential and rhetorical questions on both sides as to how and why this has remained the case. In other words, preexisting perceptions, past intricacies, and historical baggage effectively prevented the two from exercising formal relations. A comprehensive assessment of facts on the ground as a point of departure has yet to inform policy deliberations.

A baseline to this argument is the fact that Eritrea attained *de facto* independence in 1991, sanctioned by a controversial 1993 referendum. Since then, it has joined the community of world states, of which Ethiopia proved the foremost facilitator. Eritrea has earned and rightly deserves a fair share of equal treatment and a taste of accountability. In this regard, no preferential treatment or countervailing of formal procedures should be reserved for its sake, in particular by Ethiopia. Eritrea has requested this and Ethiopia has repeatedly obliged. The operating theater is supposed to accommodate both parties on an equal footing, leaving no room for mismanagement and double standards in the execution of bilateral relations. Delicacies, subtleties, and undercurrent realities informing their interactions equally demand careful scrutiny of the guiding principles; and extra vigilance in practical applications is required across the divide.

Unfortunately, the July 1993 agreement, though relatively detailed and later augmented by additional protocols and the establishment of the JHMC in September the same year, soon proved to be unethical, whimsical, and irrational in most indexes. Hindsight provides the tool to appraise the conduct of the deal as well as its execution on both sides. It is now evident that the preconditions for later altercations were inadvertently laid during these earlier times. The two sides chose to bend the rules as long as it served their purpose and put immediate party interests before that of the nation-state. This, in particular, was evident on the part of Ethiopia's leaders, who appear to have been hell-bent on appeasing and ingratiating themselves to their compatriots in arms in Eritrea.

A central consideration dictating their interactions, as was provided for in the 1993 agreement, was the desire to pursue similar goals in matters pertinent to the entire region encompassing the Horn and the Middle East.[17] Ethiopia and Eritrea soon aligned their political and security agendas in dealing with regional issues (Somalia, Sudan, IGAD, and PTA) as well as the OAU, the UN, and similar multilateral organizations. Transcending

---

17 MoFA. Ethio-Ertra yegara Commission 1, 3. Protocol Agreement of Cooperation on Foreign Affairs between the Transitional Government of Ethiopia and the Government of the State of Eritrea, 27 September 1993; MOU on the Implementation of the Ethio-Eritrean Protocol Agreement on Foreign Affairs, 13 May 1994.

conventional norms, statements, decisions, and even policy recommendations coming out of Addis Ababa and Asmara were verbatim copies with almost no significant differences in wording and tone. However, it soon became evident that the whole process hinged only on prior consultations, with no overarching principles as well as policy and strategic frameworks guiding their interactions.[18]

Indicative of the non-normative approach in the conduct of Ethiopia-Eritrea accord was the protocol for cooperation on diplomatic and consular services. Both agreed to represent the other in third countries or international forums and also to issue joint visas. Though circulars outlining this were circulated to their respective embassies and representatives abroad, practical problems soon started to emerge in the application of the procedures. The protocol entered into action without specifying types of consular services (mainly related to citizenship), without identifying countries eligible for the service, without outlining the financial and logistical details governing the process, and without preparing the vital legal documents mandating that service providers expedite consular affairs.[19]

Foremost in the agenda driving the 1993 accord was the perceived bondage between the TPLF and EPLF, who assumed the singular role of unilaterally dictating proceedings in their respective governments. Grandiose political and economic designs somehow enabled the two vanguard political entities to prevaricate on norm-references, which rather require caution and institutionalization. As a result, affairs of state were left to political power-mongers brandishing complementary ideological frameworks. Interstate relations, supposed to transcend party lines, were hijacked by specific groups; the fates of the two people and countries were left to a few decision makers; and, as a result, a legacy of suspicion, prevarication, and superficiality prevailed in ensuing interactions.

Ethiopia-Eritrea relations in the post-1991 period often have hinged on shared adversaries, past or present. In this regard, eliminating the military junta (the *Derg*, 1974-91) long infused a sense of shared mission, thereby determining their collective disposition in matters pertinent to local affairs, the region, and beyond.[20] Following their accession to power, the two, in collaboration with like-minded allies and sponsors from within and abroad,

---

18 Documents prepared by the two governments in relation to the revitalizations process of IGAD in 1996 corroborate this assertion.

19 MoFA. Ethio-Ertra Yegara Commission 2, 6. African Directorate to the Office of the Minister 12 April 1995. Ethio-Ertra yegara Commission 2, 5. To Consular Section of the Ministry of the Interior, 24 April 1995.

20 Milkias, "U.S. Foreign Policy towards Africa," 58–81.

earnestly advocated the introduction of new dispensations presumably tenable to the whole region. Some of the proposals and initiatives succeeded, while others faltered. When assessed critically, though, the baseline informing their ill conceptions of the overall dynamics and the subsequent resistance to these initiatives emanate from the very predisposition of their collective viewpoints, which they endeavored to impress on others *ad infinitum*. Other equally pertinent considerations and subtleties, usually associated with good governance, democratization, and adherence to international norms, which ought to be seriously appraised, were simply discarded or taken for granted.[21]

Rather, the ruling political factions in Ethiopia and Eritrea inadvertently put themselves in a situation unable to withstand alternate realities. Resistance to their version of political, economic, and social arrangements soon emerged on multiple levels, cornering them collectively and separately. Bilaterally conceived ideas of regional peace, security, and cooperation likewise were met with counterproposals and initiatives. More daunting a challenge to the Ethiopia-Eritrea joint venture came from within in the form of serious discord between the two parties.[22] Practical considerations soon prevailed, testing the resilience and applicability of unsolicited concessions and designs. Simply put, while rushing into the 1993 agreement the rulers of Ethiopia and Eritrea disregarded the cardinal rule governing interstate relations by not abiding by established norm-references and the rule of succession of states. Rather, governments in Addis Ababa and Asmara readily dominated the discourse analysis and narrative in ways befitting their preconceived ideas and notions.

It required a jostling realization, particularly on the part of Ethiopia, to break the slumber. In less than five years, practical considerations made it abundantly clear to Ethiopian rulers that they were losing out on the cheap bargain they had stumbled onto in 1993. The JHMC couldn't pick up the pieces of the various negotiations and consultations it had conducted; rather, it became apparent that Ethiopia was on the losing end as a result of the concessions it had readily made to Eritrea.[23]

It soon became evident that Ethiopia had compromised the integrity and interests of the state at the expense of past camaraderie and illusions of common bondage. Before the second round of consultative meetings of the JHMC in Asmara in 1995, disagreements on interpretation and

---

21   Mengisteab and Okbazghi, Anatomy of an African Tragedy, 277–85; Bereket, "While Waiting," 8–26.

22   Tekeste and Tronvoll, Brothers at War,12–18.

23   MoFA. Ethio-Ertra yegara Commission 2, 6. Ambassador Awalom Abdu (Ethiopian embassy, Asmara) to African Directorate, 13 September 1995.

implementation of the various protocols and agreements manifested. For those involved in the process, the honeymoon period was over, and the stark reality of tensions and even conflict loomed on the horizon. A resort to violence and war had been long simmering, and it was only a matter of time for it to occur.[24]

In the buildup to the 1998 war, Ethiopia endeavored to wriggle out of a tight situation that was basically of its own making. Eritrea, for its part, pressed Ethiopia hard, demanding full execution and delivery in accordance to the spirit and tenets of the accord. In a way, the fact that the two parties came to grips with the complexities informing interstate relations, and also that they gradually developed distinct tastes and appetites in handling regional and global matters, had contributed to the impasse.[25] An accord that primarily hinged on abstract notions, emotional grounds, and unsolicited frameworks simply faltered when met with practical challenges and realities. All that remained was a spark that could easily ignite the already volatile and highly charged environment. Claims to the previously insignificant portion of the common boundary readily provided the excuse, which the belligerent parties blew out of proportion. In a dramatic turn of events, the love affair soon turned into unjustifiable bloodshed and wanton destruction, with adverse effects on the immediate region.[26]

Even then, the managerial aspect of war as instrument of statecraft on the part of Ethiopia left all wanting for more wisdom and farsightedness. Short of the frantic display of punctured ego and unleashing the might of the nation-state to punish Eritrea for breaching the trust bestowed on it so irrationally, Ethiopia fell below standard in most indexes. Protracted war and conflict, astronomical human, material, social, political, and economic sacrifice, polarizing strategic goals governing bilateral and regional affairs, meaningless concessions, the inability to capitalize on the win on the war front, the tendency to prevaricate on national interests, and the farcical track record on the diplomatic front all came to define the 1998–2000 war period and subsequent developments.

More dramatic in this regard were the blunders associated with the Algiers Agreement of 2000 and the management of the binding decisions

---

24 Tekeste and Tronvoll, Brothers at War, 25–35; Plaut, Understanding Eritrea, 28–31; Wrong, "I Didn't Do It for You," 366.

25 In this regard, discord emerged on how to deal with Sudan, Somalia, and the Great Lakes region, and a competition of sorts developed on who assumed the upper hand in dictating proceedings. See Johnson, Root Causes of Sudan's Civil Wars, 102, and Prunier, Africa's World War, 67.

26 Leenco, "Ethiopia-Eritrea War," 369–88; Plaut, Understanding Eritrea, 31–32.

of the Eritrea-Ethiopia Boundary Commission of 2002.[27] The entire process leading to and following these legally binding procedures bespeaks negatively of the statesmanship of Ethiopian leaders of the time.[28] As was the case during the honeymoon times of the early 1990s, the postwar period has equally shaped the future trajectories of both countries as well as the region. Akin to their time-tested proclivity for grand posturing, the border issue accorded center stage as the primary and at times sole issue contributing to their discord.[29] No serious attempt was made to resolve the flagrant conflict in its totality, with due emphasis on underlying economic factors driving them apart by the day. This selective representation ultimately handicapped the farcical peace process that ended up frustrating both parties.

Rather, the two keenly advanced complex policy frameworks, in the process deterring any attempt at reexamining their losing streaks for two decades. Frantic gestures at characterizing the other irrelevant and any reconciliation attempt inconsequential, the crass destabilization missions launched against each other on multiple fronts, projection of their conflicts into the affairs of the region, proxy wars undertaken in Somalia, intense diplomatic debacles, and the resultant sanctions regime imposed on Eritrea, to mention only major cases in point, all testify to the level and nature of the conflict situation the belligerent parties and others in the immediate vicinity were forced to endure. Both Ethiopia and Eritrea simply barricaded themselves, hoping that the other might succumb to pressures and through perseverance one of them would be vindicated.

Geopolitical upheavals in the region and the larger world long have necessitated a reexamination of the Ethiopia-Eritrea situation at the state level. There were even attempts within Ethiopia to redress the protracted

---

27 Algiers Agreement of 2000, https://www.files.ethz.ch/isn/125337/1392_ Algiers%20Agreement.pdf; Permanent Court of Arbitration: EEBC Statement by the Commission, in International Legal Materials 46 (January 2007), 155–60; EECC Decision 7 Guidance Regarding Jus Ad Bellum Liability, in International Legal Materials 46 (November 2007), 1121–26; EECC: Partial Award, Jus Ad Bellum, Ethiopia's Claims 1–8, in International Legal Materials 45 (March 2006), 430–35; Permanent Courts of Arbitration, EECC: Partial Award, Civilian Claims, Eritrea's Claims 15, 16, 23,& 27–32, in International Legal Materials 44 (May 2005), 601–29; EECC: Partial Award on Prisoners of War (Ethiopia's Claim 4), in International Legal Materials42 (September 2003), 1056–82; EEBC: Decision Regarding Delimitation of the Border Between the State of Eritrea and the Federal Democratic Republic of Ethiopia, in International Legal Materials 41 (September 2002), 1057–1134.

28 Abbink, "Badme and the Ethio-Eritrean Border," 219–31.

29 Bahru, "Ethio-Eritrean Border/Boundary," 391–405.

stalemate with Eritrea. But it was yet again developments in Ethiopia that made the current thaw possible. The political infighting within EPRDF that ultimately removed TPLF from center-stage has basically facilitated the operating theatre for the peace process. Unique as it may sound, the process yet proved that the messenger is more important than the message. Whatsoever the case, after twenty years of discord Ethiopia and Eritrea have decided to renew their relations in July 2018, thereby ushering a new phase in their complex relationship. The manner in which the current rapprochement was handled and executed took observers and pundits by surprise. Though long overdue and righteous, again an element of surprise, haste, and secrecy continues to shroud the Ethiopia-Eritrea affair. Eritrea simply followed suit with every intention to benefit from and contribute towards potential transformations in Ethiopia (specifically the demise of the TPLF), with a keen eye on scoring the utmost points in the diplomatic, political, and economic spheres.

In an alarmingly striking parallel, the interests and viewpoints of those at the helm of power remain central to the process, with little or no transparency and institutional mechanisms guarantying resilience and comprehensiveness. One cannot dismiss elements of local political consideration on both sides as well as indirect pressures by third parties that have dictated the course of events. Likewise, Ethiopia and Eritrea appear intent on remodeling the sub-region and even the continent anew, taking themselves as a nucleus. To what extent this yields positive results remain to be seen. But already existing subtleties, dispositions, and perceptions appear to be frayed among fellow states in the region. Of course, objective realities dictating interstate relations now are distinct from those in the 1990s. Nonetheless, there still is no escaping the high probability of the two countries progressing along a similar course, one way or the other influencing the peace process.[30] They have been endowed with a second chance, and, if squandered, another one might not present itself readily or could come at a higher price later on.

Security/Defense Considerations

Defense and security sector coordination was the other significant pillar of the September 1993 agreement. The joint Ethiopia-Eritrea defense agreement stipulated coordination in training, intelligence sharing at the highest possible level, and closer cooperation in technical aspects. On the technical side, the abundance in their respective armories of Russian and

---

30 Tronvoll, "Opinion: Putting Humpty Dumpty Together Again";de Waal, "Future of Ethiopia"; Plaut, "Eritrea and Ethiopia Have Made Peace"; Zere, "Isaias Out of Character."

Eastern European weapons, specifically finding spare parts and overhauling obsolete arsenals, made it essential to collaborate. There also existed mutual understanding on security and intelligence fronts, with equally unreserved provisions for closer cooperation, information sharing, and the avoidance of visa restrictions.[31] In order to expedite the 1993 protocol agreement, a three-tier structural provision consisting of a high-level joint committee, a joint coordinating committee, and a facilitation committee was put in place. The later committee in turn consisted of training and education and intelligence and technical subcommittees.

Differences started to surface on how to proceed with these uncharacteristically overindulging provisions in rather complicated sectors of security, intelligence, and defense. These problems basically manifested during the period of unbridled cordiality. Members of the joint ministerial commission soon found themselves grappling with delicate issues hitherto considered inconsequential and trivial. The earliest snub occurred in relation to Eritrean dissident elements residing in Ethiopia, which the former demanded should be disavowed or even extradited. As far as Ethiopia was concerned, since these elements were political in character, any future deliberation on the matter should be directed not to the defense but rather the political committee.[32]

More practical and pressing challenges occurred in relation to security, consular services, dual citizenship, the movement of respective citizens, and residence permits. What began as a pure gesture at solidarity gradually devolved into a security dilemma and nightmare, progressively pitting government agencies in both countries against each other. Broadly speaking, the situation unraveled, with grave consequences for Ethiopia, around the issue of citizenship. Eritrea allows dual citizenship, with a universal identification card for all its subjects. This is not the case in Ethiopia, for the post-1991 dispensation empowers ethno-federal identity groups at multiple levels. Problematic in this regard was the sheer inability of Ethiopians, with the exception of those belonging to the Tigray region, to enter Eritrea, while Eritreans enjoyed unrestricted access to every

---

31 MoFA. Ethio-Ertra yegara Commission 2, 5. Asamenew Bedane (Ministry of Defense) to MoFA on the Ethiopia-Eritrea Joint Defense Committee, 4 January 1994.

32 MoFA. Ethio-Ertra yegara Commission 2, 6. Mahteme Solomon (Minister of Justice) to MoFA, 7 November 1995. Following the extradition agreement of March 1995, Eritrea also insisted on avoiding extradition of their respective citizens to a third country, which Ethiopia found difficult to execute in the context of similar agreements it had reached with other countries.

corner of Ethiopia. One simply has to contextualize this in terms of the socio-economic and political irregularities it generated in the relationship between the two countries.

Provisions granting freedom of movement to Eritreans, for the preferential application was inadvertently sanctioned by the 1993 agreement, gradually created acute security concerns for Ethiopia.[33] This manifested at three levels: dual citizenship, travel documents (passports), and residence permits. Ethiopia disallows dual citizenship, while Eritreans can have multiple nationalities. The 1993 agreement simply fell short of providing a legal framework on how to accommodate Eritreans of dual citizenship. This created a gaping loophole utilized by Eritrea, with dire complications for Ethiopia. Eritreans can easily enter Ethiopia without a visa, then produce another passport to exit the country. This directly countervails Ethiopia's immigration law that strictly requires exit visas unless otherwise stated. More consequential, in this regard, was the involvement of a great number of Eritreans of other nationalities in economic activities specifically reserved for their kin in Ethiopia. This created a situation whereby not only major import-export and the service sector but also retail businesses in Ethiopia became dominated by Eritreans of dual citizenship.

Some of these challenges were also of Ethiopia's doing. Most Eritreans hold Ethiopian travel documents that were issued willingly while Eritrea was transitioning to statehood. No institutional attempt was made on the part of Ethiopia to scrap these later on. Rather, Eritreans continued to utilize them and even get new ones. Only they had to get residence permits in Addis Ababa and apply for Ethiopian passports. Given the love affair between the two governments, this was the easiest thing to achieve in those times. Ethiopia's missions abroad also continued to issue Ethiopian passports to Eritreans, simply because there was no ruling dictating otherwise. Of course, the 1993 agreement provided for the issuance of residence permits within six months of its signing to citizens of one country residing in the other. Eritrea applied this to the letter, but nothing of the sort occurred in Ethiopia. All these specifics gradually fed into the dire situation that later unfolded between the two countries.

Alarmingly, these essential considerations are visibly missing from the current rapprochement between Ethiopia and Eritrea. Gestures at remedying the past discord were in full display, but the initiative fell short of even recognizing these delicate hurdles. If the peace process is to endure, these issues will require careful scrutiny and serious application. Dual citizenship

---

33 MoFA. Ethio-Ertra yegara Commission 2, 6. Kenfe Gebremedhin (Head, Ministry of Internal Affairs) to MoFA, 8 November 1995.

and associated complexities require policy frameworks. Ethiopia has to establish compatible arrangements or ascertain that Eritrea provides alternative mechanisms accommodating Ethiopia's political and legal requirements in this regard. Issues revolving around residence permits and related complexities also require expedient resolutions for the current accord to prosper.

The time for trading favors on the basis of camaraderie or cheap political gains is over. Rather, the two countries and governments need to take into stock these details and resolve them comprehensively. No doubt the two have suffered from the mismanagement of these issues, and therefore extra vigilance and farsightedness has to be the primary *modus operandi*. The integrity and interests of the states, the very resilience of the initiative for peaceful coexistence and cooperation, and by projection the peace, security, and development of the sub-region hinges on how these dynamics are handled in the near future.

Economic Imperatives

All the above problems play second fiddle to the economic underpinnings dictating Ethiopia-Eritrea relations. Economic considerations, with their various applications, remain at the very core of the conflict and central to the ongoing rapprochement. As was the case in other sectors, the 1993 agreement provided for the highest form of economic cooperation leading to complete integration between the two countries. They even pledged to harmonize and even integrate their macroeconomic, monetary, and trade policies through stages. Practical commitments included, among others, utilizing the *birr* as a common currency, defining the exchange rate for their respective currencies, and creating a free economic zone.[34]

The holistic approach to economic cooperation and integration was expected to materialize hierarchically, with the creation of a Free Trade Area (FTA) as the first stage. The FTA was expected to materialize in three stages, with each country maintaining its own currency. During the first phase, they planned to eliminate all barriers deterring the exchange of local goods and services. In phase two, uniform tariffs on imported items and

---

34 Agreement of Friendship and Cooperation between the Transitional Government of Ethiopia and the government of the State of Eritrea, Addis Ababa, 30July 1993 (personal collection). Initial attempts to sign trade protocols were made in April 1992 and January 1993, but in both instances the two governments failed to reach an agreement on a quota system and modalities on transferring commodities to third countries. See MoFA, Ethio-Ertra yegara Commission 1, 1. Ministry of Trade to MoFA, 18 August 1993; Dr. Abdulmajid Hussein (Minister of External Economic Cooperation) to MoFA, 20 August 1993.

services were to be created. The third phase was supposed to totally cast away bottlenecks impeding the free movement of capital and labor between the two countries. In this regard, the Ethiopia-Eritrea economic cooperation agreement of 1993 stipulated, among other things, that the two countries would harmonize monetary policies in as far as a common framework was applied, remove barriers to the free movement of goods and services between them, harmonize tariffs, sales taxes, excise taxes, and profit taxes, and synchronize investment policies and provide national investors of both countries equal treatment.

In view of the intended establishment of the FTA, the two governments agreed to adopt mutually accepted targets of money supply on a yearly basis, that the official exchange rate of *birr* in Ethiopia should also be applicable in Eritrea, and that the *birr* marginal rate derived from the foreign exchange auction market conducted by the National Bank of Ethiopia should be applicable in both countries for export transactions. They also agreed that the existing free flow of goods between them, which applied to locally produced goods, should exclude exportable goods, with the exception of goods destined for domestic consumption and goods imported from third countries, unless the full range of import taxes were levied by the importing states. The same agreement stipulated that in case Eritrea terminated the use of the *birr* as its currency, the two states should exchange the appropriate information in advance so as to ensure a smooth and orderly transition to the use of separate currencies.[35]

Interesting to observers, irrespective of the overarching desire of the two governments to completely integrate their economies, was the total absence of policy frameworks, at least on the part of Eritrea, vital to the very implementation and success of the initiative. The earliest effort on the part of Eritrea to formulate macroeconomic policies, procedures, and laws governing its trade and investment occurred in late 1994. Ethiopia's members of the JHMC and ancillary units had yet to study Eritrea's new policy documents and adjust their approaches accordingly. Indicative of the larger trend, no practical commitments were undertaken to realize the high-flying agenda of economic integration between the two or in the sub-region.[36]

Irrespective of these irregularities, however, a full-fledged informal economy crystallized between Ethiopia and Eritrea, tilting in favor of the

---

35 MoFA. Ethio-Ertra yegara Commission 1, 3. MOU on Transitional Issues before the Adoption of Different Currencies, April 1994; MOU on Investment, April 1994.

36 If anything, one can associate a trifle of semblance of success in this regard to the revitalization of IGADD to IGAD in March 1996.

latter. Preferential treatment for Eritrean businessmen and commodities, tax evasion, contraband, currency manipulation, and other transgressions jeopardized the resilience of the already deeply flawed accord. Gradually, the task of handling delicate economic realities became far too complex and problematic. The TPLF's design to industrialize Tigay, with the alleged goal of replicating Eritrea's economic model, created a firestorm in the relationship between the prominent ruling factions in each country.[37] Simply put, Ethiopia and Eritrea rushed into the agreement, inadvertently jeopardizing their future trajectory and setting the course for the inevitable conflict. From the outset it was never a question of if but when, and at least Ethiopia's experts braced for the worst well in advance of the second meeting of the joint commission.

In less than a year, the trade and customs arrangements put in place began to face challenges. Initial attempts by the two governments at the ministerial level (Asmara, October 1994) to resolve the situation amicably failed to yield the desired result. These problems continued to spiral towards the negative until full-fledged conflict broke out four years later. Eritrea's new economic strategy reemphasized the imperative to revamp the export sector, with Africa and the Middle East as its primary markets. In other words, Eritrea repositioned itself as the center of the capital and labor market connecting Africa and the Middle East. Achieving this, in turn, hinged on designing a fiscal policy that basically aimed to manipulate probable price hikes in the export sector through the issuance of Eritrean currency.[38]

Specifically, this new approach by Eritrea introduced additional elements in taxation, the movement of commodities, and customs services. These included excise and sales taxes as well as customs tariffs. At the same time, the 12 percent tax unilaterally imposed on Eritrean goods by the Tigray region at the Zalambessa border crossing continued to be problematic, and Eritrea protested vehemently. Eritrea also demanded cap on indirect taxes on third-party goods and the avoidance of routine customs checks on transit shipments. But these requests generated a cold rebuttal from Ethiopia. All these initiatives for economic cooperation and integration resumed in the absence of a common classification of trading goods as per the SITC method, where no agreement was reached on common instruments for data collections

---

37 Tekeste and Tronvoll, Brother's at War.

38 MoFA. Ethio-Eritra yegara Commission 2, 5. Report on problems faced in relation to the implementation of trade and customs agreements. Prepared by Ethiopia's Ministry of Trade, October 1994.

and without setting up verification mechanisms defining the exchange of trade data.[39]

More serious signs of trouble emerged in January 1995, specifically associated with procedures on how to expedite debt and other payments between commercial and national banks of the two countries. Cognizant of the controversy, the governor of the National Bank of Ethiopia notified the Transitional Government of Ethiopia prime minister's office. To his frustration, though, no concrete response was forthcoming, and the issue was deliberately sidelined.[40]

At exactly the same time, Eritrea demanded sole mandate for its oil corporation in procuring spare parts for its Assab refinery and urged Ethiopia to forward payment in foreign currency. Ethiopian authorities vehemently opposed this proposal, for it countervailed the joint mandate set by the original agreement and created a dangerous precedent whereby Eritrea would next insist on a similar payment arrangement for crude oil purchases and processing and even other trading items. Any altercation in this regard would also negate existing rules deterring foreign currency transfer through a third party. Ethiopia's documents reveal that for the 1995 fiscal year a total of 20 million *birr* ($4 million) was allocated for the purchase of chemicals, spare parts, and other materials, out of which Eritrea was demanding an equivalent in foreign currency of 15.9 million *birr*.[41]

The second meeting of the JHMC (Asmara, March 1995) exposed more of the same problems in the relationship between the two countries, and demonstrated the differences in approach and interpretation of critical economic issues. These differences primarily revolve around critical questions like the creation of an FTA, port utilization, and maritime transit. As far as Ethiopia was concerned, for the relationship with Eritrea to crystallize, challenges faced in these areas need to be addressed properly and urgently. Nonetheless, issues like how to apply excise and sales taxes on Eritrean commodities (local as well as imported) entering Ethiopia, and how to equate the transit tax imposed on Eritrean goods crossing Tigray

---

39 MoFA. Ethio-ertra yegara Commission 2, 5. Dr. Duri Mohammed (Ministry of Planning and Economic Development) to the Office of the President of Eritrea. Institutional and Policy Framework for Strengthening Economic Cooperation Between Ethiopia and Eritrea, 6 March 1995.

40 MoFA. Leykun Berhanu (governor, National Bank of Ethiopia) to Dr. Duri Mohammed (Ministry of Planning and Economic Development), 23 January 1995.

41 MoFA. Nesredin Mohammed (vice governor, National Bank of Ethiopia) to Ministry of Mines and Energy, 22 March 1995; Izedin Ali (Ministry of Mines and Energy) to the Office of the Prime Minister, 14 April 1995.

with similar goods coming out of other regional states in Ethiopia destined to Eritrea remain basically unresolved.[42]

Major fault lines in the economic sector, most long existing and some emerging, assumed center stage during the fourth meeting of the JHMC (Addis Ababa, 18–19 August 1996). Going into the meeting, there were serious concerns among Ethiopian officials regarding sluggish process in realizing economic integration as well as complications in relation to excise, sales, and transit taxes. Both had agreed, during the third meeting of the JHMC, to form an FTA and established a secretariat responsible for its implementation. Technical committees were also assigned to deal with: a) value added criterion (rules of origin) for goods originating from both sides to be eligible for free movement and to establish methods and procedures of applying the criterion; and b) to design common formats for the collection of trade statistics and develop procedures for the regular exchange of information.

The Ethiopian side outlined activities it had undertaken in accordance with the agreement, including the study it carried out on the institutional arrangement of the FTA and the term of references developed for the technical committees on value added criterion and trade statistics. Eritrean officials proposed a review of the FTA rationale and the operational difficulties encountered to that point and came up with a recommendation on how to proceed with the realization of the FTA. Central to their change of mind was the protectionist trend they observed regarding Ethiopia's trade policy.[43]

After heated debate, with a view to remove major obstacles to the smooth implementation of the agreement, both sides agreed to set up yet another joint committee. This committee was mandated to review the implementation of the agreements signed by the two countries in the field of economic cooperation, identify major constraints facing the effective implementation of the agreements, propose measures to facilitate the implementation of the agreements on economic cooperation; and produce a report within three months.

Thorny issues associated with the transfer of money, the question of debt, and related matters were also on the agenda. Discussions were held regarding the settlement of debts owed by one side to the other and the

---

42 MoFA. Ethio-Eritra yegara Commission 2, 6. Ambassador Awalom Woldu (Ethiopia's ambassador to Eritrea) to African Affairs Directorate, 13 September 1995; African Affairs Directorate to minister of Foreign Affairs, 25 September 1995; Dr. Tekeda Alemu (minister for Foreign Affairs) to Office of the Prime Minister, 9 October 1995.

43 MoFA. Ethio-Eritra yegara Commission 2, 6. Minutes of the 4th JHMC, September 1996.

transfer of the birr to Ethiopia when Eritrea's new currency, the *nakfa*, became operational. The Ethiopian side simply noted that the issue of the transfer of the birr was being deliberated at a higher level. The Eritrean side pointed out that the *nakfa* would be issued in due course and that in the meantime the Eritrean government would instruct the concerned institutions to come up with modalities as to how the issue of money transfer and debt would be handled. A final decision on the matter was simply postponed pending another report by the respective authorities.[44]

Participation of nationals of both countries in equal bi-national trade activities emerged as a point of divergence during the meeting. Ethiopia's delegation pointed out the challenges Ethiopians residing in Eritrea were encountering in getting new trade licenses or renewing old ones. They further stated that businessmen were requested to pay 1.5 percent transit tariff on goods they imported through the port of Massawa. Eritrea interjected, claiming that trade licenses issued to Ethiopians before independence could easily be renewed. The problem, it argued, was the issuance of new licenses. The delegation expressed Eritrea's readiness to issue trade and investment licenses to Ethiopian residents in Eritrea as long as the Ethiopian government was ready to do likewise.

In the ensuing debate, Eritrea suggested that trade and investment should be open to resident nationals of both countries without restrictions made on foreigners. The Ethiopian side insisted that it would have to make restrictions, particularly on banking and insurance. Both sides failed to concede on the issue, relegating it to another reviewing committee supposedly studying the ways, means, and implications of what resident nationals of both countries would be allowed in sectors open only to nationals. In the meantime, both sides agreed to instruct all concerned institutions to permit resident citizens of both countries to obtain trade and investment licenses of their choice, except in areas reserved for nationals.

Similar pressing problems were identified in the transport and communication sectors. Ethiopia highlighted pitfalls in specific areas, including, among others, the standing request for landing areas for cars, fuel tankers, and the like at the port of Assab; the handling of import-export goods at the ports; and the payment of the 1.5 percent tariff tax and the need for banking services at the port of Assab. Eritrea admitted to implementation problems in various areas of trade, transport, and transiting, but instead of dealing with them piecemeal it proposed the creation of another review committee to come up with concrete proposals for the JHMC to consider.

---

44 Ibid.

Apparently, two years in advance, the parties were faced with a stalemate and unable to amicably resolve their differences during the final ministerial meeting.

The progression of events fast spiraled out of control, dragging the countries towards the inevitable conflict and confrontation that combusted in May 1998. During the height of the Eritrea-Yemen conflict over the Hanish Islands, Eritrea denied Yemeni vessels carrying Ethiopia's cargo entry to the port of Assab. Since May 1997, Eritrea began to unilaterally undertake quality control and assurance procedures of Ethiopia's coffee exports passing through Assab. In November 1998, Ethiopia employed foreign currency as the sole payment mechanism for every trade and transaction with Eritrea. Starting January 1, 1998, Eritrea canceled the transit and port utilization agreement of September 1993. In direct violation of the previous arrangement, and without duly notifying Ethiopia, Eritrea deregulated the transit services, allowed customs clearing agencies in both countries to work in linkage, and unilaterally granted Eritrean Shipping and Transit Agency Services (ERSTAS) total rights to prepare bills of lading, import notifications, and freight manifests.[45] Finally, in May 1998, the fateful two-year war broke out.

Going forward with the current rapprochement, these critical issues require careful consideration and resolution. From the outset it appears that primary attention is being focused on reversing the stalemate but with little attention to the overriding factors that have frustrated good relations for the last two decades. Any attempt at the resumption of economic relations, specifically related to port utilization, cross border trade, economic cooperation, and integration should be handled carefully if the current accord is to endure and prosper. Bottlenecks and points of disagreement on how to address taxation, port utilization, foreign currency, commodity exchange, and the movement of people and goods need expeditious handling. Both outstanding issues as well as new dynamics require grounded approaches, executed in manners judicious and suitable for both parties.

Unfortunately, such deliberations appear to be missing from the current dispensation. Apparently, these delicacies seem to have been left for future consideration, which in turn appears not to be happening soon. As is always the case with developing countries, political considerations, economic scale, and appropriation of the upper hand remain at the very center of their rapprochement. Unless Ethiopia and Eritrea find room to settle this properly and expeditiously, they endanger the very resilience and

---

45   MoFA. Ethio-Eritra yegara Commission 7. Ethiopian Maritime and Transit Services Enterprise to Ministry of Transport and Communication, 15 December 1997.

comprehensibility of the peace process. For long, economic imperatives have informed political considerations. In the absence of comprehensive solutions to these practical hurdles, the peace process risks the danger of relapse. Leaving the fate of the much-anticipated rapprochement to run its course along whimsical and emotional lines, with the new dynamics and the new actors dictating proceedings irrationally, might prove dangerous and consequential.

The Way Forward

Expeditious execution of the Ethiopia-Eritrea rapprochement remains an absolute necessity for both countries. In retrospect, it appears perfectly clear that both actors have taken a leap of faith, with little or no grandiose plans on how to manage or implement the peace process. Coming out of incessant animosity and an entrenched track record of destabilizing one another, expecting a fertile operating theater whereby peace, stability, and trust prevails unhindered might be asking too much too soon. Ample room is required for all the dynamics to simmer and the dust to settle. Without doubt, by the mere gesture of accord, the two governments have significantly altered the status quo, which no one fathomed even a short while ago.

Nonetheless, there equally exists the urgency for caution, craft, and foresight on both sides if the process is to yield the desired result. Peace can be aspired to but should not be conceived as an end result in itself. In a volatile region where relations unravel constantly, one always has to factor-in all the dividends, including the potential benefits and fallout associated with the management and implementation of peace. Conventional wisdom dictates that all sorts of interaction—employing economic, political, or military tools of engagement—can be alternately applied as exigencies dictate, irrespective of the misnomer often attached to the method. Ample precedents highlight economic or military options as best tools for advancing strategic interests, at times even better than a meaningless peace. In other words, both parties are required to heed the overall objectives they aspire to attain, with due attention to matters beyond short-term gains.

No doubt, Eritrea unilaterally reaped the fruits of mending ties with Ethiopia, in spite of the fact that it did little to initiate the process. Rather, leaders in Asmara rightly perceived an opening whereby to score political and strategic points, striking against perceived or actual adversaries in Ethiopia and the sub-region as well as reinstating Eritrea into the community of world states. The uncharacteristically speedy lifting of the stifling sanctions regime, the correlated charm offensive to restore Eritrea's image in the region and beyond, and the euphoric display of accord basically disregarding the critical points of discord informing two decades of animosity all seemingly boosted the image and stature of the government of President Isaias in the short run. All these developments perfectly feed into the carefully crafted narrative of Eritrea's perseverance against Ethiopian hegemonic tendencies and the vindication of the former. Contrary to this, Ethiopia apparently ascribed to the literal values of peace, with unflattering notions of political settlement locally and economic cooperation regionally. It soon dawned on both parties that far greater and complex issues dictate proceedings.

Within three months of the commencement of the accord in June 2018, diplomatic relations resumed, borders opened, and telecom and air transport connections were reestablished. But the whole issue has begun to lose momentum, testing the resilience of the initiative and process. It has reached a point now that with the exception of telecom and air connectivity, other sectors, including the lukewarm consular services, has been significantly reversed. Apparently, practical rules of engagement and operational guidelines governing their interactions, including border management, economic interactions, and strategic alignments, have been visibly tested. The only constant in this dynamics has been the personal relationship of the two leaders, which by itself is waning and waxing over the last year.

The whole saga has now reached a point where bilateral affairs appear frozen, and frayed subtleties and sensibilities in the sub-region were left properly unaddressed. What was initiated with full prospects for peaceful coexistence, regional integration, and continental cohesion soon reached a point where more confusion reigns on the way forward. Ownership of strategic considerations guiding their interaction appears to be progressively slipping out of the grasp of the two actors, seemingly manipulated and dominated unilaterally (apparently by Eritrea) or third parties hailing from the region and beyond (Gulf States and company).

Few considerations remain vital for the peace process to prosper and yield the desired result. Politically, recent reform initiatives in Ethiopia have to crystallize, with proper settlement of internal fault lines and misgivings. Ethiopia should first put its house in order, more so the ruling coalition, the EPRDF/Prosperity Party, and the government need to ascertain cohesion and the rule of law internally before any act of external interaction. No other external entity, in particular Eritrea, should be allowed to meddle in the domestic affairs of Ethiopia, and any attempt to utilize relations with Eritrea as a tool to propagate a political agenda of sorts should be strictly disavowed. Strategizing bilateral affairs on account of political gains locally or at the expense of the other party, if any, has also to be avoided. In a similar vein, for a meaningful and lasting rapprochement to materialize, parallel initiatives at democratization and political liberalization have to take root in Eritrea as well.

Any comprehensive peace and economic integration, as recently envisaged by the two parties, will only be realized if the political theater in both countries embraces and upholds basic principles and tenets associated with the rule of law, respect for human and democratic rights, and adherence to international norms. Finding common ground addressing their diverse approaches to governance, political economy, and foreign interaction should be prioritized. Going forward with the accord, both parties have to indulge in a serious appraisal of the potential political, economic, and demographic altercations being witnessed in Eritrea at the moment.

Likewise, there is an urgent need to take into account all the concerns, perceptions, and diverse viewpoints in each country and the sub-region, basically aiming at a negotiated settlement of at least primary fault lines hindering the way forward. Ethiopia and Eritrea need to first put in order their multifaceted internal problems before envisioning any meaningful rapprochement, and any ploy to seek untoward advantages at the expense of the other should be avoided at all cost. Likewise, one should not be allowed to meddle in the affairs of the other or exploit the current dispensation to alter long-established norm references governing interactions among states in the region.

Acceptable rules governing equal economic interactions need be put in place. Rules of engagement, as well as operational guidelines dictating cross border trade, port utilization, exchange rates, taxation, and investment, have to be carefully devised in ways guaranteeing mutual benefit and sustainability. Preferential treatment, the tendency to manipulate one another unnecessarily, and putting economic relations at the mercy of political whims should be altogether avoided. There exists ample historical precedent where this was the case, and it is high time the two governments drew proper lessons from past irregularities.

Obviously, economic realities in the two countries have dramatically altered during the last two decades, more so in favor of Ethiopia. The once bustling and thriving economy of Eritrea has stagnated, but Ethiopia's has transformed significantly. Moving forward, this reality has to be properly equated, with Ethiopia assuming the added burden of reinvigorating Eritrea's economy with carefully calibrated and mutually rewarding policy orientations. It is incumbent upon Ethiopia again to impress upon Eritrea their shared destination to grow and prosper and also to realize that all the strategic, political, and developmental imperatives in the region hinge on how Ethiopia handles and executes its affairs with Eritrea. If somehow both parties fail to realize and execute this properly, it remains in their best interest to avoid the matter altogether. After all, it was the economic matrix that proved central to their fateful discord. In this regard, addressing the major fractures and fault lines comprehensively, irrespective of political considerations, and applying the economy of scales at a macro level might prove vital to the way forward with the rapprochement.

Strategic, security, and multilateral affairs also require proper handling. Gulf States, particularly the UAE and Saudi Arabia, have approached the Ethiopia-Eritrea accord from their own immediate geostrategic interests of ascertaining total domination over Red Sea shores. All the drive for speedy rapprochement, the lifting of UNSC sanctions on Eritrea, and all the endorsement of the proceedings can be explained within this broader context. No doubt Eritrea has reaped the utmost benefit from the process; but what this entails to Ethiopia in the medium and long run remains to be seen. Likewise, any untoward ploy by Eritrea to reassert its security presence unilaterally in Somalia, and even Ethiopia, should not be totally disregarded.

Likewise, the speed and manner in which the Ethiopia-Eritrea rapprochement was handled and executed has unnerved partners in the sub-region and beyond. Existing arrangements informing interstate relations in the Horn of Africa have been affected as a result, and the sub-regional body (IGAD) and the AU were inadvertently left out of the loop. Ethiopia, in particular, has to reassess the wisdom in this approach, more so in the interest of the political and economic agendas the current leadership openly espouses towards the region in general. Any guise of vindictiveness or total disregard of long-existing alignments might endanger the very resilience and success of the peace process between Ethiopia and Eritrea. Far greater, strategically sound and accommodative of the diverse security, economic, societal, and political viewpoints of countries in the region and the continent have to be integrated in the policy formulation and implementation process. It remains incumbent on Ethiopia and Eritrea to accommodate these realities.

It has now become evident that peace between any given countries in the volatile region of the Horn, including Ethiopia and Eritrea, need to simultaneously address the concerns and misgivings of fellow states in the region and the overall global dynamics at large. More specifically, political, economic, and geostrategic dimensions of all concerned parties should be entertained in the management and implementation of the process. Time has provided Ethiopia and Eritrea a rare opportunity to chart a new course in their relationship. Only the necessary willpower and careful investment is required to realize peace and cooperation in bilateral and multilateral settings. Achieving this in turn demands foresight, perseverance, and the knack to see the bigger picture. They can't afford to squander it, for there might not be another chance in the foreseeable future or it might come at a much higher price for both parties.

Bibliography

Abbink, Jon. "Badme and the Ethio-Eritrean Border: The Challenges of Demarcation in the Post-War Period." *Africa: Rivistatrimestrale di studi e documentazione dell' Institutoitalian per l'Africa e l'Oriente* 58, no. 3 (2003): 219–31.

Alemseged Abbay. "'Not with Them, Not without Them': The Staggering of Eritrea to Nationhood." *Africa: Rivistatrimestrale di studi e documentazione dell' Institutoitaliano per l'Africa e l'Oriente* 56, no. 4(2001): 459–91.

Bahru Zewde. "The Ethio-Eritrean Border/Boundary: A Seesaw Puzzle." *Society, State and History: Selected Essays.* Addis Ababa: Addis Ababa University Press, 2008.

Belete Belachew Yihun. "The Recent Ethiopia-Eritrea Diplomatic Thaw: Challenges and Prospects." *Horn of Africa Bulletin* 29, no. 3 (2018).

_____. "The Conduct of Ethiopia's Foreign Policy: Back to the Future." *Africa Spectrum,* forthcoming

Bereket Habte Selassie. *While Waiting or Working for Change: Things to Do and Pitfalls to Avoid in Eritrea.* Lawrenceville, NJ: Red Sea, 2015.

Cliffe, Lionel. "Regional Dimensions of Conflict in the Horn of Africa" *Third World Quarterly* 20, no. 1 (1999): 89–111.

de Waal, Alex "The Future of Ethiopia: Developmental State or Political Marketplace?" Occasional Paper, World Peace Foundation, 20 August 2018, https://sites.tufts.edu/reinventingpeace/files/2018/08/The-future-of-ethiopia-20180817.pdf.

Iyob, Ruth. "The Ethiopian-Eritrean Conflict: Diasporic vs. Hegemonic States in the Horn of Africa, 1991–2000." *Journal of Modern African Studies* 38, no. 4 (2000): 659–82.

Johnson, Douglas H. *The Root Causes of Sudan's Civil Wars: Peace or Truce.* Suffolk: James Currey, 2012.

Kohen, Marcelo G. 2013. State Succession in Matters of International Responsibility (Provisional Report). Published in the *Yearbook of the Institute of International Law.* Tallinn Session - Volume 76. file:///C:/Users/user%201/Downloads/Kohen_succession_final_report.pdf (Accessed 28 August 2019)

Leenco Lata. 2003. "The Ethiopia-Eritrea War," in *Review of African Political Economy,* Vol. 30, No. 97, pp. 369- 388.

Mengisteab, Kidane and Okbazghi Yohannes. *Anatomy of an African Tragedy: Political, Economic and Foreign Policy Crisis in Post-Independence Eritrea.* Trenton, NJ: Red Sea, 2005.

Milkias, Paulos. "U.S. Foreign Policy Towards Arica with Emphasis on Ethiopia and Eritrea" *International Journal of Ethiopian Studies* 1, no. 2 (2004):58–81.

Mosley, Jason. "Eritrea-Ethiopia Rapprochement and Wider Dynamics of Regional Trade, Politics and Security." *Horn of Africa Bulletin* 30 (July-August 2018): 7–11.

Muller, Tanja. "Back to Square One between Eritrea and Ethiopia." *Horn of Africa Bulletin* 30 (July-August 2018): 22–25.

Plaut, Martin. *Understanding Eritrea: Inside Africa's Most Repressive State.* New York: Oxford University Press, 2016.

_____. "Eritrea and Ethiopia Have Made Peace. How It Happened and What Next," *The Conversation*, 10 July 2018. http://theconversation.com/eritrea-and-ethiopia-have-made-peace-how-it-happened-and-what-next-99683.

_____. 2018. "Where Now for the Horn?" *Horn of Africa Bulletin* 30, no. 3 (2018):12–14.

Prunier, Gérard. Africa's World War: Congo, The Rwandan Genocide, and the Making of a Continental Catastrophe. New York: Oxford University Press, 2010.

Reid, Richard. "Ghosts of the Mesafint: Contemplating Conflict in Eritrean-Ethiopian History." *Northeast African Studies*, n.s., 10, no. 3, The Horn of Africa between History, Law and Politics (2003):189–211.

_____. "Old Problems in New Conflicts: Some Observations on Eritrea and Its Relations with Tigray, from Liberation Struggle to Inter-State War." *Journal of International African Institute* 73, no. 3 (2003):369–401.

_____. "Caught in the Headlights of History: Eritrea, the EPLF and the Post-War Nation State" *Journal of Modern African Studies* 43, no. 3 (2005):467–88.

Shumet Shishagne. *Unionists and Separatists: The Vagaries of Ethio-Eritrean Relations,1941–1991.* Los Angeles: Tsehai, 2007.

Sturma, Pavel. "Succession of States in Respect of State Responsibility." Report of the International Law Commission Sixty-Eighth Session (July 2017).doi: 10.18356/91a57727-en.

Taddia, Irma. "Post-Twentieth-Century Eritrea." *Northeast African Studies*, n.s., 5, no.1 (1998):7–29.

Tekeda Alemu. "The Conundrum of Present Ethiopian Foreign Policy—in Search of a Roadmap for Ethiopia's Foreign and National Security Policy and Strategy." Special Issue, *CDRC Digest* 4, no. 1 (2019): 5–11, http://www.cdrcethiopia.org/index.php/resorces/publications/send/2-cdrc-digest/25-cdrc-digest-january-2019.

Tekeste Negash and Kjetil Tronvoll. *Brothers at War: Making Sense of the Eritrean-Ethiopian War.* Suffolk: James Currey, 2000.

Tekeste Negash. *Eritrea and Ethiopia: The Federal Experience.* New Brunswick, NJ: Transaction, 1997.

_____. "Italy and Its Relations with Eritrean Political Parties, 1948–1950" *Africa: Rivistatrimestrale di studi e documentazionedell'Institutoitaliano per l'Africa el'Oriente* 59, no. 3/4 (2002):417–52.

Tekie, Fessehatzion. *Shattered Illusions, Broken Promises: Essays on the Eritrea-Ethiopia Conflict* (1999–2000). Lawrenceville, NJ: Red Sea, 2002.

Tronvoll, Kjeti. "Opinion: Putting Humpty Dumpty Together Again: The Restoration of EPRDF?" *Addis Standard, 26 March 2019, http://addisstandard. com/opinion-putting-humpty-dumpty-together-again-the-restoration-of-eprdf/*.

Woldemariam, Michael. "The Eritrea-Ethiopia Thaw and Its Regional Impact," *Current History* (May 2019):181–87, http://www.currenthistory.com/ Woldemariam-CH2019.pdf.

Woldemikael, Olivia Asmara. "The Promise and Pitfalls of the New Peace for Eritrea." *Horn of Africa Bulletin*, 30 (July-August 2018):16–19.

Wrong, Michela. *I Didn't Do It For You: How the World Betrayed a Small African Nation.* London: Fourth Estate, 2005.

_____."When Peace is a Problem." *New York Times*, 8 June 2018, https://www. nytimes.com/2018/06/08/opinion/ethiopia-eritrea-border.html.

Zere, Abraham T. "Isaias Out of Character: Why Eritreans Are Getting Nervous." *African Arguments*, 18 July 2018, https://africanarguments.org/2018/07/18/ why-eritrea-nervous-isaias-abiy-ethiopia/.

Zewde Retta. *Ya Ertera Guday* (1941–1963). Addis Ababa, 1999.

2

GOOD PROSPECTS FOR PEACE BETWEEN ERITREA AND ETHIOPIA

Tekeste Negash

Background

The series of changes that took place in both countries during the last seventy years have created favorable conditions for a novel dialogue around border issues. It is important to bear in mind the chronology of changes as well as the complex factors that led to those changes. Eritrea was part of the Ethiopian empire from 1952 until 1974, and then it continued its rebellious presence within Ethiopia until 1991, through the military regime that replaced the late emperor Haile Selassie. It became independent (de facto) in 1991, and at the same time Ethiopia managed to get rid of the military regime led by Mengistu Haile Mariam (1974–91). Both countries made a new start in 1991. After a short spell of good relations, Eritrea and Ethiopia went to war from 1998 to 2000 over their disputed border. The state of no war and no peace that prevailed since 2000 was finally resolved in June 2018 when Ethiopia unilaterally decided to accept the boundary delimited and virtually demarcated in 2002 by the United Nations Ethiopia-Eritrea Boundary Commission.

"From now onwards, anyone who says that the Eritreans and Ethiopians are two people has not understood the truth. Eritreans and Ethiopians are one people in two countries." This is a free translation of the statement in Tigrinya of Isaias Afewerki, president of Eritrea, during his first visit to

Ethiopia on July 14, 2018.[1] The president further stated that he mandated Dr. Abiy Ahmed, the prime minister of Ethiopia, to continue the work of uniting the two countries. Asked about his best memories/achievements in life, President Isaias stated that signing peace with Ethiopia as one of them.[2]

Can we take the above statements seriously, coming as they do from a person who fought against Ethiopia for over fifty years, or can we dismiss them as the utterances of a senile leader soon to exit the political scene? As I shall attempt to explain in this paper, I argue that the views of President Isaias on Eritrean/Ethiopian relations need to be taken seriously. I strongly believe he has significant support inside Eritrea; the overwhelming joy that Eritreans showed at Dr. Abiy's first visit to Asmara in early July 2018 can certainly be read as a positive sign.[3] The warm reception of President Isaias in Ethiopia and the positive treatment of Eritrean refugees in Ethiopia could also be taken as important factors in the construction of peace.[4] Yet the question remains: How do we read the new phase of Eritrea-Ethiopia relations and what are the prospects for a sustainable peace between the two countries? My view, which is also the main premise of this paper, is the following: There are now sufficient conditions for a new (reconfigured) Eritrean-Ethiopian border that reflect the wishes/desires of the population of both countries and their leaders.The most important condition is, of

---

1   President Isaias talked in Tigrinya while Prime Minister Abiy functioned as his Amharic translator.

2   Yosief GebreHiwet commented on the above description as follows: "It seems to me that too much is being invested in the statement, 'We are one people.' I bet Isaias says that when he visits Sudan, too."

3   The inhabitants of Asmara were told two days in advance of the coming of Dr. Abiy. It has also to be commented that the first row of women who greeted Abiy at the Asmara airport were organized and mobilized by the state. However, the spontaneous reactions of joy in the streets of Asmara, as captured by the Ethiopian Broadcasting Corporation, were, I believe, far beyond what Eritrean leaders expected to see. My friends from Eritrea told me that even the stones were happy with Abiy's visit and his message/sermon of unity and peace.

4   By the middle of 2018 there were about 150,000 Eritrean refugees in Ethiopia. The Ethiopian government treated Eritrean refugees very well indeed; they were allowed to work anywhere, and up to 3,000 Eritrean refugees were admitted to the various colleges and universities of the country. The more than 50,000 Eritreans who moved to Ethiopia during the first six weeks of the opening of the border (between September and November 2018), which had been closed for nearly twenty years, were accepted as brothers and sisters by the people of Tigray. I was in Mekelle in the beginning of October 2018, and I was able to witness the warm reception the Eritreans were given by the people of Tigray.

course, the statement of President Isaias, but how did this condition come about? How do we explain this new narrative? I think it is when we to try to grasp the constant and changing features of Eritrean–Ethiopian relations from the late 1950s onwards that we can appreciate the implications of President Isaias's statement.[5]

Hence, I have organized this paper as follows: I shall first deal with what I call the prelude to Badme,[6] where I sketch the relations between the two countries from 1991 to 1998. I shall then present in general terms the role of Eritrea and Eritreans in Ethiopia from the inception of the federation until the demise of the imperial system. I shall then outline the destruction of the economic base, first due to the thirty years war of liberation and second due to the overwhelming ignorance of President Isaias on the logic of economic growth. This section is followed by a brief account on the multiple links between the two countries both before and after Badme. Here I shall try to dwell on the structural features in terms of continuities and discontinuities in the history of Eritrean-Ethiopian relations over the last seventy years. And finally, fully aware of the dangers of dealing with the present (difficult to grasp and even more difficult to use as a basis for prediction), I shall put forward my views on the prospects for peace between the two countries.

A great deal has been written on the role of the United Arab Emirates in facilitating the peace treaty through generous financial aid. The then Ethiopian foreign minster, Dr. Werkneh Gebeyehu, has not only acknowledged but also warmly thanked the United Arab Emirates for its role in sealing the peace treaty between Ethiopia and Eritrea. But I believe peace in one form or another would have come due to the radical political changes that took place on the wake of the ascension to power of Dr. Abiy as prime minister in early April 2018. The series of changes that took place in both countries would have, sooner or later, created some conditions for the ending of the war, as neither peace nor war are permanent conditions.

The Ethiopian government that up to the end of March 2018 was dominated by the TPLF (pejoratively called Weyane), was replaced by the OPDO, led by Dr. Abiy (half-Oromo and half-Amhara). In a matter of few days, the TPLF lost its dominant position and was literally pushed back to Tigray province, where it continues to exercise unchallenged hegemonic power.

---

5   The reader may rightly suspect that I have dwelt so much on the statement and hence given more credit to President Isaias than he might deserve. I strongly believe that similar views are held by hundreds of thousands of Eritreans, only they are not allowed to express them.

6   The small village at the border that was allegedly the cause of the 1998–2000 war.

A great deal has also been said and written about President Isaias and his style of governance. But for me who has followed his policies towards Ethiopia since the early 1970s, Isaias has demonstrated a remarkable consistency of vision on the nature of relations he wished to see between his country and Ethiopia, namely some kind of union.

Prelude to Badme, 1991–1998[7]

Soon after independence in 1993, Isaias expressed his interest in economic, political, and social integration with Ethiopia. Recently, Mesfin Hagos, a former senior commander of the EPLF, revealed that Isaias had already put forward in early 1991 a plan for keeping Eritrea within Ethiopia and thus forming a government with the EPRDF.[8] On April 25, 1993, that is, only a few weeks before the formal declaration of independence, Isaias told foreign journalists in Asmara that he would "not rule out very close economic ties or even the establishment of a confederation with Ethiopia."[9] The Asmara Pact of 1993, a series of agreements entered between the two countries, had the intention of eventually integrating them in all spheres. By the end of 1995, Isaias stated openly that the two countries were developing relations where boundaries would be meaningless. Eritrea's ambassador to Ethiopia, Halie Menkorios, went even further and stated that as "forming an independent state was never the ultimate goal of our long struggle, integration would be easier with Ethiopia, as we share common history and culture and have also lived together under a common political system."[10]

Eritrea and Eritreans were comfortable with Ethiopia and Ethiopians up to the end of 1997. The EPLF moved freely inside Ethiopia, and Eritreans (both those who were firmly settled and those who arrived after independence) enjoyed equal rights as Ethiopians. Eritreans were separate people, if and when it suited them. They also behaved and expected to be

---

7   The official reason for the 1998–2000 war was the forced occupation by Eritrean forces of the village of Badme. Eritrea claimed that Badme was within its boundary, although it had been administered by Ethiopia since imperial times. The border was delimited but not demarcated. Italy showed little interest in demarcating the border, as it had ambitions of colonizing the Ethiopian Empire. See the pioneering work of Federica Guazzini, Le ragioni di un confine coloniale.

8   Mesfin Hagos, interviewed by Yohannes Tsegay Berhe of SBS, July 19, 2018. According to Mesfin, Isaias is a person concerned primarily with maintaining power over the organization.

9   Africa Confidential 34, no.9, April 30, 1993.

10   Tekeste, Eritrea and Ethiopia, 176; Reporter 1 no. 2, September 18, 1996.

treated as Ethiopians if they so wished. Many Ethiopians perceived the Eritreans as having the cake and eating it at the same time.

Such privileged status of Eritreans caused negative reactions among the population of Addis Ababa in particular and Ethiopians in general. Many Ethiopians called for either the expulsion of Eritreans from Ethiopia or curtailment of their privileges, since they had rejected their Ethiopian brothers and sisters and voted for a separate future. This view was not fully supported by the Ethiopian government of the time—a government dominated by the TPLF—although it was fully aware that Eritreans (those organized by the EPLF) were deriving economic advantages at the expense of Ethiopians and their economy. Here we can briefly cite two practices that provoked many Ethiopians. The first was that the Eritrean foreign exchange bureaus gave more birr to the dollar than what Ethiopian banks offered, while the Ethiopian birr was the only currency for both Eritrea and Ethiopia. The second issue was the re-exporting of Ethiopian coffee from Massawa and Eritrea pocketing the foreign currency. These and other instances might not have been of vital importance by themselves. What made them assume more gravity was, I believe, that the Ethiopian government failed altogether to see them as malpractices that should not continue. The Ethiopian government continued openly to defend Eritrea and its ambitions in Ethiopia, while secretly it expressed its opposition to a whole range of Eritrean activities and ambitions in Ethiopia.

Between 1991 and 1996, the Ethiopian political scene was dominated by four major discourses. The first was the wisdom, or mistake, in reconfiguring the country along ethnic borders and hence the pre-eminence of identity politics. The politicization of ethnicity was commonly described in the Addis Ababa of the early 1990s as a killing virus worse than HIV/AIDS. But the idea of reconfiguring the country along ethnic lines was initially supported by many nationalities (such as the Oromo, Somali, and other ethnic groups in the south of the country). The ideology that Ethiopia was an empire made up of forcibly incorporated nations was first developed by the Ethiopian Student Movement.[11] It was, however, widely, though mistakenly, believed that the culprit for the politicization of ethnicity was the TPLF, which dominated and controlled the newly founded EPRDF. Besides of course the Eritrean liberation fronts (ELF and EPLF) who considered Ethiopia a colonial power, the Oromo political organizations as well as the Somali activists had the same view as that of the TPLF. What singled out the TPLF was that, first, it was the leading organization that put into effect the major

---

11   For a full study of the history and legacy of the Ethiopian Student Movement, see Bahru, *Quest for Socialist Utopia*.

slogan of the EthiopianStudent Movement, and secondly, it implemented it such that it suited it.[12]

The second discourse was the privileged position given to Eritrea and Eritreans. Many people in Addis Ababa believed that Eritrea and its inhabitants were rewarded for breaking away from Ethiopia. Ethiopia was being invaded by an Eritrean diaspora and by Eritrean enterprises managed by the powerful EPLF. It was at the end of 1995 that Isaias described relations between the two countries as moving towards complete union. However, his vision was certainly not reflected on the ground, where the role of Eritrea and Eritreans in the Ethiopian political scene was so hotly and widely debated that the Ethiopian government could no longer ignore it. A specific issue was the question of the citizenship of Eritreans. Many Ethiopians asked their government to deal with the question—an issue that the TPLF-dominated government was also keen to settle but in its own good time.

The third discourse was the reorganization of the Ethiopian political economy in favor of the TPLF as the dominant member of the coalition of organizations that made up the EPRDF. The government, dominated as it was by the TPLF, did indeed encourage donors to pay attention to Tigray (a very poor, marginalized province). It is also true that it favored its own NGO, EFFORT, which eventually became an important actor especially in the transport and construction sectors of the national economy. It is, however, important to mention that in those dramatic years, that is between 1991 and 1997, rumors, facts, and politics were all ingredients widely circulated and difficult to disentangle from one another.

The fourth discourse was the power struggle between the EPLF, led by Isaias, and the TPLF, led by Meles Zenawi (1991–2012), on the role of Eritrea and Eritreans in the Ethiopian economic sphere. Independent Eritrea was better equipped to play a share in the Ethiopian economy compared to the newly established autonomous region of Tigray. It has to be recalled that nearly 40 percent of all industrial and manufacturing activities of Ethiopia were located in Eritrea.[13] It is true that the wars fought by the EPLF and the TPLF against the Ethiopian regime of the period (1974–1991, also known as the Derg) had devastated the fragile economies of both regions. Using their comparative advantage, Eritreans (supported by their government)

---

12   The literature is voluminous on this issue. However, the best source on the ideological basis of the politicization of ethnicity (in the form of the national question) is Addis, Autocracy to Revolution.The recurring criticism against the federal structure put in place by the TPLF is that it was not federal. The regions were easily manipulated by the TPLF, and crucial power remained in its hands.

13   See Tekeste, Eritrea and Ethiopia, 139.

were, however, quickly capturing the emerging markets in Ethiopia. The perception of Eritrea and Eritreans playing a very active role in or even dominating the Ethiopian economy was out in the open in Addis Ababa in the early 1990s.

At the same time, the Ethiopian government led by Meles Zenawi initiated a series of economic development programs to strengthen the position of Tigray in the Ethiopian economy. The TPLF-dominated government began to build similar factories (such as for the manufacture of leather goods, drugs, and textiles) as those in Eritrea. The Eritrean government reacted sharply to what it called the duplication of manufacturing companies and the creation of unnecessary competition between Eritrea and Tigray. The TPLF fought to lift Tigray from its position as a neglected and poor on the periphery of Ethiopia. I think we can safely argue that the Eritrean government had either little sympathy for or very little knowledge of the objectives of the TPLF and its long war against the Ethiopian regime.

Short of solid communication based on mutual trust, the only way for the TPLF to develop its region was to capture the position of Eritrea as the second manufacturing zone of the country.[14] The Asmara Pact of 1993, the final objective of which was the economic and eventual political integration of Eritrea and Ethiopia, was frustrated to a large extent by a lack of common purpose as to the way forward. While Eritrea continued to build on its comparative advantage and demandeda free hand in the Ethiopian economy, the TPLF-dominated government in Addis Ababa was devising ways of curtailing Eritrean presence and influence in Ethiopia.

By 1997, the TPLF-dominated government in Addis Ababa, feeling strong and secure, introduced a new trade system with Eritrea, which if put into practice would effectively push the latter away from the Ethiopian economy. From 1998 onwards, the Ethiopian government decided that trade between the two countries would be managed by the letter of credit system, with the US dollar as the currency of trade.

From the middle of 1997, the Eritrean government felt it had been pushed out from the Ethiopian economic sphere by the TPLF-dominated government. The refusal of the Ethiopian government to allow the nakfa—the new Eritrean currency—parity with the birr was further interpreted as a hostile act.

In early 1998, Isaias gave a long interview where he summed up his views on what went wrong in Eritrean-Ethiopian relations. Here are some of

---

14 See Tekeste and Tronvoll, Brothers at War, 37.

the main issues as my colleague Kjetil Tronvoll and myself recorded them. I quote:

> Eritrea has no intention of creating a new wall between the Eritrean and north Ethiopian people, who had a long common history. Transaction costs of implementation were bound to be very high, and many mistakes were bound to be committed in attempts to implement inherently unfeasible policies. Such mistakes could have adverse effects on the relations between the two peoples. Other alternatives ought to be identified.

> Ethiopia's policy discriminated against Eritrea. Ethiopia did not implement a similar system on its borders with Djibouti, Somalia, and Kenya.

> The aim of Ethiopia's new policy was to prevent Eritrea from participating in the Ethiopian economy—for example in the agro-industry, transport, and finance sectors.

> Ethiopia was creating manufacturing establishments as import substitutes. The letter of credit system was devised in order to prevent competition from Eritrean establishments. Ethiopia's policy was purely protectionist.

> The protocol agreements on economic harmonization and trade had reached a dead end. The two countries failed to agree on common investment policies.

Isaias concluded that the deadlock should not continue indefinitely, that the Eritrean and Ethiopian people are bound to live together and that "we cannot change geographical and historical links that bind the peoples of the two countries."Finally, Isaias said that Eritrea, while respecting Ethiopia's policies, would continue to look for better alternatives.[15]

The interview with President Isaias was published in April 1998. It reflected that relations between the two countries had been deteriorating for some time. The meetings of the joint ministerial committee of January 1997 clearly pointed out that they had failed to agree on major issues related to trade harmonization and investment. As Isaias clearly stated, Eritrea was being pushed from the Ethiopian economy. The introduction of a new birr and the refusal of the Ethiopian government to trade with the nakfa on an equal footing with the birr were tantamount to a declaration of war.

In the book that I published with Kjetil Tronvollin 2000, I asked why both governments sacrificed the lives of thousands of their citizens over

---

15   Tekeste and Tronvoll, Brothers at War, 37.

Badme, a border village of some relatively marginal square kilometers of land. It is now nearly twenty years since the official ceasefire and one year since the peace agreement between President Isaias and Prime Minister Abiy. Although it was Eritrea, by invading disputed territory, that initiated the 1998–2000 war, both countries soon agreed that the war had very little to do with border issues, no matter how important these might be. The Eritrean government stated repeatedly that it would not reach an agreement so long as the TPLF remained the dominant organization in Ethiopia. The Ethiopian government pursued the policy of isolating Eritrea in the hope that its economy would implode from the inside; the Ethiopian government believed that it was only a question of time. The no war, no peace phase could only come to an end under two circumstances. The first was the fall of the Eritrean regime led by Isaias, and the second was the fall of the TPLF from itscommanding heights in Ethiopian politics.

The rise of Dr. Abiy Ahmed in early April 2018 provided the proof that many people had suspected over the last twenty-seven years that the Ethiopian government was indeed dominated by the TPLF. The no war, no peace stalemate was resolved, and leaders of both countries affirmed and reaffirmed that the Eritreans and Ethiopians were one people. The border (as a cause of conflict) between Eritrea and Ethiopia dissipated into thin air. In front of Isaias, the newly elected Abiy told the Ethiopian people that the border was destroyed (made redundant), and a new bridge of love was constructed over it. How did we come to such radical views about the relations between the two countries? I believe that there are both material and nonmaterial conditions for such statements. I also believe that a closer reading of the making of Eritrea and its transformation during the last seventyyears is very important in order to understand the positions of Isaias and Abiy on the common destiny of the Eritrean and Ethiopian people. From the iconic statement of Isaias I draw one conclusion: all that has been written by Eritrean nationalists on the history of Eritrea since its creation as a colony in the late nineteenth century has to be rewritten again.[16]

I am fully aware that writing the history of Eritrea from the 1950s until the present within the parameters of this format is a project that opens itself, quite rightly, to criticism from all quarters. It is nonetheless worth the effort because the statement by Isaias on the unity of the two people cannot be understood without a good grasp of what has gone on in Eritrea since and after it became an Italian colony. Whether Isaias survives long enough to see the formation of a political union of some sort between Eritrea and

---

16 The statement by Isaias not only challenges the colonial thesis as the basis for the creation of an independent Eritrea but also nullifies it altogether.

Ethiopia is of no great significance. What is important, according to my reading of the history of the region, is that the material conditions and the series of changes that took place in Eritrea since its "forced" incorporation into the Ethiopian Empire in the early 1950s will continue to create favorable conditions for closer relations between the two countries.

Many aspects of modern Eritrean history are heavily contested, owing to the proximity of the events that are compounded by the lack of intellectual rigor/ethics of most Eritrean authors.[17] Even more treacherous is the attempt that I am about to undertake, which is to use a personal reading of the past to say something useful about the foreseeable future.[18] Even though we know how history is made (nothing is predetermined; most of the present is a continuation of the past plus a reaction of sort to unforeseen events, also called conjunctures), we have no way of predicting human action. This is because unforeseen events may prove so strong that they force or bring about a new direction or orientation to the flow of history or organized collective existence. A quick glance at the modern history of Eritrea makes two things clear. First, we can know something useful as to what happened in the past. We have the theories and methods of carrying this out. Second, the record of human existence (history) is made by people under conditions they do not fully control, owing to the occurrence of conjunctures.[19]

Legacies of Colonialism

Since the premise for the existence of good prospects for peaceis based on the changes that have taken place both in Eritrea and in Ethiopia, it is important to sketch, albeit briefly, what has changed, when, and how. Let us

---

17 Okbazghi, Pawn in World Politics; Gaim, Eritrea: A Dream Deferred; Redie, "Complex Roots"; Gebrehiwot Tesfagiorgis, Emergent Eritrea; Kidane, Anatomy of an African Tragedy; Iyob, Ethiopian-Eritran Conflict; Bereket, Conflict and Intervention; Gebremedhin, Peasants and Nationalism. There are two theoretical assumptions common to these authors. First, Eritrea, like other African colonies, ought to have been independent. Second, the United States is mainly responsible for Eritrea's incorporation with Ethiopia. Both assumptions are theoretically and empirically faulty but were driven through by massive distortion of the economic and political processes that prevailed in Eritrea during the crucial decade of decolonization (1941–52) and condoned by the pervasive anti-Ethiopia climate that prevailed during the Cold War.

18 Gaddis, Landscape of History, 30.

19 Karl Marx once remarked that history is made by people but not the way they like it.

begin with the federation of Eritrea to Ethiopia in 1952. The diplomatic and political dynamics that led to the union in a federal structure has been studied by two groups of scholars. The first group, which John Sorensen describes as Eritrean nationalists, argued that Eritrea, like any other African colony, should have been granted its independence.[20] They argue that Eritrea was a pawn in international relations and that it best fit the geopolitical interests of the United States to appease Ethiopia. One of the most intransigent proponents of this view is undoubtedly Okbazghi Yohannes. The second group, represented by Amare Tekle, Lloyd Ellingson, Erlich Haggai, Shumet Sishagne, and myself, argued that the Eritreans played a significant role in shaping their history.[21]

The 1952–62 phase of Eritrean history has been studied within the context of the narratives and counter-narratives in defense or against the various armed movements to separate/free Eritrea from Ethiopia. Very few people have studied the role of Eritrea within the Ethiopian economy and the social and economic role of the great majority of Eritreans inside Eritrea and in other parts of Ethiopia. In this section I shall argue that Eritrea and its inhabitants (the great majority) had the best deal in Ethiopia during theimperial period. The Eritreans were the most dominant political, economical, and social group in the country after the small ruling clique of Amhara. Their share of power and privileges was far greater than their demographic size.[22]

However, before I start to catalogue the impact of the comparative advantages of Eritrea and Eritreans, I shall recapitulate the positive legacies of Italian and British colonialism that the Eritreans brought with them when they joined Ethiopia. Probably one of the lasting impacts of both Italian and British colonialism is the expectation and partial realization of a European/ Italian lifestyle. Close contact between the Italian and Eritrean communities was enhanced by two factors. The first was the huge number of Italians in a very small geographical location, namely the Eritrean highlands, a region of about twenty thousand square kilometers. Second was the need of the Italian population for various services, such as domestics at home and at

---

20 Sorensen, Discourses on Eritrean Nationalism and Identity.

21 Amare, Creation of the Ethio-Eritrean Federation; Ellingson, Eritrea; Erlich, Struggle over Ethiopia; Shumet, Unionists and Separatists; and Tekeste, Eritrea and Ethiopia.

22 In 1962, the Ethiopian population was estimated to be 20 million, whereas that of Eritrea was estimated at about 1 million. Eritreans made up about 5 percent of the Ethiopian population. Fifty years later, the Eritrean population is about 3 million, while that of Ethiopia has reached just over 100 million.

the workplace. We also need to recall that the Eritreans were given political and economic privileges as a reward for their contribution to the occupation and pacification of Ethiopia between 1935 and 1941. The demise of Italian colonialism further contributed to the emergence of many Eritreans in sectors of the economy such as trucking, machine maintenance, and general services.

Modern education was another sector where the Eritreans had a comparative advantage in relation to other Ethiopians. Italy destroyed the two modern schools established by Emperor Menelik (1908) and Emperor Haile Selassie (1925) and killed as many as 50 percent of the approximately two thousand students who graduated from them. At the time of the Italian invasion, four thousand pupils were attending fourteen government schools in the capital. At that time, some forty Ethiopian students were studying abroad at government expense.[23]And when Italy belatedly started to open new schools for Ethiopians, they were of much poorer quality. The educational policy of Italy was not to educate but to produce future soldiers for Italy. This is fully documented in a classic paper by Richard Pankhurst.[24] The educational landscape in Eritrea was slightly better. After a year of closure (1935–36), schools reopened, and an average of two thousand students continued their studies, the most ambitious of them completing a program equivalent to four years of elementary school.[25] There were more children in Eritrean schools than in the entire Ethiopian empire in 1941, largely because Eritrea was peacefully (in colonial parlance) ruled for more than forty years.

The educational landscape built by the Italians was demolished both in Eritrea and Ethiopia by the British administering authority in 1941. The few sources on the subject, however, indicate that it was easier to rebuild the schools and start new ones in Eritrea than in Ethiopia. In the 1944–45 academic yearthere were 28 schools in Eritrea, with a total enrolment of 2,045.[26] Only 8 schools were for Muslim Eritreans, whereas the rest were for Christians. During the same academic year and throughout the Ethiopian Empire, there were 120 government schools, 450 teachers, and 19,000 students.[27] Although Eritrea had yet to be united with Ethiopia, such comparative figures are useful in demonstrating that there were more

---

23 Ethiopia Observer 5, no. 1,p. 61.

24 Pankhurst, Education in Ethiopia.

25 Tekeste, Italian Colonialism, 82–83.

26 Guazzini, Le ragioni di un confine colonial, 148.

27 Ethiopia: The Official Handbook (1969):113.

Eritreans in the modern school system than Ethiopians. It has also to be recalled that Eritrea existed as one of six provinces of Italian East Africa, where the same educational policies were uniformly implemented. There is another aspect that it is worthwhile to remember: the population of Ethiopia was at least twenty times more than that of Eritrea.

The 1947–50 years were very formative years indeed. Guided by the British Military Administration, Eritreans debated matters that concerned their future. The Eritreans were in one way or another influenced by the British, by the Italians, and by the Ethiopians. We know quite a lot about the role played by Great Britain and Italy in forming or shaping political opinion in Eritrea. What we know less about is first Ethiopia's role in its support for the Unionist Party on the grounds of historical links, and seconds, its claim as a landlocked country to sea access, a claim with a good chance of support by the Four Powers.[28]

Eritrea as the Industrial Center of the Ethiopian Empire, and Addis Ababa Spoke Tigrinya by Night, 1952–74

Eritrea did not become an independentstate as the Italian community had wished; or it was not partitioned into two (between the Anglo-Egyptian Sudan and Ethiopia) as the Muslim League of western Eritrea had desired. It is indeed important to remember that Ethiopia did not claim the whole of Eritrea. The maximum claim of Ethiopia was the Eritrean highlands, including access to the sea, and the minimum claim was just access to the sea.[29] By a twist of history, Ethiopia ended up acquiring the whole of Eritrea. Those who had fought for the independence of Eritrea from the 1960s onwards argued that it was the combined strategies of the United States and Ethiopia that led to the UN federal resolution of 1950. Amare Tekle (as early as 1964), Erlich Haggai (1983), John Markakis(1978), and myself since 1997 have argued that it was the Eritrean Unionist Party's persistent campaign that tilted the balance in favor of union with Ethiopia. It has to be emphasized once again that the Unionist Party fought only on behalf of the Christian population in the three regions of Eritrea (namely Seraye, Hamassien, and Akeleguzay).

---

28 The role of Ethiopia in Eritrean politics between 1947and 1950 has yet to be written, notwithstanding my attempts to do so. See for instance my articles of 1991 and 2004.

29 Spencer, Ethiopia at Bay; Amare, Creation of the Ethio-Eritrean Federation; Tekeste, Eritrea and Ethiopia.

For the Italian community, the implications of the federation of Eritrea with Ethiopia were very clear. Eritrea had become part of Ethiopia. The Italian community, which was about seventy thousand strong in 1940, dwindled to about seventeen thousand by 1952. Many of them had been repatriated, and some of them moved to Ethiopia. From 1952 to 1956, the Italian population was further reduced to eleven thousand. The departure of every Italian may not, as I wrote in 1997, have literally meant the loss of three Eritrean jobs, but there could be no doubt that the shrinking Italian community had adverse effects on the economy. Many of those who could not find employment in Eritrea found their way to Ethiopia, where skills they'd acquired from the Italians were much needed.

The modern sector of the Eritrean economy was under the control of the Italian community. In the beginning of 1958, there were 10,200 Italians in the country. Without exception, all the manufacturing establishments (many of which were established during colonial times) were owned and run by Italians. The Eritreans, as in the colonial period, waxed and waned with the economic situation of Italian firms. Although many Italian firms had to close due to stiff competition from European producers soon after the Second World War, their economic position and performance picked up from 1955 onwards. Some of the notable agro-industrial establishments (De Nadai, Melotti, and Barattolo) experienced their intensive period of expansion after 1955.[30]

Contrary to allegations made by those who have studied the federation period, the economic situation of Italian firms improved considerably with the implementation of the federation. According to a survey carried out by the British consulate in Asmara in April 1959, the federation had more to offer than the earlier British administration; at the end of 1958 there were 627 industrial activities, as opposed to 456 in 1956.[31] So although the Italian-dominated modern sector of the Eritrean economy picked up momentum after 1956, its impact on the living conditions of the majority of Eritreans was not sufficiently pervasive. Italian firms may have altogether provided employment for about twenty thousand Eritreans according to estimates made by the Italian consulate in Asmara in 1959.[32]

---

30 Asmara was the financial and industrial center of Italian East Africa. See Tekeste, Italian Colonialism, 52.

31 Tekeste, Eritrea and Ethiopia, 123.

32 Tekeste, 124. In 1953, the Eritrean government employed 7,188 people, with 4,023 in the police force. See also the table produced by George Lipsky(1962) on industrial establishments in Ethiopia and Eritrea.

Eritrean migration to Ethiopia was virtually impossible during the large part of the Italian colonial period, from 1890 to 1935. Yet many Eritreans, especially those who wanted more education and freedom, secretly left for Ethiopia. Unfortunately, we do not have figures, but their number must have been quite high,since the colonial governor of Eritrea complained that educated Eritreans preferred to move to Ethiopia rather than stay in Eritrea.[33] The Italian invasion of Ethiopia in 1935 opened up the Ethiopian empire for all those Eritreans who for one reason or another were not active in the colonial army. It has to be remembered that Eritrea, including Tigray, was organized as one of six provinces of Italian East Africa. It has also to be remembered that the Eritreans were given special privileges in the labour market as a reward for their contribution to the colonization of Ethiopia. Many Eritreans were already well inserted when the Italians were defeated in 1941.

The British who ruled over Eritrea from 1941 to 1952 did very little to control the in-and-out migration of Eritreans. From the Ethiopian side, the policy of Emperor Haile Selassie was to treat all Eritreans in Ethiopia as Ethiopian citizens or as his subjects.[34] Not only did the emperor rehabilitate fully the Eritrean colonial soldiers (known as *banda*),[35] he also tried to keep as many Italians as possible in the country on the belief that they would help him develop his country. By the beginning of 1950, the Eritrean population in all parts of Ethiopia might have been between 100,000 and 120,000.[36] More than 2,000 Eritreans were gainfully employed in Ethiopian public service, and the most prominent staff of the Ministry of Foreign

---

33 See Tekeste, Italian Colonialism, 150.

34 In 1948, Bereket HabteSelassie was sent for further studies to London by the Ethiopian government as one of the country's promising citizens. See his memoirs, Crown and the Pen, 83. See also the contents of thecampaign that Emperor Haile Selassie carried out during the 1940–41 war of liberation as documented and reported by Steer, Sealed and Delivered.

35 Shiferaw Bekele reminded me, quite correctly, that Eritrean colonial soldiers were called either askaris or Hamasienoch (those from Hamassien). The term banda was given to the approximately 300,000 Ethiopian soldiers recruited by the Italian Fascist state from 1939 onwards; the risk that Ethiopia, under Fascist rule, might have to face the British Empire without the support of Italy became imminent. When Italy entered the Second World War in June 1940, the British cut communication lines (Suez Canal) and thus isolated Ethiopia from getting support from Italy. Italy did not secure its communication lines with Ethiopia—its major African colony—and was least able to defend its possessions against the combined British and Ethiopian assaults.

36 Ethiopia claimed parts of Eritrea on the grounds of historical links.

Affairs were from Eritrea.[37] It is important to put the Eritrean population in Ethiopia in 1950 in relation to the population of Eritrea, which in 1950 was about 700,000.[38] Nearly 20 percent of the Eritrean population lived and worked in Ethiopia in 1950.

With the coming of the federation, Eritreans, now as full citizens of the Ethiopian Empire, moved in even bigger numbers to Ethiopia. They had two main advantages: first, they had gained skills owing to their close contact with the Italians; and second, they had greater access to modern education. Let us look in general terms at the advantage Eritrean youth had in relation to the rest of the population.

In 1959–60 the enrollment landscape looked as follows:

> Enrollment in government schools in the empire: 181,163; in Eritrea: 32,387.
>
> Enrollment in mission schools in the empire 20,497; in Eritrea: 6,612.
>
> Enrollment in private schools in the empire: 14,790; in Eritrea: 9,110.[39]

In 1959–60 there were 581 government elementary schools, out of which 154 were in Eritrea. In the empire, including Addis Ababa, there were 28 secondary schools out of which 3 were in Eritrea. In the provinces there were 14 secondary schools in total.

(The total number of students stood at 224,934, out of which 48,111 were from Eritrea.) Nearly 30 percent of all the students in the empire were Eritreans.[40] The largest non-Amhara group at the newly established Addis Ababa University (AAU) were Eritreans; between 1963 and 1968, nearly 17 percent of those who passed the Ethiopian School Leaving Certificate Examination (ESLCE) were Eritreans.[41]

The Ethiopian educational landscape was no doubt dominated by Eritrea and its inhabitants. The number given above does not include the children of Eritrean families that resided in all the provinces of the empire. It would not be an exaggeration to state that up to 1960, one out of three students of the

---

37   Tekeste, Eritrea and Ethiopia,60.

38   According to the census of 1939, Eritrea had a total population of 614,353. The Tigrinya speakers constituted 54 percent of the population. See Tekeste, Italian Colonialism, 150.

39   Ethiopia Observer 5(1962):63.

40   See also the table on enrollment in government schools in Eritrea, 1955–62, produced by Teshome Wagaw(1979):101.

41   Haile, "Problem ofAdmission," 119, cited by Markakis, National and Class Conflict, 119.

empire was Eritrean. Eritrea, it has to be kept in mind, was a tiny province with a population of slightly over 700,000, whereas Ethiopia in 1960 might have had a population between 18 and 22 million. The Eritrean population, whichconstituted less than 5 percent of the Ethiopian population, had so much comparative advantage due to its colonial experience.

I think it is relevant to see at close range the advantage that Eritrea gained during the imperial period, from 1952 to 1973. In 1959 there were 4,334 secondary school students in the Ethiopian Empire, out of which 984 were from Eritrea. Or we can deconstruct the figures in a slightly different way. There were 3,350 secondary school students in the Ethiopian Empire and 984 secondary school students in the autonomous region of Eritrea.[42] And here we can see that nearly 30 percent of all secondary school students were either Eritreans or were from Eritrea. This number is extremely large when seen in relation the demographic position of Eritrea within Ethiopia. Eritrea, with its population of less than 5 per cent, had an outsized presence in the public sphere of the Ethiopian polity during the imperial period in general but more so during the so-called decade of federation, from 1952 to 1962.

The presence of the Eritreans in high political positions was also considerable, once again in view of the small demographic size of the region, as was documented by Christopher Clapham in the 1960s.Between 1941 and 1966, out of the 138 individuals holding high office in the central government,85 were from Shoa, 7 from Tigray, 19 from Eritrea, and 6 from Wällega. In 1966, out of the 68 high officials in the empire, 9 were from Eritrea, 5 were from Wällega, and 2 from Tigray. (About 15 percent of all officials were from Eritrea.) It has to be remembered that these were high officials (such as ministers). Eritreans were heavily represented in the intermediate levels of the imperial bureaucracy.[43] In the context above, one can certainly argue that Eritrea was decolonized and its citizens were represented in the Ethiopian economic, social, and political spheres much more than what their demography would indicate. The anecdote that Addis Ababa spoke Tigrinya by night had, according to me, more substance in the sense that many Eritreans with good-paying jobs could afford the expenses of going out in the evenings.

In my earlier work, I have described the 1941 to 1970 period as the golden age of Ethiopian education, where there was a direct correlation between investment in education and employment.[44] The country was being

---

42 Levine, Wax and Gold, 294. The table is illustrative.

43 Clapham, Haile Selassie's Government, 77.

44 Tekeste Negash, Crisis of Ethiopian Education, 1990.

modernized, and there was a great need for young, schooled people. A good primary education (up to grade eight) was more than enough to get a good-paying job. Salaries for schooled workers were quite highin relation to the cost of living and per capita income of the population at large.[45] In a period where virtually every schooled boy and girl got a good job (most of these jobs were in cities and small towns), we can easily imagine a landscape where there were Eritreans everywhere, and it was not an exaggeration at all when my relatives in the mid-1960s told me that Addis Ababa spoke Tigrinya by night.[46]

From its inception in 1950 (as a university college) and later from 1961 as Haile Selassie University, AAU's greatest challenge was to get students and retain them. Job opportunities were so plentiful that it was difficult for the university to persuade its students to be patient enough to complete their studies. Few students saw the advantages of pursuing their education at the tertiary level.[47]

By 1970, the Ethiopian public and private sector was fully staffed, and secondary school graduates began to face unemployment. And by 1974 up to 25 percent of secondary school graduates were unemployed.[48] Modern education did not even reach more than 10 percent of the school-age population in the country and yet the Ethiopian economy was so much based on subsistence agriculture that it could not absorb the steadily growing graduates from Ethiopian schools. By this time, however, tens of thousands of Eritreans with eight years of schooling or more were gainfully employed.

---

45 The initial salary of a university graduate in the 1960s was 400 birr; a new car could be purchased for 2,000 birr and a hundred kilograms of teff (staple cereal) could be bought for less than 20 birr. I was a student at the University of Asmara between 1967 and 1972. I followed salaries and prices, as I was in the pipeline for a good job. My first employment was at Asmara University in 1972, and my initial salary was just 400 birr.

46 I contacted about a dozen of my diaspora relatives who lived and worked in Addis Ababa and other cities, and they confirmed they had a great time and that it was the Derg that shattered and robbed them of their Ethiopian citizenship. Between 1965 and 1967, on my way to Jimma Agricultural Technical School to do my secondary education, I stayed in Addis on several occasions and hence could witness the privileged position of the Eritrean community.

47 See the table on the number of grade 12 students and those who sat for the ESLCE from 1951–52 to 1960–61, Teshome Wagaw, 1990:99.

48 Desta Assayehegn, 1979:71, quoted in Tekeste, 1990:8.

The Fall of Haile Selassie and the Steady Decline of Eritrea and Eritreans in Ethiopian Affairs, 1974–1991

Not all Eritreans benefitted from being united to Ethiopia. The Christian Eritreans (or commonly known as the highlanders) were the great beneficiaries. The Muslims of western Eritrea were not easily absorbed into the Ethiopian economy, owing to their peripheral location (agro-pastoralism as the dominant mode of survival) and the culture gap. Moreover, it has to be recalled that the inhabitants of western Eritrea did not want to join Ethiopia, and the Ethiopian state was not keen to incorporate them. Western Eritrea was joined to Ethiopia by UN decision. Both the Unionist Party in Eritrea that fought for reunion with Ethiopia, and the Ethiopian government, had clearly stated that the inhabitants of western Eritrea were free to either join Sudan or declare their independence. And it was exactly in the western parts of Eritrea and by those Eritreans who voted to be independent (both from Ethiopia and Sudan) that the first armed resistance against Ethiopian administration started in the autumn of 1961.

I shall not dwell in depth on the history of Eritrean resistance for independence/liberation or separation from Ethiopia at length, partly because such a narrative does not provide useful information on the subject and partly because there is a sufficient number of studies; suffice it to mention the work edited by Basil Davidsonin 1988 and the exhaustive studies by Haggai Erlich (1983), Gebru Tareke (2009), and the by far most comprehensive study of John Markakis (1987).[49]From its inception in 1961 until 1974, Eritrean armed resistance against Ethiopia was dominated by the ELF, whose leading members were Muslims of western Eritrea. The ELF believed that Eritrea was predominantly a Muslim country annexed/ colonized by a Christian monarch. Consequently, the ELF, through its charismatic leaders, Ibrahim Sultan and Osman Saleh Sabbe, sought assistance from the Arab world and got it. The ELF put the message that the abolition of the federation in 1962 by Emperor Haile Selassie and the incorporation of Eritrea as one of the provinces was an act of colonialism by a black power over a small, Muslim, ex-Italian colony.

The Eritrean question as part of the Muslim struggle against the hegemony of the West (led by US imperialism and the Zionist state of Israel) gave rise in 1970 to a countermovement led and managed by Christian Eritreans. In a manifesto issued in 1971, this movement, known as the Eritrean People's Liberation Forces, made its position

---

49 Davidson and Cliffe, eds., Long Struggle of Eritrea; Erlich, Struggle over Eritrea; Gebru, Ethiopian Revolution.

clear from the outset. It accused the ELF of wrongly portraying Eritrea as an Arab and Muslim country and that the ELF killed or eliminated the Christian Eritreans in its ranks.[50] Here is how Markakis described it:

The manifesto did not conceal that its authors were Christians, but stressed that it was not religious sentiment that brought them together. "We are freedom fighters, not prophets of Christianity," they proclaimed. Confronted with an unenviable choice— to perish at the hands of Muslim fanatics or to surrender to Haile Selassie—they chose to fight both enemies, "to sit on the edge of the blade" as they put it. The manifesto refuted the Arab identification favoured by some elements in the ELF, and rejected the adoption of Arabic as an official language since it was not the spoken language of any group in Eritrea. . . . We and our Objectives became the revolutionary gospel of the Eritrean People's Liberation Front.[51]

This new movement had the upper hand because it had a better human resource base, the Eritrean highlanders, most of whom were Christians who had better education and training and were accustomed to recognizing and respecting political hierarchy.[52]

Eritreans were used to a lifestyle based on an economy dominated by the presence of the US military base at Kagnew Station in Asmara(1953–72) and the Italian community. The five thousandsoldier-strong base kept the urban economy going. The approximatelyten thousand-strong Italian community managed to give a certain amount of urban flavor to the city of Asmara and also gave employment to several thousand Eritreans. Contact between American soldiers and Eritrean youth (mainly in drinking places), as well as contact between the Italian community and the Eritreans of Asmara transformed the youth of Asmara (the Asmarinos) to be the most sophisticated citizens of the Ethiopian Empire. By the end of 1974, the base was closed, and most of the Italian community, scared by the socialist rhetoric of the Derg, which had recently taken power, left Eritrea for good.

---

50   Eritrean People's Liberation Forces, 1971.

51   Markakis, National and Class Conflict, 132–33.

52   The Tigrinya-speaking inhabitants of Eritrea (the great majority of whom are Christians) number more than the other eight ethnic groups (predominantly Muslim) put together. Hence the demise of the ELF in 1982 meant that the EPLF and its cadres felt and behaved like the new and legitimate owners of all of Eritrea. No non-Christian ethnic group can on its own challenge the expansionist policies of the EPLF in western Eritrea, hitherto inhabited by non-Christian/Abyssinian ethnic groups. The expansion of Tigrinya or Abyssinian culture throughout the entire Eritrean landscape is one of the unintended outcomes of the armed resistance against union with Ethiopia started by the ELF in the early 1960s.

We can date the beginning of the decline and eventual collapse of the Eritrean economy to two major factors, namely, the closure of Kagnew Station in 1973 and the mass exodus of the Italian community in 1975. Thus from1975 until 1991, the comparative advantage that Eritrea had up to 1974 was steadily erased, and by 1990 Eritrea lost virtually all its advantages.

The 1974 revolution in Ethiopia created new conditions in Eritrea. In the ensuing power vacuum, which lasted from February 1973 until November 1974, thousands of Eritreans joined both liberation fronts. The more Christians joined the ELF, the more it lost its hegemonic narrative of Eritrea both as a Muslim and Arab nation. From 1976 onwards the balance of forces were clearly in favor of the EPLF.

In 1982, the EPLF and the newly established Tigray People's Liberation Front (TPLF) in a joint military move pushed the ELF out of the Eritrean scene. The joint military operation had far-reaching consequences. The assistance of the TPLF enabled the EPLF to dominate the Eritrean scene. It has to be remembered that, notwithstanding the rhetoric of scientific socialism, both the EPLF and TPLF were founded on principles of Christian/Abyssinian culture.

The EPLF might have eventually defeated the ELF because of the latter's impossible ambition to create an organization that would accommodate both Christians and Muslims. While the joint EPLF and TPLF military assault against the ELF hastened the process of demise, the assault and subsequent victory contributed to the consolidation of the hegemony/supremacy of Tigrinya/Christian culture in Eritrea. In this sense, the joint EPLF/TPLF assault can be described as a Tigrinya (Christian) crusade against the weakly organizedMuslim communities. Since 1982, the Muslim regions of Eritrea came under the firm grip of the EPLF and Tigrinya as the hegemonic culture. The outmigration of Muslims from western Eritrea gained momentum followingthe military demise of the ELF. This is a subject more fully discussed in the next section of this paper.

The ELF ceased to exist as a fighting force in 1982 but left a powerful legacy behind it, and that is that Eritrea was colonized by Ethiopia. The best representative of this legacy is Basil Davidson, who in two powerful articles (1980 and 1988), writing as he did after the demise of the ELF, bought the colonial thesis of the ELF but not its religious dimension.[53] The other narrative put forward, by Haggai Erlich (1983), is that the Eritrean armed resistance was supported by neighbouring states such as Egypt and the Sudan as well as some states in the Middle East (mainly Syria and Iraq) but the Ethiopian

---

53 Davidson, Cliffe, and Bereket, Behind the War; Davidson and Cliffe, Long Struggle of Eritrea.

imperial government had by and large succeeded in both neutralizing foreign support and maintaining internal control over Eritrea. The conflict in Eritrea was manageable and was defined as low-intensity conflict.

The vulnerable situation that prevailed in the country in the immediate wake of the revolution of 1974, with widespread internal rebellion and outright invasion of Ethiopia by Somalia in 1977, was a major factor in the militarization of Ethiopia as never before witnessed. Once Somalia, thanks to the massive support of arms and soldiers from Russia and Cuba, was defeated, the Ethiopian regime led by Mengistu Haile Mariam decided to solve the Eritrean question militarily, that is in the same way Mengistu did in Somalia. The first offensive against the combined forces of the EPLF and ELF took place in the beginning of 1978. This was a daunting challenge because with the exception of Massawa and Asmara, the rest of the country was under the control of both the EPLF and ELF. As the Ethiopian armed forces pushed their way forward, the Eritrean liberation fronts either destroyed materials they deemed would benefit the enemy or plundered property (various types of machinery) for future use. Eritrea and its society witnessed massive social, economic, and political upheaval from 1974 to 1978.

The sphere of rule of the Ethiopian state was limited only to Massawa and Asmara, where several military intelligence units (army, navy, air force, security) carried out extrajudicial killings in the few areas under their control. A chain of command was only established in 1979. In the countryside, the Eritrean liberation fronts spread a reign of terror accompanied by the massive forced recruitment of boys and girls.[54]

By 1980, Eritrea had lost a great deal. Certainly up to 100,000 of its youth were either in the Eritrean liberation movements or had left Eritrea. The school system was completely disrupted. As GebruTareke noted in his brilliant article of 2002, the Eritrean economy "had been seriously disrupted as most of the factories had lain idle since 1977. The few that remained in operation did so only at or near 30 percent capacity."[55] From 1980 to 1989, the Ethiopian state turned Eritrea, where more than 150,000 Ethiopian soldiers were stationed, into the main theater of war. At least six major offensives to push and defeat the EPLF were recorded, each bringing massive

---

54   Indeed thousands of young people from the cities joined the Eritrean fronts between 1974 and 1977. While those who joined the ELF could leave it, those who joined the EPLF had no chance whatsoever of either leaving or deserting the organization. From 1977 until 1991, the EPLF resorted to forced recruitment of Eritreans in the same way as the military regime in Ethiopia.

55   Gebru, From Lash to Red Star, 475.

destruction of human life and material resources. The Ethiopian state was at war not only against the Eritrean liberation fronts but also indirectly against the Eritrean people, as it failed to involve them in a meaningful way.[56] Determined to solve the Eritrean conflict by arms, as it had in Somalia, the Ethiopian state turned Eritrea into a militarized zone. The Eritrean people found themselves squeezed between two highly authoritarian regimes. The Eritrean liberation fronts forced people to support them (at the risk of being considered enemies), and the Ethiopian state was all too ready to punish and kill anyone suspected of aiding or supporting the Eritrean rebels.

The political situation in Ethiopia had greatly improved since 1979 (with the formation of a political party organizing committee), and the Ethiopian state weathered the great famine of 1984–85 without any social unrest. The situation in Eritrea was different. Those harassed by the Ethiopian state left Eritrea, and many were encouraged/forced by the Eritrean liberation fronts to join the fronts, leaving their homes and families behind. Between 1980 and 1991, Eritrea was emptied both of its people and its resources.

By the end of the 1980s, Eritrea had lost its privileged position as the literate house of Ethiopia.In a pioneering article published in 1992, Habtamu Wandimu revealed that Eritrea lagged behind in comparison with other provinces of the country.[57]

The literacy rate of 1970 (18 percent for Eritrea and 8.5 percent for the rest of the country[58]) remained stagnant in Eritrea, while other regions, such as Arsi, Wellega, Sidamo, and north Omo experienced dramatic growth. Eritrea lost the advantage it had because of the war of "liberation." There was also another loss that Eritrea as a society suffered. The great majority of those who left Eritrea (either forced or of their own volition) were not encouraged by the EPLF and its supporters to pursue their academic studies. The perfect supporter was the one who paid his/her regular financial due to the EPLF and asked no questions (of a democratic nature).[59]

---

56 The first and last effort on the part of the Ethiopian state to involve Eritrea in resolving the conflict was in 1974 when General Aman Andom, head of the Ethiopian military junta, was given the mandate to seek a peaceful solution. His approach was not appreciated, and he was killed on November 23, 1974. The Eritrean liberation fronts were jubilant at his death; they were concerned that Aman's continued presence might create a wedge among the Eritreans.

57 Habtamu, "Inequality of Opportunity," 7.

58 Brooks, "Literacy in Ethiopia," 16–41.

59 Even the doyen of Eritrean nationalism, Bereket HabteSelassie, kept his mouth shut for over twenty-five years over the EPLF human rights violations he witnessed in 1976,for fear of being branded either an infantile intellectual leftist or an outright

The thirty years of war of "liberation from Ethiopia" left Eritrea with the loss of at least sixty-five thousand dead and most probably double that number wounded. More Ethiopians died to keep Eritrea within the Ethiopian fold. According to my estimate, up to three hundred thousand Ethiopians died. However, the impact of these losses was felt, I would argue, much more in Eritrea, owing to its demographic size. Hard figures are difficult to get; they do not exist as yet, and they have to be reassembled using many types of sources—a task far beyond the scope of this paper. Nearly half a million Eritreans from the western region were in Sudan, many of them since 1967. The generous asylum policies adopted by Ronald Reagan and Margaret Thatcher led to thousands of Eritreans and Ethiopians migrating to the United States and the United Kingdom. Once again, I think we can argue with great plausibility that these migrations affected Eritrea much more than Ethiopia because of the different demographic realities.

The thirty years war also left a legacy of the invincibility of the Eritrean People's Liberation Front. The EPLF, admittedly with the crucial support of the TPLF, had defeated the Ethiopian army successively, first at Nakfa in 1982, then at Af Abet in 1988, and later in early February 1990 when the EPLF won its second and most important victory by seizing the city and port of Massawa. Gebru Tareke wrote that "the result was as methodical as the earlier one, conducted in utmost secrecy, with utmost speed, and utmost concentration of forces."[60] Eritrea became independent in 1991 but paid a very heavy price for it. Whether independence was worth the price would depend on the balance of forces and on the strength of the links (historical, geographical, and economical) that bind the two countries.

On the occasion of an international conference on challenges of economic development, held in Asmara on July 21–22, 1991, Isaias described the situation of Eritrea in the following incisive words:

> It is sad, but true, to say that Eritrea has no economy today, devastated as it is by the thirty years of war and deliberate scorched-earth policy. In addition to the war, the manpower and economic resources of the country have been depleted by recurrent drought and other natural calamities. As there is virtually nothing, the first priority of the task is to formulate and lay the foundation for an initial economic framework.

And regarding education, Isaias continued:

> Generations have been deprived of education, and our professional and skilled manpower has been paralyzed and made to lag behind.

---

traitor to the cause. See Crown and the Pen, 317–18.

60   Gebru, Ethiopian Revolution, 292.

This is a very serious situation that requires immediate attention.[61]

Unfortunately, Isaias's perceptive assessment passed unappreciated by Eritrean scholars. I quote:

> *The newly born state of Eritrea is destined to play a key regional economic role in the Horn of Africa, over the medium and long run. . . . Eritrea is facing a challenge and opportunity of rehabilitation, restructuring, and transformation of war–devastated economy. Its potential for economic growth and development is immense. Its comparative advantage stems from its natural resources, location, and the availability of a talented, hard-working, and ingenuous population.*[62]

The same diaspora scholar went to the extent of fabricating the resources of the country that would certainly have shocked Isaias. I quote:

> Industry in Eritrea was relatively developed, and by 1960 there were more industries in Eritrea than the whole of Ethiopia, Somalia, Sudan, and Djibouti put together. Eritrean industries were providing various consumer and industrial items. The quality of products produced in Eritrea was considered high and in great demand and appreciated by consumers in Eritrea, Ethiopia, Djibouti, and Sudan as well as others.[63]

Moreover, many diaspora Eritreans painted a future for Eritrea President Isaias would not have even imagined. In the first international conference on economic challenges, organized in Asmara in July 1991, one of the architects of the conference wrote:

> At the initial stages Eritrea can play the lead role and provide the nucleus for close economic cooperation and integration of the economies of the area. In this regard much can be learned from the strategy adopted by Singapore. Eritrea has a strategic location in terms of land, sea, and air communication links with Sudan, Ethiopia, Djibouti, and Somalia. Eritrea's location becomes even more significant when the other neighbouring country across the sea, Yemen, is considered as part of the group. Thus Eritrea, taking advantage of its geographic location, becomes the regional hub. Singapore has used the hub strategy with much success.[64]

---

61 Keynote address by Isaias, July 21, 1991. Reproduced in Gebre, ed., Emergent Eritrea, xxii–xxvi.

62 Yohannes, Regional Economic Cooperation, 13.

63 Yohannes, 5. In the first place, the information is a product of his imagination. But even if it were true, he ought to have mentioned that industries in Eritrea were owned by Italians and could only remain in Eritrea as long as they could export to Ethiopia. Many of the industries in Eritrea moved to Ethiopia to save on transportation costs.

64 Berhe Habte-Giorgis, 1993:42.

The Asmara conference of July 1991 revealed a very serious gap of perception as to the potentials of Eritrea. While Isaias described the damage of the thirty yearsof war on the Eritrean economic and social fabric, Eritrean diaspora scholars painted a future for Eritrea that had no correspondence with the reality on the ground. How could a country whose economy has, according to its leader, been completely destroyed and whose manpower potential was ravaged by neglect, drought, and natural calamities be described at the same time as a country that had all the potential to emerge as a hub like Singapore? Eritrea has been served badly by its intellectuals.[65]

Ethiopia and Eritrea: Unequal Partners, 1991–2018

Between 1974 and 2018 both Eritrea and Ethiopia experienced notable changes in their demographic composition. The inhabitants of western Eritrea (mostly Muslim) were successively pushed or driven out of their villages and settlements. This was largely due to the fact that most of the war between the Ethiopian army and the Eritrean Peoples Liberation Front took place in the western parts of the country. There was also another factor; the EPLF has been either unwilling or incapable of encouraging the return of the approximately half a million Eritreans from the Western region.[66] Either by design or by default, the Tigrinya speakers of Eritrea have repopulated most of the regions previously inhabited by the Muslim communities of western Eritrea.

Although no census has been conducted in Eritrea, there aresufficient indicators to postulate the following: The Tigrinya population (who share common history, culture, and geography with northern Ethiopia) have not only increased their demographic power over the other eight quite small and Muslim ethnic groups but they have also spread throughout the country. The thirty years of war for independence acquainted many highlanders to the climate of western Eritrea, and moreover, many were pushed both by increasing demographic pressure and a government policy of resettlement. The political implication of the consolidation of all power in the hands of the Tigrinya speakers is bound to be considerable. Crudely speaking, the Tigrinya frontiers have now extended far beyond the mountains of Keren.

65　I hesitate to extend the term intellectual to the great majority of Eritrean diaspora writers because they do not fulfill the essential requirements of the term, namely a person who examines an issue without any preconceived ideas as to its outcome.

66　Gaim, Eritrea.

There is also another indicator of the demographic decline of Eritrea, namely school enrollment. It is said that Eritrea is composed of nine different ethnic groups. This might be true, but the lion's share of the resources is under the control of the Tigrinya ethnic group. The Tigrinya districts had in 2015–16 a total enrollment of slightly more than 51,000 in the secondary school system, whereas the remaining eight ethnic communities had a combined total of less than 25,000 enrolled students. Nearly 80 percent of all secondary school students are from the highlands—that is from the Tigrinya-speaking areas of the country.[67] The dominant position of the Tigrinya speakers in the education system can hardly be overestimated. Eight out of ten students in the secondary education sector (those from gradesnine to twelve) in Eritrea are Tigrinya speakers. The remaining eight ethnic groups—the majority of whom are Muslims—cannot in any meaningful way compete with the Tigrinya-speaking group for two reasons: first, each of the ethnic groups are too small compared to the Tigrinya, and second, they do not communicate with each other easily. The fact that the great majority of the eight ethnic groups are Muslims does not necessarily translate into effective bonds of solidarity.[68]In a long interview, Gunther Schröder pointed out that more than 30 percent of the population in the northern Red Sea region and more than 20 percent in the Afar region have fled to Sudan and Ethiopia, respectively. The government replaced the loss by settling people from the Tigrinya-speaking regions of the highlands. Schröder mentioned the case of Gash and Barca—a region that has experienced more than 30 percent growth. The new migrants are peasants from the Tigrinya-speaking regions of the country. Tigrinya-speaking Eritreans are moving into the previously Muslim/non-Tigrinya regions, while the indigenous inhabitants (Schröder's term), mostly Muslims, are moving out to Sudan and Ethiopia.The use of Arabic as a lingua francahas been rejected by the Eritrean government since1993.[69]

Although we can strongly argue that Eritrea is under the firm grip of the Tigrinya-speaking group at the expense of the remaining eight non-Tigrinya ethnic communities, we also notice that the country has experienced considerable demographic decline, especially since 2001. The main circumstantial evidence is gross enrollment, as shown in table 1.

---

67   Eritrea Education Sector Analysis(2017):46.

68   Interview with Eri Medrek on Eritrean TV from North America, August 24, 2019. Schröder put the population of Eritrea at 3.2 million, thus providing additional confirmation to my assessment.

69   Arabic was rejected on the grounds that it is not the native language of Eritrean Muslim ethnic communities.

Table 1. School enrollment in Eritrean public schools

Year	Primary (1–5)	Middle (6–8)	Secondary (9–12)
2011–12	334,245	167,928	95,152
2012–13	349,652	155,526	110,369
2013–14	361,604	152,005	115,422
2014–15	361,684	147,031	95,217
2015–16	353,859	141,746	87,664

Source: Eritrea: Education Sector analysis, 2017:44–46.

In 2014–15 there were about 362,000 students at all primary schools in Eritrea. A year later, enrollment had gone down to 354,000. There were 10,000 children fewer in 2015–16 compared to 2014–15. The Ministry of Education was cognizant of the decline but did not provide any explanation. The primary education sector is made up of the first five years of schooling.The next stage is middle school (grades 6–8). In 2011–12 the total enrollment at middle schools stood at 168,000. In 2015–16, total enrollment declined to 142,000. There were 25,000 fewer students in 2015 compared to 2011. This is extremely worrying. It is a trend that should not happen under normal circumstances. A possible explanation is that Eritrea is undergoing a demographic decline. Unfortunately, we do not know, since Eritrea hasn't carried out a census since gaining independence in 1993.The same trend of decline in enrollment is also shown at the secondary level (grades 9–12). In 2011–12 there were 95,000 students enrolled at secondary schools. In 2015–16 enrollment went down to about 88,000. Here again there was a decline of about 8,000 students.[70]

How much can we learn about the stagnancy or decline of the demography of Eritrea from gross enrollment figures? Enrollment figures through the first eight years of schoolingdo reflect the demographic size of a country in a rather satisfactory manner. In the case of Eritrea in 2015–16, there were about 500,000 students in grades 1 to 8. Net enrollment stood at about 75 percent. This would mean that the total school age

---

70 In the 2018–19 academic year, 98,000 students from Tigray took the NSCLE, given at the completion of ten years of primary education. The comparative for Eritrea would be about 20,000. There are five times more students in secondary schools in Tigraythan in Eritrea. This huge gap indicates two things: first, net enrollment in Eritrea is very low, and second, Eritrea is undergoing demographic decline while Tigray is experiencing the opposite.

population of 6–13 year olds is about 625,000. Assuming that as many as 650,000 children areunder 6 years of age, we get a figure of 1.3 million under 14 years of age, which in turn constitutes up to 42 percent of the total population.[71]In Ethiopia in the academic year 2014–15, there more than 18 million students in primary schools (grades 1–8).[72] Now what does this figure say about the population of Eritrea as a whole? I believe it says quite a lot. The population of Eritrea is most likely to be around 3 million.[73] This figure has to be taken with great caution until Eritrea is in a position to carry out a census. Moreover, this figure does not include all those who have left Eritrea, between approximately 800,000 and 1 million. However, the figure of 3 millionpeople currently residing in Eritrea, according to me, makes a great deal of sense given what we know about the history of the country.[74]

While the Eritrean population remained stagnant or even declined, the population in Ethiopia kept growing at a rather alarming rate. Ethiopia's population, estimated at 104 million(2018) isthirty times bigger than that of Eritrea.[75]

---

71 The estimate for Ethiopia is that 41 percent of the population is fourteen years and younger.

72 World Education News and Reviews: Education in Ethiopia, posted by Eric Roach, November 15, 2018.

73 This estimate does not include Eritreans abroad. The estimated number of Eritreans, most of them from western Eritrea, is 500,000. Another 300,000 Eritreans have fled to Ethiopia since 2003. A significant number of them did so soon after the opening of the Eritrean-Ethiopian border on September 11, 2018.

74 In 1940, Eritrea had a population of 660,000. The British estimated the population at about 750,000 in 1950. The population grew similar to other parts of Ethiopia from 1950 until 1974. It is most probable that the population of Eritrea, as in most parts of Africa, might have doubled during this period. I would imagine that the transformation of Eritrea as a theater of war must have affected the demographic growth of Eritrea, although we have no idea by how much. The end of the war against Ethiopia in 1991 and the seven years of peace must have improved the demographic deficit, but this trend was thwarted by the 1998–2000 war. The period from 1998 until the present is one of great hardship for the Eritrean population, where the great majority of youth (sixteen and above) spend many years of their lives doing national/military service with no pay other than a small amount of pocket money. Eritrea was on a state of no war, no peace with Ethiopia from 1998 until 2018—a twenty-year period that certainly had a negative impact on its demography.

75 In Ethiopia, too, the demographic growth was spread unevenly. The demographic growth was much more vigorous among the Oromo as compared to other ethnic groups. The Oromo population increased from 18 million in 1994 to 27 million in

The path that Eritrea followed, with disastrous consequences, is captured by Yohannes Okbazghi, Yohannes and Kidane Mengisteab, former staunch supporters of the EPLF. In their major work: Anatomy of an African Tragedy: Political, Economical and Foreign Policy Crisis in Post-Independence Eritrea, published in 2005, the authors write:

> *Eritrea has largely remained an exception to the liberalization process, taking place in Africa. Its economy is highly regulated. As already noted, it is one of the few African countries that have not allowed political parties and the private press. Eritrea also remains a country devoid of a constitutional rule, where the executive is unencumbered by any checks from a functioning legislature or judiciary. The government's ability to change its policies at whim has created an acute "sovereignty paradox" problem. The government's ability to change its policy at any time has, for example, made the risk of uncertainty for investors, both domestic and foreign, very high.[76]*

The authors sum up their analysis of Eritrea's future as follows:

> Lack of respect for the muted civil society and the fractured opposition groups along the risks the government faces in the event of change have made the government recalcitrant. Given the loss of popularity it has faced over the last several years, the PFDJ runs a high risk of losing power in implementing the constitution and conducting multiparty elections. Loss of political power is also likely to bring about loss of the party's economic power, as the party's extensive ownership and control of economic assets would be incompatible with the constitution's spirit, even if the constitution fails to make an unequivocal provision on the issue.
>
> Under these conditions, the prospects for change in the country in the short to intermediate runs remain uncertain. Furthermore, given the weakness of civil society organizations and the opposition groups, it is difficult to predict which kind of change, if any, might take place. Absence of institutions and civil society organizations, which is one of the critical legacies dictatorial regimes leave behind, often tend to reduce changes to a mere recycling of the elite.[77]

2007, whereas the Amhara population increased from 14 million in 1994 to 17.2 million in 2007. The Oromo population increased by 42 percent while that of the Amhara increased by 25 percent. This aspect of uneven demographic growth merits moreattention; it would be worthwhile indeed to look into the dynamics of unevenness, such as the linkages between resource base, political stability, and demographic growth.

76   Kidane and Okbazghi, Anatomy of an African Tragedy, 279.

77   Kidane and Okbazghi, 283.

I believe no one can explain better the decline that Eritrea has experienced since 1991 than Bereket HabteSelassie. I quote:

> *Eritrea's economy is in utter shambles. The slogan of self-reliance, which had served a useful purpose during the armed struggle, has not only outlived its usefulness; it has become a straightjacket from which the economy cannot extract itself. Moreover, the "command economy" inherited from the Ethiopian government (Dergue) has not been abandoned by the PFDJ, which is itself principally led by recovering Marxist-Leninist ideologues. Private enterprise that had been promised under a "mixed economy" has not been encouraged— far from it. The government's vaunted idea of a Singapore-style development project has failed. To begin with, the conditions that vaulted Singapore to a first class economy do not apply to Eritrea. Eritrea's economy—agriculture, livestock, light industry—does not provide a sufficient base for a "takeoff."[78] The hopes pinned on marine resources, minerals and tourism, which were expected to draw foreign investment and provide employment, have been shattered on the rock of wrong policies and disastrous politics, and consequently could not attract the expected investment."[79]*

> *The vast majority of the members of the Diaspora are the escapees of the last ten years. Their epic story is testimonial to the human spirit—to courage, determination, persistence and ingenuity—a characteristic that defines Eritreans.[80] A few of these heroic escapees have joined one more of the political parties, some have joined the civic organizations. The vast majority remain outside of the groups, tending to go with the flow and concerned with daily problems of survival, and wishing to forget the harsh life that they left behind. Many indeed express extreme sentiments about their experience and do not want to be reminded of it, or even of Eritrea. They boldly assert that they have amply paid their dues and tell recruiters of political parties or civic organizations to spare them preaching about nation and people, which to them sounds utterly sanctimonious. They are bitter and it is anybody's guess as to whether they can be eventually induced to recover their faith in the nation they left behind. Many*

---

78 Bereket Habte Selassie kept silent in 1991 when the Singapore syndrome was widely and loudly debated. According to me, an intellectual worth some salt would have pointed out at the earliest moment the glaring distortions of such a perception.

79 Bereket HabteSelassie, While Waiting or Working for Change, 9.

80 Italian colonial rule used similar logic to drive a wedge between the Eritreans and the Ethiopians. They told the Eritreans that they were more civilized than their Ethiopian cousins. The Italians did this because they wanted the Eritreans to help them pacify their new colony of Ethiopia. Bereket HabteSelassie, however, appears oblivious to the damage he is doing to Eritreans by defining them in such a way. There is nothing that defines Eritreans as separate from the rest of the Ethiopian population other than that they speak Tigrinya—a language also spoken in Northern Ethiopia.

seem to see their future in their adopted country of refuge, not in the nation they
left behind. This is indeed one of the saddest aspects of the current Eritrean
reality. It raises some serious questions with deeper implications for Eritrea's
future."[81]

For once I fully agree with the analysis provided by Bereket HabteSelassie.
The future of Eritrea hangs in the balance.

Encouraging Prospects for New Relations

The two countries have indeed diverged so much that political and
diplomatic sensitivity on the part of Ethiopia is required in its dealings with
Eritrea. A very important marker in a positive direction is the creation of a
pool of knowledge in Ethiopia on the complex and complicated history of
Eritrea and its various stages of transformation. Any Ethiopian policy on
Eritrea has to recognize that there are three actors whose feelings and fears
need to be taken into account. These are the Eritrean political leadership,
Eritreans abroad (diaspora), and Eritreans inside the country.

Already on the eve of the independence of Eritrea, the leaders of
both countries floated the idea of confederation. Attempts were made to
establish institutional infrastructures to enhance economic and eventually
political integration. At the bottom of this discourse, was according to me
a strong current of irredentismamong the population of both countries, but
especially among Ethiopians. In broad terms, we can describe the irredentist
undercurrents as follows: Many Eritreans, especially among the Tigrinyans,
believe that they were part of the Ethiopian nation; they fought for it, and
they died for it as well.[82]Whereas the majority of Ethiopians considered
Eritrea as part of Ethiopia once under a brief European colonial rule; and
the return of Eritrea to Ethiopia (that is the irredentist position) was logical
and just a question of time.

The now famous statement of President Isaias on July 14, 2018, can
certainly be read as a confirmation of an irredentist view. Now, of course
this reopens the question as to the nature of the war between Eritrea and
Ethiopia (defined by the Eritrean political leadership as colonial) for a new

---

81 Bereket, 25.

82 The Italians admitted that the Eritrean followers of the Orthodox faith continued
to express feelings of irredentism—a view that their country ought to be free from
Italiancolonialism and reunited withEthiopia. For more on the politics of the 1930s
see, Tekeste, Italian Colonialism, 127–31.For the 1941–52 period and the various
forms of irredentist movements, see Tekeste, Eritrea and Ethiopia, 37–68.

assessment.[83] I shall leave the question as to the nature of irredentism from the Eritrean side[84] as a subject that merits a separate study and concentrate on Ethiopian irredentism and how it might impact the formation of the country's foreign policy.

Many Ethiopians did not and still do not accept the reasons why Eritrea opted to fight for so long to break away from Ethiopia. The belief that Eritreans are as good as any other Ethiopians and that there are still strong links that bind the two peoples is very strong. This irredentist stand is highly criticized by Eritrean nationalist scholars who accuse Ethiopia either of lingering hegemonic ambitions or blatant refusal to accept the fact of Eritrean independence. However, it is not the Ethiopian government that refused to accept the independence of Eritrea; it is rather the people of Ethiopia.[85]Eritrea, its peoples, its history and culture are daily manifested in all corners of Ethiopia, thus keeping alive as well as strengthening the irredentist movement. The history of the region before and after colonialism is quite well known by many people throughout Ethiopia. The presence of Eritreans in all walks of life and the absence of any significant difference between the Eritreans and the rest of the majority of the Ethiopian population further strengthen irredentism. The opening of the Eritrea-Ethiopia border in September 2018 (although the border was closed some months later) and the spontaneous reaction of the Eritrean and Ethiopian population to the move was no doubt one of the strong manifestations of irredentism from both sides.[86]

---

83   The question as to whether the thirty years war was justifiable has been a subject of intense debate (from 2009 to 2011 at Asmarino.com) between Yosief Gebrehiwet and supporters of the PFD J, the political organization that succeeded the EPLF. I have urged Yosief Gebrehiwet to put together his huge collection of articles on this subject, and I do hope that he soon brings himself to this important task. See especially his most poignant writings: "Eritrean Independence," parts one and two.

84   On the irredentist movement in Eritrea during the 1940s, see Ellingson, Eritrea, and Tekeste, Italian Colonialism; "Unionist Party"; Eritrea and Ethiopia; and Shumet, Unionists and Separatists.

85   The formal independence of Eritrea was made possible by the early support of the Ethiopian government. Led by the TPLF, the Ethiopian state (1991–2018) was not keen at all to build on the historical/cultural links that bound the countries. On the contrary, the TPLF-led government attempted to treat Eritrea as any other country—a policy to which the Eritrean president strongly objected. Ruth Iyob, in her highly construed 2000 article on differences between Eritrean and Ethiopian nationalisms misses the point of irredentism completely.

86   The border was closed about six months after it was opened. The Eritrean government has not given any reason. However, its critics claim that Eritrea closed

Ethiopian irredentist undercurrents are interpreted differently by the three different groups. Eritrean nationalist scholars (most of them in the diaspora) describe it as "Ethiopia's failure to come to terms with the inexorable reality of Eritrea's independence and the existence of a separate identity and nationhood destined to exist in the neighbourhood of Ethiopia."[87] Another Eritrean diaspora scholar interpreted the Eritrean-Ethiopian relations from 1952 onwards as follows:

> The similarity among the three regimes is striking. The purposeful social and economic dislocation have the hallmarks of previous Ethiopian rulers of Eritrea, except the TPLF has been brutally more efficient than Emperor Haile Selassie and Colonel Menghistu. All three share something in common: a pathological jealousy of Eritrea's economic progress and an obsessive compulsion to drag it to Ethiopia's level. In the 1950s, at the time of the Federation, the Emperor could not stomach that Eritrea was more economically advanced than his beloved Shoa and its decrepit capital, Addis Ababa. He made sure Eritrea was brought to Shoa's level in less than ten years. Menghistu continued the emperor's politics of envy by grounding Eritrea's economy to the floor. The TPLF came to power with a huge chip on its shoulder about Tigray's underdevelopment, and immediately sought to remedy the situation at Eritrea's expense. The assault on Eritrea's infrastructure and industrial and agricultural enterprises that have come on the wake of the invasion is a well thought out plan to economically cripple Eritrea.[88]

---

the border first in order to stem the constant migration of its youth to Ethiopia and second to deny its archenemy, the TPLF, access to the Eritrean economy. Nearly 100,000 young people have left Eritrea for Ethiopia since September 2018. Moreover, the opening of the border revealed the huge gap between the Eritrean and north Ethiopian economies. The Eritrean government was not pleased to hear Eritreans say after a visit to Mekelle (the regional capital of Tigray) that the latter has become like Dubai. On August 2, 2019, the Ethiopian prime minister explained the reasons for the closure of the border. The pressure of Eritreans wanting to migrate to Ethiopia as well as the lack of trade harmonization were among the important reasons he gave. He fully understood the move taken by the Eritrean government to temporarily close the border. According to me, the danger that Eritreans would leave their country en masse is a real one.

87   Redie, "Complex Rules," 28. Redie writes as if nations and states are permanent conditions and not products of external and internal factors (conjunctures) always subject to unforeseen and unforeseeable futures; these are basic sociological premises, and I cannot understand why he chose to ignore them.

88   Tekie, Shattered Illusions, 272.

Typical of Eritrean diaspora scholars, Tekie contradicts himself, without, however, being aware of his untenable reasoning. He wrote:

> Ethiopian officials have repeatedly defended their position on trade with Eritrea as no different from their trade with other countries, say Kenya, for example. This is misleading. Eritrea is not just another country, a neighbouring country, with whom Ethiopia has trade ties. None of Ethiopia's trading partners have trading ties as integrated and as intertwined as Ethiopia's is with Eritrea. History, location, and happenstance have contributed to the creation of an economic region that transverses political boundaries so much so that economically northern Ethiopia and Eritrea are like Siamese twins, joined at the back and naturally looking in opposite directions. Their separation is technically possible as long as the nerve system that connects the two is not carelessly severed.[89]

The opinion of the vast majority of the Eritrean people, and especially those from the highlands, can be surmised from the way they received the news of the opening of the border and the warm reception that they received in Ethiopia. While the Eritrean government has, in the words of Isaias Afwerki, virtually endorsed the irredentist viewpoint on the unity of the Eritrean and Ethiopian people.

How should Ethiopia treat Eritrea, its people, and its resources? This is a huge subject, the ramifications of which can only be sketched at this stage of our knowledge. Many more people and conferences would be required to exhaust the question from all its complex and complicated aspects. With great trepidation I shall outline my views, firmly based, I hope, on the unfolding of the history of the region since the 1950s and fully aware that both Eritrea and Ethiopia are in the midst of great social and political upheaval with an unpredictable future.

The cornerstone of Ethiopian policy on Eritrea ought to be the eventual union of the Eritrean and Ethiopian people without infringing on any instruments of international law. Eritrea is not a foreign country as far as the majority of Ethiopians are concerned. And I think one can also say that Ethiopia is not a foreign country for the majority of the Eritrean people. The late emperor Haile Selassie is accused (though I have not been able to ascertain the truth of the allegation) of being interested in the territory of Eritrea and not its people. The opening of the border aroused the deep feelings of unity that lay buried for so long. Irredentist sentiments (in both countries) are deep and cannot be easily derailed by statements (such as that alleged to Emperor Haile Selassie) or

---

89 Tekie, 5–6. It is quite hard to find a text filled with as careless a depiction of the economy and society of Eritrea as that of Tekie Fessehatzion.

even by decisions of leaders such as Emperor Menelik and his complicity with Italy in the making of Eritrea.[90]

The greatest problem for Eritrean diaspora communities (of course not all of them) is the widespread belief in Ethiopia that the greater part of Eritrea was part and parcel of Ethiopian political history. Eritreans cannot accuse Ethiopians of holding the belief that the Eritreans are their brothers. Some Eritreans (most of them in the diaspora) might have succeeded in breaking clean from any connections with Ethiopia and its culture by denying any value to the cultural and political links that existed between the peoples of the region. But many Eritreans still cherish the cultural, historical, and geographical links they have with the rest of Ethiopia and its people. Even Bereket HabteSelassie, after forty years of denial, eventually came to talk in 2017 about intangible things that unite Eritrea and Ethiopia, and he proposed a special formula (confederation) as a good solution. However, of far more importance was the reaction of the Eritrean people on the occasion of the opening of the Eritrean-Ethiopian border on September 11, 2018; it was a resounding demonstration of the links that had endured a long separation.

The Ethiopian state should take serious consideration of the irredentist undercurrents in Ethiopia as well as in Eritrea. A most effective demonstration of an irredentist policy is the extension of citizenship to Eritreans who are currently residing in Ethiopia if they so wish. This measure would undoubtedly be welcomed by the Eritreans in Eritrea and by those in Ethiopia. And I strongly believe that the great majority of Ethiopians would welcome such a pro-unity stand by their government.

The great majority of Eritreans have lost the privileges they had during the 1991–97 period. Many of those who were suspected of wrongly exploiting Ethiopia and its resources were expelled in the wake of the 1998 war. A great deal has happened since then. Eritrea, like Tigray, is a resource-poor region on the verge of desertification. The strength of Eritrea lies in its human power—a population more accustomed to migrate in search of labor and a better livelihood. The extension of citizenship to all Eritreans residing in Ethiopia would not in any way infringe on any instrument of international law; the practice of extending citizenship to anyone who has resided in a country lawfully

---

90 Emperor Menelik allowed Italy to occupy the three highland districts of Hamasien, Seraye, and Akele Guzay, for which he was severely criticized. See Tekeste, "No Medicine," 1–25. Fifty years later, the people of the three highland districts pursued a highly successful irredentist movement by creating a political party that advocated immediate union with Ethiopia as early as 1942. So much is acknowledged by Trevaskis, Eritrea. See also Tekeste, 1994.

for a number of years is common in nations like Sweden and Norway. The Ethiopian government need not wait for a reciprocal measure from the Eritrean government. The extension of citizenship to Eritreans in Ethiopia would have wide ramifications and would play a positive role in the current discourse in Ethiopia about the intricate relations between the citizen and the state.

The Eritreans in the diaspora, like Redie and Ruth Iyob, would most likely accuse Ethiopia of pursuing its hegemonic ambitions. Many others would also oppose such a move from Ethiopia for fear that it might somehow affect the chances of their relatives and friends to seek asylum in Europe and North America.[91]

Although it is very difficult to preempt the attitude of the Eritrean government, I do not think that it would recant its strategic wish of achieving some form of union with Ethiopia. Furthermore, it would not go as far as dictating its wishes on the Ethiopian government without entering into a reciprocal engagement.

Given the skewed balance of forces, Ethiopia would be tempted to think primarily in terms of exercising hegemonic power such as a visible presence in the Red Sea and pursuing policies that put the interests of the state (security and big business) at the expense of the interests of ordinary people. It would be a great tragedy if that were to be the main pillar of Ethiopian policy in and around the Red Sea. It is only when Ethiopia succeeds to gain the confidence of the Eritrean and Tigrayan people that it can evolve a Red Sea policy that is commensurate with its size and need. The objective of unhindered access to the Red Sea cannot be achieved unless it is manifestly clear that it is reflective of the interests of the majority of the people straddling the Red Sea coast.

A second challenge is reviving the Eritrean economy from its current state of collapse. The Eritrean economy is in a shambles, and there is no private sector worth the name. The Eritrean economy is that of a war economy where every resource is under the control of the state. The Eritrean state defined the 1998–2018 period as a period when the country was besieged not only by Ethiopia but also by powers such as the United States. Major economic activities are carried out by state-controlled enterprises. Foreign investment is allowed only in collaboration with either the state or enterprises owned by the state.

---

91 A careful reading of the last reflection of Bereket HabteSelassie hints that the life of an asylum seeker or refugee in Europe is worth dying for compared to eking out survival in Eritrea. The description of Eritrea as an authoritarian state by the European Union contributed greatly to the exodus of Eritreans to Europe, thus turning the country, with its miniscule population, into a giant producer of refugees.

The economic policy of the Eritrean regime has been described by the growing opposition in the diaspora as an evil policy master minded by Isaias to keep the Eritrean population on the throes of starvation. His enemies further argue that he would do everything to remain in power, since liberalizing the Eritrean economy would weaken his position and eventually make his hold over the people difficult, if not impossible.

For many years I entertained the view that Isaias was genuinely incompetent (illiterate) on the logic of economic growth, the fundamental principles of which are the accumulation of capital by a wise exploitation of labor. The only system that Isaias knew was the one that he developed in the war front (that is from 1970 until 1991) and he continued with it even during the few years of peace, that is, from 1991 until the outbreak of war in 1998.

The depopulation of the country that was the outcome of the national service program (where young people were forced to carry out unpaid labor for an unlimited number of years on the grounds that Ethiopia might launch another war of attrition) can only be conceived and stubbornly carried out by a leader who has no clue as to the economic implications of such a waste of human resources.[92] Most of the Eritrean opposition groups argue that Isaias considers Eritrea and its human and material resources as his own private property where the citizens have duties and very few rights. A closer look at the way he has managed the Eritrean economy and society since 1998 and at the arbitrariness of his actions in closing the border six months after it was formally opened, tempts me to conclude that the well-being of his population and the stability of his country are not the reasons he is still in power. However, it has to be remembered that Isaias does not work in a vacuum. He has an army of followers both inside the country and in the diaspora, albeit in dwindling numbers, who support his informal style of rule.[93]

The economic mess that the system of President Isaias has brought about is indeed a challenge for Ethiopia. Unless Ethiopia takes this aspect of the Eritrean economy into serious consideration, the temptation for Ethiopian

---

92 The peace accord between Eritrea and Ethiopia signed in July 14, 2019, made it amply clear that the conflict between the two countries had very little to do with border demarcation. President Isaias could have managed to reach a similar deal with the Ethiopian government soon after the formal conclusion of the UN task of demarcating the border (2002) but refused to do so because he did not want to negotiate with an Ethiopian government led by the TPLF.

93 Plaut, Understanding Eritrea.

business and capital to claim more space would be irresistible.[94]Such a hegemonic approach to Eritrean political economy could in turn be viewed, especially by Eritreans in the diaspora, as a second Ethiopian colonization of their country.

Yet the future trajectory of relations between the two countries rests heavily on Ethiopian shoulders. In the 1940s, many Eritreans wanted to join Ethiopia, and they did. Between the 1960s and 1980s, many Eritreans fought to break away from Ethiopia, and they succeeded. From 1993 until the end of 1997, the Eritrean regime led by Isaias tried to redraw the map by creating some form of union with Ethiopia where borders would be meaningless but failed because the Ethiopian government of the time (1993–2018), dominated as it was by the TPLF, did not want it. With the downfall of the TPLF (since April 2018), the Eritrean regime is calling for some form of union, and it has very good reasons. The regime has come to realize that the destiny of Eritrea and its citizens is intertwined with Ethiopia and Ethiopians. This time, however, the initiative does not lie in the hand of Eritrea and its inhabitants.

Whether Eritrea succeeds to establish a confederal relation with Ethiopia depends on the political climate in Addis Ababa. At the moment (September 2019), the situation in Ethiopia can be described as follows: There is a weak central government surrounded by quite strong regional/ethnic states. Some of the regions, Tigray and Oromia, for example, are so strong that they have the power to hold the federal government at bay. A strong federal government is a precondition for managing Eritrea-Ethiopia relations towards a direction of greater integration at all levels. This is all the more truesince any such move would be challenged by the Eritreans in the diaspora—for many of whom the continued crises in Eritrea is a condition for seeking asylum in Europe and North America. The pacification of relations between Eritrea and Ethiopia on the one hand and the return to the normal way of doing things would close the door for young Eritreans to make the journey to Europe, thus affecting the fate of hundreds of thousands of people involved in the migration syndrome: many Eritreans abroad would like to help their close relatives to flee (providing the pull factor) and many Eritreans would seek to get rid of the authoritarian arm of their government (encouraging the push factor). This may sound cynical and insensitive to the genuine plight

---

94 Ethiopia has to devise ways of building Eritrean economic capacity in Ethiopia that would eventually expand to Eritrea. Ethiopia is so big (and economically more stable) and Eritrea is so small (in economic terms) that managing relations between the two countries cannot be left to market forces. Ethiopia has to build institutional capacity to deal with the integration of the Eritrean economy.

of people (not all Eritreans who flee their country do so for only economic reasons) but a lot of people would have remained at home had the conditions been barely bearable.

Is Ethiopia up to the challenges sketched above? This is obviously a very difficult question to answer for the simple reason that it is impossible to know for certain the future policy orientations of the Ethiopian government of the day. Ethiopia is in the middle of profound social and political upheaval, where the policies of the TPLF-led government (1991–2018) are rejected and new ones are in the process of evolving. Nevertheless, few words can be said on the capacity of the current prime minister, Abiy Ahmed, and what he might be able to achieve if he were to remain in power for another ten years or long enough,as his predecessors.[95] In sharp contrast to former Ethiopian rulers such as Mengistu Hailemariam (1974–1991) and Meles Zenawi (1991–2012), Dr. Abiy Ahmed has a much deeper knowledge of the people of Tigray and by extension of the Tigrinya population in Eritrea.

While Mengistu gave priority to military solutions to even non-military issues, Meles, being himself from Tigray, had a highly politicized image of his region. Operating within the logic of the right of nations and nationalities to self-determination, including secession, Meles and his political organization, the TPLF, attempted to develop Tigray as an autonomous unit within greater Ethiopia. The depiction of Tigray as a highly oppressed region did not match the perception of the majority of the people of Tigray who, in the words of Abiy, just wanted to live their lives as before.

The TPLF image of Tigray eventually created conflict between TPLF and the great majority of the people of Tigray. The TPLF's attitude towards the people of Tigray resembles the attitudes of President Isaias Afewerki and his party towards the Eritrean people. The people of Tigray have many issues that they would like to take up with the TPLF but at present at the mercy of the same organization. This image also created conflict between the people of Tigray(wrongly suspected as beneficiaries of government policies) and the rest of the Ethiopian population.

Only a few days after coming to power, Abiy outlined the political orientation he would follow in northern Ethiopia and by extension Eritrea. As far as Tigray is concerned, Abiy stated that what the people aspire to is to live peacefully with the rest of the Ethiopian people as they did before, that is during the imperial period.[96] The imperial system

---

95   Once in power, Ethiopian rulers rule for an average of seventeen years.

96   Apart from the first Woyane rebellion in 1943, Tigray was peaceful throughout the

is gone for good, and neither the repeated statement by the people of Tigray to live their lives as they did before nor the prime minister's endorsement of such aspirations imply a return to the past. But what is implied is quite clear. It is the opening of Ethiopia to all its citizens and the renegotiation of the importance of citizenship over other rights such as identity rights. Abiy stands a good chance of getting the support of the people of Tigray if he can ensure their free movement throughout the country. In the meantime, I am greatly troubled by the highly destructive discourse on the breakup of Tigray that is currently gaining ground fanned by social media.[97]

In the case of Eritrea, the recognition of irredentist undercurrents in both countries can, I believe, be used as a building block to construct sustainable policies of integrating Eritrea. I believe that Abiy has the knowledge to deal with the challenges sketched above. I hope that other looming issues of governance willnot fully absorb his attention and force him to leave Eritrea and its future to the winds of fortuitous events.

Acknowledgments

This article would not have been written had it not been for the gentle but firm guidance and encouragement of Dr. Belete Belachew Yihun. On August 24, 2019, I presented the main points of this paper at a small seminar in London organized by the Eritrean Education and Publication Trust. Several of the participants did not agree with my views but expressed their respect for divergent opinion. I thank the participants of the seminar: Abdu Abdella Suleiman, Eyob Tsegai, Habtegiorgis Abraha, Hassan Ibrahim, Ismail Mussa, Meseret Beyene, Petros Tesfagiorgis, Salah al Zain, and Wolde Selassie Asfaw. I am most grateful to Berhane Woldegebriel, the chairperson

---

reign of Emperor Haile Selassie (1941–74). Up to 1974, up to a million people from Tigray migrated to other parts of Ethiopia and hence benefited themselves and the communities they lived in.

97 The idea of Tigray breaking away from Ethiopia has no basis in the history of Tigray and its population. My fear is that some activists from Mekelle (I refrain from using the term intellectuals) are following the destructive script from Eritrea, briefly described in the following words: Eritreans can make it alone and better. This logic brought great damage to Ethiopia but a total destruction of the social, economic, and political fabric of Eritrean society. I hope other activists will challenge the emerging destructive narrative and succeed in showing the history of Tigray and the role that Tigray and Tigreans played (and continue to play) in the making of the multiethnic Ethiopian polity. I hope to return to this subject at a later date.

of the Eritrean Education and Publication Trust for inviting me to deliver the paper. Michael Ståhl (associate professor emeritus) has, as always, read the paper and given me invaluable comments. To Yosief GebreHiwet, I am greatly indebted for his extensive and exhaustive comments on the paper, posted to me on October 12, 2019. He strongly disagreed with my description of President Isaias. I have incorporated some of his comments and left the rest for others to judge. As always I am greatly indebted to Shiferaw Bekele (professor emeritus and a member of the Ethiopian Academy of Science) for a very critical reading of the paper.

Bibliography

Addis Hiwet. *From Autocracy to Revolution,* London: Review of African Political Economy. 1975.

Amare Tekle. *The Creation of the Ethio-Eritrean Federation: A Study in Post-War International Relations*, Denver: University of Denver PhD thesis, 1964 .

Bahru Zewde. *The Quest for Socialist Utopia: The Ethiopian Student Movement c.1960-1974.* Addis Ababa: Addis Ababa University Press, 2010.

Berhe Habte-Giorgis. "The Direction of the Eritrean Economy: Some Thoughts about Strategy", in *Emergent Eritrea: Challenges of Economic Development,* edited by Gebrehiwet Tesfagiorgis, 1993.

Bereket HabteSelassie. *Conflict and Intervention in the Horn of Africa.* New York: Monthly Review Press, 1980.

Bereket HabteSelassie. *Eritrea and the United Nations and other essays.* Trenton, NJ: Red Sea Press, 1989.

Bereket HabteSelassie. *The Crown and the Pen: the memoires of a lawyer turned rebel.* Trenton, NJ: Red Sea Press, 2007.

Bereket HabteSelassie. *The making of the Eritrean constitution: The dialectics of Process and Substance.* Lawrenceville, NJ: Red Sea Press, 2003.

Bereket HabteSelassie. *While waiting or working for change: Things to do and pitfalls to avoid in Eritrea.* Lawrenceville, NJ: Red Sea Press, 2015.

Bereket HabteSelassie. *Wounded Nation: How once a promising Eritrea was betrayed and its future compromised. Volume 2 of the Crown and the Pen.* Trenton, NJ: Red Sea Press, 2011.

Brooks, Kenneth. "Literacy in Ethiopia", *Journal of Ethiopian Education, 4:1* (1970): 16-41.

Clapham, Christopher. *Haile Selassie's Government.* London: Longman, 1969.

Davdison, Basil and Lionel Cliffe, eds. *The Long Struggle of Eritrea for Independence and Constructive Peace.* New Jersey: Red Sea Press, 1988.

Davidson, Basil, Lionel Cliffe and Bereket HabteSelassie. *Behind the War in Eritrea.* London: Spokesman, 1980.

Dawit WoldeGiorgis . *Red Tears: War, Famine and Revolution in Ethiopia.* Trenton, NJ: Red Sea Press, 1989.

Desta Assayehegn. *Schooling for Alienation. The Ethiopian Experience.* UNESCO, Paris: International Institute for Educational Planning. 1979.

Doornbos, Martin and Alemseged Tesfai, (eds). *Post-conflict Eritrea :Prospects for Reconstruction and Development.* Trenton, NJ: Red Sea Press, 1999.

Ellingson, Lloyd. *Eritrea: Separatism and Irredentism, 1941-1985.* East Lansing, PhD Thesis, Michigan State University, 1986.

Eritrea, *Education Sector Analysis.* 2017.

Erlich, Haggai. *The Struggle over Eritrea, 1962-78.* Washington: Hoover International Studies Press, 1983.

Ethiopia: The Official Handbook. Nairobi, Kenya: University press of Africa, 1969.

Fessehatzion, Tekie. *Shattered illusions, Broken promises: Essays on the Eritrea-Ethiopia conflict (1999-2000).* Lawrenceville, NJ: Red Sea Press, 2002.

Gaddis, John Lewis. *The landscape of History: How Historians map the past.* Oxford: Oxford University Press, 2002.

Gaim Kibreab. Eritrea: A *Dream Deferred.* London: James Currey, 2009.

Gaim Kibreaba. *Refugees and Development in Africa: The case of Eritrea.* Trenton, NJ: Red Sea Press, 1987 .

Gebre Hiwet Tesfagirgis, ed. *Emergent Eritrea: Challenges of Economic Development.* Trenton NJ: The Red Sea Press, 1993.

Gebru Tareke. "From Lash to Red Star: The pitfalls of counter-insurgency in Ethiopia, 1980-1982". *Journal of Modern African Studies,* 40:3(2002): 465-498.

Gebru Tareke. *The Ethiopian Revolution: War in the Horn of Africa.* New Haven and London: Yale University press, 2009.

Gewald, Jan-Bart. "Making Tribes: Social engineering in the Western Province of British Administered Eritrea, 1941-52". *Journal of Colonialism and colonial History, 1:2 (*2000).

Guazzini, Federica. *Le ragioni di un confine colonial: Eritrea, 1898-1908.* Torino: L'Harmattan Italia, 1999 .

Habtamu Wondimu. " Inequality of Opportunity for Higher Education in Ethiopia: A challenge to a Plural Society", *The Ethiopian Journal of Education,* 13:2 (1992): 7.

Haile Wolde Mikael. "The Problem of Admission to the University through the School Leaving Certificate Examination". Haile Selassie University, Faculty of Education, 1969 .

Jordan Gebremedhin. *Peasants and Nationalism in Eritrea: A Critique of Ethiopian Studies.* Trenton, NJ: The Red Sea Press, 1989.

Kidane, Mengisteab and OgbazghiYohannes. *Anatomy of an African Tragedy: Political, Economic and Foreign Policy Crisis in Post-independence Eritrea.* Trenton, NJ: Red Sea Press, 2005.

Killingray, David with Martin Plaut. *Fighting for Britain: African Soldiers in the Second World War.* Suffolk: James Currey, 2010.

Kohn, Margart and Keally McBride. *Political Theories of Decolonization: Post-colonialism and the problem of foundations.* Oxford: Oxford University Press, 2011.

Labanca, Nicola. *Oltremare. Storiadell'espansione coloniale italiana.* Bologna: Il Mulino, 2002.

Lenco, Lata. "The Ethiopia-Eritrea War". *Review of African Political Economy,* 97 (2003):369-388.

Levine Donald. *Wax and Gold: Tradition and Innovation in Ethiopian culture.* Chicago: Chicago University press, 1965.

Lipsky, George. *Ethiopia: Its People, its society, its culture.* New Haven, 1962.

Markakis, John. *National and class conflict in the Horn of Africa.* Cambridge: Cambridge University Press, 1987.

Owen, George and Bob Sutcliffe, eds. *Studies in the theory of Imperialism.* London: Longman, 1972.

Pankhurst, Richard."Education in Ethiopia during the Italian Fascist Occupation (1936-40)", *International Journal of African Historical Studies, 5:3 (1962): 261-96.*

Plaut, Martin. *Understanding Eritrea: Inside Africa's Most Repressive State.* Oxford: Oxford University Press, 2016.

Pool, David. *Eritrea: Africa's Longest War.* London: anti-Slavery Society, Human Rights Series, number 3 (1980).

Puglisi, Giuseppe. Chi E`?Dell'Eritrea. Asmara, Agenzia Regina, 1952.

Redie Bereketaeb. "The Eritrea-Ethiopia conflict and the Algeries Agreement: Eritrea's March down the rod of isolation", in Reid, Richard, ed., *Eritrea's regional role and foreign policy: Past, present and future perspectives.* London and Washington: Chatham House and Brookings Institution Press, 2009.

Redie Bereketeab. *State-building in Post-Liberation Eritrea: Challenges, Achievements and Potentials.* London: Adonis and Abbey Publishers, 2009.

Redie Bereketeab. "The complex roots of the second Eritrean-Ethiopian War: Re-examining the causes", *African Journal of International Affairs, 13, 1-2 (2010): 15-59.*

Robinson, Roland. "Non European foundations of European Imperialism: Sketch for a theory of collaboration". *Studies in the theory of Imperialism,* edited by Owen, Roger and Bob Sutcliffe. London, 1972.

Ruth Iyob. *The Eritrean Struggle for independence: Domination, Resistance, Nationalism.* Cambridge: Cambridge University press, 1993.

Ruth Iyob. "The Ethiopian-Eritrean conflict: diasporic vs. hegemonic states in the Horn of Africa, 1991-2000". *The Journal of Modern African Studies*, 38:4 (2000): 659-682.

Schumpeter, Joseph. *The Sociology of Imperialism*. 1919 (1950)

Sherman, Richard. *Eritrea: The Unfinished Revolution*. Praeger, 1980.

Shumet Sishagne. *Unionists and Separatists: The vagaries of the Ethio-Eritrean relations, 1941-1991*. Hollywood: Tsehai Publishers, 2007.

Sorenson, John. "Discourses on Eritrean Nationalism and Identity: A Review Article", *The Journal of Modern African Studies*, 29:2 (1991): 301-317.

Spencer, John. *Ethiopia at Bay: A Personal Account of the Haile Selassie Years*. Michigan: Reference publications Inc., 1983.

Steer, G.L. *Sealed and Delivered*. A book on the Abyssinian Campaign. London: Hodder and Stoughton, 1942.

Teka, M. Edwin. *Instability in the Horn of Africa: An assessment of the Ethiopia-Eritrean conflict*. MA thesis defended at the Naval Postgraduate School. Monterry, California, 2010.

Tekeste Negash and Kjetil Tronvoll. *Brothers at War: making Sense of the Eritrean-Ethiopian War*. Oxford: James Currey, 2000.

Tekeste Negash. *No medicine for the bite of a white snake: Notes on Nationalism and Resistance in Eritrea, 1890-1940*. Uppsala: Distributed by Nordic Africa Institute, 1986.

Tekeste Negash. *Italian colonialism in Eritrea, 1882-1941: Policies, Praxis and Impact*. Stockholm: Almqvist & Wiksell International, 1987 (second printing 1997).

Tekeste Negash. "The Unionist Party and its strategies of irredentism". Proceedings of the Eleventh International conference of Ethiopian Studies, 1991.

Tekeste Negash. *Eritrea and Ethiopia: The Federal Experience*. Uppsala: Nordic Africa Institute; New Brunswick, NJ: Transaction Publishers, 1997.

Tekeste Negash. "Adwa and the History of Eritrea: some issues of interpretation". *Adwa: Victory Centenary Conference, 26 February to 2 March, 1996*, edited by Abdussamad Ahmed and Richard Pankhurst. Addis Ababa: Institute of Ethiopian Studies, 1998.

Tekeste Negash. *Crisis of Ethiopian Education: Implications for nation-building*. Uppsala: Uppsala University Department of Education and Nordic Africa Institute, 1990.

Tekeste Negash. "The Eritrean Unionist Party and its strategies of Irredentism, 1941-50", in Bahru Zewde, Richard Pankhurst and Taddese Beyene, eds. *Proceedings of the 11th International conference of Ethiopian Studies*. Addis Ababa: Addis Ababa University Press and Institute of Ethiopian Studies, 1994.

Tekeste Negash. "Towards new premises in Eritrean historiography". A paper read at the XIV International Conference on Ethiopian Studies. Addis Ababa, November 6-10 (2000).

Tekeste Negash. "Italy and its relations with Eritrean political parties". *Africa: Rivistatrimestrale di studi e documentazionedell'Istitutoitaliano per l'Africa e l'Oreinte.*, (2004): 417-452.

Tekle M. Woldemikael. "Language, Education and Public Policy in Eritrea", *African Studies Review 46:10 (*2003): *117-136.*

Tesfatsion Medhanie. *Eritrea and Neighbours in the New World Order.* Bremen: Bremen Afrika-Studien, 1994.

Teshome Wagaw. *The Development of Higher Education and Social Change: An Ethiopian Experience.* East Lansing, MI: Michigan State University Press, 1990.

The Horn of Africa Bulletin, 1993 (number 3).

Trevaskis, Kennedy. *Eritrea: A Colony in Transition,* Oxford: Oxford University Press, No Date.

Volterra, Alessandro. "Disertori e patrioti. Soldatiafricanitraguerra e passage di fronte (1935-36)", in *Colonia e postcolonial come spazidiasporici: Attraversamenti di memorie, identittà e confine nelcornod´Africa,* edited by UoldelulChelatiDirar and others. Roma: Carocci, 2012.

Weitzberg, Keren. *We do not have borders: Greater Somalia and the predicaments of belonging in Somalia.* Athens: Ohio State Press, 2017.

World Education News and Reviews: Education in Ethiopia, posted by Eric Roach, November 15, 2018.

Yohannes Habtu. " Regional economic cooperation and integration propsects for development in the Horn of Africa: The case of Eritrea and its immediate neighbors", in Gebre Hiwet Tesfagiorgis, ed. *Emergent Eritrea, (*1993*): 3-15.*

Yosief Gebrehiwet. "Eritrean Independence: Is it worth all the sacrifice". *asmarino. com* (2009-06-17 and 2009-07-16).

Young, John. "The Tigray and Eritrean Peoples Liberation Fronts: A History of Tensions and Pragmatism", *The Journal of Modern African Studies,* 34:1 (1996): 105-120.

Zaccaria, Massimo. *Anche 'io per la tuabandiera: Il V battaglioneascari in missionesulfrontelibico (*1912). Ravenna: Giorgio Pozzieditore, 2012.

3

PROSPECTS FOR MAINTAINING THE NEW ERITREA-ETHIOPIA PEACE
Lessons from the Past

Senai W. Andemariam

The Sinuous Eritrea-Ethiopia Relationship: Pre-1991

This paper does not intend to interrogate the legitimacy of the respective debates on whether what is now Eritrean territory historically and legitimately belonged, in part or as a whole, to what is now Ethiopia proper. For purposes of its objectives, this chapter will make an introductory reference to the sinuous relationship between the two entities since the declaration of Eritrea as an Italian colonial territory. The history of the creation of what is now the State of Eritrea is at least different from that of almost all African countries that obtained their independence and sovereignty through an immediate succession, mostly in the 1960s, from their respective European colonizers.

The 1890–1941 Period

The Wuchalie (1889) and Addis Ababa (1896) treaties provided for Emperor Menelik II's recognition of Eritrea as an Italian colony and Italy's reciprocal recognition of Ethiopian sovereignty. The 1900, 1902, and 1908 treaties between Italy and Ethiopia then followed to draw (without full delineation or demarcation) the border between colonial Eritrea and

Ethiopia.[1] Despite the continuance of confusion and misunderstanding on the status of some areas in the border (such as Badme and Irob),[2] the territorial integrity of both entities was maintained until October 1935 when Mussolini, intending to establish his long-desired Italian East Africa colony embracing Eritrea, Ethiopia, and Somalia, invaded Ethiopia, and Emperor Haile Selassie I was forced to flee to the United Kingdom.[3] With the extension of World War II to the African continent, British forces led the dislodging of Italian control of Eritrea, Somalia, and Ethiopia by 1941. Whereas the British maintained, on a temporary basis, a military administration in Eritrea (1941–52), they allowed the emperor to return to Ethiopia and run the territory he left in 1935.[4] The British administration continued in Eritrea until the fate of formerly Italian colonies (Libya, Italian Somalia, and Eritrea) was attempted to be decided by a consortium of the Allied powers and, that failing, by the international organization that would be established after the end of the war—the United Nations. With its control of "Greater Somalia" (i.e., British and Italian Somalia), Eritrea, and Ethiopia, Britain would later on make varying proposals on the fate of Eritrea and Somalia.[5]

The Fate of Eritrea Decided: 1945–1950

When the Council of Foreign Ministers (CFM) of the victorious Allied powers failed to agree on the fate of the three former Italian colonies, they sent commissioners to gather economic and sociopolitical facts to help make a more informed decision. Between 8 November 1947 and 3 January 1948, the commissioners stayed in Eritrea and gathered the necessary information. Two reports were produced by the commissioners. The reports were bifurcated between US-Great Britain and France-USSR observations, although both reports attested to large support for independence, some support for union with Ethiopia, and smaller support for Italian rule or surrender of the western lowlands to Sudanese sovereignty. The divergence of the respective wishes of the Eritrean political parties already established before the arrival of the commissioners is largely attributed to the starkly

---

1   EEBC, Decision Regarding Delimitation of the Border between the State of Eritrea and the Federal Democratic Republic of Ethiopia (13 April 2002), paras. 2.6–2.7; Negash and Tronvoll, Brothers at War, 23–25.

2   Negash and Tronvoll, Brothers at War, 23–25.

3   3Wrong, I Didn't Do It for You, 70–73; Yohannes, Eritrea, a Pawn, 89–177.

4   As narrated in detail by Retta, YeErtraGudday, 363–414. See also Negash and Tronvoll, Brothers at War, 7–8.

5   Wrong, I Didn't Do It for You, 127, 160–64.

differing geographic, ethnic, social, religious, and proprietary interests of the leaders and members of the parties.[6] The CFM considered the two reports on 15 September 1948. Inability by the Allied powers to agree on the wishes of the inhabitants of the Italian colonies and a series of—some surprising— shift of positions by the Allied countries led the CFM, and the Allied powers, to refer the case of the Italian colonies to the United Nations.[7]

The fate of the three Italian colonies continued to be debated at the UN General Assembly (UNGA). Regarding Eritrea, the positions varied from self-determination and independence to partition (between Ethiopia and Sudan) to trusteeship (under Italy, Ethiopia, United Nations, or the Four Powers) and eventually to the dispatch of a UN inquiry commission to visit Eritrea and comeback with a recommendation.[8] After receiving the recommendations of the inquiry commission, the UNGA, in the evening hours of Saturday, 2 December 1950, by a majority vote of forty-six members (ten against), passed the famous/infamous Resolution 390-A (V) to federate Eritrea (as an autonomous unit) with Ethiopia. The resolution called for the appointment of a commissioner to implement the Federal Act (of the resolution)[9] by, inter alia, producing a constitution for the Eritrean federal government.[10] The sinuous relationship between Eritrea and Ethiopia thus started.

The Federation and Its Dissolution: 1952–1962

The Bolivian jurist Eduardo Anze Matienzo was appointed commissioner and prepared the constitution for the Federal Government of Eritrea. A 68-member Constituent Assembly was elected to approve Matienzo's constitution. The assembly approved the constitution on 15 July 1952, elected Tedla Bairu as chief executive of the Eritrean government and thus triggered the establishment of the federal arrangement. Emperor Haile Selassie then approved the Federal Act on 11 August 1952 and endorsed the Eritrean constitution as well as its government on 12 September 1952. The

---

6   Tesfai, Aynfelale, 103–266.

7   Yohannes, Eritrea, a Pawn, 78–88.

8   For a detailed narration, see Yohannes, Eritrea, a Pawn, 89–136; Retta, YeErtraGudday, 284–99; Wrong, I Didn't Do It for You, 161–68; Iyob, Eritrean Struggle for Independence, 64.

9   The resolution had fifteen articles. The first seven articles, which regulated relations between Eritrea and Ethiopia, are historically known as the Federal Act. Negash, Eritrea and Ethiopia, 70.

10   Retta, YeErtraGudday, 299–321.

ceremony of the replacement of the Union Jack by Eritrean and Ethiopian flags on 15 December 1952 formalized the birth of the federation.[11]

The rivalry already in motion between the pro-independent and pro-union forces in Eritrea soon reflected itself in, inter alia, the Eritrean Assembly's deliberations, the assembly's interpretation of the Eritrean constitution, the relationships between the chief executive and the assembly, the chief executive and the representative of the Ethiopian emperor, the assembly and the Eritrean Supreme Court, and the Eritrean and Ethiopian governments as well as the jurisdiction of the Eritrean and Ethiopian courts. Following a difficult tenure, Bairu resigned on 29 July 1955 and was replaced by Asfaha Woldemichael. On the morning of Wednesday, 15 November 1962, the Eritrean Assembly, in what is still a controversial narration, resolved, by acclamation, to immediately dissolve the federation and unconditionally unite Eritrea with Ethiopia. Emperor Haile Selassie readily endorsed the resolution.[12] Concerned Eritreans continued to petition and remind the United Nations, until the 1980s, to denounce Ethiopian "annexation" of Eritrea.[13]

Struggle for Eritrean Independence: 1961–1991

The complex events that transpired between 1941 and the early 1960s, mainly those during the federal era, are mainly credited with the launch of the thirty-year-long war for Eritrean independence.[14] The increasing move towards the dissolution of the federation[15] had already convinced independence-seeing Eritreans to organize themselves towards the creation of a fully independent Eritrea.[16] On 2 November 1958, the Eritrean Liberation Movement (*Haraka*) was established in Port Sudan as a clandestine movement composed of cells of seven—hence the name *maHbershewAtte* (group (assembly) of seven)—with the aim of launching a peaceful termination of Ethiopian rule, preferably by a police-led coup, although it later attempted to launch an armed guerrilla fight. In July 1960, a group of Eritrean students

---

11 Retta, 329–59.

12 Retta, 360–505; Negash, Eritrea and Ethiopia, 78–106, 112–38; Wrong, I Didn't Do It for You, 177–89.

13 Wrong, 191–96.

14 As contained, among others, in the three-volume narration by Tesfai: Vol. 1 (2001), Vol. 2 (2005), and Vol. 3 (2016). See also, Bereketeab, Revisiting the Eritrean National Liberation Movement; Iyob, Eritrean Struggle.

15 Presented in much detail in Tesfai, Ertra.

16 Yohannes, Eritrea, a Pawn, 189–95.

and political exiles in Cairo established the Eritrean Liberation Front (ELF) with the aim of launching an armed struggle to create a democratic republic. Eleven people armed with a British .303 rifle, five Italian rifles, and five swords began armed guerrilla warfare on 1 September 1961 under the leadership of Hamed Idris Awate. Eventually, the warriors were put under the leadership of the ELF, whose Supreme Council sat in Cairo, with Sheik Idris Mohammed Adem, the former president of the Eritrean Assembly (1955–56) as its president.[17] By presenting itself as part of the Muslim world and Eritrea's cause as part of the pan-Arabic movement, the ELF was able to get military training and weaponry support from Arab countries, particularly Syria and Iraq,[18] and played the communist tune to get support from Cuba and China.[19] In 1965, the ELF divided its field structure into five geographic units following the model of Algeria's Front de Libération National. The division was more or less structured along the ethnic and tribal affiliations of the ELF's political and military leaders. After eliminating the ELM's nascent soldiers in a battle in 1965, ELF fighters remained the only fighting force in Eritrean fields, for a while.[20]

A series of events between 1965 and 1969 led to the internal disintegration of the ELF army and the formation of three splinter groups from within it. Two of these splinter groups finally merged and formed the Eritrean People's Liberation Front (EPLF) in September 1973, with some military support from Libya. Until around 1981, the two dominant forces in the Eritrean fields were the EPLF and ELF proper. After many years of mistrust (there were intervals of joint military action against Ethiopia) and fighting, the EPLF finally dislodged the ELF from Eritrea in August 1981 and remained as the only military and political force in the Eritrean fields for the coming ten years, when it liberated Eritrea.[21]

At around the same time the Socialist Marxist military group the Derg overthrew Emperor Haile Selassie, young university students from Tigray formed the Tigray People's Liberation Front (TPLF). Since its inception in 1975, the TPLF had a close, and at times tense, on-and-off relationship with

---

17 While Idris Mohammed Adem was president of the ELF, Idris Ghelawdewos, a law student at Cairo University, was in charge of military affairs and Osman Saleh Sabbe, a school director from Hirgigo (near Massawa), was in charge of foreign relations.

18 Negash, Eritrea and Ethiopia, 36, 71 (n. 1), 149; Iyob, I Didn't Do It for You, 108–10.

19 Markakis, "Nationalist Revolution," 59.

20 Markakis, 56–58.

21 Markakis, 59–63, 66–67.

the EPLF. At best, their relationship was based on "tension and pragmatism" owing to differences in ideology, politics, and military doctrine.[22] Necessity, however, drove them to ally their military operations in finally defeating the ELF (1981) and the Derg (1991). With the EPLF controlling the whole of Eritrea and the Ethiopian People's Revolutionary Democratic Front (EPRDF), a coalition of politico-military groups formed with the TPLF at its helm, controlling Ethiopia in May 1991, it was agreed during peace talks in London (May 1991) that Eritrea's de facto independence should be formalized by a referendum in 1993 to grant Eritrea full de jure independence from Ethiopia.[23] The April 1993 referendum achieved that. The conduct of the referendum still provokes the long-held debate on whether Eritrea's route to independence was through a process of decolonization or self-determination.[24]

The Sinuosity Continues Post-1991 and Ends with a Ruinous War: 1991–2000

The uneasy relationship between EPLF and TPLF leaders continued even after they sat on their respective power seats in Asmara and Addis Ababa. The uneasiness even extended towards strong opinions by one country over the political administration of the other. For instance, Eritrean authorities continued to staunchly oppose the ethnic-based Ethiopian federal constitutional structure,[25] while the TPLF continued to support the right of Eritrean ethnic groups to secede from within Eritrea as a matter of their right to self-determination.[26]

It All Begins with Fraternity

In the few years after the EPLF and TPLF assumed control of Eritrea and Ethiopia, respectively, common and mutual Eritrean-Ethiopian (or rather EPLF-TPLF) interests prevailed over the serious differences, and both countries formed what appeared to be a healthy relationship at all levels. In July 1993, an Agreement of Friendship and Cooperation was signed between the two governments, foreseeing activities of mutual advantage in practically every field with the ultimate goal of "gradual evolution of the two economies and societies into a higher level of integration in accordance

---

22 Negash and Tronvoll, Brothers at War, 12–18.

23 Metaferia, Ethiopia and the United States, 77–80; Whitney, "Ethiopian Seeks."

24 Mohammed-Ali, "Eritrea's Case."

25 Negash and Tronvoll, Brothers at War, 15–16.

26 Prime Minister Meles Zenawi interview with Assenna, 25 February 2011.

with . . . the commitment of both countries to bring about regional economic integration and political cooperation" (Art. 1).[27] The July 1993 agreement further targeted the gradual elimination of all trade barriers between the two countries and the harmonization of customs policies as well as the use by Ethiopia of Assab and Massawa as free ports (Art. 4). It allowed free movement of people and called for the harmonization of immigration laws (Art. 5). It also included agreements for cooperation and/or consultations in the financial and monetary fields (Art. 9), realization of common objectives in matters of foreign policy (Art. 10) and regulation of border areas (Art. 12).[28]

The July 1993 agreement was followed by the September 1993 Asmara Pact, a consortium of twenty-eight protocol agreements ranging from a defense pact to harmonization of trade and financial rules. A joint ministerial committee was established to meet once a year to review the progress and implementation of the protocols.[29] The relationship between the two governments was hailed as exemplary, and the two leaders (Isaias Afwerki of Eritrea and Meles Zenawi of Ethiopia) were identified as examples of a new generation of visionary African leaders.[30] The combined works of both governments were noticed not only domestically (such as Ethiopia's supplying of documentary and related evidence in Eritrea's maritime dispute with Yemen and Eritrea's assistance in confronting domestic opposition forces in Ethiopia) but also internationally (their joint operations in supporting South Sudanese independence forces[31] and their intervention in the Democratic Republic of the Congo).[32]

Said relationship was not, however, strongly institutionalized in both countries, partly owing to a dearth of human resources. It was also not strong enough to tackle the abovementioned serious differences. Hence, the historical suspicion between the EPLF and TPLF started to slowly resurface in the relationship between the two countries. Two major causes have been identified as the principal reasons for the subsequent two-decade-old hostilities between the two countries: border and economic issues.

---

27 Tesfai, "Cause of the Eritrean-Ethiopian Conflict," Part I.

28 Tesfai, "Cause of the Eritrean-Ethiopian Conflict," Part I.

29 Tesfai; Negash and Tronvoll, Brothers at War, 31–32.

30 Wrong, I Didn't Do It for You, 15–16.

31 Johnson, Root Causes, 102.

32 Prunier, Africa's World War, 67.

Causes of the War

Border incidents

In 1984 the EPLF and TPLF agreed to suspend border negotiations until the end of their struggles.[33] An incident that occurred sometime before August 1997 put to the limelight the lack of trust in keeping the 1984 pledge. On 16 august 1997, Isaias wrote a letter to Meles that Ethiopian forces crossed into Adi Murug, an Eritrean village, and forcibly occupied it. Isaias sent a second letter to tell Meles that Ethiopian forces did the same with the village of Badme, the casus belli of the 1998–2000 military conflict, and requested Meles to handle the matter. Meles responded that his forces were not within disputed areas and that both countries needed to solve border disputes in accordance with earlier agreements. Sometime in November 1997 a joint border commission consisting of political, military, and security officials from both sides was established to settle the border problems. The commission met only twice. The second meeting was held on 8 May 1998. In a conflictingly narrated set of events, however, Eritrean and Ethiopian forces engaged in a military clash in the environs of Badme on 6 May 1998, two days before the 8 May meeting was held in Addis Ababa. With Badme as the flashpoint, a major battle was launched on 12 May 1998, sparking the catastrophic war that continued until May 2000. The two-year war would claim around 100,000 lives from both sides in addition to countless physical and psychological harm, massive deportations, internal displacements, and damage to property.[34] Both parties blamed each other for instigating the war.[35]

The economic cause

A number of writers have identified economic tension as one of the main reasons—Meles claimed it was the main reason[36]—for the beginning of the border war. Except for the free use by Ethiopia of Eritrean ports and the use of a common currency, the Ethiopian birr, until Eritrea issued its own currency, the 1993 Asmara Pact never progressed as expected. In fact, the differences between both sides were so deep that by the beginning of 1997 "there was virtually nothing of substance left of the Asmara Pact of 1993."[37] The Eritrean national currency, the nakfa, entered the market in November

---

33   Negash and Tronvoll, Brothers at War, 25–26; Reid, "Old Problems," 386–90.

34   Negash and Tronvoll, Brothers at War, 25–29; Plaut, Understanding Eritrea, 28–30; Wrong, I Didn't Do It for You, 363–66.

35   Dybnis, "Was the Eritrea-Ethiopia Claims Commission," 257–58.

36   Prime Minister Meles Zenawi interview with Assenna, 25 February 2011.

37   Negash and Tronvoll, Brothers at War, 35.

1997 before both countries could agree on the process of its issuance. The launch of the nakfa left two key questions unanswered: the manner of the return to Ethiopia of birr that was within Eritrean territory as of November 1997 and the currency (currencies) to be used for post-nakfa trade between the countries, including trade at the border. Both countries had different views on these issues, and before they could settle their differences military conflict began.[38]

The regional dimension

The conflict went beyond the borders of the two countries and had a regional dimension. Such a dimension was reflective of the desires of the two warring parties not only to win the war against the other but also to influence and buy friends within the region. In Somalia, for instance, Eritrea, intending to outflank Ethiopia, supported the warlord Mohamed Farrah Aidid and Ethiopia supported Aidid's rivals. When Eritrea actively supported the Oromo Liberation Front fighting against the power in Addis Ababa, Ethiopia similarly renewed relations with Sudan to encourage various Eritrean opposition groups, including the Eritrean Islamic Jihad based in the Sudan. Eritrea also accused Djibouti of siding with Ethiopia.[39]

Other factors

Some observers also refer to other reasons that may have contributed to the outbreak of the war. Lata, for instance, identifies "the divergence of the ideologies of the groups ruling the two entities, differing visions and nature of state types, the contrast between democracy in one state and authoritarianism in the other."[40] Plaut also refers to the cultural perception of Eritreans of Tigrayans and vice versa, communication barriers, and a culture of secrecy and the clash between machismo and the "Spartan complex" in the EPLF and TPLF.[41]

---

38 Negash and Tronvoll, 32–36; Plaut, Understanding Eritrea, 30–31; Wrong, I Didn't Do It for You, 366.

39 New World Encyclopedia (2017).

40 Lata, "Ethiopia-Eritrea War," 369.

41 Plaut, Understanding Eritrea, 31–32.

Algiers Crafts the Peace Formula: June and December 2000

Initial Efforts to End the Conflict

Efforts to end the conflict and secure normalization began almost immediately after the outbreak of the conflict in May 1998. A US-Rwanda initiative that began on 3 June 1998 was finally rejected by Eritrea, which had qualms about the US team's mandate which, Eritrea believed, went beyond negotiation toward a peace plan the elements of which Eritrea was also not happy about (for instance, the proposal to have Eritrean troops withdraw from Badme may have been taken to mean that Eritrea was the aggressor).[42]

A framework agreement initiated by a high-level delegation of four African heads of state and the chairperson of the Organization of African Unity (OAU) was initially rejected by Eritrea in December 1998 but later accepted by it in February 1999. When implementation of the framework agreement was followed into details by modalities (July 1999) and technical arrangements (August 1999), Ethiopia, unhappy with the conditions Eritrea put on the technical arrangements, rejected the arrangements and so ended the OAU initiative.[43]

The UN Security Council (UNSC) also followed up with a series of resolutions (1177 (1998), 1226 (1999), 1227 (1999), 1298 (2000)) to, inter alia, identify the conflict as a serious threat to peace and security in the region (hence the possibility for taking action under Chapter VII of the UN Charter); call the warring parties to avoid taking steps that would aggravate the conflict; support the OAU initiative; and, finally, impose a military embargo on both parties.[44] Between 1998 and 2008 (until it adopted Res. No. 1827 (2008) to terminate the UN Mission in Eritrea and Ethiopia (UNMEE)) the UNSC adopted twenty-eight resolutions in relation to the Eritrea-Ethiopia conflict.[45]

Despite the claim that the Intergovernmental Authority for Development (IGAD) attempted to mediate between Ethiopia and Eritrea during the

---

42 Negash and Tronvoll, Brothers at War, 56–60; Plaut, Understanding Eritrea, 34–36.

43 Negash and Tronvoll, Brothers at War, 60–70, 72–82; Plaut, Understanding Eritrea, 34–36.

44 S/RES/1177 (1998); S/RES/1226 (1999); S/RES/1227 (1999); S/RES/1298 (2000); Guttry, "UN Mission in Ethiopia and Eritrea," 79.

45 Dybnis, "Was the Eritrea-Ethiopia Claims Commission," 264.

1998–2000 war,[46] IGAD played no discernible role in the peace process that stopped the border war, nor would it, or the guarantors and witnesses of the Algiers Agreement, later on show any notable and persistent endeavor to normalize the relationship between the two countries following a rise in the stalemate between them following the April 2002 decision of the Eritrea-Ethiopia Border Commission (EEBC). After referring to the Eritro-Ethiopian and Eritro-Djiboutian conflicts, Frank noted that:

> Regarding conflict mediation, the failure of the regional organizations, notably [IGAD], to initiate such action calls into question the ability of these regional security brokers to accomplish one of their fundamental tasks.[47]

The Algiers Agreements of 2000

Bouteflika Succeeds with the Peace Effort

The then chairperson of the OAU, President Abdulaziz Bouteflika of Algeria, spearheaded the design of a couple of agreements that formally ended the two-year war. On 18 June 2000 the two countries signed the Agreement on Cessation of Hostilities to cease military conflict immediately, to allow a UN peacekeeping mission, the UNMEE, to be stationed in a twenty-five-kilometer Temporary Security Zone within the entirety of Eritrean territory with a mandate to oversee the ceasefire and assist in the demarcation process.[48]

On 12 December 2000, the Algiers Peace Agreement was signed. This comprehensive peace restoring formula called for the establishment of three dispute settlement organs with respective mandates:

1. An independent and impartial body established to determine the origins of the conflict (Article 3).
2. A Border Commission to delimit and demarcate the border based on pertinent colonial treaties (1900, 1902, and 1908) and applicable international law (Art. 4).
3. A Claims Commission with a mandate to decide through binding arbitration all claims for loss, damage, or injury by one government against the other and by nationals (including both natural and juridical persons) of one party against the government of the other party or entities owned or controlled by the other party (Art. 5).

---

46   For instance, Demeke, "Conflict Resolution," 248–57.

47   Frank, "Ripeness," 113–38.

48   UN Doc. S/RES/1430 (2002).

Moreover, the International Committee of the Red Cross was given the responsibility of handling prisoners of war. Plaut noted that the Algiers Agreement, the institutions it created, and the other relevant institutions made up "a gold-plated peace agreement, drawn up with the best of intentions by skilled negotiators from across the globe."[49]

Non-Implementation of the Algiers Agreement

The EEBC was the first of the three Algiers Agreement organs to carry out its functions. Based on the 1900, 1902, and 1908 Ethio-Italian treaties, applicable international law, and the 1964 OAU Summit Resolution AHG/Res. 16(1) on the applicability of colonial borders existing at independence, the EEBC worked for ten months and on 13 April 2002 came up with a decision that delimited the entire border between Eritrea and Ethiopia.[50] Badme was awarded to Eritrea. The original plan was to finish demarcation within six months of the date of the delimitation award.[51] As of the writing of this chapter (more than seventeen and a half years later), however, the EEBC decision remains not fully implemented in many forms, with both parties contributing to its nonenforcement.[52] Most remarkably, no demarcation has happened yet, and Ethiopia, whose army continues to be stationed at Badme, has not transferred sovereignty over Badme and its environs to Eritrea.

Although the position of the current Ethiopian government, led by Dr. Abiy Ahmed Ali, is not clear on the issue, his two predecessors (Meles Zenawi and Hailemariam Dessalegn) had been following the so-called five-points proposal regarding the demarcation process. In a 25 November 2004 speech before the Ethiopian parliament, Zenawi unveiled a five-point proposal whereby Ethiopia accepted the boundary decision in principle, with the

---

49 Plaut, Understanding Eritrea, 41.

50 EEBC, Decision Regarding Delimitation of the Border between the State of Eritrea and the Federal Democratic Republic of Ethiopia (13 April 2002).

51 UN Doc. S/2008/54.

52 See the following regarding Ethiopia's contribution on nonenforcement of the border decision: UN Doc. S/2008/148, Annex; UN Doc. S/2006/992, enclosure, para. 10; UN Doc. S/2008/226, para.15; UN Doc. S/2008/226, para. 18; Mukur, "PM Melles Zenawi's"; UN Doc. S/2003/257/Add.1; UN Doc. S/2007/580; UN S/2002/977; Eritrea-Ethiopia Boundary Commission, Sixth report on the work of the Commission, Annex 1, para. 10; Eritrea-Ethiopia Boundary Commission, Sixteenth report on the work of the Commission, Annex 1. See the following regarding Eritrea's contribution on nonenforcement of the border decision: UN Doc. S/2006/992; UN Doc. S/2004/116 (Annexes I-III); UN Doc. S/2008/156; Jibril (2003), pp. 633-677.

precondition that talks and dialogue be held between the parties regarding on-ground implementation of the demarcation.[53]Eritrea consistently insisted on a literal demarcation of the delimitation coordinates before any negotiations could resume with Ethiopia. Following the July 2018 peace deal between the two countries, however, Ethiopian troops continue to be stationed in Badme and its environs, while peace and cooperation talks continue between the two governments. Eritrea points fingers at machinations of the TPLF in explaining why the reverse has happened, that negotiations have begun with Ethiopian troops continuing to occupy parts of Eritrean.

The Eritrea-Ethiopia Claims Commission (EECC) began its work in March 2001 and divided its assignment into two phases: to decide on the merits of the numerous liability claims[54]; and, if liability were established, determine the amount of damages.[55] After four rounds of hearings between November 2002 and April 2005, the EECC produced a total of fifteen partial and final awards (eight on Ethiopian claims and seven on Eritrean claims), with the final set released on 19 December 2005.[56] Among others, the EECC found that Eritrea unlawfully invaded Ethiopian-controlled territory at the start of the conflict; unlawfully conducted or permitted the killing, rape, or abduction of civilians and the looting of property; abused or provided improper care and treatment to Ethiopian prisoners of war; and failed to provide expelled civilians with appropriate protection and treatment. The EECC also found that Ethiopia

---

53 Mukur, "PM Melles Zenawi's". The five points are:
   Resolution of the dispute between Ethiopia and Eritrea only through peaceful means;
   Resolution of the root causes of the conflict through dialogue with the view to normalizing relations;
   Acceptance by Ethiopia, in principle, of the Boundary Commission decision;
   Agreement by Ethiopia to pay its dues to the Boundary Commission and to appoint field liaison officers; and
   Immediate start of dialogue with the view to implementing the Boundary Commission's decision in a manner consistent with the promotion of sustainable peace and brotherly ties between the two peoples.

54 The issues included: lawfulness of the initial resort to force; treatment of prisoners of war and civilian internees; legality of means and methods of warfare used; treatment of diplomatic personnel and premises; seizure and destruction of private property; damage related to ports; pension and treatment, including deportation, by each side of the nationals of the other. Matheson, "Eritrea-Ethiopia Claims Commission."

55 Kidane, "Civil Liability," 26; EECC, Final Award, Eritrea's Damages Claims, para. 6; EECC, Final Award, Ethiopia's Damages Claims, para. 6.

56 EECC (all decisions and awards), available at https://pca-cpa.org/en/cases/71/.

failed to give proper treatment and protection to Eritrean prisoners of war; engaged in looting and unlawful destruction of property; improperly detained or expelled civilians; and violated diplomatic immunity of Eritrean diplomats and its embassy.[57]

Proceeding to the damages phase, the EECC calculated the damages due to each party and granted, on 17 August 2009, Ethiopia seventeen *jus ad bellum* (Eritrea was found by the commission of violating the *jus ad bellum*) and nineteen *jus in bello* Eritrean violation damages totaling US$174,036,520.[58] Likewise, the EECC granted Eritrea nineteen *jus in bello* Ethiopian violation damages totaling US$161,455,000, with an additional US$2,065,865 in respect of claims presented on behalf of five individual claimants, hence a total of US$163,520,865.[59] Except for initial statements by both parties accepting, despite reservations, the EECC liability and damages awards, no progress has been registered to date on implementation of the decisions. Since the parties opted for a state-to-state claims process, there was no clear mechanism on how individuals on whose behalf the damages were litigated can/will collect their share of the awards.

The third Algiers organ, the fact-finding body, should also be mentioned. Logically, this body should, by laying out the "factual" background, have been established and carried out its mandate before the EEBC and EECC could embark on the "legal" aspects of the dispute. For example, in the *jus ad bellum* award, the EECC, in asserting jurisdiction, controversially[60] sidelined the fact that its finding on whether Eritrea resorted to the use of force in violation of Article 2(4) of the UN Charter was not based on the works of the fact-finding body and made its own "factual" analysis of the events that immediately led to the launch of battles in May and June 1998. It accordingly ruled against Eritrea.[61]

The "No Peace-No War" Years

With the nearly total non-implementation of the Algiers Agreement, the two countries jumped into sixteen years (2002–18) of diplomatic hostility, proxy wars, and a few direct military clashes. For some observers, the two

---

57   As summarized by Matheson, "Eritrea-Ethiopia Claims Commission."

58   EECC, Final Award, Ethiopia's Damages Claims, 106.

59   EECC, Final Award, Eritrea's Damages Claims, 96.

60   Grey, "Eritrea/Ethiopia Claims Commission," 699–721; Berhe, "Ethio-Eritrea Claims Commission," 2171–88.

61   EECC, Eritrea/Ethiopia, Partial Award, Ius Ad Bellum, Ethiopia's Claims 1–8, paras. 6–20.

regimes entered into what looked like a zero-sum game of dominance. Eritrea called these sixteen years of impasse the years of "no peace, no war." Each government hosted and supported political and armed opponents of the other.[62] Ethiopia used its diplomatic arm to convince IGAD and the African Union to call for the imposition of UNSC sanctions against Eritrea in December 2009 for Eritrea's involvement in Somalia and Djibouti. Ethiopia also used its influence in IGAD to make it impossible for Eritrea to rejoin IGAD in August 2011 after Eritrea had unilaterally suspended its participation in IGAD in April 2007 in protest of Ethiopia's intervention in Somalia.[63] As the years progressed, however, none of the two appeared to prevail, and the mutual hostility slowly wore on them. The increasingly expensive cost of keeping the other weaker seemed to have proven it inevitable that the hostility would not continue forever. The February-March 2018 domestic events in Ethiopia would show how eager each party was to quickly end the hostility, forget all that was the past, and fully look into the future. The February-March 2018 events referred to here are the mass protests in Ethiopia, the resignation of Prime Minister Hailemariam Dessalegn, and the coming to power of Dr. Abiy Ahmed.[64]

The Pandora's Box of Good Tidings: The Rapprochement of 2018 and the Asmara/Jeddah Agreements

Expected or otherwise, Abiy (2 April 2018)[65] and the EPRDF Executive Committee (5 June 2018) publicly made known their intent to rekindle peace efforts with Eritrea by promising "to fully implement the Algiers Agreement and the ruling of the EEBC under the Algiers Agreement."[66] This call seemed to clear the fog of suspicion through which Asmara initially looked at Abiy's government.[67] And on 20 June 2018, Eritrea's Isaias publicly accepted Abiy's

---

62 Puddu, "Border Dispute," 173–80; Bereketeb, "Eritrea-Ethiopia Conflict," 98–128.

63 Andemariam, "In, Out."

64 Bereketaeb, "Ethiopia-Eritrea Rapprochement," 23–26.

65 Hussein, Full English Transcript.

66 Ethiopian Broadcasting Corporation, "Ethiopia Decides."

67 The suspicion manifested itself on 14 May 2018 when the Eritrean government, reacting to a meeting between Abiy and then Sudanese leader Gen. Omar Hassan al-Bashir, released a strongly worded statement rejecting an Abiy-Bashir agreement "to extend support to . . . Eritrea's armed opposition groups in order to enable them to properly execute their objectives" and provide said groups with material support and requisite facilities. Eritrea Profile, 16 May 2018, p. 1; Mumbere, "Sudan,

offer for peace by declaring "game over" for the "vultures" of Ethiopia (a reference easily decoded to refer to the TPLF's leadership and its sympathizers).[68] A senior Eritrean diplomat told the author that it was Abiy's full embrace of the Algiers Agreement that prompted Isaias to accept Ethiopia's olive branch.[69] Asmara and Addis soon ecstatically accepted Ethiopian and Eritrean leaders, and the warming up appeared so rapturous. Isaias advisor Yemane Ghebreab told the audience at the reception hall in Addis Ababa in Amharic that with the joyous welcome he and Eritrea's foreign minister, Osman Saleh, received on their entry into Addis, "It does not look like we have been separated for twenty years" (*author's translation*) (ለሃያ ዓመታት ያህል ተለያይተን የቆየን አንመስልም).

On 9 July 2018, Abiy and Isaias signed a five-article Joint Declaration of Peace and Friendship in Asmara. Through the declaration the two governments: (1) announced the end of the state of war between them; (2) agreed to cooperate in political, economic, social, cultural, and security issues; (3) announced the resumption of links in transport trade, communications, and diplomatic ties; (4) pledged the implementation of "the decision on the boundary between the two countries"; and (5) committed themselves to jointly endeavour to ensure regional peace, development, and cooperation.[70]

The Asmara Declaration was followed by a 16 September 2018 Agreement on Peace, Friendship and Comprehensive Cooperation signed in Jeddah, Saudi Arabia.[71] The Jeddah Agreement more or less copies the Asmara Agreement in seven articles and it: declares the end of the state of war between the two countries and heralds the start of a new era of peace, friendship, and comprehensive cooperation (Article 1); adds defense, trade, and investment to the five areas of cooperation listed in Asmara (Article 2); calls for developing joint investment projects, including the establishment of joint special economic zones (Article 3); provides that the two countries will implement the EEBC decision (Article 4); binds both countries to work for global peace and security on top of the Asmara commitment to labor for regional peace and security (Article 5); commits both countries to combat terrorism as well as trafficking in people, arms, and drugs (Article 6); and

---

Ethiopia Accused." In short, Eritrea viewed Abiy as continuing the hostile policy that his predecessors pursued against it.

68   Eritrea Profile, 23 June 2018, p. 3.

69   Informal discussion with a senior Eritrean diplomat (25 March 2019). As also stated by Müller, "Borders and Boundaries," 10.

70   Eritrea Profile, 11 July 2018, p. 2.

71   Eritrea Profile, 19 September 2010, p. 2.

calls for the establishment of a High-Level Joint Committee as well as subcommittees as required to guide and oversee the implementation of the agreement (Article 7).

The rapprochement opened the gate for a series of positive steps caused directly as a result of, or contributed to by, it: embassies were opened in both capitals; Ethiopian Airlines resumed its regular flight to Asmara and Eritrean Airlines started flying to Addis; visa-free arrivals were permitted to nationals of one country at the airports of the other; for a few months the border between the two countries was opened with no restriction for persons and merchandise to cross; leaders and high delegates of Horn of Africa and neighboring countries crisscrossed capitals for diplomatic advances; and regional, continental, and international organizations heartily welcomed this rapprochement, which has been viewed as possessive of huge potential to contribute to peace and prospect in the region.

Even if not operationalized yet, the Asmara/Jeddah Agreements seem to have laid very general principles for a better *future* relationship between the two countries. The only reference to the *past* is the commitment to abide by the decision of the EEBC. Section 6 interrogates the wisdom of this apparent delink from the past and full vigor to only look into the future.

Look into the Future, Not the Past

This section argues that if there is any lesson to be learned from the pre-1998 Eritrea-Ethiopia relationship (Section 2) it is that the 2018 peace deal is best served by either putting one of its legs in the past or by consciously forgetting the past. Two important "past" issues are identified here: implementation of the Algiers Agreement and acknowledgment of responsibilities by each country for disruptive steps (some contrary to public international law) it may have taken during the years of impasse.

A Space for the Algiers Agreement in the Asmara/Jeddah Agreements

As noted above, Prime Minister Abiy and his government made a peace offering to Eritrea by pledging "to fully implement the Algiers Agreement and the ruling of the Eritrea Ethiopia Border Commission under the Algiers Agreement," and Eritrea accepted the offer. Read literally, therefore, Ethiopia and Eritrea made a promise to: co-initiate the work of the fact-finding body; oversee the withdrawal of Ethiopia troops from areas belonging to Eritrea under the EEBC decision; and co-initiate the process of dispatching money owed to each other under the EECC's awards. Again read literally, there was no need for Ethiopia to redundantly pledge to implement "the ruling of the

[EEBC]" if it promised to "fully implement the Algiers Agreement," which contains the EEBC as one of its elements. Was this an honest inadvertence or an intentional emphasis? If intentional, why emphasize the EEBC ruling? Is this because as the years went on, the main preoccupation in the minds of both governments was the border ruling? Was it because the recurrent Eritrean petition at many international fora had been the call for Ethiopia to withdraw its troops from Badme and its environs, and Ethiopia wanted to highlight its notice of Eritrea's call? In fact one may even argue that the intense focus on the border ruling during the 2002–18 period made it look like implementing the Algiers Agreement meant implementing the border ruling. Badme means Algiers?

Such apparently confusing reference not only reflected itself in said Ethiopian call to Eritrea but also in the Asmara/Jeddah Agreements. In Asmara and Jeddah, both governments pronounced "the end of the era of war and the beginning of the era of peace" between the two countries (Articles 1 and 1, of the Asmara and Jeddah documents, respectively). Moreover, the two governments promised to honor the new era of peace by, inter alia, implementing the boundary ruling of the EEBC (Articles 4 and 4 of the Asmara and Jeddah documents, respectively). There is no mention in Asmara and Jeddah of implementing the EECC awards and the establishment of a fact-finding body.

From a legal point of view, therefore, one may inquire about the relationship between the Algiers Agreement and the Asmara/Jeddah documents and even between the Asmara Declaration and the Jeddah Agreement. Under contemporary rules of international law, if a new treaty that governs the *same subject matter* covered by a previous treaty has been concluded, the previous treaty is deemed to be supplanted by the new one.[72] Article 59 of the Vienna Convention on the Law of Treaties (VCLT) provides that if parties to a treaty conclude a new treaty related to the same subject matter, the former is believed to be terminated, as long as the parties intend to be governed by the new treaty. The subject matter covered by Algiers and Asmara/Jeddah is almost the same, at least in intent—in other words, to craft a means for the end of conflict between both countries. Algiers and Asmara/Jeddah declare the end of the state of war[73] and pledge to respect

---

72 Shaw, International Law, 947.

73 If Algiers declared the end of war, why would Asmara and Jeddah, eighteen years down the road, again pronounce the end of war? Are we to read, therefore, the countries were in a state of war between 1998 and 2018? If so, does this mean that Algiers has completely failed and, therefore, been fully replaced by Asmara/Jeddah? Does this also mean that there was never been a "no peace, no war" situation during

the territorial integrity of the countries. There is, however, a very crucial difference between the two: whereas Algiers looked into the *past* through investigation of the origin of the conflict, the setting of the border as it existed under international law and colonial treaties, as well as payment of damages caused as a result of the war, Asmara and Jeddah look into the *future* by crafting means for cooperative development and security. A very literal reader may understand Asmara's and Jeddah's explicit reference only to the EEBC ruling as having rendered the works of the EECC and the establishment of the fact-finding body irrelevant.

The answers to the question of the status and relevance of Algiers Agreement in the new peace deals, therefore, vary. One may argue that since the essence of the two sets of treaties is the same, the Algiers Agreement has been *replaced* by the new agreements, except as it applies to the implementation of the EEBC decision. Another may argue that since the temporal scope of Algiers (past) and Asmara/Jeddah (future) is different, the Algiers Agreement continues to be in force and the mention of the EEBC in the Asmara/Jeddah Agreements is only an emphasis of the most contentious of the outstanding issue of the past—the demarcation of the common border. A third argument may be made that the Asmara/Jeddah Agreements are the logical continuations (or extensions) of the Algiers Agreement in forming one big peace package in that they build on the Algiers mandate of addressing the key issues of the conflict (i.e., investigating the cause of the conflict, clarifying the border, and paying damages) by crafting a means of consolidating the Algiers-obtained peace (i.e., post-normalization cooperation in trade, investment, tourism, defense, and security as well as regional and global peace).

Whichever argument may be made about the status and relevance of the Algiers Agreement, one cannot deny the indispensability of fully addressing the three Algiers elements because they are the very foundations for the type of peace that is intended to be consolidated between the two countries. The statement by Abiy before the Ethiopian parliament that by inviting Eritrea to peace he was simply keeping up with the works of his two predecessors must be understood to mean that Addis Ababa has no other intention but to honor the Algiers Agreement.[74]

Experience from the pre-1998 relationship between the two countries appears to show that a "complete forgetting of the past to move together to the future" may not work. On the evening of 23 May 1993 (the eve of Eritrea's day of formal independence), the late Meles Zenawi, standing before Isaias

---

the 2002–18 years of impasse?

74   PM Dr. Abiy Ahmed Speech in Parliament—Full (2018).

Afwerki, invited dignitaries, and thousands of Eritreans assembled in the September 1 Square, entreated Eritreans and Ethiopians with the words 'ቀስ፟ና ኣይ ሕክኽ' (*let's not to lick our wounds*). This was a petition to let bygones be bygones, or, as the Tigrigna proverb goes, ኣብጎቦሎ ኃፋስ ይስይ፣ ኣብርዐሎሎው ሕጀ ይስይ (closely translated to mean, *Let the wind carry away that which is on the hill and may the flood carry away that which is in the stream*). Such crucial issues as the inclusion of the Red Terror and accusations of genocide committed by Ethiopia in Eritrea[75] and the concomitant redresses to Eritreans were left to be blown away on the wind of the new Eritrea-Ethiopia fraternity (or the EPLF and TPLF fraternity, to be specific). And the world witnessed what happened five years later. If there are two lessons this new atmosphere of peace and friendliness has to learn from the 1991–98 peace, they are that a proper settling of past accounts (under the Algiers Agreement) needs to be done as the countries march together towards the future and the butter of fraternity at the top of the pyramid (the leaders of both countries) needs to quickly melt and percolate down into the entire pyramid (the institutions and peoples of both countries).

Acknowledgment of Responsibility for Wrongs Done During the Impasse

That the two countries have singularly or jointly not implemented the Algiers Agreement has been established in the previous sections. In the years between 2002 and 2018 the two countries were also involved in mutually offending activities through sporadic direct military confrontations, proxy wars, and support of politico-military groups opposed to the other government. All these acts translate themselves into what in public international law parlance is called state responsibility. In other words, all these acts/omissions cannot be passed over as mere political or strategic machinations in a vicious zero-sum game; they entail a wide array of legal responsibilities under international law.

In 2002, the UNGA adopted the Articles on the Responsibility of States for Internationally Wrongful Acts (ARSIWA), a compendium of rules for determining responsibility attributed to states for their internationally wrongful acts and for identifying the consequences of such acts. Although not developed into a binding treaty, most of the provisions of ARSIWA have attained the status of customary international law—they can be referred to and deemed binding even in the absence of a treaty or, in the case of a treaty, against any state that is not a party thereto.[76]

---

75 Tiba, "Mengistu Genocide Trial."

76 For a comprehensive analysis of ARSIWA, see Crawford, International Law.

Article 2 of ARSIWA lays out the conditions for determination of state responsibility: (a) there has to be an action or omission attributable to the state under international law; and (b) such act or omission must constitute a breach of an international obligation of the state.[77] Without the need to dwell on the issue of *sequence* of the respective breaches by Eritrea and Ethiopia,[78] it may be concluded that these two ARSIWA elements have been met during the 2002–18 years of impasse: (a) the acts or omissions mentioned regarding nonenforcement of the Algiers Agreement and the other acts of mutual hurt are all attributable to both Eritrea and Ethiopia; and (b) such acts or omissions definitely constitute respective breaches, regardless of the magnitude of the breach, of their international obligations under the Algiers Agreement, and other relevant obligations under international law (for instance the obligation not to interfere with the integrity and independence of other states). International law provides for many remedies for damages caused as a result of breaches of the rules of state responsibilities. These include the right to request reparations, the right to terminate or suspend the operations of a treaty for material breach, and the right not to carry out one's obligations if the other party has not carried out its obligations.

This chapter does not intend to indicate how Eritrea and Ethiopia can each pursue their right to seek remedies for breaches of international law obligations by the other. Such pursuits may be unwise given the atmosphere of good neighborliness being strived for. It may also be argued whether the Asmara/Jeddah declarations of the end of the state of war and hostility, added to the now-famous Isaias statement, "ኣይከሰርናን" (*we have not suffered any loss*),[79] may be read to mean that the two countries have decided not to raise any issue of attribution of responsibility for hurtful acts they had directed at each other. However, such a waiver cannot be presumed given

77 International Law Commission, Vol. II (1976):75 ff; International Law Commission, Vol. II (2001):68.

78 Under the contemporary rules of state responsibility, the sequence of breaches by the states involved often determines whether the state that breached its obligations after and as a result of the breaches of the other can be held responsible for violating its treaty obligations. Under Articles 22, 49–54 of ARSIWA, for example, a state has no obligation to be bound by a bilateral treaty (in our case the Algiers Agreement) if it can clearly establish that the other state initially violated the treaty and hence is able to justify its subsequent breaches of the treaty as countermeasures. Countermeasures, if properly notified, are, by reason of the earlier breach by the other state, not deemed violations of the treaty. Could Eritrea or Ethiopia use this justification in defending their acts or omissions?

79 Uttered during the dinner he hosted for Abiy his delegation at Asmara Municipal Hall during the latter's maiden visit to Eritrea on 8 July 2019.

the scantiness of acts that show both countries have consciously waived their rights under international law to seek remedies for breach of the rules of state responsibility. Enforcement of the new peace formula is better served if sometime in the immediate future both governments could, by official word or deed, indicate their acknowledgment, at least, or assumption of responsibilities for their respective breaches of the Algiers Agreement and other relevant obligations under international law. Such an act is not only reflective of the responsibility that each government owes the nationalities of both countries, but also one more step to show that a lesson has been leaned from the past practice of *let's not lick our wounds*.

Conclusion

Admittedly, this chapter may have read too much into the very few, broadly worded, and only a year-long Asmara and Jeddah Agreements in discovering the desire and common intent of both governments, especially as far as the status of the Algiers Agreement and their views on state responsibility. All deference needs to be given to the good faith of both governments to establish peace. In the absence of any publicly available sources regarding the drafting of the Asmara/Jeddah Agreements, as well as explanations by the governments regarding the rationales and substances of these agreements, however, all that we have at the moment as the basis for the issues raised in this chapter are the texts of the two agreements and the circumstances of their conclusion. Even if such sources and explanations were available, as far as the issues raised by this chapter, they would still need to be reconciled with the texts of these agreements, to which the analyses in this chapter have tried to remain faithful.

This chapter has argued that since the 2018-and-forward era is an uninterrupted continuation of the 1998–2018 period, the *forward-looking* 2018 agreements must pick up from where the rules that guide the previous period (i.e., the Algiers Agreement and the rules of state responsibility) have stopped. By not fully reflecting the interrupted Algiers process and pledging to its full implementation, the Asmara/Jeddah Agreements may have left some interests unaddressed and impact the attainment of their objectives. If the "lofty" objectives[80] of the new era are to be attained under the Asmara/Jeddah peace formula, the grievous past of these two countries has to properly end in accordance with the very formula designed to end it (the Algiers Agreement) and the general rules of state responsibility.

---

80 As the preamble to the Jeddah Agreement has called the objectives of the new peace deal.

Bibliography

Agreement on Cessation of Hostilities between the Government of the Federal Democratic Republic of Ethiopia and the Government of the State of Eritrea, Algiers, 18 June 2000, https://www.refworld.org/pdfid/4a54bbecd.pdf (accessed 27 July 2019).

Agreement between the Government of the Federal Democratic Republic of Ethiopia and the Government of the State of Eritrea, Algiers, 12 December 2000. https://pcacases.com/web/sendAttach/786 (accessed 27 July 2019).

Andemariam, Senai W. "In, Out or at the Gate? The Predicament on Eritrea's Membership and Participation Status in IGAD." *Journal of African Law* 59, no. 2 (2015):355–79.

Bereketeab, Redie. "The Eritrea-Ethiopia Conflict and the Algiers Agreement: Eritrea's Road to Isolation." In *Eritrea's External Relations: Understanding Its Regional Role and Foreign Policy*, edited by Richard Reid. London: Chatham House, 2009.

———. *Revisiting the Eritrean National Liberation Movement, 1961–1991*. Trenton: Red Sea, 2016.

———. "The Ethiopia-Eritrea Rapprochement: Peace and Stability in the Horn of Africa," *Policy Dialogue* 13. Uppsala: Nordic Africa Institute, 2019.

Berhe, Isaias Teklia (2016). "The Ethio-Eritrea Claims Commission on Use of Force: Issue of Self-Defense or Violation of Sovereignty." *World Academy of Science, Engineering and Technology International Journal of Law and Political Sciences* 10, no. 6 (2016): 2171–88.

Claussen, Kathleen. "Invisible Borders: Mapping Out Virtual Law?" *Denver Journal of International Law and Diplomacy* 37, no. 2 (2009): 257–78.

Crawford, James. *The International Law Commission's Articles on State Responsibility: Introduction, Text and Commentaries*. Cambridge: Cambridge University Press, 2002.

Demeke, M. A. "Conflict Resolution Responses of IGAD and AU to the Somalia Crises." *International Journal of Political Science and Development* 2, no. 10 (2014): 248–57.

Dybnis, Ari. "Was the Eritrea-Ethiopia Claims Commission Merely a Zero-Sum Game? Exposing the Limits of Arbitration in Resolving Violent Transnational Conflict." *Loyola of Los Angeles International and Comparative Law Review* 33, no. 2 (2011): 255–86.

Eritrea Profile (2018). Press Statement. Eritrea Profile (vol. 25, no. 22, 16 May 2018).

Eritrea Profile (2018). President Isaias's Speech on Martyrs' Day. Eritrea Profile (vol. 25, no. 31, 23 June 2018).

Eritrea Profile (2018). Prime Minister of Ethiopia Dr. Abiy Ahmed Visits Eritrea: Ethiopian Delegation Expressed Appreciation for Warm Reception: State

Dinner in Honor of Abiy Ahmed. Eritrea Profile (vol. 25, no. 38, 11 July 2018).

Eritrea Profile (2018). Joint Declaration of Peace and Friendship between Eritrea and Ethiopia. Eritrea Profile (vol. 25, no. 38, 11 July 2018).

Eritrea Profile (2018). Agreement on Peace, Friendship and Comprehensive Cooperation between the Federal Democratic Republic of Ethiopia and the State of Eritrea. Eritrea Profile (vol. 25, no. 58, 19 September 2018).

Eritrea-Ethiopia Boundary Commission (13 April 2002), *Decision Regarding Delimitation of the Border between the State of Eritrea and the Federal Democratic Republic of Ethiopia*. https://www.refworld.org/cases,EE_BCOM,4a54bbec0. html.

Eritrea-Ethiopia Boundary Commission, *Sixth Report on the Work of the Commission* (26 August 2002).

Eritrea-Ethiopia Boundary Commission, *Sixteenth Report on the Work of the Commission* (24 February 2005).

Eritrea-Ethiopia Claims Commission (all decisions and awards), https://pca-cpa. org/en/cases/71/ (accessed 18 July 2019).

Ethiopian Broadcasting Corporation. "Ethiopia decides to fully accept Algiers Agreement," 5 June 2018, http://www.ethiopia.gov.et/-/back-ethiopia-decides-to-fully-accept-algiers-agreement-ebc-june-5-2018 (accessed 23 July 2019).

Frank, K. K. "Ripeness and the 2008 Djibouti-Eritrea Border Dispute." *Northeast African Studies* 15, no. 1 (2015): 113–38.

Grey, Christine. "The Eritrea/Ethiopia Claims Commission Oversteps Its Boundaries: A Partial Award?" *European Journal of International Law* 17, no. 4 (2006): 699–721.

Guttry, Andrea de. "The UN Mission in Ethiopia and Eritrea (UNMEE)." In *The 1998–2000 War between Eritrea and Ethiopia*, edited by Andrea de Guttry, HHG Post, and Gabriella Venturini. The Hague: TMC Asser Press, 2009.

Hussein, Hassen. Full English transcript of Ethiopian Prime Minister Abiy Ahmed's Inaugural Address. Opride, 3 April 2018, https://www.opride. com/2018/04/03/english-partial-transcript-of-ethiopian-prime-minister-abiy-ahmeds-inaugural-address/ (accessed 28 July 2019).

International Law Commission. *Yearbook of the International Law Commission* (Vol. II). New York: United Nations, 1976.

———. *Yearbook of the International Law Commission* (Vol. II). New York: United Nations, 2001.

Iyob, Ruth. *The Eritrean Struggle for Independence: Domination, Resistance, Nationalism, 1941–1993*. Cambridge: Cambridge University Press, 1995.

Jibril, Nejib. "The Binding Dilemma: From Bakassi to Badme—Making States Comply with Territorial Decisions of Judicial Bodies." *American University International Law Review* 19, no. 3 (2003): 633–77.

Johnson, Douglas H. *The Root Causes of Sudan's Civil Wars: Peace or Truce.* Suffolk: James Currey and Kampala: Fountain Publishers, 2011.

Kidane, Won. "Civil Liability for Violations of International Humanitarian Law: The Jurisprudence of the Eritrea-Ethiopia Claims Commission in The Hague." *Wisconsin International Law Journal* 25, no. 23 (2007): 23–87.

Lata, Leencho. "The Ethiopia-Eritrea War." *Review of African Political Economy* 30, no. 97 (2003): 369–88.

Markakis, John. "The Nationalist Revolution in Eritrea." *Journal of Modern African Studies* 26, no. 1 (1998): 51–70.

Matheson, Michael J. Eritrea-Ethiopia Claims Commission: Damage Awards. *Insights* (ASIL) 13, no. 13 (2009), https://asil.org/insights/volume/13/issue/13/eritrea-ethiopia-claims-commission-damage-awards.

Metaferia, Getachew. *Ethiopia and the United States: History, Diplomacy, and Analysis.* New York: Algora, 2009.

Mohammed-Ali Osman, Abdu. "Eritrea's Case: Secession or Decolonization?" unpublished LL.B. senior thesis presented to the School of Law, College of Arts and Social Sciences, Eritrea (copy with author), 2018.

Mukur, Natsenet. "PM Meles Zenawi's Five-Point Peace Proposal. Dehai (30 November 2004), http://dehai.org/demarcation-watch/articles/Natsenet_Mukur_Melleses_five_point_ proposal.html (accessed 23 July 2019).

Müller, Tanja. "Borders and Boundaries in the State-Making of Eritrea: Revisiting the Importance of Territorial Integrity in the Rapprochement between Eritrea and Ethiopia." *Review of African Political Economy* 46, no. 160 (2019), DOI: 10.1080/03056244.2019.1605590.

Mumbere, Daniel. Sudan, Ethiopia Accused of Agreeing to Support Armed Eritrean Opposition Groups. *Africa News*, 16 May 2018. https://www.africanews.com/2018/05/16/sudan-ethiopia-accused-of-agreeing-to-support-armed-eritrean-opposition-groups//.

Negash, Tekeste. *Eritrea and Ethiopia: The Federal Experience.* New Brunswick, NJ: Transaction, 1997.

Negash, Tekeste and Kjetil Tronvoll. *Brothers at War: Making Sense of the Eritrea-Ethiopia War.* Oxford: James Currey and Athens: Ohio University Press, 2000.

Plaut, Martin. Eritrea to Pay Ethiopia Millions. BBC News, 18 August 2009, http://news.bbc.co.uk/2/hi/africa/8208285.stm.

———. *Understanding Eritrea: Inside Africa's Most Repressive State.* New York: Oxford University Press, 2016.

Tenaadam. "PM Dr. Abiy Ahmed Speech in Parliament—Full, 18 June 2018, https://www.youtube.com/watch?v=wJnC2aX4jP8 (accessed 23 July 2019).

Prunier, Gérard. *Africa's World War: Congo, the Rwandan Genocide, and the Making of a Continental Catastrophe.* New York: Oxford University Press, 2009.

Puddu, Luca. "The Border Dispute between Ethiopia and Eritrea, c. 1998–2016."

In *The Dynamics of Conflicts in Africa in the Early 21ˢᵗ Century*, edited by János Besenyő and Viktor Marsai. Budapest: Dialóg Campus, 2018.

Reid, Richard. "Old Problems in New Conflicts: Some Observations on Eritrea and Its Relations with Tigray, from Liberation Struggle to Inter-State War." *Africa* 73, no. 3 (2003): 369–40.

Retta, Zewde. *YeErtraGudday (The Eritrean Affair (1941–1963) During the Reign of Emperor Haile Selassie I)*. Addis Ababa: Mega, 1999.

———. *YeQedamawi Haile Selassie Mengst (The Government of Haile Selassie I)*. Addis Ababa: Shama, 2013.

Shaw, Malcolm N. *International Law* (6ᵗʰ ed.). Cambridge: Cambridge University Press, 2008.

Tesfai, Alemseged. "The Cause of the Eritrean-Ethiopia Conflict." *Dehai*, 1998, http://dehai.org/conflict/articles/alemsghed.html (accessed 20 July 2019).

———. *Aynfelale (tr. Let Us Not Be Separated), 1941–1950* (Vol. 1). Asmara: Hdri, 2001.

———. *Federation Ertrams Ethiopia: KabMatienzoksabTedla (tr. The Federation of Eritrea with Ethiopia: From Matienzo until Tedla), 1951–1955* (Vol. 2). Asmara: Hdri, 2005.

———. *Ertra: KabFedereshn nab GobeTanSewran (tr. Eritrea: From Federation up to Annexation and Revolution), 1956–1962* (Vol. 3). Asmara: Hdri, 2016.

Tiba, Firew K. "The Mengistu Genocide Trial in Ethiopia." *Journal of International Criminal Justice* 5, no. 2 (2007): 513–28, doi:10.1093/jicj/mqm021.

UNSC Resolution No. 1177, S/RES/1177 (26 June 1998).

UNSC Resolution No. 1226, S/RES/1226 (29 January 1999).

UNSC Resolution No. 1227, S/RES/1227 (10 February 1999).

UNSC Resolution No. 1298, S/RES/1298 (17 May 2000).

UNSC Resolution No. 1430, S/RES/1430 (14 August 2002).

UNSC Resolution No. 1827, S/RES/1827 (30 July 2008).

UN Doc. S/2002/977 (30 August 2002), Progress Report of the Secretary-General on Ethiopia and Eritrea.

UN Doc. S/2003/257/Add.1 (31 March 2003), Progress Report of the Secretary-General on Ethiopia and Eritrea.

UN Doc. S/2004/116 (13 February 2004), Letter Dated 13 February 2004 from the Permanent Representative of Eritrea to the United Nations Addressed to the President of the Security Council.

UN Doc. S/2006/992 (15 December 2006), Special Report of the Secretary-General on Ethiopia and Eritrea.

UN Doc. S/2007/580 (28 September 2007), Letter Dated 27 September 2007 from the Permanent Representative of Eritrea to the United Nations Addressed to the President of the Security Council.

UN Doc. S/2008/54 (29 January 2008), Letter Dated 29 January 2008 from the Chargé d'affaires of the Permanent Mission of Eritrea to the United Nations Addressed to the President of the Security Council.

UN Doc. S/2008/148 (4 March 2008), Letter Dated 3 March 2008 from the Permanent Representative of Eritrea to the United Nations Addressed to the President of the Security Council.

UN Doc. S/2008/156 (5 March 2008), Letter Dated 4 March 2008 from the Permanent Representative of Eritrea to the United Nations Addressed to the President of the Security Council.

UN Doc. S/2008/226 (7 April 2008), Special Report of the Secretary-General on the United Nations Mission in Ethiopia and Eritrea.

Whitney, Craig R. Ethiopian Seeks to Form Temporary Government. *New York Times*, 29 May 1991, https://www.nytimes.com/1991/05/29/world/ethiopian-seeks-to-form-temporary-government.html (accessed 23 July 2019).

Wrong, Michela. *I Didn't Do It for You: How the World Betrayed a Small African Nation*. London, Fourth Estate, 2005.

Yohannes, Okbazghi. *Eritrea, a Pawn in World Politics*. Gainesville, FL: University of Florida Press, 1991.

4

THE ETHIOPIA-ERITREA RELATIONSHIP
Reflections on Pending Legal Disputes

Wondemagegn Tadesse

Introduction

There are indications that neither the armed conflict nor its resolution has been about the application of international law relating to boundary or other disputes between Eritrea and Ethiopia. It has been mostly political (rivalry among those in power), economic (the extent to which economic arrangements should have benefited each), or socio-cultural (lack of gratitude, for example, of the ruling elites towards one another in contrast to their loyalty during their joint armed struggle). Such political analysis is made elsewhere, and this chapter will not go into factors other than law—international law to be specific.

Regarding international law, there were a few legal regimes regulating bilateral as well as transit relations of the two states, at least until the war broke out. As an outcome of the commencement of the war, however, none of the bilateral arrangements survived so as to protect state, governmental, and private interests, including the interests of non-belligerents. The bilateral agreements regulated transit and port services, air services, and trade. There were also some aspects of the bilateral relations that never had clearly articulated legal regimes. The Eritrea-Ethiopia boundary regime was one. While there were "colonial" treaties, at least Eritrea was never a party. Nevertheless, absence of bilateral regimes for such relations has not meant the relations were beyond the reach of law. In addition to the bilateral agreements, indeed, peacetime, general, and specialized rules of international law must have applied before the outbreak of the war. So did rules of international humanitarian law and to some extent international human rights law after the outbreak of the armed conflict.

Based on rules of international law (and in some cases in contravention of the same), the Parties have been trying to resolve their disputes, initially boundary disputes, afterwards disputes regarding unlawful/lawful use of force, then claims and counterclaims of liabilities and damages caused by violations of international law, and so on. These same disputes arguably exist today, although the Parties are apparently pursuing their resolutions in a more friendly and conciliatory manner.

This chapter will explore the major legal disputes briefly and provide reflections on the way forward. A three-part contribution, the first section will deal with the boundary dispute and the Eritrea-Ethiopia Boundary Commission (EEBC). The damages and claims disputes of the Parties occasioned by violations of international law owing to the commencement and conduct of war and the Eritrea-Ethiopia Claims Commission (EECC), established to arbitrate those claims, will be highlighted in the second section. In the final section, humanitarian and human rights law issues and transit and bilateral trade considerations will be touched upon.

The Boundary Dispute, the EEBC, and the Current State of the Dispute

Background to the Boundary Dispute and the EEBC

As far as public statements are concerned, boundary disputes between Eritrea and Ethiopia were the raison d'être for the Eritrean-Ethiopian War. That was what at least the international community understood and wanted to understand. What was the boundary dispute all about? For this chapter, there is no need to go back millennia to trace the boundaries of the two states. It is enough to note that before colonialism there were not as such international boundaries between them (mostly because they were not separate territories), that colonialism brought colonial boundary treaties separating Ethiopia and Eritrea (the latter administered by a colonial power), that following the end of WWII Eritrea became part of Ethiopia (with colonial boundaries no longer mattering), that after decades of civil war Eritrea seceded in 1990, that Eritrea obtained recognition as a state without proper boundary delimitation and demarcation, and that in 1998 armed conflict between Eritrea and

Ethiopia began, with boundary disagreement presented as a cause.[1] The main point from this historical narrative is that following the independence of Eritrea, the more than 1,000-km-long boundary between Ethiopia and Eritrea was neither delimited nor demarcated. The independence was the result of decades of civil war and there was not much of an opportunity and incentive at the beginning to have a clear international boundary. Arguably the solidarity of the ruling elites in both countries continued, and there was no reason to rush for delimitation and demarcation.

In any event, they went to war owing to boundary disputes. The war ended, unfortunately but not unexpectedly, with no boundary solution, at least a mutually agreed upon or internationally acceptable (in law or practice) international boundary. The principal document ending the war was the Algiers Agreement of 12 December 2000 (AA hereinafter), negotiated with the involvement and assistance of several players, including the Organisation of African Unity (OAU). In addition to cessation of hostilities, commitment to peace, and so on, it established the EEBC to arbitrate the boundary dispute by outlining principles and instruments for the EEBC's consumption. According to the AA, the EEBC's mandate was to "delimit and demarcate the colonial treaty border based on pertinent colonial treaties (1900, 1902, and 1908) and applicable international law." In addition to its mandate, composition, and other clauses, the AA made the EEBC's findings final and binding and required the Parties to respect border determinations of the EEBC. It also established the EECC, to which we shall come back in the next section.

This section will also engage major challenges associated with legal principles used and unused in the resolution of the boundary dispute, particularly *uti possidetis* and *ex aequo et bono*. In the final sub-section, reflections on possible ways forward, relying on the Jeddah Agreement, will be made.

The EEBC's Performance

Following its establishment based on the AA, the five-member EEBC[2] reviewed memorials and counter-memorials (both parties arguing their territorial claims by mostly relying on colonial treaties and subsequent

---

1   This is a very simplified summary presented for the purpose of legal analysis of the current state of the boundary dispute and is not intended in any way to exclude other nuanced narrations that might be brought forward for historical or other purposes. For further reading on the War, see, Tekeste Negash and Kjetil Tronvoll (2000), Brothers at War: Making Sense of the Eritrean-Ethiopian War, Oxford.

2   According to Algiers Agreement, each state appointed two commissioners, who in turn appointed the fifth member, who became President of the EEBC.

state practices), adopted rules of procedure and other directives (regulating matters ranging from proceedings before the EEBC to the opening of field offices and final compliance with boundary determinations), used the services of UN organs and missions, particularly the UN Cartographer as its secretary and United Nations Mission in Eritrea and Ethiopian (UNMEE) (among the latter's initial responsibilities of overseeing compliance with the peace agreement, it was tasked with demining and administrative and logistical support to field offices), passed the Delimitation Decision (DD) and "virtual" demarcation and did other tasks it deemed necessary for the resolution of the boundary dispute as mandated in the AA.[3]

Engaging all those tasks and determinations is not useful in this brief essay. In terms of outcome and relevance to the resolution of the boundary dispute, the most remarkable work of the EEBC was the DD, passed in April 2002. The Decision, which was made after review of memorials, counter-memorials, oral arguments, and evidence submitted, consisted of eight chapters of technical and legal analysis and dozens of maps. The chapters narrated in elaborate manner procedural and substantive introductions, including descriptions of the three Sectors of the boundary, applicable principles of international law, separate chapters for each Sector (Central, Eastern, and Western Sectors), boundary lines within rivers, and finally *Dispositif*, the operational part of the DD pointing out the lines of delimitation of all the Sectors, with forty-one "points" marked on three varied scales of maps in the DD). Some of these components of the DD will be picked up later; but it should be noted that this Decision, which identified territorial boundaries of the two states on paper, marked a central step in the process of the boundary dispute resolution, at least before the EEBC. As will be explained later, the DD was disputed, but at least the process was a success and was to the satisfaction of the Parties as well as the EEBC. If things had been as planned, what should have and would have followed was the second and last stage, namely demarcation, which is the emplacement of permanent structures or pillars on the ground.

The EEBC and What Went Wrong

Initially and until the EEBC passed its DD in April 2002, EEBC's proceedings were going as planned. Both parties claimed to have accepted the DD and there was a lot of hope, with both celebrating the DD. An apparent misunderstanding of the DD by either of the Parties could have contributed

---

3   Article 4.7 of Algiers Agreement; Resolution 1430 (2002), adopted by the Security Council at its 4,600th meeting, 14 August 2002; Rules of Procedure of the EEBC; the various Reports of the EEBC.

to the celebratory mood by both. Because of the DD's complexity of maps and points and narrations, quick understanding of everything might have been difficult, without careful studies, leading to premature celebrations. Following its Decision, the EEBC continued its usual business and issued Demarcation Directives on July 8, outlining principles and rules relating, among others, to objective of demarcation, composition of demarcation team, establishment of field offices in both territories, assistance by UNMEE, information regarding operations, liaison, freedom of movement, demarcation process, mine clearance, construction of pillars, sectoral maps, and special direction for specific locations.[4] In about a year following the DD, the Eastern Sector was almost completed when issues began with the Central and Western fronts. Owing to their three constitutive colonial treaties, it should be noted that there have been three Sectors of the boundary, namely the Central, Western, and Eastern Sectors, corresponding to the three colonial boundary agreements of 1900, 1902, and 1908, respectively, between Italy and Ethiopia.

Problems with the arbitration started to emerge with Ethiopia's initial "Request for Interpretation, Correction and Consultation."[5] Ethiopia's Request, which it considered to be about points of determination during demarcation, related to consistency in analysis of the parties conduct along the boundary, identification of principles during demarcation for river confluence points, carrying out field surveys to locate geographical features, existence of geographical error regarding Fort *Cadorna*, and so on. The EEBC, however, dismissed the Request as inadmissible, arguing that Ethiopia's elaborate request amounted to an appeal, a request for an amendment to the DD affecting the latter's binding quality and not as such a request for interpretation or clarity. Afterwards, acrimonies began and Ethiopia started referring to the DD as "illegal, unjust and irresponsible," particularly referring to *Badme* and some aspects of the Central Sector. The EEBC was not oblivious to Ethiopia's concerns but explained that Ethiopia's *Badme* claim was not supported by evidence and that its hands were tied about the alleged "anomalies and impracticalities," a point which will be taken up later.[6]

---

4   These are most of the terms the EEBC used in its Demarcation Directions. See the Delimitation of the Border (Eritrea-Ethiopia): Demarcation of the Eritrea/Ethiopia Boundary Directions, 8 July 2002.

5   The challenges are detailed in the more than two dozen reports of the EEBC. For a summary, see Statement by Ethiopia Eritrea Boundary Commission, 29 November 2006, available at http://www.pca-cpa.org/.

6   EEBC, Sixteenth Report on the Work of the Commission, covering the period from

It is not necessary to detail the back and forth between Ethiopia and the EEBC and later between Eritrea and the EEBC. But according to the Commission and United Nations (UNs)-Secretary-General (SG) reports,[7] both states used multiple methods to frustrate, right or wrong, the work of the EEBC. These included failure to attend meetings called by the EEBC and denying access to EEBC's officers working on the ground. Both had committed in the AA to assist the EEBC in the process of boundary demarcation.[8] That did not happen, and failure to cooperate, which started with Ethiopia, culminated in both parties withdrawing support and cooperation from the EEBC in various ways. There was not much of a dispute on the Eastern Sector, and Ethiopia, despite its reservations, agreed to demarcation of this Sector while subjecting the other two to further "interpretation"; but Eritrea refused to the demarcation of the Eastern Sector unless all the Sectors were simultaneously demarcated unconditionally based on the DD.[9]

Four years passed, with little progress. The plan was to finalize the settlement as soon as possible, with submissions of claims and evidence in forty-five days, a delimitation decision in six months, and final demarcation "expeditiously."[10] The EEBC, convinced that demarcation was not to continue as planned and that it could not function for an indefinite duration— both concerns were legitimate at the time, adopted an alternative approach. It argued,

> Modern techniques of image processing and terrain modelling make it possible, in conjunction with the use of high resolution aerial photography, to demarcate the course of the boundary by identifying the location of turning points (hereinafter called "boundary points") by both grid and geographical coordinates with a degree of accuracy that does not differ significantly from pillar site assessment and emplacement undertaken in the field.

That is the "virtual demarcation" left behind by the EEBC at the time it declared mission accomplished and dissolved itself around the end of

---

15 December 2004 to 28 February 2005.

7   There were dozens of reports each by the EEBC and the Secretary-General of the UN; the EEBC's reports were concerned with boundary issues while the SG's related to all issues, including boundary issues, claims, humanitarian situation, peace keeping and demining.

8   Article 4.14 of the Algiers Agreement.

9   EEBC, Sixteenth Report on the Work of the Commission, covering the period from 15 December 2004 to 28 February 2005.

10   Algiers Agreement, Articles 4(8), 4(12), and 4(13).

2007.[11] This is a demarcation done on paper by a list of coordinates. That was unusual for resolution of boundary disputes under international law. Demarcation is actual emplacement of pillars on the ground. Nevertheless, the EEBC justified its virtual demarcation on the principle of effectiveness, international practice, and on the lack of any other option to discharge its mandate in the AA.[12] Once the EEBC in 2006 came up with the virtual demarcation of boundary coordinates and maps,[13] it waited for twelve months for the parties to agree or seek assistance from the EEBC to resume demarcation, the absence of either of which made virtual demarcation effective beginning 30 November 2007.[14] The parties neither agreed nor wanted the EEBC to resume, making the virtual demarcation effective, at least as far as the EEBC was concerned.

Relevant Legal Principles

There are three major stages of any boundary dispute resolution in international law (the same applying to the Ethiopia-Eritrea boundary): determination of applicable principles, delimitation, and demarcation. Delimitation, which is the determination of boundary lines on paper, was performed by the EEBC with its passing of the DD. It has been briefed in the previous section. With regard to demarcation, which is the third and last stage, the task has not yet been completed. Even taking the virtual demarcation as some sort of demarcation, there still should be the emplacement of pillars on the ground, which should then finalize demarcation. Issues associated with the current state of demarcation will be highlighted in the next section. What should not be omitted is the first stage of setting legal principles for the determination of the boundary dispute. It is no less important since determinations of both delimitation and demarcation rely on these principles. This section will highlight two principles that helped and could still help in the boundary dispute resolution: *uti posseditis* and *ex aequo et bono*.

---

11   The last Report of the EEBC covered the period between September and December of 2007. See Eritrea-Ethiopia Boundary Commission, Twenty-sixth Report, covering the period from 27 September to 31 December 2007.

12   Statement by Ethiopia Eritrea Boundary Commission, 29 November 2006, available at http://www.pca-cpa.org/.

13   The maps, according to the EEBC, can be consulted at the Permanent Court of Arbitration in The Hague and the UN Cartographic Section; see Ethiopia Eritrea Boundary Commission, Press Release, Permanent Court of Arbitration, The Hague, 30 November 2006, available at http://www.pca-cpa.org/.

14   Ibid.

The first two paragraphs of Article 4 of the AA determine the legal principles applicable to the boundary dispute. Here are the paragraphs:

> *Consistent with the provisions of the Framework Agreement and the Agreement on Cessation of Hostilities, the parties reaffirm **the principle of respect for the borders existing at independence** as stated in resolution AHG/Res. 16(1) adopted by the OAU Summit in Cairo in 1964, and, in this regard, that they shall be determined on the basis of pertinent **colonial treaties [(1900, 1902 and 1908)]** and applicable international law[15] [Emphases added].*

> *The Commission shall not have the power to make decisions **ex aequo et bono**.[16] [Emphasis added.]*

According to these clauses, the principle of *uti posseditis*, which states boundaries that existed during colonial times should continue as international boundaries, is the pillar in the boundary dispute resolution. The principle is not a new creation by Ethiopia and Eritrea. As a matter of fact the Algiers Agreement, as can be seen from the paragraph above, recognizes the OAU Cairo Declaration of 1964, which is a landmark declaration in the formation of states in Africa, recognizing this principle as applying to Africa. It was long used for boundary disputes following decolonization in Africa and elsewhere. That was the option the continental organization (OAU) chose and African states agreed. At the time, the other available option, which was redrawing African colonial boundaries based on self-determination or sociolinguistic identity or something else and which affected almost all African states, would have been a disaster, possibly resulting in perpetual war throughout the continent.[17]

According to the files of the EEBC, the principle appeared to have been applied consistently throughout the Sectors. As a result, one could safely assert that it is this principle that determined the delimitation, resulting in the "anomalies" that led eventually to Ethiopia's refusal to comply with EEBC's DD. This requires a few words on difficulties associated

---

15   Algiers Agreement, Article 4(1).

16   Ibid, Article 4(2).

17   More on *uti possidetis*, see for example, S. Ratner (1996) "Drawing a Better Line: *uti possidetis* and the Borders of New States," American Journal of International Law 90 (4). For critique on the principle's application to Ethiopia-Eritrea boundary dispute and the principle's origin and development, see this Author's unpublished Master's Thesis: *Uti Possidetis* and the Ethiopia-Eritrea Boundary Dispute, Master's Thesis (Unpublished), November 2006, University of Oslo. For the alternative of redrawing boundaries, particularly in African context, see Saadia Touval (1972), The Boundary Politics of Independence in Africa.

with a strict application of the principle. It is not to suggest that the parties should retract the application of the principle. As a starting point, there is no doubt as to the utility of the principle. The principal merits of its application, its simplicity and pragmatism, are without match.[18] Rather, since the parties in any case are to negotiate on the finalization of the boundary disputes, they should enter with an understanding of major flaws of the principle.

One criticism against the principle relates to its meaning. Generally there are two possible approaches to seeing *uti possidetis*: *de jure* and *de facto*.[19] The argument basically is that the principle's application, at least in Ethiopia's case, did not take into account realities on the ground, *de facto uti possidetis*. *De jure uti possidetis*, which is principally found in colonial treaties, becomes decisive at the cost of reality on the ground, which is to say *de facto uti possidetis*.[20] As a result, the application of *uti possidetis* in the Eritrea-Ethiopia boundary dispute could be said to have relied essentially on *de jure*, owing to the express identification of the colonial treaties in the AA, with little regard to actual control of territories at the time the treaties were concluded.

The second argument is that the application of the principle has not taken into consideration the special circumstances of the Eritrea-Ethiopia boundary as well as their colonial background. In this connection, few points should be noted. First, the colonial treaties were not colonial treaties bargained and agreed upon by equal colonial powers, at least in the sense known at the time. Ethiopia was the weakest party in terms of bargaining and the ability to survey its territorial boundaries. As a result, the colonial treaties might not have reflected the actual territories administered. Second, Ethiopia and Eritrea became one country, and developments, at least good faith developments, following this federation should have been taken into account if the boundary that should remain is a boundary that existed at the time of dissolution. Third, and related to the second, the colonial treaties were long abrogated, at least during the Italian invasion, and they should have been kept as such.[21] Again, while the principle might have

---

18 Gbenga Oduntan, International Law and Boundary Disputes in Africa (London: Routledge, 2015), 336.

19 For more on these approaches of *uti possidetis*, see Wondemagegn T., *Uti Possidetis* and the Ethiopia-Eritrea Boundary Dispute, Master's Thesis (Unpublished), November 2006, University of Oslo.

20 Gbenga Oduntan, International Law and Boundary Disputes in Africa (London: Routledge, 2015, p198.

21 Ibid, p201.

been useful for Africa at the time to address the multiple boundary claims, its time might have passed and may no longer be suitable for African boundary disputes.[22]

Despite the application of *uti posseditis*, the boundary resolution could have still ended with both parties gaining what they essentially wanted. But that did not happen, mainly because another principle mentioned in the AA is excluded from the legal arsenal of the EEBC. This exclusion could be said to have limited flexibility and frustrated potential progress in the demarcation phase. It was the prevention of the EEBC from using *ex aequo et bono* (literally meaning equitable and good), which the AA expressly ruled out. It was not and is not quite clear why the parties ruled out *ex aequo et bono*. It could be because of the general understanding of sources of international law, which disfavor the principle unless the parties expressly agree to its use.[23]

As the EEBC rightly pointed out on several occasions, the prohibition of the principle was among the major obstacles. Exclusion of *ex aequo et bono* is also taken by some as the most damaging part of the AA.[24] Had the principle been available for the boundary determination, the EEBC could have introduced flexibility and rectified anomalies, while at the same time granting both parties the amount of territory they wanted. The parties, in their future negotiation, are advised not to preempt the application of this principle.

What Now

Recent developments regarding Ethiopia and Eritrea are widely known. The Jeddah Peace Agreement concluded between Prime Minister Abiy and President Isaias (2018), the reunion of Ethiopian and Eritrean families separated for two decades because of the War, leaders visiting each other's capitals and communities, the resumption of daily flights, and people enthusiastically traveling both ways are nothing less than miraculous. These are indications of future potential in the continued and peaceful relationship between the two states. The Jeddah Agreement marked the moment for the current promising relationship between the two states. In this agreement, the parties committed to:

---

22   Ibid, p336. Its suitability for African boundary disputes has long been challenged.

23   Article 38, Paragraph 2 of the Statute of the ICJ (Article 38 is an authority for sources of international law) reads: *This provision shall not prejudice the power of the Court to decide a case ex aequo et bono, if the parties agree thereto.*

24   Gbenga Oduntan, International Law and Boundary Disputes in Africa (London: Routledge, 2015), p199.

- Peace, friendship and comprehensive cooperation;

- Comprehensive cooperation in the political, security, defense;

- *Economic, trade, investment, cultural and social fields on the basis of complementarity and synergy;*

- *Joint Investment Projects, including the establishment of Joint Special Economic Zones;*[25]

Indeed the Jeddah Agreement has also an important clause in connection with the boundary dispute. Like the AA, the principal area of concern for the Jeddah Agreement has been expectedly the resolution of boundary disputes. A clause relating to the matter commits the parties to "implement the Eritrea-Ethiopia Boundary Commission decision."[26] While the clause appears good, a close examination of the determinations of the EEBC raises a few concerns. Three of them are worth highlighting here. The first is which decision the parties are referring to, the DD of 2002 or the virtual demarcation decision of 2007? Second, how is the demarcation to be executed? The third relates to institutional mechanisms for the resolution of the dispute.

Before reflecting on these three, one preliminary point should be noted. As pointed out elsewhere, there are three parts of the boundary, often called Sectors: Central, Western and Eastern Sectors. From the proceedings before the EEBC as well as the parties' statements, the Eastern Sector is not disputed. Neither the DD nor the demarcation related to it is disputed, and this Sector could be easily demarcated—pillars placed on the ground—as long as the parties wish to continue the boundary demarcation. Immediate demarcation of it is a possibility, although this demarcation might need to wait for the other two Sectors for comprehensive settlement. Hence the boundary Sectors that are likely to pose challenges are the Central and Western.

As explained in the previous section, there are two determinations by the EEBC that the parties might have referred to in the Jeddah Agreement. One is the DD and the other is the virtual demarcation. To begin with the first, there is no doubt that the parties were referring to the DD. That was the decision the parties unequivocally accepted, at least at the beginning. It was the decision in which the parties fully participated in the process as well as substance. But implementing it might have difficulties, as Ethiopia feared. Although Ethiopia expressed its support for the DD, and only later in the

---

25 Jeddah Agreement, Articles 1 and 2.

26 Jeddah Agreement, Article 3.

demarcation phase that it raised reservations, Ethiopia's concerns were also about the DD. Before implementation of this decision, the parties might need to negotiate regarding its anomalies.

In this connection, the EEBC itself acknowledged the possibility of anomalies in the DD, except that it claimed to lack authority but to work based on the laws given to it. Even it suggested of the possibility of the parties agreeing to empower it to vary the DD. As the EEBC reiterated on several occasions, almost in all its reports to the UNSC through the SG, once it became clear that Ethiopia was not to agree with the strict application of the DD, at least regarding the Central and Western Sectors, it claimed to have lacked the authority to vary boundary lines marked in the DD.

The EEBC foresaw the possible occurrence of special challenges in the demarcation phase. In its Demarcation Directions relating to the "division of towns and villages," the EECC pointed out that it "has no authority to vary the boundary line. If it runs through and divides a town or village, the line may be varied only on the basis of an express request agreed to between and made by both parties."[27] In this connection, although the EEBC denied Ethiopia's request for consideration of those situations, there appeared instances where it used equity in deviating from the DD in its virtual determination.

For example in its virtual demarcation, the EEBC implied that there are differences between its "coordinates" for the virtual boundary and those in delimitation decision, although they are not "significant," and also that clarity was introduced to the coordinates from the DD (in the areas of Tserona and Zalambessa as envisaged in the DD).[28] Again, the EEBC did state that some of the elements in Ethiopia's request might be considered in the demarcation, and it kept Ethiopia's request and Eritrea's observations in the files while dismissing Ethiopia's request as inadmissible.[29] However it is not clear to what extent the EEBC heeded Ethiopia's request in its virtual demarcation.

If it were up to the EEBC, Ethiopia and Eritrea would now have the virtual boundary, with the list of boundary coordinates, explanatory

---

27   Delimitation of the Border (Eritrea-Ethiopia): Demarcation of the Eritrea/Ethiopia Boundary Directions, 8 July 2002.

28   That was identified in the literature. See for example, Gbenga Oduntan, International Law and Boundary Disputes in Africa (London: Routledge, 2015), who, for example, identifies this use and argues that the EEBC's claim that equity was not to be used is not quite accurate.

29   EEBC decision regarding the "Request for Interpretation, Correction and Consultation," submitted by the Federal Democratic Republic of Ethiopia, 13 May 2002.

comments, and forty-five maps illustrating the boundary points. It is not evident the parties had these coordinates in mind when they concluded the Jeddah Agreement. The clauses relating to the boundary were so general that they could be interpreted to permit both ways. While the virtual demarcation might be useful, particularly relating to boundaries that were not disputed, its complete acceptance might not be in the parties' best interest, at least not Ethiopia's. Several criticisms could be mounted against the virtual boundary.

One general criticism is whether the virtual demarcation was in the EEBC mandate. The EEBC, as explained earlier, instead of leaving the matter as it stood for future determinations, wanted to finalize the matter and went on with virtual demarcation. It could have stopped at the delimitation decision and dissolved, and probably the commissioners' eagerness to contribute to peace and "fulfill their mandate" might have resulted in the unexpected step of marking boundary coordinates. This unfortunately appears beyond their mandate. While the EEBC argued that virtual demarcation was supported in practice, it presented little evidence that it was a rule in international law or that it was permitted under the AA.

Second, the virtual demarcation, in any case, cannot replace the actual demarcation, and the EEBC's determination on this point could not resolve the matter once and for all. The EEBC admitted this fact, except that it had no choice. Third, as long as there is the DD, based on which the EEBC said it issued the virtual demarcation, there is no reason for both parties not to agree to the setting aside of the virtual demarcation. Fourth, there could also be errors in the virtual demarcation since both parties disregarded the determination and were not willing to provide feedback. For example even Eritrea had expressed the possibility of raising a number of questions regarding "meaning, content and implications" regarding the virtual demarcation, although it also admitted the exercise to be a significant step.[30] Fifth, as Ethiopia argued, the map coordinates' demarcation did not reflect the reality on the ground, since surveys were not carried out as required for actual demarcation of boundaries. As a result of these and other factors, complete reliance on the virtual demarcation is not advised. Indeed, the virtual demarcation is one of the documents that should be studied in further negotiation of the boundary dispute and could be used for all Sectors except those contested owing to anomalous outcomes, such as *Badme*.

The third point that should be raised in connection with the boundary resolution under the Jeddah Agreement is what institutional mechanisms to employ. Now everybody knows the EEBC no longer exists and cannot be

---

30 A letter by the President of Eritrea to EEBC, as quoted in the Report of the Secretary-General on Ethiopia and Eritrea, 7 April 2008.

brought back given the acrimonies and all that led to its dissolution without conclusion of the demarcation. As a result, the parties have a number of choices. One is bilateral negotiation, mostly with the involvement of experts, to be decided on the bases of the parties' domestic laws and procedures. This is in line with their prime responsibility to resolve their boundary disputes. In the SC's language, "Eritrea and Ethiopia bear the primary responsibility for achieving a comprehensive and lasting settlement of the border dispute and normalizing their relations."[31]

The other possibility is inviting the UNs to assist in the negotiation or participate as observer. Engaging the UNs is particularly important, since international assistance might be necessary in terms of technical assistance as well as humanitarian and other help needed in case the actual demarcations are likely to affect the livelihood of communities. Financial assistance might as well be necessary during demarcation, which is likely to be a costly process. For example, during the life of the EEBC there was a fund established to cover expenses associated with delimitation and demarcation, including compensation for the commissioners.[32] In this connection, the SG in his report recognized the possibility of the "movement of communities, some reconstruction of community facilities, and some understanding between the parties regarding cross-boundary movement," during demarcation.[33] This is not to suggest communities should be moved from one territory to another. As a matter of fact, the parties need to do their utmost to ensure communities stay where they are irrespective of their citizenship. If necessary, open and common boundaries could be considered, which will be noted later. In the end, the parties might allow a third party; but one important lesson should be for the parties to avoid binding third-party arbitration and finality clauses. Their relationship is complex and utmost flexibility and innovation should be allowed.

In the end, whether on the basis of the virtual demarcation, DD, or another agreement, actual demarcation might be necessary. The objective of demarcation, as the EEBC itself stated, is to set "on the ground pillars identifying the course of the line decided" in the DD or in a few cases foreseen by the DD "determine more precisely the delimitation line" of the DD.[34] That has not occurred. In further actions following the Jeddah

---

31   Resolution 1798 (2008), adopted by the Security Council at its 5829th meeting, 30 January 2008.

32   Establishment of a Trust Fund for Delimitation and Demarcation by Resolution 1177 (1998), adopted by the Security Council at its 3895th meeting, 26 June 1998.

33   Progress report of the secretary-general on Ethiopia and Eritrea, 6 March 2003.

34   Delimitation of the Border (Eritrea-Ethiopia): Demarcation of the Eritrea-Ethiopia Boundary Directions, 8 July 2002.

Agreement and further negotiation, the challenges raised by Ethiopia should be taken into account. Challenges regarding the division of villages and roads are not new to boundary disputes. The delimitation of boundaries in cases of straddling villages and communities has been said to be difficult, complicating boundary dispute resolutions in general.[35] In such cases, what is often suggested is mutual agreement.[36]

These would have been ideal if they were made before boundary decisions, but at least in terms of *Badme* and related issues, that should still be a possibility. As Gbenga Oduntana argues in the African context citing the case of Cameroon and Nigeria, for example, post-litigation processes are possibilities.[37] Important principles suggested in this resolution include confidence-building measures, high-level political determination, flexibility, engaging well-meaning international partners, inhabitants first and the protection of human rights (avoiding discrimination and respecting freedom of movement no matter what), good faith, avoidance of manifest injustices such as splitting up school compounds, separating families from their subsistence, and maintaining permanent structures.[38]

Considering the current positive atmosphere in the bilateral relationship, the parties could work out exemplary boundaries. In all these efforts, bringing to the table an equitable settlement might be useful. Open boundaries are possibilities in areas where immediate solutions cannot be found for internal, political, or other reasons. Physical demarcation might still be necessary, but that should not be considered the end of the world. The President of the EEBC did suggest, for example, that the parties work out open boundaries if there are manifest absurdities, for example a line cutting through a village or across a road several times and nationals of one country cultivating their fields in the other.[39] It should be noted that as long as the parties are acting in good faith, it is not an absolute necessity that the boundaries are demarcated and pillars emplaced. The two states have lived without demarcation for a century, and they could do the same for the foreseeable future.

It is possible to undertake a comprehensive study of the current state and past developments, including developments in the last twenty years, since

---

35 Gbenga Oduntan, International Law and Boundary Disputes in Africa (London: Routledge, 2015), pp352–54.

36 Ibid.

37 Ibid.

38 Ibid.

39 Twenty-fifth report of the EEBC (covering from 10 July to 26 September 2007).

the War began. The documents to be studied include the DD, the virtual demarcation (including the marked points and maps), and documents presented by the parties on various occasions. Alleged intentional population movements and settlements should also be studied, not with the purpose of resettling or moving the people back but for a complete understanding of the situation. Movement of persons of Ethiopian origin to Eritrean territory has been alleged by Eritrea. The EEBC agreed with Eritrea's allegation and ordered Ethiopia to comply with the order.[40] The people allegedly moved might have lived in that area before, during, or after colonial times and only afterwards moved to Ethiopia; their movement, if any, might have been part of measures to rectify. As a result, despite intent of the government of Ethiopia in the alleged movement and despite accuracy of the allegations, population movement should be discouraged unless there is evidence that the people were moved despite their wishes and they still wanted to move back.

Claims, the EECC, and the Current State[41]

Background

It should be noted that the two commissions established by the AA are distinct: one dealing with boundary disputes relating to the delimitation and demarcation of the international boundaries of Eritrea and Ethiopia (the EEBC, discussed above) and the other on claims, the EECC, which is the subject of this section. Apart from appearing in the same AA, there is not any formal relationship between the two. As the EECC rightly indicated in one of its awards, its findings have been irrespective of boundary delimitation/demarcation and decisions by the EEBC.

The EECC began its operation in March 2001 in two phases: the liability phase, which was finalized in December 2005 and the damages phase, which was completed in 2009. After nine long years of filings of memorials, counter-memorials, oral statements, and consultations, the EECC found both Ethiopia and Eritrea liable for some claims, while relieving them from others. The EECC's establishment, mandate, and procedure were regulated by the AA,

---

40   EEBC, Determinations, 7 November 2002.

41   This section of the chapter substantially borrows from the Author's yet unpublished article submitted for publication to International Law Series, School of Law, AAU: "Ethiopia-Eritrea Claims for 'Loss, Damage or Injury' and the Claims Commission: Lessons for the Future, November 2019."

rules of procedure of the EECC, and international law.[42] It was composed of four arbitrators, two members appointed by each Party and one President selected by the four arbitrators appointed by the Parties.[43] Decisions and awards were agreed to be final and binding; the parties also agreed to honor all the decisions and promptly pay EECC's monetary awards.[44]

The mandate of the EECC as outlined in the AA has been to decide on "all claims for loss, damage or injury" against each other or each others' nationals.[45] Relying on general statements of the AA, which refers to "violations of international humanitarian law, including the 1949 Geneva Conventions, or other violations of international law," the rules of procedure took the ICJ Statute as authoritative and provided the following as sources:

- Customary International Law;

- The four Geneva Conventions of 1949, as a matter of customary

---

42 EECC, Rules of Procedure: it outlines the nature of "Decisions," the types of awards it could make, the binding nature of decisions and awards, applicable law (Article 19), which is a verbatim copy of the ICJ Statute; procedures for individual consideration of claims (governments on their behalf plus claims in excess of $100,000, and any other meriting individual treatment such as claims seeking to prove actual damages); mass claims procedure; also providing proof of acts or omissions, attributable, and a violation of international law; random sampling of evidence; determination of compensation.

43 Appointment by the SG of the UN of any of the Arbitrators was a possibility in the AA, where the Parties failed to nominate any of the Arbitrators within the specified time. Likewise the SG was mandated to appoint a President where Arbitrators selected by the parties were not able to appoint the President. However, the SG did not have the opportunity to exercise his authority. Indeed there was a vacancy created by resignation of a member appointed by Ethiopia in 2001, which was filled in due time. On the procedure of appointment, see EEBC, it is Article 4(4) & (6); on the filling of the vacancy left open by resignation, see Report of the Secretary-General on Ethiopia and Eritrea, 5 September 2001. The procedure for the Boundary Commission was the same; one vacancy left by resignation in 2001 of a member appointed by Eritrea was filled in due time. Another opportunity had presented itself in 2007 by a passing away of a member appointed by Ethiopia. Ethiopia refused appointment on the ground that it made little difference since the EEBC already claimed to have completed its tasks. Despite the EEBC's advice for the SG to appoint, the SG avoided the issue, partly probably for the same reason as Ethiopia and partly not to further antagonize any of the Parties. See AA, Article 5 (2) & (3) and Report of the Secretary-General on Ethiopia and Eritrea, 23 January 2008.

44 Article 5(17) of the Algiers Agreement.

45 Algiers Agreement of 12 December 2000, Article 5.

international humanitarian rules as well as treaty obligations [since Eritrea acceded to the Geneva Conventions on August 14, 2000, this date served as the marking point for invocation as either customary law or treaty law][46];

- The Vienna Convention on Diplomatic Relations of 1961;

- International HRs law, e.g. ICCPR and ICESCR.[47]

In addition to Article 5(1) of the Algiers Agreement, the first decision of the EECC elaborated on its mandate and the temporal scope of its jurisdiction.[48] On the basis of the relevant documents, the EECC temporal jurisdiction included claims between May 1998 and 12 December 2000, the duration of the armed conflict. As a result, all claims of *jus in bello* presented by both parties were considered to fall within temporal jurisdiction. Moreover, it had temporal jurisdiction on some claims after December 2000, as long as they were related to the armed conflict or its disengagement. In addition to the temporal jurisdiction, some claims were also dismissed for filing out of time. The deadline for filing, 12 December 2001, was crucial for some claims that would otherwise have been considered by the EECC.[49]

Claims, Liabilities, and Compensation

There were a number of claims made by the parties. According to EECC files, Eritrea filed a total of thirty-two claims and Ethiopia eight. Despite variations in numbers, both parties' claims were largely similar. All Ethiopia's claims were on behalf of the government, while Eritrea also presented a few claims on behalf of named individuals. The claims, filed under six categories, related to the unlawful expulsion and the unlawful displacement of natural persons from their residences; injuries suffered by prisoners of war and by civilians; the loss, damage, or injury of persons not covered by the other categories; and governmental loss, damage, or injury.[50] In consultation with the parties, the EECC set out to consider the claims in two phases: liability and damages, with the first dealing with the

---

46 Partial Award, Prisoners of War, Eritrea's Claim 17, between the State of Eritrea and the Federal Democratic Republic of Ethiopia, The Hague, 1 July 2003.

47 ECC, Rules of Procedure.

48 EECC, Decision Number 1: The Commission's Mandate/Temporal Scope of Jurisdiction.

49 Article 5(8) of the Algiers Agreement provides for one year from the effective date of the agreement. Claims not filed within the period but falling within the jurisdiction of the EECC were made to be extinguished.

50 EECC, Decision Number 2: Claims Categories, Forms and Procedures.

ascertainment of liabilities and the second, assuming that liabilities are established, with the assessment of damages and compensation or other reparations due.

Liabilities found include *jus ad bellum* liability against Eritrea, a controversial finding in which Eritrea was found to have violated Article 2(4) of the UN Charter by initiating a war in a manner contrary to international law.[51] The other is the finding that both parties violated international humanitarian law relating to the protection of prisoners of war. Ethiopia's violations included beatings or other unlawful abuse at capture or its immediate aftermath, deprivation of footwear during long walks from place of capture to detention, loss of personal property, health conditions that seriously and adversely affected or endangered health, provision of diet that was seriously deficient in nutrition, and delay in repatriation.[52] While Eritrea's violations included most of what Ethiopia did, remarkable additions were refusals of visits to detention places, registrations, interviews, and services by the International Committee of the Red Cross (ICRC); failure to allow complaints about living conditions; the seeking of redress; and punishment for attempting to complain.[53] There were also liabilities found regarding diplomatic claims, such as searching diplomats and their luggage, ransacking the embassy residence (by Ethiopia), and the brief detention of a diplomatic member and withholding of a box of diplomatic correspondence (by Eritrea).[54] There were a number of civilian and other complaints to which both parties were found to be liable.

---

51 EECC Partial Award: *Jus Ad Bellum*, Ethiopia's Claims 1–8, 19 December 2005; Article 2(4) of the UN Charter reads, "All Members shall refrain in their international relations from the threat or use of force against the territorial integrity or political independence of any state, or in any other manner inconsistent with the Purposes of the United Nations." See also, Christine Gray, "The Eritrea/Ethiopia Claims Commission Oversteps Its Boundaries: A Partial Award?" *European Journal of International Law* 17, no. 4 (2006), 699–721.

52 Partial Award, Prisoners of War, Eritrea's Claim 17, between the State of Eritrea and the Federal Democratic Republic of Ethiopia, The Hague, 1 July 2003.

53 Partial Award, Prisoners of War, Ethiopia's Claim 4, The Hague, 1 July 2003.

54 Partial Award, Diplomatic Claim, Ethiopia's Claim 8, The Hague, 19 December 2005 and Partial Award, Diplomatic Claim, Eritrea's Claim 20, The Hague, 19 December 2005; on international standards for protection, see also: Vienna Convention on Diplomatic Relations of 1961.

Table 1, Some of the Liabilities on Both Sides Regarding Civilian and Other Claims[55]

Ethiopia's Liabilities	Eritrea's Liabilities
Loss of property by nonresident Eritreans	Beating of civilians
Loss of businesses and property by Eritrean expellees	Killings, injuries, abduction, forced labor, and conscription of civilians
Looting, burning, stripping, destruction, etc. of buildings, businesses, government buildings, police stations, courthouses, bakeries, villages, livestock, cotton factories, and tobacco plants	Unexplained disappearances
Failure to prevent rape of women	Looting and destruction of property, including houses and livestock
Aerial bombing of a reservoir	Intentional and indiscriminate killings of civilians
Unlawful displacement	Failure to prevent rape of women
Damage to or destruction of Eritrean hospitals and other medical facilities and loss of medical supplies	Looting and destruction of government buildings and infrastructure
Damage to cultural property	Failure to protect Ethiopian civilians in Eritrea from threats and violence
Forcible expulsion of population	Wrongful detention and abusive treatment of Ethiopian civilians in Eritrean custody
Arbitrary deprivation of Ethiopian nationality of dual nationals in third countries	Failure to protect the property of Ethiopian detainees expelled from Eritrea
Wrongful expulsion of dual nationals	Internal displacement

---

55   Sources: Partial Award, Loss of Property in Ethiopia, Owned by Non-Residents, Eritrea's Claim 24, 19 December 2005; Partial Award of 17 December 2004 in Eritrea's Claims 15, 16, 23, and 27–32, 17 December 2004; Partial Award, Western Front, Aerial Bombardment and Related Claims, Eritrea's Claims 1, 3, 5, 9–13, 14, 21, 25, and 26, The Hague, 19 December 2005; Partial Award, Western and Eastern Fronts, Ethiopia's Claims 1 and 3, The Hague, 19 December 2005.

Failure to provide humane and safe treatment for expellees	Looting and destruction of government buildings and infrastructure
Imprisonment of Eritrean civilians on security charges or detaining them for unknown reasons under harsh and unacceptable conditions	Failure to protect Ethiopian civilians in Eritrea from threats and violence

There were a number of claims that were dismissed for one reason or another. Four factors account for the dismissal of many. First is lack of jurisdiction, principally of temporal jurisdiction (only claims related to the duration of the war and as related to the war). The second is filing out of time (filing after 12 December 2001). A clear case, for example, is Ethiopia's claim of delays in the repatriation of its prisoners of war, which was rejected for being filed out of time while Eritrea's similar claim was accepted.[56] The other, which accounts for the dismissal of several of the claims and sub-claims, was lack of evidence. The other ground was the missing legal element, the finding that no violations of international law occurred, regardless of establishment of the facts.

Ethiopia's dismissed claims include Eritrea's diversion of Eritrea-bound[57] claims based on violations of the five bilateral agreements, as the EECC found no violation of international law and as such treaties are suspended during armed conflict;[58] Ethiopia's ports claims of properties detained at the Ports of Assab and Massawa (the claim of unlawful expropriation by Eritrea of 135,000 tons of dry cargo, including aid shipments and new vehicles, and 33 million liters of fuel)[59]; Eritrea's dismissed claims include: an unlawful, indiscriminate, and disproportionate bombing campaign; the prevention of displaced persons from returning and indirect displacement;[60] and pension claims.[61]

---

56 Partial Award, Prisoners of War, Eritrea's Claim 17, between the State of Eritrea and the Federal Democratic Republic of Ethiopia, The Hague, 1 July 2003 and Partial Award, Prisoners of War, Ethiopia's Claim 4, The Hague, 1 July 2003.

57 Partial Award of 17 December 2004 in Eritrea's Claims 15, 16, 23, and 27–32.

58 Partial Award, Economic Loss Throughout Ethiopia, Ethiopia's Claim 7, The Hague, 19 December 2005.

59 Around 95 percent of the cargo was at Assab; see Ports Claim.

60 Partial Award, Western Front, Aerial Bombardment and Related Claims, Eritrea's Claims 1, 3, 5, 9–13, 14, 21, 25, and 26, The Hague, 19 December 2005.

61 Final Award, Pensions, Eritrea's Claims 15, 19, and 23, The Hague, 19 December 2005.

Regarding compensation, the EECC granted, with few exceptions, monetary compensation where the occurrence of damages was proven. In a few cases, it also ruled its findings as satisfaction, particularly where no damage was shown.[62] In the determination of compensation, the EECC considered, among others, the parties' limited economic resources (according to the EECC, for example, Ethiopia's compensation claims amounted to three times Eritrea's gross national product); parties' obligations under international human rights law; the maintenance of peace, which might be affected by extensive compensation; [63] the nature and seriousness of the unlawful acts;[64] the level of evidence (considered in a later section);[65] and constraints in time and resources.[66] With all factors considered, the EECC awarded reparations (monetary compensation or mere finding as satisfaction) for nineteen items under *jus in bello* and eighteen for *jus ad bellum* damages in favor of Ethiopia. In final awards, Ethiopia's total monetary compensation was $174,036,520.[67] Regarding compensation for Eritrea, sixteen items were counted for monitory compensation, two findings as satisfaction, and four items on behalf of named individuals for Ethiopia's violations of *jus in bello*. [68] Total monetary compensation for Eritrea was $161,455,000 on behalf of the state and $2,065,865 on behalf of named individuals.[69] Unsurprising from the EECC's counting of factors to limit the amount of compensation, the total compensation is just a fraction of what the parties requested (0.16 percent). Ethiopia's claims amounted to around $14 billion, while Eritrea's equaled $6 billion. They were not granted even 1% of their requests. Indeed, the EECC had foreseen the possibility that the compensation/awards might not reflect the actual damages both parties suffered.[70]

Overall, the EECC's granting of compensation in the second phase was not as sweeping as it seemed in the liability phase. The constraints

---

62 EECC, Decision Number 3: Remedies.

63 EECC, Final Award, Ethiopia's Damages Claims, 17 August 2009.

64 EECC, Final Award, Ethiopia's Damages Claims and Final Award, Eritrea's Damages Claims, The Hague, 17 August 2009.

65 EECC, Final Award, Ethiopia's Damages Claims.

66 Ibid.

67 Ibid.

68 EECC, Final Award, Eritrea's Damages Claims.

69 Ibid.

70 Ibid.

in connection with evidence, the EECC's engagement with systemic and not individual violations, and time and resources were important in the determination. Regarding Ethiopia's *jus ad bellum* claim, the EECC was not prepared to grant the extensive damages sought. It adopted the criteria of "proximate cause," reasonably foreseeable, as legal causation in determination of damages for violations of *jus ad bellum,* excluding enormous amounts of damages Ethiopia requested. The EECC admitted the existence in history of extensive damages, like in the case of Germany towards Israel. But the EECC pointed out that extensive damages have been awarded either as victor's justice, which the EECC was not established to administer, or as moral or political duties (instead of demands by state responsibility). Accordingly, the EECC argued, extensive damages, as invoked by Ethiopia, were not supported by international law.[71]

What Now

Since the parties did not say anything in the Jeddah Agreement about the claims, one might arguably say issues of claims will not arise now. But this is not the right approach on the way forward. Two arguments would support the opposite approach. First, justice requires that the parties address the issues of claims in a transparent and fair manner. Even when they wish to extinguish, they should expressly say so. Second, the parties are resuming their comprehensive relationship, and there are a number of lessons to be obtained from negotiation and review of the EECC's awards. Third, there are third-party actors, including private citizens, on how they should behave in the future relationship, while they are using each other's territories, doing business, and living in each other's territories. If that is the case, there are several challenges that they have to address. Fourth it is also important that all the resources of the arbitration are not wasted for nothing. In the following paragraphs, those challenges will be highlighted.

Unimplemented Awards

Despite the Algiers Agreement and the parties' commitment to implement decisions of the EECC promptly, the enormous expenses of the arbitral proceedings, and other factors, the awards of the EECC were not executed. It is around a decade since the final awards were granted. As a result, one principal issue if the parties take Claims seriously is whether to implement the awards or not, to totally abandon them or not, and to renegotiate or not. The parties' failure of implementation was not a surprise

---

71   EECC Decision Number 7: Guidance Regarding *jus ad Bellum* Liability.

as such. By the time the EECC was granting its partial and final awards between 2005 and 2009, their relations were at the lowest point since the War, owing to their inability to resolve the boundary dispute.

It is unfortunate the recent agreement between Eritrea and Ethiopia does not include anything about the EECC's awards or other pending claims.[72] What to infer from this omission? The agreement's silence on claims should not be interpreted to mean they are not relevant. It is a framework agreement on peace and friendship with a few clauses on urgent matters such as the boundary issue, which was a cause for the stalemate. As a result, there is still room for the parties to negotiate on outstanding issues of claims, including EECC awards. The Agreement envisages the establishment of a High-Level Joint Committee as well as subcommittees,[73] and one subcommittee could look into the possibility of implementing the EECC awards. Disregarding the decisions and awards of the EECC would not be appropriate considering the resources spent so far. Any negotiation on claims should start or at least include the awards.

Little Regard for the Victims

Despite compliments by the EECC that the parties were able to observe international humanitarian law, all serious violations were committed against civilians, POWs, and properties. In violation of international rules of *jus ad bellum* and *jus bello*, lives were lost, people were injured, and property was destroyed. In short, there were a number of war victims that should have been compensated for their losses, injuries, and damages. Despite the suffering of individual victims, they were beneficiaries of neither the claims proceedings nor other schemes that might have mitigated injuries and losses caused by the War. For this, the Algiers Agreement is partly to blame in its adoption of more or less the traditional arbitral model of state-to-state complaints. Despite its declaration to address the socioeconomic impacts of the war on civilians, the Algiers Agreement has not permitted individuals to appear before the EECC. It was only the parties, on behalf of themselves or their citizens, which were allowed to bring claims before the EECC.[74] Since there was no obligation, but rather discretion, to bring claims on behalf of individual victims, Ethiopia's claims of compensation, for example, were

---

72 Agreement on Peace, Friendship and Comprehensive Cooperation between Eritrea and Ethiopia (the Jeddah Peace Agreement between Eritrea and Ethiopia), 16 September 2018.

73 Article 7 of the Jeddah Agreement.

74 Article 5(8) of the Algiers Agreement.

on behalf of the state only, with none on behalf of its nationals.[75] Again upon the EECC's admission, the compensation granted was more about damages against the state and not compensation for civilian victims.[76] With few exceptions, Eritrea's claims were also largely on its behalf. Arguably, the Algiers Agreement could have adopted a better approach that allowed individuals to present their claims before the EECC.[77] The results would probably have been better, at least to individual victims. Moreover, the constraints in terms of time and resources also contributed to the states limiting their claims to interstate claims.

Indeed, under the circumstances, including time, resources, and constraints, the EECC could have done little to ensure the humanitarian objectives of the claims proceedings were met, except to regularly remind the parties of these objectives. To its credit, the EECC, on several occasions, requested the parties not to keep out of sight the importance of benefiting civilian victims through the proceedings.[78] In one of its decisions related to war victims, it specifically appealed to the parties to find resources, including compensation to be granted to benefit the various categories of war victims through relief programs such as "health, agricultural and other services."[79] That would have been useful, except that the parties did not embrace the suggestions.

The parties might have designed programs distinct from the claims proceedings at the time through aid, governmental budgets, and other schemes. Civilian victims on the front lines would not have probably recovered from the devastating losses and injuries and displacements without assistance. These activities might be accounted for in the final settlement of claims.

Lesser Damages, Claims Dismissed, and Claims Extinguished

As explained in the liabilities and damages section above, the totality of damages has not been established. Upon the EECC's admission, the awards have not reflected the totality of damages owing to evidence, restrained by resources and time. It is only a fraction of the claims the EECC was able to

---

75   EECC, Final Award, Ethiopia's Damages Claims.

76   Ibid.

77   Ari Dybnis, "Was the Eritrea-Ethiopia Claims Commission Merely a Zero-Sum Game?: Exposing the Limits of Arbitration in Resolving Violent Transnational Conflict, *International and Comparative Law Review* 33, no. 2 (2011).

78   EECC, Final Award, Ethiopia's Damages Claims.

79   EECC, Decision Number 8: Relief to War Victims.

award. As noted above, the combined award of compensation is less than $500 million, while the parties' combined claims were around $20 billion. In this connection, two categories of claims can be identified: those dismissed but not extinguished and those dismissed and extinguished.

Claims Dismissed but Not Extinguished

If negotiations were to happen today, there are two categories of claims that should be taken into account, apart from liabilities and damages found by the EECC. The first is the category of claims dismissed for lacking temporal jurisdiction: claims related to acts and omissions before the start of the armed conflict and those that arose afterwards. Depending on the gravity of the violations, these claims could be negotiated. The other category relates to claims dismissed owing to the legality of acts and omissions during the armed conflict. Once armed conflicts end, as is the situation now, those claims could revive under international law and become subject to negotiation. Ethiopia's ports and Eritrea's pension claims could fall under this category. In the case of the ports claims, Eritrea promised to return the balance. The parties need to negotiate the matter, make inventory, and if possible ensure the return. The same could be suggested regarding the pension claims.

Claims Dismissed and Extinguished

There were a number of claims the EECC dismissed, claiming they were extinguished as mandated by the Algiers Agreement. They include claims filed out of time and claims for which evidence was lacking. While it is difficult to revive the latter claims, claims filed out of time could be renegotiated in good faith.

In summary, there are two possibilities available to the parties today: to abandon the claims in total or to fully or partly address them. Abandonment, as noted elsewhere, is not wise. The claims, both awarded and yet to be claimed and negotiated, run into billions of dollars. It would also be an irresponsible act to ignore all civilian victims, hoping they will all go away or they were gone already. Indeed it has been two decades since losses, injuries, and damages occurred, and raising them now might look difficult. But the passage of time should not be a bar, at least to recognizing past violations and rectifying damages if there are still individual victims suffering. Statutory limitations may not apply under the circumstances.[80]

---

80 Convention on the Non-Applicability of Statutory Limitations to War Crimes and Crimes against Humanity, New York, 26 November 1968; Basic Principles and Guidelines on the Right to a Remedy and Reparation for Victims of Violations of

Moreover, settling the claims in a transparent and fair manner is also about the future. It is an emerging practice that individuals should also have a remedy for breach of international obligation,[81] at least by way of recognition of wrongs done to them. The lessons would also help in future relationships. Future armed conflicts are unlikely to occur, but it is not in the realm of the impossible. The lessons from the claims would also help peacetime relationships.

Assuming that the parties want to address the issue of claims, comprehensive negotiation and settlement are crucial going forward. There are a number of challenges to address, which were noted in the previous sections. The evidentiary challenges persist, now that two decades have passed, with documents destroyed, property spoiled, and damages repaired. But the parties could negotiate in good faith; hence they should avoid complete denials as they did before the EECC.

It is this author's opinion that any negotiation on claims should start with EECC findings and damages. The parties should expressly acknowledge the excellent job the EECC has done, despite the unfortunate circumstance that none of its findings have so far been implemented. That is not, of course, the EECC's fault. But this is not to suggest that the parties need to agree on each and every finding of the EECC. As a matter of fact, reasonable disagreements might exist as to some of them. For example, there appears to be some inconsistency in EECC's determinations where it finds Ethiopia liable for not providing compensation for trucks and buses requisitioned but not returned to their owners, while implying that issues of return of Ethiopia's stranded properties at the ports would fall beyond the EECC's temporal jurisdiction. This is simply to suggest that the EECC's findings should be considered final on factual determinations.

While respecting the EECC's findings, however, the parties need not feel constrained by any of the previous findings. The High-Level Joint Committee and its subcommittees, established by the Jeddah Agreement, could be a good forum for negotiation. Mutually agreed upon settlements are not excluded, despite the EECC, particularly considering the fact that nothing came out of the EECC by way of implementation. Moreover, the Algiers Agreement expressly allows the settlement of "outstanding claims, individually or by categories, through direct negotiation or by reference to another mutually agreed settlement mechanism."[82] Implementing the awards

---

International Human Rights and Humanitarian Law (2000), Article 6.

81 Dinah Shelton, *Remedies in International Human Rights Law*, Third Edition (London: Oxford University Press, 2015).

82 Agreement between the Government of the Federal Democratic Republic of

in ways parties see fit, the parties could negotiate on remaining issues such as claims and pension. Monetary compensation may not be necessary owing to the passage of time, for example. Recognition of wrongs might as well serve as satisfaction. The author is not aware of the current state of war victims. But their stories and concerns should be recognized and documented in a final settlement of Claims.

Owing to a long mutual history, largely shared cultural and religious practices, and geopolitics, the fates of the two states are intertwined. As a landlocked state, Ethiopia would benefit from a peaceful, mutually beneficial, principled relationship. If the parties are committed, they could and should create an exemplary relationship in terms of peace, friendship, and trade. One good example that could be mentioned in this regard is Eritrea's reluctance to invoke the application of laws of war against Ethiopia's Ports Claims. Although it was not prevented from confiscating governmental properties during the war, Eritrea did not claim to have the right to confiscate governmental properties as permitted by customary international law. That was an exemplary gesture. Although customary international law does not appear to create a special legal regime, where properties of landlocked states that happen to be in a belligerent territory in the exercise of transit rights are accorded special treatment, Eritrea pointed out before the EECC that it was willing to return even governmental properties, together with private property. Again, whatever the motives, the unilateral action by the Ethiopian government granting restitution or proceeds of properties to Eritreans and considering them like nationals for their exercise of ownership of property and carrying out business is also exemplary.[83]

In their ongoing negotiations, there are a number of factors to consider. Current opinion of the parties is one. Claims before and after the war, dismissed for lack of temporal jurisdiction, such as violations of diplomatic immunities, should also be considered. Even some claims the EECC considered extinguished, such as those filed out of time, should factor in the negotiations.[84] Consultations with affected people, particularly those whose lives are still impacted, are crucial. Studies and assessments regarding some

---

Ethiopia and the Government of the State of Eritrea [Algiers Agreement], Article 5 (16).

83 Council of Ministers Directive to Enable Eritreans Deported from Ethiopia Due to the Ethio-Eritrea War Reclaim and Develop Their Properties in Ethiopia [Unofficial Translation], 2009.

84 According to Algiers Agreement Article 5(8), claims which should have been submitted to the EECC but not submitted or not submitted within the deadline are said to be "extinguished," in accordance with international law.

of the claims, such as survey of Ethiopian properties detained at the ports in order to transfer balances as promised by Eritrea, are important. Also needed are assessments of the types of entitlements and whether pensioners are still interested in the claims in order to implement Ethiopia's recognition of a fair and agreed-upon regime of pensions.

As indicated in the Algiers Agreement, among the principal objectives of the claims' substance and procedure has been to offset the negative impacts of the war on the civilian population, including deportees.[85] That objective has not been fulfilled, for there were no remedies coming out of the Algiers Agreement and the EECC process. But this may not include remedies being granted out of the Algiers' process, such as the return of property of Eritrean citizens by the Ethiopian government. There were also a number of initiatives to alleviate the humanitarian disaster encountered by UN organs, civil societies, governments, and others.[86] Return of refugees and internally displaced persons, demining activities, supply of emergency food, reintegration through restoration of social services such as health and education, reconstruction activities, water supply, emergency interventions, and so on are some of the activities carried out through the concerted efforts of all, particularly with the assistance of the United Nations, such as through UNMEE, quick-impact projects through the Trust Fund, the UN Humanitarian Assistance country offices, UNHCR, World Food Program, WHO, UNDP, UNICEF, and UNOCHA's consolidated appeals and local and international nongovernmental organizations.[87]

Hence, the suggestion is that not all the damages done would outlive the present. Many of them might have been addressed already, despite the parties' reluctance to execute the EECC's decisions on compensation. Instead, the suggestion is for the parties to factor everything that went on in connection with loss and damage and resolve the claims issues.

Other Legal Issues of Concern

There are also other legal issues of concern that the parties need to take into account in their commitment to a peaceful relationship.

---

85   Algiers Agreement, Article 5(1).

86   For example, there was a Trust Fund for Supporting Peace Process, from which a number of small humanitarian projects were designed and executed. See, for example, Progress Report of the Secretary-General on Ethiopia and Eritrea, 13 December 2001.

87   See for example, Ethiopia and Eritrea progress reports of the secretary-general, 9 August 2000 and 13 December 2001.

International Human Rights and Humanitarian Laws

The first relates to the humanitarianism expected from both in their engagement towards one another. Whether in peacetime or during conflict, states should respect basic standards in their conduct towards citizens of another. Respect for human rights and international humanitarian law is expected from both. Some of these principles are in the Algiers Agreement both parties expressly recognized. For example, the Algiers Agreement requires both parties to release and repatriate all POWs and to "release and repatriate or return to their last place of residence all other persons detained as a result of the armed conflict" without delay, in cooperation with the ICRC.[88] They also agree to "afford humane treatment" to each other's citizens.[89] But that did not occur, as can be seen from the files of the EECC, as well as a series of reports by the SG. True, the EECC spoke in good terms of the parties' adherence to international humanitarian law. But that might be about diplomacy. Both parties, at least on the basis of the EECC's findings, were responsible for egregious violations of human rights and humanitarian law. As indicated in the second section, relating to claims, the parties were found by the EECC to have violated numerous principles and standards of international humanitarian law.

The UN SG has long reported on the humanitarian situation around boundary areas and cities, frequently expressing its concerns of violations of human rights and humanitarian laws. Delays in the repatriation of POWs, despite appeals by the UNs and other organs, displacements, discrimination, ill treatment, long detentions, cross-border abductions, and expulsions were all committed.[90]

In this connection, the parties should learn from their mistakes and be able to abide by human rights and humanitarian laws in their future relationships. In the current peace initiative, the parties need also to admit the commission of all those violations, addressing both civilian and military victims. They need to commit for the future as well on the basis of human rights and humanitarian law.

---

88 Article 2(1) of the Algiers Agreement.

89 Article 2(3) of the Algiers Agreement.

90 See for example, Ethiopia and Eritrea Report of the Secretary-General, 9 August 2000; 13 December 2001 Progress report of the Secretary-General on Ethiopia and Eritrea; and Resolution 1398 (2002), adopted by the Security Council at its 4494th meeting, 15 March 2002.

Transit Rights and Bilateral Trade

As one can see from the EECC's liabilities and awards, none of the parties were held responsible for violations of bilateral peacetime agreements. At the time the Eritrea-Ethiopia War broke out, around five bilateral treaties operated relating to transit and port services, air services including traffic, trade (including trade in goods and services), and commercial road, all of them signed in 1993.[91] Ethiopia's claims in connection with violations of the bilateral agreements were all dismissed on the grounds that belligerents are entitled to suspend such kinds of agreements during war. As a result, Ethiopia's claims for economic loss because of alleged violations of these treaties were dismissed. Ethiopia's ports claims were also dismissed, mainly relying on a related legal principle that armed conflict justified suspension of Ethiopia's transit rights.

While these might be right under the current state of international law, the traditional understanding might need reassessment. The agreements are not mere bilateral agreements. They are partly to implement the transit right of a landlocked state, which is allowed under international law. Moreover, according to the International Law Commission, armed conflicts need not necessarily suspend or terminate treaties.[92] From this, stronger arguments could be made for the bilateral agreements, such as those between Eritrea and Ethiopia, as they are not ordinary agreements that could be fully suspended owing to commencement of war. Considering the parties' relationship as transit and landlocked states, at least transit relations should not be subject to immediate suspension and termination. In this connection, the parties could introduce into their new bilateral agreements a clause recognizing their special relationship as transit and landlocked states, which should allow for the continuation of the relationship even during armed conflicts, at least suspension with adequate notice. This would provide confidence to engage for all, private, multinational, and others, without the need to panic owing to threats of conflict between the two states.

As bordering states, the fates of the two states are locked. While they would be legitimately terminated under traditional international law, to build confidence the parties might need to design a special regime that

---

91 The bilateral agreements referred to in the claims are the following: Transit and Port Services Agreement of September 27, 1993; Protocol Agreement of September 27, 1993, on traffic between Ethiopia and Eritrea; Air Services Agreement of September 27, 1993; the Trade Agreement of September 27, 1993 and its Protocol of September 27, 1993 (on trade in goods and services), and the Commercial Road Agreement of September 27, 1993.

92 ILC, "Effects of Armed Conflicts on Treaties," 1985.

would regulate their relationships no matter what. They should recognize that their bilateral relations should be designed on the basis of this formula. According to the Jeddah Agreement, they are to undertake a comprehensive assessment of their relationship, and these special factors need to be taken into account in this assessment. The parties might also become parties to UNCLOS, committing in theory and practice, creating an exemplary relationship.

5

EXAMINING THE ROLE OF STATE AND NON-STATE ACTORS FOR SUSTAINABLE PEACE BETWEEN ETHIOPIA AND ERITREA

Wegahta K. Sereke and Daniel R. Mekonnen

Introduction

Following the advent to power of a reformist and overly ambitious new prime minister in Ethiopia (Abiy Ahmed), Eritrea and Ethiopia opened a new chapter of their most recent history, heralded by the adoption of a landmark reconciliation agreement signed on 9 July 2018 in the capital city of Eritrea. The treaty, officially known as the Joint Declaration of Peace and Friendship or the Asmara Declaration,[1] enabled both countries to break away from an intense animosity of twenty years and make a symbolic move to a much-anticipated peaceful coexistence and collaboration.

The rapprochement has received widespread appreciation, for it signals the dawn of a new era that ends the unfortunate suffering of two decades experienced by peoples of both countries in general and those who live in the common border areas in particular. While a full account of the background of the twenty-year animosity is beyond the immediate objectives of this

---

1   Available at http://www.shabait.com/news/local-news/26639-joint-declaration-of-peace-and-friendship-between-eritrea-and-ethiopia (accessed on 16 May 2019).

contribution, a short introductory remark needs to be made by way of providing context.

Historically, the conflict started in May 1998, at least according to official accounts known to the international community.[2] However, it is believed to have roots going back earlier than May 1998, stretching as far as to 1997. In our understanding, the major factors that triggered the border conflict have never been resolved in a holistic manner. Officially known as a "border conflict," the animosity was at its highest peak between May 1998 and June 2000, when it reached the level of a full-fledged international armed conflict. In spite of a formal resolution of the conflict by major agreements signed in June and December 2000 and a number of arbitral awards resulting from these agreements, the two countries remained in a prolonged state of hostility until the adoption of the Asmara Declaration on 9 July 2018.

It is true that the Asmara Declaration was followed up by another agreement signed on 16 September 2018 in Jeddah, Saudi Arabia, fully known as the Agreement on Peace, Friendship and Comprehensive Cooperation between the Federal Democratic Republic of Ethiopia and the State of Eritrea "Jeddah Declaration."[3] Context wise, there is no major difference between the two agreements. They are complementary. We believe that the Asmara Declaration has greater historical significance in the sense that it is the first such official document heralding the end of the twenty-year animosity and signed in one of the most important capital cites for the conflict (the capital cities being Asmara and Addis Ababa).

The most devastating aspect of the twenty-year antagonism lies in the fact that never in the history of the two countries has their common border been as sealed as it was during the period between May 1998 and September 2018. That is why the rapprochement is widely seen as a harbinger of the dawn of a new era for the peoples of the two countries. The rapprochement has great potential not only in ushering in a lasting peace between the two countries but also in changing favorably the overall situation of peace and security in the entire Horn of Africa, a region known for its recurrent armed conflicts.[4] Among other things, the rapprochement has paved the way for the resumption of official diplomatic relations between Ethiopia and Eritrea; the recommencement of direct air flights between their capital cities; and the reopening of major common border crossings such as Zala Ambesa-Adigrat,

---

2   Mekonnen and Tesfagiorgis, "Causes and Consequences."

3   Available at http://www.shabait.com/news/local-news/27076-agreement-on-peace-friendship-and-comprehensive-cooperation-between-the-federal-democratic-republic-of-ethiopia-and-the-state-of-eritrea- (accessed on 16 May 2019).

4   Mekonnen and Tesfagiorgis, "Causes and Consequences."

Assab-Debay, Sima-Burie, and Omhajer-Humera.[5] However, we also note that almost all of these border crossings were closed a few months after their opening, prompting several questions about the sustainability of the rapprochement, as will be seen in the remaining parts of this contribution.

Thus far, several commentators have opined in different forums about the positive aspects of the rapprochement. There is no doubt that the rapprochement is a step in the right direction. It has generated a lot of optimism in a region that has been deprived of peace for a prolonged period of time. On the other hand, there has been very little discussion about the shortcomings of the rapprochement and those aspects of the process that require urgent improvement. Recognizing the rapprochement as an admirable step that needs to be preserved, in the remaining parts of this essay our contribution will address two major areas of concern that are believed to be of paramount importance for a sustainable peace between the two countries. Improvement in these areas of concern is a key factor in order to make sure that the dividends of the rapprochement are sustained on a long-term basis.

The problems we discuss are related to a major imbalance we observe in both countries in terms of the role that can be played by state and non-state actors in strengthening the rapprochement. The problem is most visible, as will be seen below, on the Eritrean side. In order to be specific, we will discuss one major example of a state actor and another major example of a non-state actor, which in our view are not playing any role in the rapprochement as would be naturally expected in the normal course of things. From state actors, we will discuss the role that should have been played by the nonexistent parliament of Eritrea. From non-state actors, in particular civil society organizations (CSOs), we will use a case of the Eritrean Law Society by way of demonstrating the complete absence of meaningful contribution by non-stators.

In so doing, our observation pays particular attention to the asymmetric relationship between the two countries, in which context the peace process is taking place. Ethiopia as a country is undergoing a nearly fundamental process of political reform. It is also a country with relatively robust national institutions (such as a functioning national parliament). Eritrea has none of this. From the very beginning, one key problem area observed in the rapprochement was the lack of institutionalization of the peace process. This

---

5   Aaron Maasho, "Ethiopia, Eritrea Reopen Border Points for First Time in 20 Years," Reuters, September 10, 2018, https://www.reuters.com/article/us-ethiopia-eritrea/ethiopia-eritrea-reopen-border-points-for-first-time-in-20-years-idUSKCN1LR0FX.

problem is extremely complicated on the part of Eritrea, where it can be said there are no meaningful national institutions (in particular a parliament). We emphasize the role of a parliament, that being a key state institution for democratic oversight in all matters of national interest. Matters of war and peace lie at the heart of such national interest for any given country. Therefore, from the viewpoint of state actors, our contribution examines the role that can or should have been played by the national parliament of Eritrea) in the ongoing rapprochement with Ethiopia.

The second dimension of our discussion will be based on the presumed role that can be played by non-state actors and particularly by what are known as CSOs. In the current context, non-state actors are understood as organisations or initiatives that are not formally affiliated with the state.[6] In its broader sense, the term may refer to corporations and nongovernmental organizations, among other things. For purposes of this article, the focus is on CSOs. Before examining the critical role of state and non-state in the ongoing rapprochement, we will discuss the following general observations about the respective position of both governments by way of providing context to the overall political situation in each country.

The Overall Political Situation in Ethiopia and Eritrea

One key feature of the ongoing rapprochement is that it is a result of a fundamental process of political transformation that is taking place in Ethiopia itself, a process that began with the advent to power of a new and reformist prime minister in April 2018. Be that as it may, over the past twenty years, Ethiopia and Eritrea have suffered major setbacks in their democratization efforts, leading to deep-seated political crises in their internal political dynamics. In the case of Eritrea, the problem includes gross human rights violations as sufficiently reported by several sources, the most authoritative of which is the UN Commission of Inquiry (COI) on Human Rights in Eritrea.[7] In the case of Ethiopia, the problem included political crackdown, such as the widely reported shooting of demonstrators in the post-election violation of 2005, as well as similar shootings of demonstrators in recent years, related to the political unrest stemming from disagreements about the implementation of a new master plan for Addis Ababa.[8]

---

6   ESCR-Net, "Non-State Actors," 2019, https://www.escr-net.org/resources/non-state-actors.

7   First COI Report, A/HRC/29/42, 4 June 2015; Second COI Report, A/HRC/32/47, 8 June 2016.

8   BBC, "Ethiopian Protesters 'Massacred'," October 19, 2006, http://news.

In both countries, the political crisis was partly aggravated by the prolonged hostility that persisted since May 1998. Although both countries suffered similar problems in their internal political dynamics, the manner in which each ultimately addressed these problems and the way it entered rapprochement is markedly different.

Ethiopia started the new peace process with a commitment aimed at redressing issues of major discontent at the local level, namely by taking the significant and very bold steps of broadening the national political landscape. Specific actions included releasing thousands of political prisoners, decriminalizing exiled political organizations, including those engaged in armed rebellion, and many other reform-oriented steps taken by Prime Minister Abiy Ahmed and widely popularized by his philosophy of *medemer*, stemming from an "Amharic word for coming together, or synergy."[9]

In contrast, the political situation in Eritrea remained intact, with no sign of change in widening the political space in the country. As reported widely, due to an internal political crisis that dates to September 2001, Eritrea has a very sad record of political repression, which has been the subject of condemnation by regional and international actors, including an international COI established by the UN Human Rights Council.[10] This means that the peace process is taking place in the context of a huge imbalance in terms of the internal political dynamics of the two countries, thus casting heavy shadows on its sustainability—due to the imbalance experienced on the Eritrean side. Similar observations have been made most recently by two major Eritrean initiatives: a group of sixteen thought leaders and scholars who convened in Nairobi, Kenya, and a major publication released by the Eritrean Law Society (ELS). We will return to the observations made by these initiatives in the latter parts of this contribution.

The Absence of Major State Institutions in Eritrea

As far as Eritrea is concerned, the rapprochement is taking place in the context of a complete breakdown of the rule of law, at the center of which

---

bbc.co.uk/2/hi/africa/6064638.stm; Human Rights Watch, "Ethiopia: Brutal Crackdown on Protests," May 5, 2014, https://www.hrw.org/news/2014/05/05/ethiopia-brutal-crackdown-protests; Maasho, "Ethiopia, Eritrea Reopen Border."

9   World Economic Forum, "Abiy Ahmed: A Conversation with the Prime Minister of Ethiopia," YouTube video embedded in "Ethiopian Prime Minister Abiy Ahmed Wins Nobel Peace Prize," October 11, 2019, https://www.weforum.org/agenda/2019/10/ethiopia-prime-minister-abiy-ahmed-wins-nobel-peace-prize/.

10   First COI Report, 2015; Second COI Report, 2016.

lies the absence of a major state institution that is deemed essential both for matters of peace and security as well as for the requirements of democratic accountability and transparent governance. It is important to highlight that as a mater of factual reality, since February 2002 Eritrea has not had a functioning parliament. To the knowledge of the authors, Eritrea is the only country in Africa that has no functioning parliament, regardless of the democratic-nondemocratic or accountable-non-accountable nature of such a parliament. This observation requires further explanation.

The absence of a functioning parliament in Eritrea, as a matter of one of the three major and conventional state organs, is very problematic. This issue is part of the post-2001 political crisis of Eritrea. Before February 2002, Eritrea had a transitional parliament officially known as the National Assembly. The parliament was convened for the last time in February 2002, after which it was unilaterally dissolved by the state president, whose actions are not subject to any form of checks and balances.[11]

In this context, all major national affairs of the country are literally conducted in a manner that resembles the performance of the private business of the state president, the only person who has the ultimate say on any matter of national interest, including matters of peace and security. This practice is contrary to basic requirements of democratic accountability, a function essentially performed by parliaments as the most important and highest representatives of the will of the people.

It is a matter of general knowledge that parliaments are key state institutions having the ultimate say in matters of major national interest, such as matters of peace and security. Even by the standards of operational Eritrean laws, the general assumption in this regard is not different. As shown recently by a major publication of the ELS on this issue,[12] operational Eritrean laws are very clear about the specific and unique role the Eritrean parliament should have played in the ongoing rapprochement with Ethiopia.

The main reference in this regard is Proclamation No. 37/1993, officially known as Proclamation to Provide for the Establishment, Powers and Functions of the Government of Eritrea. According to the relevant provisions of this law, on matters of peace and war, such as the newly signed rapprochement agreement with Ethiopia, the state president is duty bound to act in a manner that takes into account the requirements of democratic oversight envisaged in several provisions of Proclamation No. 37/1993.

---

11 Weldehaimanot and Mekonnnen, "Nebulous Lawmaking Process," 171–93.

12 ELS, "Stakeholder Report."

The provisions of the law cited above, as discussed adequately by the ELS publication,[13] oblige the state president, among other things, to obtain prior approval from the Eritrean parliament before the conclusion of major agreements with the government of another country. This means that in spite of its declared good intentions, as far as Eritrea's national interest and laws are concerned, certain procedural aspects of the rapprochement are fundamentally antithetical to what has been stipulated by operational Eritrean laws.

In other words, the above observation means that as far as the internal political dynamics of Eritrea is concerned, the manner in which the rapprochement is taking place is bereft of the basic requirements of democratic accountability. In addition to the above concerns emanating from the lack of respect to operational Eritrean laws, this issue is very much related to the broader debate on the role of democratic accountability and transparency in peacemaking and peace-building operations, in particular the need to promote policy considerations that are cognizant of the requirements of the twin terms of security sector reform (SSR) and security sector governance (SSG). While this issue is equally important to both Eritrea and Ethiopia, the lack of clarity on how this is to be handled is by far more noticeable in the former than the latter.

The objective of making states and people safer (sustainable peace) is better served by a political environment that gives the utmost respect to the requirements of SSR and SSG. In the current context, we understand SSR as a:

> process by which countries formulate or reorient the policies, structures, and capacities of institutions and groups engaged in the security sector in order to make them more effective, efficient, and responsive to democratic control, and to the security and justice needs of the people. This policy takes note that security sector reform is sometimes expressed as security sector governance, security sector transformation, security sector development, or security sector review, as well as security and justice reform.[14]

SSR is an integral part of any peace process. As a political process, SSR aims at improving state and human security. It does this "by making security provision, management and oversight more effective and more accountable,

---

13 ELS, "Legal Analysis."

14 African Union Policy Framework on Security Sector Reform (SSR), January 27–28, 2013, p. 5, https://issat.dcaf.ch/download/60132/986021/AU_SSR_policy_framework_en.pdf; see DCAF, Geneva Centre for Security Sector Governance, https://www.dcaf.ch/about-ssgr.

within a framework of democratic civilian control, rule of law and respect for human rights."[15] A key component of SSR is the application of the principles of good governance to the security sector.[16] Eritrea does not have the most important state institution needed for the operationalization of good governance. It is unequivocally clear that the Eritrean government's approach to the rapprochement is not compliant with existing normative frameworks on SSR, particularly those developed by the United Nations and other multilateral actors, including the African Union.

The concept of SSR is supplemented by its twin term of SSG, which refers to "the process by which accountable security institutions supply security as a public good via established transparent policies and practices."[17] One of the leading global think tanks on this topic, the Geneva Centre for Security Sector Governance, notes that accountability for the security sector is performed by democratic oversight mechanisms, involving "the participation of a range of stakeholders including democratic institutions, government, civil society and the media."[18] This is the main objective of SSG. By subordinating security institutions to oversight mechanisms, vetting, and lustration and making their actions complaint with the requirements of accountability and transparency, both SSR and SSG help in reinforcing the rule of law.[19] In terms of these key requirements, there has been no tangible progress in Eritrea one year since the conclusion of the rapprochement agreement in July 2018.

There is also no known plan in Eritrea on how the government will address the challenges of SSR and SSG in the future. Evolving literature on this topic, cited above, suggests that both SSR and SSG presuppose a political system based on respect for the rule of law and the tenets of an accountable and transparent government system. The political situation in Eritrea is far from this. Seen in light of this and other critical shortcomings, the sustainability of the ongoing rapprochement with Ethiopia remains precarious. In the next section, we will discuss another glaring shortcoming, which is the nonexistence of any role that could have been played by non-state actors.

---

15 DCAF 2019.

16 DCAF, 2019.

17 DCAF, 2019.

18 DCAF, 2019.

19 DCAF, 2019.

The Role of Non-State Actors[20]

While the presence of institutions at the formal level alone is not a guarantee for the success of a peace process (unless such institutions are backed by a strong political will for change), the authors argue that it is a very essential starting point in terms of the requirements of institutionalizing peacemaking and peace-building efforts. This observation is equally important to the presence or non-presence of non-state actors as role players in peace processes. The recurring message in this contribution is that the Eritrean experience in this regard remains despondent, even looking at how the three most important and traditional state institutions operate at practical levels: the executive branch, the judicial branch, and the legislative branch. The challenge is not different for non-state actors.

Traditionally, peacemaking and peace building are regarded as intrinsic purviews of state actors. This is due to the fact that political, military, and legal actions that underpin peace processes are primarily undertaken by states—either unilaterally, as part of a coalition, or through regional or intergovernmental organizations.[21] This observation has greater validity in the twenty-year animosity between Eritrea and Ethiopia and the rapprochement of the present time. The conflict and rapprochement have been primarily driven by the governments of both countries.

Following earlier recommendations made by peace and conflict scholars, such as Bah,[22] we argue that non-state actors also have a role to play in peacemaking and peace-building processes. By definition, peacemaking refers to the process of bringing about peace by reconciling conflicting parties.[23] Peace building is a process that comes after peacemaking, or in situations that are susceptible to conflict, with the aim of strengthening a society's capacity to manage conflict in nonviolent ways.[24] In the current experience of Eritrea and Ethiopia, especially on the part of Eritrea, there is little to no room for any role that can be played by non-state actors, in particular CSOs.

---

20 Much of the discussion in this section relies on Sereke, "Civil Society Space."

21 Bah, "Civil Non-State Actors," 314.

22 Bah, 314.

23 Julian Ouellet, "Peacemaking," Beyond Intractability, September 2003, https://www.beyondintractability.org/essay/peacemaking.

24 Interpeace, "What Is Peace Building?" 2010, https://www.interpeace.org/wp-content/uploads/2010/08/2010_IP_What_Is_Peacebuilding_Do_No_Harm_Conflict_Sensitivity_And_Peacebuilding.pdf.

There is also a growing academic and non-academic literature emphasizing the role that can be played by non-state actors, in particular CSOs, in modern peace-building processes. For example, a study conducted by CIVICUS (a global alliance of civil society organizations and activists) recognizes CSOs as key role players in peace processes and post-conflict situations, in which context they are believed to play a role by addressing "social, economic, and political issues, through securing livelihood and providing services, creating social capital," and, most importantly, "counterweighting state and corporate power."[25]

For purposes of clarity, our contribution adopts the following working definition of civil society: "a broad spectrum of organizations that cover the space between the household and the state."[26] The concept may include "charity and advocacy organizations, cultural and religious societies, informal community groups, youth and women organizations, trade unions, business and professional associations, and the media."[27]

In the period preceding the adoption of the Asmara Declaration on 9 July 2018, CSOs in both countries suffered from a tremendous amount of political repression, as reported by various rights groups and UN human rights bodies.[28] In the case of Ethiopia, for example, with the introduction of a repressive anti-civil-society law in 2009 (Proclamation No. 621), there has been a shrinking space for CSOs in the country. Moreover, in the years preceding the 2018 rapprochement, Ethiopia also experienced widespread political unrest that ultimately brought to power the new prime minister (Abiy Ahmed). Admirably, the situation changed dramatically after the coming to power of Abiy, who has thus far led the country on a path of unprecedented political transformation, opening the political space like never before seen.

In contrast, the Eritrean experience is very unpromising. As reported by various scholars (such as Kibreab, 2008), Eritrea actually offers one of the saddest examples on the entire continent of Africa when it comes to the role that can be played by CSOs in the socio-political life of a country. Indeed, as regards the presence and operationalization of CSOs in the country, Eritrea exhibits contradictory and ambivalent views.

In the conventional understanding of the term, the existence of CSOs in Eritrea is exclusively limited to cultural, traditional, or religious associations,

25 Anderson, "Exploring Civil Society," 38; Yeshanew, "CSO Law," 369–70.

26 Bayart, 1986; Yeshanew, "CSO Law."

27 Yeshanew, 369.

28 Human Rights Watch, "Ethiopia"; First COI Report, 2015; Second COI Report, 2016.

such as *ekub* (ዕቁብ) and *mahber* (ማኅበር), whose role is limited to the lowest levels of societal engagement, with no significant role in major issues of national concern, such as matters of peace and conflict.[29] Eritrea still has a very restrictive legislative framework on CSOs, which is made up of: (a) Legal Notice No. 5/1991; (b) Legal Notice No. 17/1994; (c) Proclamation No. 61/1994, and (d) Proclamation No. 145/2005.

According to operational Eritrean laws, CSOs are excluded from key societal services, which are increasingly recognized as shared domains of state and non-state actors. One such domain includes social and political activities aimed at the promotion of human rights, good governance, and democratization at local and national levels. Other domains in which CSOs throughout the world actively participate, but which are prohibited under Eritrean laws include: programs aimed at poverty alleviation, socioeconomic development, environmental and cultural preservation, conflict resolution, peace building, and transitional justice efforts.[30]

In particular, according to Article 2(1) of Proclamation No. 145/2005, the activities in which CSOs can participate are specifically limited to relief and/or rehabilitation work, such as the provision of food, water, sanitary materials, medicines, shelter, and other emergency supplies to the victims of natural or man-made disasters or displaced people. In this context, CSOs are relegated to humanitarian activities that include the restoration and reparation of damage caused by natural or man-made disasters. From this it is not difficult to understand how restrictive Eritrea's legislative framework is. In addition, there are at least two other major factors that make the government's position towards CSOs extremely hostile: 1) lack of a working constitution and 2) lack of a functioning parliament.

The only CSOs that are operational in Eritrea are what are generally known as GONGOs (government operated nongovernmental organizations). In mainstream civil society discourse, GONGOs are nothing more than government entities masquerading as CSOs with the sole purpose of camouflaging anti-civil-society government policy and practice. In corroborating the claim about the absence of a space for genuinely independent CSOs in Eritrea, in particular independent professional associations, the following example personally known to the authors is illustrative.

The matter relates the predicament of the ELS, or the Society, which is the only professional association of Eritrean lawyers and jurists, currently

---

29 Sereke, "Civil Society Space."

30 Sereke, "Civil Society Space."

operating from exile, and in which both authors are members. Since its formal establishment in 2008, the Society has been incorporated as a nonprofit organization in the state of Virginia and later on in the state of California. Due to the extremely repressive political situation in the country, earlier efforts to establish the ELS inside Eritrea (dating back to 1998–99) were helplessly frustrated by the persecution of legal professionals who took the noble initiative of establishing the Society.[31]

The story of the ELS represents one particularly odious chapter in Eritrea's post-independence history, a practice that does not tolerate the existence of independent professional associations, including the role of such non-state actors, in nurturing the long-term objective of peaceful coexistence of Eritrea with its neighbouring countries. More than a year after the adoption of the Asmara Declaration, the Eritrean government is yet to take meaningful measures that shall make it possible for Eritrean non-state actors, in particular professional associations like the ELS, to play their rightful role in shaping policy and practice in matters of peace and war, issues which are of paramount importance both to the professional associations and the Eritrean people at large. As recently noted by a long-time observer[32] of political developments in Eritrea, there is a lot of uncertainty at to whether the new rapprochement with Ethiopia will indeed usher in a much-needed political opening in Eritrea, including circumstances that shall make it easier and possible for non-state actors to play a proactive role.

Looking into the experience in Ethiopia, one can observe that although the internal political dynamics are not yet fully settled in terms of the requirements for the consolidation of a stable democratic order, there is some space within which independent CSOs can play a role. If there were similar opportunities on the Eritrean side, it would have been much easier, for example, to initiate on both sides of the equation programs by joint independent grassroots movements that could play a proactive role in shaping policy and practice in matters that have direct or indirect relevance to the ongoing peace process. A good example would, for instance, be initiating collaborative working relationships between and among like-minded CSOs from both countries. Potential joint projects that can be implemented by a joint collaboration between the ELS and the Ethiopian Lawyers' Association (ELA) can be cited as an example.

As professional associations of the legal profession, these initiatives can play a role in areas such as the training of law enforcement personnel in

---

31 Weldehaimanot, "Undermined Law Society"; ELS, "Stakeholder Report."

32 Müller, "Will Peace . . .?"

the broader sense, capacity building in conflict resolution skills, as well as fundamentals of international human rights law and international relations. While it is true that such programs can be primarily implemented by state actors or existing educational institutions, a supplementary role always can be played by CSOs in a tailored fashion according to the needs and demands of specific circumstances. Experience from many other African countries tells us that capacity building is one major area in which CSOs, and in particular professional associations, can play a very active role. Two recent examples from July 2018 (Uganda) and September 2019 (Kenya) in which the ELS participated in regional semi-consultation and semi-capacity building programs are good examples in this regard.

The 2019 experience was a regional consultation of stakeholders that took place in Kampala, Uganda, under the theme of "Emerging Trends on Complementarity: Consultation with Stakeholders in Central and Eastern Africa," in which stakeholders from the following countries participated: Burundi, Cameroon, Central African Republic, Chad, Congo, Eritrea, Ethiopia, Equatorial Guinea, Gabon, Kenya, Rwanda, South Sudan, Tanzania, and Uganda. The consultation was organized with the aim of marking the twentieth anniversary of the adoption of the Rome Statute of the International Criminal Court (ICC). At the event, the ELS made an active contribution by making a presentation titled "The Principle of Complementarity and the Challenge of Ensuring Accountability for Crimes Against Humanity in Eritrea." The consultation was facilitated by Africa Legal Aid (AFLA).

The 2019 experience, themed "Children's Rights Litigation: Regional Workshop for Civil Society Organisations," was organised by the Gambia-based Institute for Human Rights and Development in Africa (IHRDA). A team of experts from the ELS shared views about the dire state of children's rights in Eritrea and explored potential avenues for advocacy using regional or African human rights instruments. Workshops and consultations such as these are vital not only in helping broaden the political space but also in inculcating a political culture of democratic accountability, one of the most important ingredients in laying down the foundations for a lasting and institutionalized peace process. It is true that the political space in Ethiopia, in terms of hosting and organizing such types of events, is by far broader than that of Eritrea. The problem is always on the Eritrean part, where programs such as the ones discussed above cannot be initiated independently.

Other Issues of Concern

Before concluding this chapter, we would like to engage with some major concerns that are currently expressed by different Eritrean groups, at least those concerns emanating from diaspora-based thought leaders, activists, and professional associations. Due to its long history of forced migration, Eritrea as a country is (virtually) equally lived in its national borders and in its vibrant diaspora communities, so much so the latter can be appositely described as the "alter ego of Eritrea *proper*."[33]

Ever since the signing of the new rapprochement agreement on 9 July 2018, Eritrean diaspora actors have been expressing various concerns, pointing fingers to major shortcomings that need to be addressed in a timely and more responsible fashion. One such example is a major demonstration that took place in Geneva on 31 August 2018 calling on the international community to find solutions for the shortcomings of the new peace process.

At a more substantive level, there are two major publications we can briefly discuss here in that they represent the variety of concerns raised and discussed by Eritrean diaspora actors in various forms and shapes. For ease of reference, we call the first of these publications the 2019 Nairobi Manifesto, for it was authored by a group of sixteen Eritrean thought leaders and activists[34] who conducted a series of meetings in Nairobi in the period between December 2018 and May 2019. The second publication is that of the ELS. Both documents were published on the occasion of Eritrea's Independence Day of 2019.

One common concern addressed by both documents is related to a disturbing trend of historical revisionism demonstrated on the part of some key Ethiopian personalities, including political movements and parties. Over and above some controversial public utterances and gestures made by leaders of the two countries on different occasions,[35] since the advent to power of Prime Minster Abiy, there has been a lingering expansionist sentiment among many Ethiopians. The problem with such sentiments is that they "question the very sovereign independence of Eritrea, either in whole or in part."[36] According to the ELS, "This lingering expansionist sentiment

---

33   On Eritrean diaspora studies, see in general Hepner, Soldiers, Martyrs, Traitors; Bernal, Nation as Network.

34   The full list of Nairobi Manifesto signatories, including their host countries, is: Andom Ghebreghiorgis (US), Asia Abdulkadir (Kenya), Assefaw Tekeste (US), Awet T. Weldemichael (Canada), Bereket Berhane Woldeab (Ethiopia), Habteab Yemane Oghubazgi (Switzerland), Khadeijah Ali Mohammed-Nur (UK), Meron Semedar (US), Paulos Tesfagiorgis (Canada), Sabine Mohamed (Germany), SalehYounis (US), Samuel EmahaTsegai (Canada), Sarah Ogbay (UK), UoldelulChelatiDirar (Italy), Vanessa Tsehaye (UK), and Wejdan Osman (Canada).

35   For a discussion of such an example, see ELS, "Legal Analysis," 5–9.

36   ELS, 9.

includes propagation of an unlawful Ethiopian claim over the Port City of Assab."[37]

Given that Eritrea as a country has a long history of troubled relations with Ethiopia, lingering expansionist sentiments are not at all helpful for the objective of lasting peace between the two countries, which are duty bound to treat each other as sovereign equals. This concern becomes a serious issue when one observes no meaningful action taken about it by the governments of both countries. In the 2019 Nairobi Manifesto, this concern was addressed in conjunction with another critical problem described by the authors of the document as the "Ethiopian government's bipolarism," namely "the act of promoting democratic pluralism in its home country while simultaneously perpetuating a dictatorship in Eritrea."[38] The lamentation goes further:

Some of our preexisting difficulties have worsened after the rapprochement with Ethiopia. When moral clarity and leadership was needed, the Ethiopian government has remained silent around whether it would be possible to encourage similar reforms in its neighbouring country. Regretfully, the Ethiopian government's rhetoric has been disingenuous (praising the Eritrean leadership and evoking imperialist Ethiopian sentiments that should have been laid to rest long ago), and, more worryingly, it has been tolerant or ambivalent about Ethiopian extremists who claim to have natural, legal, and historical claims to our waters.[39]

Similar concerns, related to a lack of transparency and the institutionalization of the entire rapprochement, are discussed in a separate contribution by one of the signatories of the Nairobi Manifesto.[40] In addition to the above, the other major publication we discuss here is by the ELS, which is more of a legal analysis of major issues related to the rapprochement and underscores one fundamental reality. Contrary to the widespread positive impressions felt by regional and international observers about the rapprochement, there is a growing concern and anxiety among Eritreans of all walks of life about it. The concern is prompted by the extremely high level of secrecy the Eritrean government has shown in its approach to the rapprochement. This has triggered major questions among Eritreans, questions including those about potential acts of subterfuge that may jeopardize the sovereign independence and territorial integrity of Eritrea.

---

37 ELS, 9.

38 Eritrea - State of the Nation, para. 31. Eritrea Digest (Nairobi Manifesto), May 22, 2019, https://www.eritreadigest.com/eritrea-state-of-the-nation/.

39 Eritrea - State of the Nation, para. 29.

40 Weldemichael, "Ethio-Eritrea Peace Deal."

The concerns were exacerbated by a series of negative developments that are taking place in Ethiopia, such as a lingering expansionist sentiment expressed by some political actors, as discussed above. In the absence of robust democratic institutions, such as a functioning parliament, Eritreans are left with no other option in addressing such major concerns about the rapprochement.

Another issue, which we believe is crucial for lasting peace between the two countries, is the issue of genuine reconciliation between two major political parties in both countries dominated by what we call the Tigrinya-speaking elites of both countries. These are the People's Front for Democracy and Justice (PFDJ) in Eritrea and the Tigray People's Liberation Front (TPLF) in northern Ethiopia. Relations between these two political organizations are far from normalized. As noted in another contribution by one of the current authors, common sense dictates that there must be peace first between Eritrea and Tigray (northern province of Ethiopia), the region that shares a common border with Eritrea, before talk of peace between Eritrea and Ethiopia as independent countries. This is crucial for a number of historical reasons that go beyond the most immediate objectives of this chapter. Although the same can be said about the relationship between the Afar region of Ethiopia and Eritrea, relatively speaking this remains less complex than that of the relationship between Tigray and Eritrea.[41]

Concluding Remarks

By officially ending their prolonged animosity, Eritrea and Ethiopia are entering a new era of cooperation and peaceful coexistence, by which both governments have already received widespread appreciation. It is aptly correct to give recognition to this development as a groundbreaking and very positive step in the right direction. However, this does not mean that the process is flawless.

The focus of this chapter was on the role that could be played by key state institutions, such as the nonexistent parliament of Eritrea, and non-state actors, in particular professional associations and other variants of CSOs. It is important to underscore that these role players do not operate in a political vacuum. In other words, our understanding of the internal political dynamics of both countries is very important in gauging the sustainability of the new peace process between the two countries, in a way that also measures participation of state and non-state actors in the peace process. In this regard, it is not difficult to observe that the rapprochement suffers from

41 Mekonnen, "Ethiopia's Transitional Justice."

one fundamental problem, which is an apparent lack of parity pertaining to the respective political dynamics in both countries.

Compared to the apparently sufficient level of political commitment seen on the part of Abiy Ahmed's administration, including the officially declared intent to reform the internal political landscape of Ethiopia, the Eritrean government did not display the same level of political commitment when entering into the rapprochement agreement of July 2018. That is why we believe the process started from the very beginning in the context of an asymmetric relationship between the two countries that is not an ideal milieu for a lasting peace. As far as Eritrea's national interest, which is a key factor in assessing the ingredients of a lasting peace, is concerned, we believe there is a lot that needs to be done from both sides, but more so from the Eritrean side.

There seems to be a very noticeable comparative advantage on the part of the Ethiopian government in the sense that when the latter started the new peace process with Eritrea it did so (at least in principle) by taking bold initiatives aimed at addressing critical and structural problems at the local level, so to speak, by broadening the Ethiopian political space. The story on the Eritrean side is completely different, prompting a question to the following effect: for a government that is not at peace with its own people, is it realistically possible to make peace with a neighboring country? This is the overall context within which the role of state and non-state actors in the ongoing peace process needs to be understood.

As it appears, Eritrea is expected to take some tangible and measureable steps in order to ensure the sustainability of the new peace process. Regional and international actors, including the Ethiopian government, IGAD, and the African Union, are expected to play a proactive role in this regard, in particular by encouraging the Eritrean government to take all the necessary supplementary measures deemed essential to the success of the rapprochement. This also requires an understanding, by both parties, of the following fundamental assumption. The challenges of post-conflict reconstruction, the exigencies of healing, and societal reconciliation after violent conflict are so pervasive that no state in the developing world can single-handedly overcome these challenges. On the part of Eritrea, there is an urgent need to widen its internal political landscape in ways and means that make it possible for the proactive engagement of non-state actors. It goes without saying that this would be hardly possible without introducing substantive and structural political reform in Eritrea, just like Ethiopia has done since April 2018. For this to happen, the Eritrean government needs to be encouraged and supported persistently by regional and international actors to widen the political space in the country.

Bibliography

Anderson, T. Exploring Civil Society in Conflict and Post-Conflict Countries: A Continuum to Peace. In *Civil society, Conflict and Violence: Insights from the CIVIUS Civil Society Index Project*, edited by R. A. List and W. Dörner, 35–61. London: Bloomsbury Academic, 2012.

Bah, A. B. "Civil Non-State Actors in Peacekeeping and Peacebuilding in West Africa." *Journal of International Peacekeeping* 17 (2013): 313–36.

Bayart, J. F. Civil society in Africa. In P. Chabal (Ed.), *Political Domination in Africa*, 109–125. Cambridge: Cambridge University Press, 1986.

Bernal, V. *Nation as Network: Diaspora, Cyberspace, and Citizenship*. Chicago: University of Chicago Press, 2014.

Eritrean Law Society (ELS). Legal Analysis of Potential Threats to the Sovereign Independence and Territorial Integrity of the State of Eritrea, 24 May 2019, http://erilaw.org/legal-analysis-of-potential-threats-to-the-sovereign-independence-and-territorial-integrity-of-the-state-of-eritrea/#.

Eritrean Law Society (ELS). Stakeholder Report Submitted to the 32nd Session of the Working Group on the Universal Periodic Review of the UN Human Rights Council, Third UPR Cycle of Eritrea, 2018.

Hepner, T. R. *Soldiers, Martyrs, Traitors, and Exiles: Political Conflict in Eritrea and the Diaspora*. Philadelphia: University of Pennsylvania Press, 2011.

Kibreab, G. *Critical Reflections on the Eritrean War of Independence: Social Capital, Associational Life, Religion, Ethnicity and Sowing Seeds of Dictatorship*. Trenton: Africa World Press, 2008.

Mekonnen, D. "Ethiopia's Transitional Justice Process Needs Restoration Work." *Ethiopia Insight*, 1 February 2019, https://www.ethiopia-insight.com/2019/02/01/ethiopias-transitional-justice-process-needs-restoration-work/.

Mekonnen, D. and P. Tesagiorgis. "The Causes and Consequences of the 1998–2000 Eritrean-Ethiopian Border Conflict: The Need for a Holistic Approach towards Transitional Justice. In *Regional Security in the Post-Cold War Horn of Africa*, 65–94, edited by R. Sharamo and B. Mesfin. Pretoria: Institute for Security Studies, 2011.

Müller, T. "Will Peace with Ethiopia Usher in a Political Opening in Eritrea?" *World Politics Review*, 19 February 2019, https://www.worldpoliticsreview.com/articles/27463/will-peace-with-ethiopia-usher-in-a-political-opening-in-eritrea.

Sereke, W. K. "Civil Society Space in Post-Independence Eritrea." Paper presented at the conference on *Eritrea at Silver Jubilee: Stocktaking on the Nation-Building Experience of a "Newly" Independent African Country*, Geneva, 19–20 May 2016.

Weldehaimanot, S. M. The Undermined Law Society and Legal Profession in Eritrea. *International Journal of Civil Society Law* 10, no. 2 (2012): 47–60.

Weldehaimanot, S. M. and Daniel Mekonnen. "The Nebulous Lawmaking Process in Eritrea. *Journal of African Law* 53, no. 2 (2009): 171–93.

Weldemichael, A. T. "Ethio-Eritrea Peace Deal: Implications for Regional Security." Paper presented at the *Tana High-Level Forum on Security in Africa*, 3–4 May 2019, https://drive.google.com/file/d/1xyFWmoh1_NE2I9BjzFhNC2XS858HlBfq/view.

Yeshanew, S. A. "CSO Law in Ethiopia: Considering Its Constraints and Consequences." *Journal of Civil Society* 8, no. 4 (2012): 369–84.

6

ERITREA-ETHIOPIA RAPPROCHEMENT AND ITS IMPACT ON FOREIGN POLICY

Patrick Gilkes

Ethiopia and Eritrea Agreement and Joint Declaration

The original five pillars of the July 9 Joint Declaration on Peace and Friendship, as might be expected, concentrated on Ethiopia-Eritrea relations, stressing that a state of war had come to an end and referring, broadly, to forging cooperation across numerous fields. The one mention of wider external policies came in the fifth pillar: "Both countries will jointly endeavour to ensure regional peace, development, and cooperation."[1]

No further details were provided, but Ethiopia's then foreign minister, Dr. Workneh Gebeyehu, said a day or two later that two commissions, headed by the respective foreign ministers, had already been established and subcommittees would be created to work out the details and implementation of economic, political, social, and other agreements, including the use of Assab, the sharing or leasing of ports, land and air transport tariffs, visas, the release of prisoners captured during the 1998–2000 war; and the

---

1   The five pillars of the Joint Declaration: 1) The state of war between Ethiopia and Eritrea has come to an end. A new era of peace and friendship has been opened. 2) The two governments will endeavor to forge intimate political, economic, social, cultural, and security cooperation that serves and advances the vital interests of their peoples. 3) Transport, trade, and communications links between the two countries will resume; diplomatic ties and activities will restart. 4) The decision on the boundary between the two countries will be implemented. 5) Both countries will jointly endeavor to ensure regional peace, development, and cooperation.

technicalities of the border.[2] Although the commissions and committees did meet a number of times in 2018 and produced a raft of suggestions, they failed to reach agreement on any policy initiatives or, more accurately, President Isaias failed to accept the suggestions made. In January 2019, Eritrea's minister for information, Yemane Gebremeskel, who said the Eritrea-Ethiopia Interim High-Level Committee had been undertaking consultations to regulate trade and transport relations, implied the results would shortly be made public.[3]

Three months later, President Isaias's presidential advisor, Yemane Gebreab, said Ethiopia and Eritrea were working more closely, but no specific agreements on port utilization, transport, or trade had been signed. The handover of Badme, he pointed out, had not been implemented, even though both leaders had agreed it should happen soon, and the delays, he said, were caused by Ethiopia's internal problems, including ethnic tension, the need to ensure the rule of law, economic problems, and the country's uncertain future, all of which he blamed on the TPLF.[4] By September 2019, no further progress had been made. All that had happened directly in the fifteen months after July 2018 had been some temporary border openings, the restoration of flights between Addis Ababa and Asmara, and the reopening of phone lines.

International response to the joint declaration was uniformly positive. "A tremendously positive impact on peace and security, as well as development and integration, in the Horn of Africa and the continent as a whole" (AU Commission Chairperson Moussa Faki Mahamat); "As you pursue your policy of peace in the region and rapprochement towards Eritrea, we also look forward to Eritrea rejoining the IGAD family and collectively advancing peace and development in our region" (IGAD's executive secretary Ambassador Mahboub Maalim); The recent evolution of relations between

---

2   The original post-independence Agreement of Friendship and Cooperation of Ethiopia and Eritrea of July 1993 and subsequent agreements and protocols allowed for a Joint High Ministerial Commission, as well as clusters of subcommittees and experts' committees. They, however, failed to make any progress in institutionalizing the agreement, which collapsed in May 1998.

3   3. A fourth round of the interim ministerial commission took place in Addis Ababa in February 2019, with Dr. Workneh and Osman Saleh adding comment to reports covering port utilization, transport, trade, and customs. They also discussed the formal establishment of the proposed Joint High Ministerial Commission. As of October 2019, nothing had yet been formally agreed or implemented.

4   Yemane Gebreab, Eritrean presidential advisor, talking to members of the Eritrean diaspora in Riyadh, 22 April 2019.

Ethiopia and Eritrea was "a very important signal of hope, not only for these two countries, and Africa, but for the whole world" (UN Secretary-General António Guterres); "It paves the way for enhanced regional cooperation and stability in the Horn of Africa" (former high representative of the Union for Foreign Affairs and vice-president of the European Commission, Federica Mogherini); "Peace between Ethiopia and Eritrea will further the cause of stability, security and development in the Horn of Africa and Red Sea" (US Secretary of State Mike Pompeo); and a "momentous step towards building a lasting peace [that will] . . . greatly strengthen the political and economic ties that will benefit not just the populations of both countries but also enhance security and prosperity across the Horn of Africa" (the UK). Egypt hoped the deal would be a model for all countries suffering from disputes in Africa; Turkey's view was that "it will enable a conducive environment for peace, stability and comprehensive cooperation in the Horn of Africa region."

The Joint Declaration on Peace and Friendship in July was followed by the Agreement on Peace, Friendship and Comprehensive Cooperation between the Federal Democratic Republic of Ethiopia and the State of Eritrea, signed in Jeddah on September 16 under the watchful eye of King Salman of Saudi Arabia, Crown Prince Mohammed bin Salman, and the UAE Minister of Foreign Affairs and International Cooperation Sheikh Abdullah bin Zayed Al Nahyan, as well as Guterres, who described this as a historic event: "We have seen a conflict that has lasted for decades ending, and that has a very important meaning in a world where we see, unfortunately, so many conflicts multiplying, and lasting forever."

It was hardly a coincidence that on the occasion of the signing, Prime Minister Abiy and President Isaias were honoured with the kingdom's highest award, "The Order of King Abdulaziz," for their historic achievement in bringing about peace between their two countries. The Kingdom of Saudi Arabia in an official statement warmly welcomed the new agreement and praised the leaders of the two countries "for exercising outstanding statesmanship and courage to restore the brotherly relations between their countries and laying the foundation for a new phase that will bring significant developments in the relations between the two nations in all fields." A week later, Abiy and Isaias were also given the Order of Zayed (First Class) in Abu Dhabi, "in recognition of their efforts to end the conflict between their countries and open new horizons for cooperation and coordination, and in appreciation for their role in strengthening cooperation with the UAE."

Positive Saudi and UAE support for an Ethiopian rapprochement with Eritrea had been made very clear earlier in the year. Abiy held talks in Riyadh in May with the king and crown prince, and then with Sheikh Mohamed bin Zayed Al Nahyan, crown prince of Abu Dhabi and deputy supreme commander of the UAE Armed Forces. A month earlier, Zayed had arrived in Addis Ababa heading an impressive delegation that included the deputy prime minister and ministers or state ministers of foreign affairs, the economy, international cooperation, culture, and energy, and the director general of the Abu Dhabi Fund for Development. The delegation agreed on an economic cooperation package that included an allocation by the Abu Dhabi Fund of $3 billion for sustainable socioeconomic development. The fund deposited $1 billion in the National Bank of Ethiopia to improve Ethiopia's liquidity and foreign exchange reserves; the remaining $2 billion was to stimulate the Ethiopian economy and encourage joint productive investment.

Abiy had expressed unconditional acceptance of the 2000 Algiers Agreement to bring the conflict with Eritrea to an end in his acceptance speech in April, and the EPRDF Executive Committee had endorsed this in June when he insisted it was in the interest of both countries to end the standoff and focus on development. This, he added, demonstrated the strides Ethiopia was making on the diplomatic front. In parliament, a couple of weeks later, he elaborated that diplomacy was one of the key priorities of the government. It was strengthening longstanding and historic bilateral and multilateral relationships as well as filling any gaps in its diplomatic activities. His recent visits to Djibouti, Sudan, Kenya, Uganda, Egypt, Saudi Arabia, UAE, and Somalia had been "an overwhelming success."

Following his visit to Somalia on June 16, Abiy spoke of his vision for the region. It included "a common trade area where people, ideas, goods and products move freely across borders, a future where we work to enlarge opportunities for our people and work for economic security that gives our children and grandchildren great hope; a future where we abolish trade barriers; a future where we will create a single market in our region; a future where we stimulate more products, more production, innovation and more private enterprise. . . . The resources of our region and the talent and capacity of our people can provide abundance for all, as long as we are prepared to recognize what we have and renounce fully violence and lawlessness. . . . This vision of the region offers a diversity of states, each developing all its culture, each solving its challenges according to its own way, but all tied together with a shared purpose and a respect for one another. . . . We need to adopt and implement a border and joint strategy to promote regional stability in the Horn of Africa . . . [in which] we will give equal attention to address the underlying diverse problems of violence, extremism in the region, regional conflict, lack of trade and investment and poverty."

The Jeddah Agreement made a little more of external affairs. The parties promised to contribute actively to regional and global peace and security and reiterated their commitment to the principles and purposes of the UN Charter. In Articles 5 and 6 they committed themselves to "promote regional and global peace, security and cooperation" and "combat terrorism as well as trafficking in people, arms and drugs in accordance with international covenants and conventions." They agreed to promote comprehensive cooperation in the political, security, defense, economic, trade, investment, cultural, and social fields on the basis of complementarity and synergy.

In fact, during the original discussions in Asmara, a number of other issues had been agreed to, at least in outline. The principals had decided Eritrea ought to rejoin IGAD; that Ethiopia would call for the lifting of international sanctions on Eritrea (and indeed a week later, Abiy sent a letter to the UN Secretary-General requesting the lifting of sanctions against Eritrea); and that Ethiopia would make efforts to resolve the dispute between Eritrea and Djibouti.

A series of other moves followed quickly on the Jeddah Agreement, including the signing of a Joint Declaration on Comprehensive Cooperation between Ethiopia, Somalia and Eritrea in Asmara on 5 September 2018, as well as the visit undertaken by the ministers of foreign affairs and other senior officials of these three countries to Djibouti on 6 September 2018 as part of the efforts to normalize relations and promote good neighborliness, enhance peace, security, stability and advance regional integration. The AU Peace and Security Council subsequently linked the rapprochement, the signing of the Final Revitalized Agreement on the Resolution of the Conflict in South Sudan on September 12, and progress in Somalia, all together as an example of the efficacy of "African solutions to African problems." It commended IGAD, of which Ethiopia was the chair, for its efforts to promote peace, security, and stability across the entire Horn of Africa.

One of Eritrea's main interests in accepting the rapprochement with Ethiopia was the lifting of the UN Security Council sanctions on Eritrea, and by the end of July, support for this was gathering momentum. Although the chair of the UN Eritrea-Somalia Sanctions Committee regretted Eritrea had not invited the committee to visit Eritrea, given its views on the regional situation, he told the Security Council he welcomed the Joint Declaration of Peace and Friendship signed by Isaias and Abiy on July 9 as well as the visit by Somalia's President Mohamed Abdullahi "Farmaajo" to Asmara later in the month.[5] At the UN General Assembly in September, Eritrea was able to

---

5   Ambassador Kairat Umarov, chair of the UN Eritrea-Somalia Monitoring Group Sanctions Committee, quarterly briefing to the UN Security Council, 30 July 2018.

use this to emphasize the new framework of all-around cooperation that had been set in motion and was providing a positive dividend for regional peace and security. Eritrea's representative, Nebil Said Idris, said firmly that recent historic developments made it clear the most appropriate action for the Security Council to take would be to lift sanctions, unequivocally indicating its support for these positive developments: "The Security Council should not miss another opportunity to contribute positively to regional peace and security in the Horn of Africa and the Red Sea."

Ethiopia agreed it was only appropriate and timely that the Security Council now seriously consider this.[6] Ethiopia's Ambassador Tekeda Alemu spoke of the silencing of guns in Africa fostering peace, with "this wind of change" welcomed by the region and beyond: "It is downright impossible to deny that the politics of the Horn of Africa are in the process of rapid change and with salutary implications. What was once considered impossible has been made possible thanks to the courageous and bold steps taken by the leadership of the two countries." Equally, Ethiopia was well aware this required some resolution of the dispute between Eritrea and Djibouti.

Djibouti

Djibouti was not so sure. Ambassador Mohamed Siad Doualeh, Djibouti's representative, raised concerns over Djibouti's still ongoing border dispute with Eritrea. His suggestions included asking the Security Council to urge Eritrea to engage in mediation efforts, and sending a monitoring mission to Eritrea. Eritrea, he said, must fully cooperate with the mission and provide full access to all information and records the mission wanted to review and all personnel it wanted to interview. The council should require Eritrea to account for the missing Djibouti prisoners of war and the secretary-general, in close collaboration with the Security Council, should convene an urgent meeting of the parties to facilitate a mutually acceptable means of settlement to reach a solution within four months. If this was not accepted then the issue should be referred to the International Court of Justice. Djibouti said it would support action by the Security Council to facilitate Eritrea's compliance by laying out a clear path and a reasonable timetable.

Djibouti's concerns were, and still are, threefold: the Eritrean seizure and occupation of Ras Doumeira and the Doumeira Islands in 2008; the refusal of Eritrea to provide any information about thirteen missing Djibouti

---

6   Foreign Minister Workneh Gebeyehu speaking at the UN General Assembly, September 2018.

soldiers, captured in 2008, not even whether they were alive or dead; and whether Eritrea had withdrawn support for FRUD elements for which it had been providing training and support at the Anda'ali training camp in southern Eritrea.

In September 2019, in an attempted gesture of reconciliation, Djibouti released nineteen Eritrean prisoners it had held since 2008. They have now been resettled in Canada, as Eritrea persistently refused to acknowledge that Djibouti had ever held any prisoners. Eritrea, after repeatedly denying it held any Djibouti prisoners, released four in 2016, following Qatar mediation, but has never provided any details of another thirteen Djibouti troops still missing and believed to have been captured. Qatar launched its mediation at the request of both sides in 2010 and deployed 450 peacekeeping troops in the disputed area. Its mediation made little progress and ended in 2017, a week after the decision by Saudi Arabia, the UAE, Bahrain, and Egypt to sever ties with Qatar in June 2017. Qatar withdrew the troops from the disputed frontier. It gave no reason for its decision, but it followed the action of Eritrea and Djibouti in downgrading relations with Qatar, leaving the Qatari force on the Eritrea-Djibouti border dangerously isolated, especially with Eritrea involved in Operation Decisive Storm in Yemen. There were reports that Eritrean troops immediately moved in after the Qatari withdrawal and have remained in occupation of the disputed area.

Abiy was well aware of the Eritrea-Djibouti problem; he had been in Djibouti only a few days before the agreement reached in Asmara, at the official opening of the Djibouti International Free Trade Zone on July 5. Djibouti had firmly underlined its concerns at the Security Council later in the month when its representative asked the council to urge Eritrea to engage in mediation efforts. When Eritrea's representative called for sanctions to be lifted, he made no mention of Eritrea's relations with Djibouti, although this was a major reason for the imposition of the sanctions.

While the UN and others were keen to lift the sanctions in the wake of the Ethiopia-Eritrea agreement, they did need Djibouti to accept this, and Djibouti came under considerable pressure. President Guelleh had visits from Ethiopia's foreign minister, Dr. Workneh, and from President "Farmaajo," who had made the first-ever visit of a Somali president to Asmara shortly before. While in Eritrea, he had, as requested by Isaias, called for the lifting of sanctions. Djibouti had not been pleased. Its ambassador to Somalia expressed Djibouti's "deep shock" and made reference both to Eritrea's occupation of Djiboutian territory and its denial of prisoners. Djibouti's view was that as Eritrea moved to take up a place in the region again, it should actually address resolution of its disputes with Sudan and Djibouti.

Nor was Djibouti impressed by Eritrean media comments to the effect that Djibouti would be losing most of its Ethiopian trade following the Ethiopia-Eritrea peace. It regarded that kind of gloating comment, produced by the somewhat maverick commentator Thomas Mountain, as reflecting Eritrean government thinking.[7]

The Foreign Ministers of Somalia, Ethiopia, and Eritrea visited Djibouti following the Asmara tripartite summit of Eritrea, Ethiopia, and Somalia on September 15 and the signing of their Joint Declaration on Comprehensive Cooperation. The visit was intended to initiate a dialogue between Eritrea and Djibouti, and Eritrean Foreign Minister Osman Saleh carried New Year's greetings from Isaias: "This is the season for peace in the Horn of Africa and this peace should be inclusive to all." Formally, at least, Djibouti then agreed to normalize relations with Eritrea, with Dr. Workneh describing the visit as "a historic diplomatic achievement." President Guelleh said Djibouti was ready for reconciliation and normalization of its ties with Eritrea, though he did also underline that normalization had to include a resolution of Djibouti's concerns.

Despite the lack of any sign of progress in that direction, Guelleh did then accept an invitation from King Salman and Crown Prince Mohammed to meet with Isaias in Jeddah a few days later, on September 17. The two presidents, who thanked the king for his effort at mediation, did agree to establish a new chapter of cooperation and good neighbourliness, though their body language showed little warmth. Although they shook hands, the meeting only "lasted two or three minutes, the time to exchange polite phrases"; then Isaias turned to the Saudis, thanked them for their work, and said: "Now my brother and I will continue this dialogue without intermediaries."[8] Since then, the respective foreign ministers and others have kept in touch, but movement on the major points at issue for Djibouti have been nonexistent. The two presidents have not met again.

The Jeddah meeting was, however, sufficient for the Security Council. It issued a statement a few days later welcoming Eritrea's normalization of relations with Djibouti, expressing the hope that the meeting would open a new chapter in relations between Djibouti and Eritrea, and encouraging them to continue to engage in meaningful dialogue. Despite any subsequent lack of progress, the council finally voted unanimously in mid-November to lift the sanctions imposed on Eritrea a decade earlier, passing resolution 2444 (2018) and terminating measures imposed on Eritrea by resolutions 1907 (2009),

---

7   Thomas Mountain, "Djibouti Faces Dark Days to Come," Counterpunch, 21 August 2018.

8   "Interview with President Ismail Omar Guelleh," JeuneAfrique, 4 July 2019.

2023 (2011), 2060 (2012), and 2111 (2013), including the arms embargo, travel ban, assets freeze, and individual targeted sanctions. During the debate, the United Kingdom, which drafted the resolution, underlined the importance of continuing efforts towards the normalization of relations between Eritrea and Djibouti, which were, in effect, ignored in the resolution. Ethiopia welcomed the resolution "unreservedly," noting, "The breakthrough arising from the rapprochement between Ethiopia and Eritrea is already producing unprecedented and far-reaching positive consequences and is significantly changing the political landscape of the Horn of Africa and beyond." Djibouti remained sceptical that this would make any difference to Eritrea's policies. Mahamoud Ali Youssouf, Djibouti's foreign minister, said he was optimistic that progress would be made over Djibouti's concerns, even indicating he was hopeful that Isaias would pay a visit to Djibouti "soon." He didn't, and there has been no progress in normalizing Eritrea-Djibouti relations, despite efforts by both Ethiopia and Somalia to continue to work for an effective détente. According to Guelleh, Abiy later warned him that care was needed to avoid irritating Isaias and that patience was required. Nevertheless, Abiy said he believed the situation would eventually move forward.[9] A rather less optimistic comment came from Isaias adviser Yemane Gebreab, usually regarded as providing an accurate interpretation of Isaias's thoughts: Djibouti was "not on board yet, not come out of the past."[10]

Whatever concerns might remain over Eritrea's reluctance to improve relations with Djibouti, Ethiopia is well aware of the importance of Djibouti, not least because of Abiy's underlying commitment to effective regional integration, an interest shared with Guelleh. Africa's moves towards socioeconomic and political transformation through the continental strategic framework, Agenda 2063, emphasize interconnectivity. Ethiopia and Djibouti have long understood the need for this and continue to commit themselves towards achieving full economic integration. Abiy's first trip outside Ethiopia, in April 2018, was to Djibouti. Nearly 90 percent of Ethiopia's imports pass through the port of Djibouti, and this commercial capacity has been underlined by the major infrastructure development of the 756-km-long Ethio-Djibouti electric railway, operational in 2018. It significantly augmented the importance of Djibouti's port service. Even if Ethiopia does begin to use other ports on a considerable scale, Djibouti will certainly remain the major outlet for years to come. The 238-km

---

9   "Interview with President Ismail Omar Guelleh."

10   Yemane Gebreab, Eritrean presidential advisor, talking to members of the Eritrean diaspora in Riyadh, 22 April 2019.

power transmission line to Djibouti provides for electric-based projects like the Ethio-Djibouti railway and enables Djibouti to import up to 60 mw of electricity, easing Djibouti's reliance on fossil-fuel power plants and generators and considerably reducing its energy bill. Both countries are committed to security, peace, and stability under the umbrella of regional mechanisms like IGAD. They work closely on fighting terrorism as well as addressing pressing issues such as climate change, migration, and illicit arms trafficking.

Djibouti remains confident that Ethiopia will continue to use its ports. It has numerous long-term agreements and contracts with Ethiopia. It does not believe that it can be replaced by either Massawa or Assab, and certainly not now that the Djibouti-Addis Ababa railway has been opened. In a visit at the end of May 2019, Ethiopia's minister of foreign affairs, Gedu Andargachew, emphasized to Guelleh that the strategic partnership and symbolic ties between Ethiopia and Djibouti were too well entrenched to falter in the face of challenges. He called for mapping out new areas of cooperation to provide additional impetus to strengthen relations. Guelleh reiterated his government's unwavering commitment towards ensuring that symbolic Ethio-Djibouti ties would make giant leaps forward in the years to come. Guelleh believes even if Eritrean ports open up on a large scale for Ethiopian use, Massawa will remain essentially a port for Tigray Regional State rather than Ethiopia at large, and Assab's future, lacking a railway, is questionable. Equally, though, Djibouti takes a close interest in DP World's activities in the region since it dismissed it from management of its Doraleh port. In 2018, DP World was describing Eritrea as an "attractive investment destination for logistics companies and a gateway to other nations in the region." CEO Bin Sulayem said Eritrea was going to have a major role in adding South Sudan, Sudan, and Ethiopia to the equation of DP World activity in the Red Sea. DP World has also expressed interest in developing Mombasa and creating a logistics center in Ethiopia, though for trading purposes only. Bin Sulayem claims "the UAE has no political agenda in Africa, only trade.

Djibouti will also remain a key refueling and transshipment center, as well as the principal maritime outlet for Ethiopia. Djibouti ports now have the capacity to handle 50 million tonnes a year—Ethiopia's current traffic is 18.5 million tonnes. Djibouti has modernized the old port and constructed new ports at Tadjourah, Goubet, Damerjock, and Doraleh, with both multipurpose and container ports, Lake Assai, and an oil terminal, Horizon Port. Doraleh multipurpose port is able to operate 8 million tonnes annually, and the bulk terminal can take 2 million tonnes a year. It is already supplying Mozambique and a number of East African ports. The future of Tadjourah, however, remains in doubt, as it was built to take Ethiopian potash, and that may now go out through a proposed new port in Eritrea.

In July 2019, Djibouti also launched its China-built Djibouti International Free Trade Zone, a $370 million project intended to handle $7 billion a year. Significantly, President Kagame of Rwanda was present at the opening, as was Abiy and the presidents of both Sudan and Somalia and the AU Commission chair, as well as IGAD representatives. IGAD said the zone was "a clear demonstration of regional economic integration that the member states have been working towards"; an important milestone in regional integration contributing to the realization of ongoing discussions on the IGAD free movement protocol and the African Continental Free Trade Area. Djibouti is now also specializing in hosting computer and telematics data centers with Chinese and Pakistani, French and American companies all involved. Djibouti in fact is now becoming the center of revived regional infrastructural networks such as the proposed Djibouti-Addis Ababa-Juba-Kampala Corridor).[11]

All of this feeds into China's Belt and Road Initiative (BRI). In January 2017, Silkroad Bank opened a branch in Djibouti; the Chinese EXIM Bank is also present. China's BRI sees Djibouti as a major center for pushing into northeast and central Africa, the access point for up to thirteen landlocked countries. This is a vision that Ethiopia can, and does share, as it works to create the infrastructure to link itself with Sudan, South Sudan, Kenya, Uganda, Eritrea, and Somalia. Djibouti's economic growth reached 6.8 percent in 2017 and the AfDB estimates similar figures for 2018 and 2019 and for the near future. There have been concerns over Djibouti's levels of indebtedness to China, but this has largely come from the United States and can be seen as part of US attempts to minimize Chinese influence. In fact, although Djibouti dismisses concerns, its debt to China is over 60 percent of the total national debt, but the chairman of the Djibouti Ports and Free Zones Authority is clear that Djibouti is confident about the sustainability of the loans and says the investment strategy is already paying off.[12] Foreign Minister Youssef is equally dismissive: "Other countries turned their back on us; China agreed to help us; we did not reach out to the devil, we seized an opportunity." Djibouti is clear that China's main attraction for Djibouti is that it was prepared to respond to requests for assistance over infrastructure.

---

11   An IGAD meeting in May considered a feasibility study strongly recommending the project and signed an MOU to consider ways to implement, and its place in, the BRI.

12   Eromo Egbejule, "Djibouti: Small Country, Big Stakes," Africa Report, 21 August 2018.

This, in effect, holds true for Ethiopia as well. Neither country accepts the US concerns over excessive indebtedness; both, for example, have been able to adjust the credit terms on the railway funding.

Djibouti does have other concerns related to the Eritrea-Ethiopia rapprochement, one being the future of US naval base Camp Lemonnier. The United States currently pays some $79 million a year for Camp Lemonnier, the country's only permanent base in Africa, and which now holds facilities for up to four thousand personnel. The current agreement with Djibouti has another six years to run. The US Department of Defense, and John Bolton when US National Security Adviser, has, however, expressed concern over the proximity of the Chinese military base in Djibouti, which they regarded as a potential future threat. The Department of Defense indeed made clear its interest in Massawa as an alternative to Djibouti back in the early 2000s, when President Isaias offered its use for US activity in Iraq or Afghanistan. The State Department, however, was strongly opposed. It was concerned to keep its links with Ethiopia, as well as worried by Eritrea's human rights record, including the arrest of local US embassy staff. Now with the United States rehabilitating its relationship and Eritrea "coming in from the cold," there is likely to be less opposition to any such offer, though there has been no improvement in Eritrea's human rights record. In December 2018, on a visit to Asmara, Ambassador Tibor Nagy, US assistant secretary of state for African Affairs, made it clear that while human rights was "very much" a part of US consideration in its bilateral relationship with Eritrea, he emphasized that he hoped to get to a point where relations with Eritrea were as warm and cordial as with Ethiopia. Isaias has made it clear he would be happy to have "constructive engagement" with the United States, as indeed, despite his often-aggressive rhetoric, he has always been prepared for just that. It is clear that this could include providing the United States with military facilities.

Somalia

A whole series of other diplomatic initiatives have followed the Ethiopian-Eritrean rapprochement in addition to the lifting of sanctions on Eritrea. Awareness of the potentially positive impact of peace between Ethiopia and Eritrea on the politics of the Horn of Africa spread quickly around the region. The agreement, in effect, removed a logjam on the river of diplomacy and development, underlining the value of investing in peace-building processes on a regional level. It lifted more than a decade of mistrust between regional states, opening up new ways to consider common concerns, looking at problems from a different and more optimistic direction.

One diplomatic milestone that quickly followed was Isaias's invitation to Farmaajo to visit Asmara. The readiness of Eritrea and Somalia to write a new chapter of their relationship in regional cooperation was welcomed as another sign of progress. The last effective contacts were when Isaias pulled out of IGAD in 2007 after IGAD rejected his suggestions for Somalia. He carried his annoyance over Ethiopia's military intervention to the point of providing support to Hizbul Islam, an ally of Al-Shabaab, an extremist opposition group in Somalia. Farmaajo and Isaias signed a Joint Declaration on Brotherly Relations and Comprehensive Cooperation. This noted the deep bonds of friendship between the peoples of Eritrea and Somalia and agreed on four main points: internal problems and external intervention had hindered Somalia from reaching its potential; Eritrea strongly supported Somalia's political independence, sovereignty, and territorial integrity and the efforts of the people and government of Somalia to restore the country's rightful stature and achieve the lofty aspirations of its people; Somalia and Eritrea would forge close political, economic, social, and cultural links and cooperate in defense and security; they would establish diplomatic relations and exchange ambassadors, promote bilateral trade and investment as well as participate in educational and cultural exchanges. They also agreed to work together to foster regional peace, stability, and economic integration. Farmaajo called for the lifting of sanctions on Eritrea, but if he expected Eritrea to push for an end to sanctions on Somalia, he was disappointed.

Welcoming Farmaajo "to your home," President Isaias said the region had been affected by "ethnic and clan cleavages," and the "scourges of poverty and hunger spurred by external pillage and internal thievery." This epoch was, however, now coming to an end, and the people of Eritrea, triumphing over ethnic polarization and foreign subservience, were marching forward "to crystallize a correct national and regional policy framework." The people of Somalia, he said, would as always travel with the people of Ethiopia and Eritrea. President Isaias wished President Abdullahi the "best of success in your serious endeavours to overcome all obstacles and promote all-rounded bilateral and regional partnership in the economic and security fields."

Prime Minister Abiy had made his own effort to improve Ethiopia's relations with the government in Mogadishu in June when he made an unexpected one-day visit. He unveiled a vision of a single market to tie the two countries together and spoke of intensified relations, to include the opening of reciprocal diplomatic and consular offices in major cities, the free movement of goods and services, enhancement of economic integration, the removal of all trade and economic barriers, and the development of infrastructure, including both ports and highways. At a joint press conference with Farmaajo, Abiy said they had agreed on joint investment in four key ports that could serve both the Indian Ocean and the Red Sea, though he did not name them.[13] They agreed on the construction of major road networks to link Somalia to Ethiopia, and to set up a joint technical team to consider timelines, as well as encouraging private sector investment to create jobs as part of a process to facilitate full economic integration. The importance of cooperation to counter terrorism and deal with cross-border security was also included.

The extent of the proposed cooperation alarmed Farmaajo's critics and concerned the federal member states of Somalia, already seriously worried by the way the president was responding to the elections due in four of the states in 2019. Investment in four ports and the construction of road networks were interpreted as massive concessions to Ethiopia without any apparent reciprocity. Questions were also raised over the communiqué's offering of "mutual respect for the sovereignty, territorial integrity, political independence and the unity of both nations and call upon all Somali actors to relentlessly work towards the unity and cohesiveness of Somalia." There were claims that this was near to an official statement by Somalia renouncing any territorial claims to Ethiopia's Somali Regional State.[14] As might be expected, the visit was also viewed with some concern by Somaliland.

Following this visit, already suggestive of a shift in Ethiopia's policy towards Somalia, the tripartite agreement between Eritrea, Ethiopia, and Somalia, signed in Asmara in early September 2018, made clear just how considerable this was intended to be. Abiy and Farmaajo returned from the Forum on China-Africa Cooperation (FOCAC) in Beijing via Asmara at Isaias's suggestion. The same evening, they issued a Joint Declaration on Comprehensive Cooperation between Ethiopia, Somalia and Eritrea. Like all these recent agreements, it was short on detail on what had been agreed to and even briefer on details of how to implement this "cooperation," but it underlined the aim of the three countries to facilitate economic integration. A statement from Villa Somalia later added further elements, claiming Farmaajo's vision was for the promotion of a flow of free trade and mutual economic cooperation among all the countries of the Horn. Somalia, it said, sought to play a key role in the economic and social integration of the region to foster trade and investment and improve connectivity between

---

13   The most likely ports would be Berbera (Somaliland), Bossaso (Puntland), Kismayo (Jubaland), and Mogadishu, and of these only Mogadishu is under control of the federal government. Other options would include Merka and Brava.

14   "He Came, Conquered and Humiliated Farmajo": Inside PM Abiy's Visit to Mogadishu," *Somaliland Chronicle*, 18 June 2018.

people and businesses. It would like to take the lead in facilitating a robust Horn of Africa trade bloc that would foster stronger economic stability and development for the region. In October 2018, Ethiopia's and Eritrea's foreign ministers made a joint visit to Mogadishu as part of an effort to develop the tripartite axis; both ministers also met with Italy's foreign minister, Enzo Moaveru Milanesi, during the Italian-Africa Forum in Rome later that month to discuss possible support for the tripartite link.

The second trilateral meeting of Eritrea, Ethiopia, and Somalia, taking place in Bahr Dar in Ethiopia in November, also focused on regional economic integration as well as strengthening peace and security and developing a common and aligned voice on international agendas. The meeting, reinforcing this burgeoning Eritrea, Ethiopia, Somalia axis, welcomed the impending lifting of all sanctions against Eritrea—"an act of justice that will contribute to enhancing peace, development, and cooperation in the region"—which took place a few days later. It stressed the importance of "respecting the sovereignty, territorial integrity and political independence of Somalia," and the three leaders agreed to support each other to deal with challenges they faced individually and collectively. Abiy, however, went very much further, speaking of the possibility of one president for "the new Horn" instead of three. He did not, however, suggest when this might happen, merely referring to it happening "in the future." Nor did either of his fellow leaders endorse the idea.

Ethiopian Diplomacy

Abiy has been extraordinarily active in personal diplomatic efforts, holding a series of summits with neighboring leaders, at both the bilateral and trilateral level, in his efforts to encourage and generate peace processes, generate regional peace and security, and support an agenda for integration. He puts great store in his own personal capacity to get agreement, and the award of the Nobel Peace Prize in October 2019 will certainly encourage this approach.[15] Abiy's first visit to Asmara pointed out the positive advantages of such an approach. However, the lack of progress in normalizing Eritrea-Djibouti relations has also underlined that personal charisma may not be sufficient in itself. The problems of resolving deep-seated regional disputes, the difficulties that still attend regional economic integration, let alone the prospects of political integration, and long-standing distrust, remain formidable.

---

15 The Nobel Peace Prize announcement refers to Abiy's "efforts to achieve peace and international cooperation" and his engagement in peace and reconciliation processes between Eritrea and Djibouti, Kenya and Somalia, and in Sudan.

One experienced observer of the region, for example, described Abiy's visit to Khartoum in June 2019 as "a trademark Abiy initiative, undertaken with minimum preparation or consultation, and advocating brotherly love as a solution to a political problem."[16] This was, perhaps, hardly fair, as the subsequent appointment of a special envoy to mediate and the success of the Ethiopian and AU mediation, provided the solution to the Sudan crisis, but it underlined that Abiy certainly places much more reliance on personal contact and rather less on preparation and consideration of possible repercussions.

The approach is not always successful, and even where one-to-one meetings have gone well, at least on the surface, they can generate apparently unexpected problems. The tripartite cooperation agreement between Ethiopia, Eritrea, and Somalia, for example, led to immediate concern in Somaliland, which interpreted Ethiopia's undertaking to respect the territorial integrity of Somalia as indicating a change in Ethiopia's policies detrimental to Somaliland. Since 1991, Ethiopia has, in effect, supported Somaliland, if without formally recognizing its declaration of independence from Mogadishu. It was part of a policy designed to ensure that Somalia would not be in a position to resurrect the aggressive nationalism that led to the Somali invasion of Ethiopia in 1978. After Somalia's acceptance of a federal constitution in 2012, Ethiopia was quick to establish relationships with federal member states, offering a way to balance the influence of the federal government. Equally, Ethiopia believed federalism genuinely offered a way to mitigate, if not resolve, interclan conflicts and disputes in Somalia.

It was a policy that contrasted sharply with that of Eritrea after its independence. Isaias has always seen a strong Somalia as a possible counterweight to Ethiopia. During the 1998–2000 war with Ethiopia, he armed and trained a substantial number of Oromo Liberation Front (OLF) fighters and tried to infiltrate them into southern Ethiopia through Somalia. Later in 2007, he armed over a thousand Ogaden National Liberation Front (ONLF) fighters and infiltrated them through Mogadishu into Ethiopia's Somali Regional State as well as providing arms to support ex-Islamic Courts Union elements to continue their fight against Ethiopian forces in Somalia.[17]

---

16   Alex de Waal, "Cash and Contradictions: On the Limits of Middle Eastern Influence in Sudan," African Arguments, 1 August 2019.

17   The UN Monitoring Group inaccurately reported that Eritrea had provided two thousand soldiers to support the ICU in 2006. They were not Eritrean troops but OLF and ONLF fighters trained in Eritrea. Eritrea did supply advisers to the ICU

Abiy's visit to Mogadishu in June 2018, the tripartite agreement, and Isaias's own visit to Mogadishu in December emphasized a new approach, an approach that offers greater support to the federal government and has certainly given Farmaajo increased confidence in dealing with his federal member states. At the same time, Abiy has been careful not to break with Somaliland. In December 2018, Ethiopia appointed a new consul-general in Hargeisa, Ambassador Shamsudin Ahmed. Ambassador Shamsudin is a former Ethiopian ambassador to Djibouti (2002–11) and Kenya (2011–14) from Ethiopia's Somali Regional State. He replaced a military officer, and his appointment was widely interpreted as upgrading Ethiopia's representation.

He has also made efforts to open a dialogue between Somalia and Somaliland, though to little effect. He tried to bring Farmaajo and Somaliland President Musa Bihi together for talks in Addis Ababa in February 2019. Bihi came, Farmaajo did not.[18] Somaliland subsequently laid down a list of conditions to be accepted by Somalia before any further talks took place.[19] These included an admission by Somalia that Somaliland is an independent country and an agreement that international intergovernmental organizations should use the name, map, emblem, and flag of Somaliland in project documents. Any dialogue should take place in a neutral venue with a clear agenda, including future relations, and the international community should serve as mediators. In addition, nobody from Somaliland holding positions in Somalia or who are against the statehood of Somaliland should be allowed to represent Somalia in the dialogue. In fact, Somalia and Somaliland's views of such talks have always run on parallel lines: Somalia sees them as negotiations to restore Somaliland's place in Somalia; Somaliland regards any talks as providing for its recognition as an independent state. There is no meeting of minds.

Somaliland's tougher stance, despite the attempts at mediation, is the result of two main factors. One is the deterioration of Kenya's relations with Somalia following the dispute over their maritime boundary and more recently over the reelection of Sheikh Ahmed Mohamed, "Madobe," as president of the Federal State of Jubaland in southern Somalia. One effect

---

in 2006, some of whom accompanied ICU forces to capture Kismayo in September, but they numbered no more than a dozen or so.

18 Eritrea also made a bid to encourage talks between Somalia and Somaliland in March 2019. Isaias's foreign policy team of Foreign Minister Osman Saleh and Presidential Adviser Yemane Ghebreab made a three-day working visit to Somaliland and followed this up three weeks later with a visit to Mogadishu.

19 The last round of talks, brokered by Turkey, collapsed in 2015.

of these problems has been Kenya's decision to extend its relationship with Hargeisa. Somaliland has also been encouraged by the ongoing differences between the UAE and the federal government. This has, in effect, become an extension of the crisis between Qatar and the other members of the Gulf Cooperation Council.

Kenya-Somalia

Kenya-Somalia relations have also been a target of Abiy's mediation over their maritime dispute going back to 2014 when Somalia laid claim at the International Court of Justice to a triangle of the Indian Ocean believed to be rich in oil and gas. The 65,000-sq. mile area included several oil blocks previously considered to be within Kenya's exclusive economic zone. Somalia has called for its land border to be extended to the southeast along Kenya's coastline. This would effectively mean access to Kenya would have to be through Somali and Tanzanian waters. Kenya argues the maritime border should follow the line of latitude due east as it has done previously. The ICJ ruled in 2017 that it had jurisdiction despite Kenya's objections, and after some delays the ICJ has now decided to hear the representations of the two parties in June 2020.

Kenya has been pushing for a negotiated solution to the dispute, accusing Somalia of acting in bad faith when it filed the suit claiming there was an active mediation process in progress. Kenya's cabinet secretary for foreign affairs, Monica Juma, insists a "sustainable solution has to be seen as mutual. We have preference for negotiated settlement." Kenya has also called for AU dispute resolution mechanisms to become involved. In September 2019, the AU Peace and Security Council (of which Kenya was currently a member) requested the AU chair to assist the parties as a matter of urgency, either directly or through appointment of a special envoy to reach an amicable and sustainable settlement. The council urged Kenya and Somalia to refrain from any actions that might lead to the escalation of tensions. Kenya has also made other efforts to pressure Somalia: it tried to have Al-Shabaab listed by the United Nations as a terrorist organization. It is perhaps surprising this hasn't been done before, but Kenya's intent, which was unsuccessful, was clearly aimed at putting pressure on Somalia. Listing Al-Shabaab as a terrorist organization would mean its activities would fall under UN Security Council resolution 13473 (2001). This obliges states to freeze the funds of anyone who facilitates the commitment of terrorist acts or makes any funds, financial assets, or economic resources available to terrorist organizations, whether "directly or indirectly." This would be interpreted to cover any activity by organizations in Somalia to which Al-

Shabaab might have access. It would have had a significant impact on the operation of UN agencies and humanitarian organizations, limiting their ability to access funding and preventing them from operating in areas where their activities could benefit, indirectly, Al-Shabaab members, or where Al-Shabaab might be able to seize any of their assets.

Both sides brought their ambassadors back for consultations in February, amid accusations that Somalia had been selling off blocks within the disputed area at an oil conference in London, a claim Somali denied. It was at this point that Abiy became involved in an attempt at mediation. Following a visit by President Uhuru Kenyatta of Kenya to Addis Ababa in March 2019, and then by Farmaajo a few days later, Abiy then accompanied Farmaajo to Nairobi the next day for Abiy to chair a meeting with Kenyatta. Kenya's State House did not release any official communiqué of the meeting, but Abiy's office said the parties had resolved to "amicably resolve differences and agreed to work towards peace and to take measures in addressing particular issues that escalated the tensions." Farmaajo's office said the meeting discussed recent diplomatic tensions and that Somalia and Kenya had committed themselves to strengthening their working relationship. It described the talks as fruitful and said the main agenda for the meeting was to find a solution to diplomatic differences.

Abiy's office insisted he had made no effort to mediate specifically in the maritime dispute or to try and persuade Somalia to withdraw its case from the ICJ. He had merely intended to get both sides to agree to talk again, ease tensions between the two sides, have them resume diplomatic missions, reopen their respective embassies, and work together to promote regional cooperation, resolve contentious issues through diplomacy, and maintain stability— generalities not specifics. It may have had some effect. A few weeks later, both sides were expressing "a strong desire to normalize relations" and had agreed their respective ambassadors should return to their posts.

If this was due to the meeting on March 6, the effect did not last long. Both sides continued to seize opportunities to annoy each other. In May, Kenya suspended direct flights from Mogadishu to Nairobi and insisted planes should stop at a border town for screening. It also denied some Somali MPs entry to meetings in Nairobi. In October 2019, Somalia summoned Kenya's ambassador after a Kenyan-registered plane landed in Kismayo without "official permission," noting: "Somalia strongly protests this violation and will not accept any encroachment on its air, sea and land borders. . . . The Federal Government of Somalia sees this action contradicts all principles of good neighbourliness and non-interference in the internal affairs of states."

Another element in the relationship has been the future of Jubaland, embroiled in 2018–19, like other federal member states, in disputes with the federal government over the level of autonomy for the states and control of oil, gas, and other potential resources. Jubaland is a particular problem for Kenya-Somalia relations because of Kenya's unilateral decision in October 2011 to send troops into Jubaland, to take Kismayo from Al-Shabaab, and in effect establish a buffer zone inside Somalia against Al-Shabaab and extremist elements. The Kenyan forces subsequently became part of the African Union Mission in Somalia (AMISOM) two years later. This helped Kenya manage its border, if not as effectively as hoped, as well as control Somali clan disputes in northeast Kenya. Kenya also appears to have profited from the arrangement to a considerable degree.[20]

The Jubaland authority has also served Ethiopia's interests in helping to bring an end to extremist infiltration into its Somali Regional State from the Gedo region, part of Jubaland, and activities by members of the ONLF.[21] Ethiopia accepted Madobe, a former militia commander linked to Al-Shabaab, as a legitimate figure capable of stabilizing Jubaland and helping in the construction of a federal Somalia. In August 2013, it oversaw the signing of the Addis Ababa Agreement between the Somali federal government and the interim administration for Jubaland, headed by Madobe. Ethiopia's foreign minister, Dr. Tedros, said the agreement had opened the door to the establishment of a federal state in Somalia, with leaders rising above factional interests to offer an example of political reconciliation.

The agreement laid down five principles: the Somali government to lead the federal process; respect for the provisional constitution; an all-inclusive consultative process; the supportive role of IGAD; and fighting Al-Shabaab as the primary focus of the federal government and its regional and international partners. One contentious issue was who should control Kismayo Port and Airport; equally controversial were the modalities and

---

20 There have been repeated allegations that the Kenyan military have profited substantially from their presence, being extensively involved in sugar and charcoal trading through Kismayo. The UN Monitoring Group for Somalia and Eritrea in 2013 estimated the illicit charcoal market to be worth over $360 million, "with profits divided along the charcoal trade supply chain, including Al-Shabaab." Two years later, a report by Journalists for Justice detailed Kenyan Defence Force involvement in the sugar trade, channeling it from Al-Shabaab through the port of Kismayo, past corrupt border guards into Kenya, https://foreignpolicy.com/2015/11/12/report-kenyan-military-in-business-with-al-shabab.

21 The importance of this was minimized in 2018 by the return of the ONLF to Ethiopia and its decision to limit itself to political activity in the Somali Regional State.

timetable for the integration of Jubaland militia units in the Somali national armed forces. Several aspects of the Addis Ababa Agreement have not been implemented. The Kenyan presence has allowed Madobe considerable license in his dealings with the federal government, and, more recently, in his efforts, together with other federal states' leaders to hold back federal government control.

In fact, Farmaajo has put considerable effort into arranging for his own allies to take over leadership in the states, through a series of state elections in 2018-19. Emboldened by the support of Eritrea and Ethiopia, he succeeded in South West State. At his request, Ethiopian troops based in Baidoa arrested Sheikh Muktar Robow, a former leading member of Al-Shabaab who had looked set to win the state presidency.[22] Farmaajo then attempted to prevent Madobe being reelected president of Jubaland. When Kenya made its support for Madobe clear, Farmaajo asked for Ethiopian help. Ethiopian troops were apparently involved in an attempt to replicate the arrest of Sheikh Robow. A planeload of troops was dispatched from Baidoa to Kismayo to "assist in local security." Madobe believed the troops were coming to arrest him, and the plane was refused permission to land. If Ethiopian troops had tried to arrest Madobe before the election, as they did Sheikh Robow in South West, there would have been the real possibility of a shoot-out with Kenyan forces. Kenya's foreign ministry was quick to congratulate Madobe after the election. The federal government in Mogadishu said it would not accept the results and called for a new election. The problems between Mogadishu and Jubaland, as with Puntland, looks set to continue.

Although Somali elections in 2020 and 2021 are intended, for the first time, to be "one person, one vote" rather than through clan elders and assembly voting, on past record Farmaajo is unlikely to win reelection in 2021. No Somali president has yet achieved reelection, if only because of the understanding that clans should take turns to benefit from the role of "their" president. Whatever the result, however, it is unlikely to resolve the tensions between federal government institutions in Mogadishu and the federal member states, between Mogadishu and Hargeisa, or Kenya and Somalia. The factors at issue will remain and will, in turn, impinge on the planned drawdown of AMISOM scheduled for completion in 2021. AMISOM commanders remain highly doubtful there will be sufficient capacity in the Somali national forces

---

22   It was a controversial move, strongly criticized by then UN representative Nicolas Haystom, who was then declared persona non grata by Mogadishu. AMISOM denied the troops involved were under its command.

to take over security by 2021.[23] Both Kenya and Uganda, as well as Ethiopia, have expressed their concern about a premature withdrawal, despite strong indications from members of the UN Security Council and Somalia's partners that the mission must end in 2021.

Underlying the tensions between Kenya and Somalia is also Kenya's concern over recent power shifts within the region. From Kenya's perspective, the Eritrean-Ethiopian alliance, the Ethiopia-Somali-Eritrea axis, and the removal of Omar al-Bashir from power in Sudan, has left Isaias seeing himself as the senior-most leader in the region and, in his own eyes, the most influential figure shaping politics in the Horn. Coupled with Isaias's long-term view of his own, and Eritrea's, messianic place in the region, Kenya is concerned that recent events have affected Kenya's influence as a regional peacemaker and guarantor of stability. Its concerns have not been offset by the finding of oil or by the fact that Kenya will be taking over from Ethiopia as chair of IGAD when Ethiopia finally hands it over, after thirteen years. Kenya and Ethiopia have a defense pact, dating back to the mid-1960s, aimed at curbing the ambitions of an irredentist Somalia; and as the two major regional powers, Kenya and Ethiopia, saw themselves as playing a central but noncompetitive role in IGAD and the African Union and subsequently in regional peace and security architecture and in AMISOM in Somalia. The resurgence of clan supremacist politics inside Somalia, pan-Somali nationalism following the election of President Farmaajo in 2017, and Ethiopia's apparent support for Somalia have shaken that certainty.

Nevertheless, despite possible differences over Jubaland and over the future governance of Somalia, Ethiopia still firmly sees itself as a strategic partner of Kenya, not as a competitor, operating within the parameters of regional integration. Abiy's idea of *medemer* as a call for unity, synergy, and harmony resonates with Kenya. Recent summits have revitalized the

---

23 The question of whether Somali national forces could acquire the capacity to take over from AMISOM in 2020-21 goes back to the London Conference of May 2017 when the UK, US, Kenya, and Ethiopia, together with the EU, UN and AU discussed the future of Somalia. The conference agreed on the creation of a regular army of 18,000 troops and 32,000 federal and state police to replace AMISOM. The US would be responsible for training special forces, Danab units, one battalion to be assigned to each federal member state; the rest of the regular troops would be trained by the EU, Turkey, and the UAE. Many of the 6,000 troops trained by the EU failed to join the national forces, and a majority have joined federal member state militias or local clan forces. Integration of the Turkish trained forces, and of the UAE efforts while they lasted, was more effective. AMISOM has trained no more than a third of the number expected.

Special Status Agreement of 2012 and have underlined the importance of the Moyale Joint City and Economic Zone project and of the LAPSSET Corridor project, where the first three berths should be completed by the end of next year. The advantages of partnership over competition are certainly clear, allowing for power sales and possible development synergies with Kenyatta's "Big Four" agenda, but much may depend upon how relations work out in IGAD and within the region. Kenya, like Djibouti, was angered by Ethiopia's failure to announce support for either of their respective bids for a nonpermanent UN Security Council seat.

There has also been exasperation over the distribution of, and delays in finalizing, appointments in IGAD. Indeed, this is one reason for current dissatisfaction with IGAD, which has been chaired by Ethiopia for over a decade (see below). Somalia, for example, was irritated by the appointment of a Kenyan to be the special envoy of IGAD to Somalia, the Red Sea and the Gulf of Aden. Social media comments pointed out there were no Somalis holding executive posts in IGAD, as well as emphasizing Kenya has no links with the Red Sea or the Gulf of Aden: "If Somalia isn't given its rights then it is time to leave and time to set up a regional bloc of the 'willing.' Somalia should belong to an organization that defends its national interests, and one which does not interfere in the internal affairs of Somalia, or South Sudan." In the latter part of 2019, Kenya and Djibouti both indicated their desire to hold the executive secretary position. Ethiopia also put in a bid, tied to the fact that Abiy was proposing to finally give up Ethiopia's chairmanship, and this was expected to go to Kenya.

Somalia, Qatar, and the UAE

Another continuing dimension to internal Somali politics has been the increasing involvement of members of the Gulf Cooperation Council, and the impact of the GCC crisis. Somalia has been particularly vulnerable to pressure from both sides, given its strategic location on the periphery of the Muslim *umma*, on the Gulf of Aden and because disputes between the federal member states and the federal government have left it peculiarly open to competition for influence.

Somalia's links with the Gulf have traditionally been with the UAE, with which it has extensive and long-term commercial ties. There is a large Somali commercial presence in the Emirates. However, in February 2017, Qatar literally outspent the UAE in support of the election of Farmaajo, and although he has been careful not to take sides openly in the Gulf crisis, the UAE has interpreted his neutrality, and his refusal to support the coalition in Yemen, as siding with Qatar. Farmaajo, indeed, has steadily refused both diplomatic pressure and financial inducement to break links with Qatar. The federal government in Mogadishu also, of course, has close relations with Turkey, whose presence in Somalia predates other regional actors. Ankara began sending humanitarian aid to Somalia during the famine of 2011, and President Erdogan visited the country while still prime minister. Turkey has invested substantially in humanitarian support since then, and has its largest overseas military base in Mogadishu, used for training Somali forces.

Problems with the UAE rapidly followed the election of Farmaajo in February 2017. In June, he had to appeal to donors after the UAE and Saudi Arabia decided to withhold direct budgetary support after the UAE cut its training program and support, including the provision of armored personnel carriers and other equipment for the Federal Ministry of Internal Security and Police. It also stopped payment of salaries for government security forces. Relations deteriorated further when Farmaajo seized US$9 million in cash from an Emirati plane on the tarmac at Mogadishu, accusing the UAE of meddling in local politics. The UAE said the cash was to pay for troops who had been trained; the government suspected it was to be used to pay off members of parliament or federal state politicians. Although the cash was eventually returned, the UAE closed its training program for federal troops. As UAE support declined, Qatar began to provide some military support, giving sixty-eight armored vehicles in early 2019. In mid-year, it also agreed to build a port at Hobbyo.

The UAE also responded to the refusal to break with Qatar by increasing support for the federal member states, just at the time that Farmaajo was making every effort to influence the results of forthcoming state elections. The UAE's main vehicle for support in the Horn has been the Abu Dhabi-based DP World port management and logistics company. This had a contract with the Djibouti government, but when they fell out the UAE was quick to encourage DP World to move to Berbera as an alternative option, signing an agreement to invest some $400 million to build a major port. It had earlier signed a separate deal to build an airbase and a naval base. As part of the deal, the UAE agreed to train Somaliland coastguard, police, and security services. Ethiopia took a 19 percent interest in the port development, a move that upset Mogadishu, particularly when Somaliland's foreign minister said the port could be one of the gateways to Ethiopia.[24]

President Farmaajo declared the deal with UAE to be "null and void"; and Somalia's minister of ports and marine transport said the deal was against

---

24   The UAE has announced plans to build a road connecting the port of Berbera to Tug Wajale on the Ethiopian border; Ethiopia is already working on upgrading the road from Jijiga to Tug Wajale.

hopes for unity in Somalia and a violation of the Somali constitution.[25] Somaliland and the UAE ignored such comments. In April 2019, President Bihi made his second official visit to Abu Dhabi to discuss further UAE investment in Somaliland. Somaliland sees continued UAE support as adding to its legitimacy as a political actor, as it does the recent decision of Saudi Arabia to recognize Somaliland passports, the first real indication of Saudi support for Somaliland's independence. Recognition, however, still remains a long way off.

The UAE has also continued to support both Jubaland and Puntland. During the presidency of Farmaajo's predecessor, Hassan Sheikh Mohamoud, the UAE gave vehicles to the security forces of Jubaland, supported the Puntland maritime police force, with bases in Bossaso and Eyland, and financed and trained the Puntland Intelligence Agency. It signed an agreement with Puntland authorities to operate and rebuild Bossaso port, which DP World has leased for thirty years and where it proposes to invest over $300 million. There are reports that the UAE held talks with Jubaland over setting up a military base as well as refurbishing Kismayo port.

The UAE's interest and presence in Somalia has merely been one aspect of its wider regional agenda for the Horn of Africa, the Red Sea, and the western Indian Ocean, where it sees itself becoming a major power. It has been giving extensive support for tourist, humanitarian and port construction projects in the Comoros, Madagascar, the Maldives, Mauritius, the Seychelles, Somalia, and Somaliland, and built up a number of military facilities, in particular in Eritrea, Somaliland, and Somalia. One aspect of this was the creation of a mobile Yemeni battle group operating out of Assab in Eritrea, and it has been suggested the UAE might now be prepared to use its expertise to influence the outcome of other regional conflicts.[26] The geographic spread offers some indication of the range of the UAE's strategic interests and ambitions. While much of its interest may lie in looking to see "pliant mini-states along the eastern coast of Africa," it will also try to continue to keep its links with ports around the Horn of Africa to allow it to influence trading policies and safeguard its investments as well as prevent other powers gaining influence or control. From the UAE perspective, for example, Berbera offers serious value. It is only 160 miles across the Gulf

---

25 In September 2019, President Bihi announced that the UAE had decided the airport improvement would not include military facilities but be confined to civilian traffic, presumably a response to the UAE's decision to downsize its military involvement in Yemen and support southern secessionist elements.

26 Alexandre Mello and Michael Knights, "West of Suez for the United Arab Emirates," Washington Institute for Near East Policy, 2 September 2016.

of Aden from Berbera to Aden, and the UAE currently also has a presence on the Yemeni island of Socotra. In effect, this allows the UAE potential control of the entrance to the Red Sea, with potential facilities on both sides of the Gulf. Currently, it also has its major air and naval facility at Assab for the use of the war in Yemen.

These activities by the UAE, acquiring strategic ports and military facilities, paralleled by the efforts of others, have been described as a "new scramble for Africa." Reasons include gaining access to the region's developing economies and benefiting from China's BRI largesse, as well as the war in Yemen. Of equal concern is the question of Red Sea security and, most important of all, ensuring the exclusion of rivals.

Red Sea Security

The importance of the Red Sea as a maritime waterway and of the Bab el Mandeb Strait as a potential chokepoint needs no emphasis. The Suez Canal to the north connects the Red Sea with Europe and the Mediterranean, while the Bab el Mandeb Strait connects it to the Indian Ocean and Asia. Trade passing through the Suez Canal accounts for about 8 percent of the world's total, and about four million barrels of oil and refined petroleum products pass daily through Bab el Mandeb. Its strategic importance has been most obviously visible in the growing foreign military presence in and around the Red Sea and the Gulf of Aden, centered on Djibouti, where at least seven outside powers have military bases or facilities, and others are involved though the anti-piracy Combined Task Force 151, which involves thirty-three countries.[27]

The original reason for the interest and consequent militarization of the last decade or so was the intent to counter the perceived and expanding threat posed by terrorism and piracy, concentrated in or around Somalia from 2006 onwards. At the height of Somali piracy in January 2011, 736 hostages and thirty-two ships were being held by pirates. By October 2016, no hostages or ships were being held, and the number of incidents had dropped to near zero. However, the Jeddah Amendment (2017) significantly broadened the scope of the Djibouti Code of Conduct against piracy to cover other illicit maritime activities. There is every indication that the three task forces of the Combined Maritime Forces will continue to conduct operations in the

---

27 Countries with bases in Djibouti are China, France, Germany, Italy, Japan, Spain, and the US, with Saudi Arabia still finalizing details. See Neil Melvin, "The Foreign Military Presence in the Horn of Africa Region," SIPRI Background Paper, April 2019.

Indian Ocean, the Gulf of Aden, the Red Sea, the Arabian Sea, and the Gulf of Oman.

More recently, the focus on Red Sea security has been underlined by the arrival of international commercial and military competition, with the United States concerned over China's Belt and Road Initiative. This parallels the regional focus of opposing Middle Eastern interests, with Turkey and Qatar on the one side and Saudi Arabia, the UAE, and Egypt on the other, just as the United States began to delegate its interest in regional security to regional powers Israel, Saudi Arabia, and the UAE.

Another concern has been the spillover from Saudi Arabia's and the UAE's intervention in Yemen, Operation Decisive Storm, complicated by the subsequent Gulf crisis, splitting the GCC and raising the specter of regional Sunni-Shia conflict. In fact, in the second half of 2019, the UAE began to respond to the upsurge in tension with Iran in the Arabian Gulf, along with increasing calls to end the war in Yemen, by emphasizing the possibility of looking more closely at a political solution given the continuing military failure to provide victory. Announcing the drawdown of its own forces from Yemen in mid-2019, it made it clear it wanted to see the focus shift away from military activity. This was reinforced by the capture of Aden in September 2019 by the Southern Transitional Council (STC), whose forces have been armed and trained by the UAE. The STC, which supports an independent South Yemen, said it would hold Aden until President Hadi's government removed members of Islah from the government and northern politicians/officials from positions in the south.

Although the UAE has given no indication it wants to withdraw from the Saudi-led coalition, it is clear its actions will give support to those who believe no military solution is possible in Yemen and increase the prospects of some solution that includes an independent South Yemen once again. While the UAE and Saudi Arabia may differ over tactics and the future of Yemen, they do also share the same strategic objective, to keep Yemen weak. The UAE wants a presence in Aden, either directly or indirectly, and to defeat Al-Qaeda on the Arabian Peninsula. It now sees a resurrected South Yemen as the best way to achieve this while still allowing it to keep oversight of its commercial and maritime interests in the lower Red Sea and Gulf of Aden.

The main driver of the war in Yemen has been Saudi Crown Prince Mohammed bin Salman, but the conflict against the Houthis also fits into longer-term Saudi strategic concerns over Iran and the danger of Iranian influence in an area that Saudi Arabia considers its own. Saudi Arabia would not object to a divided Yemen but does not want to see the north controlled by the Houthis. The Houthis themselves are the main critics of a divided

Yemen, regarding this as a deliberate policy to keep Yemen under Saudi or UAE control. They argue for a Yemeni-Yemeni dialogue to resolve problems and the withdrawal of all foreign troops: "Yemenis should be united against both countries. The only way to restore our sovereignty is by uniting our ranks and our guns against the foreign Saudi and Emiratis intervention in Yemen."[28]

A UAE withdrawal from Yemen will have other repercussions. The UAE has already decided not to build an airbase at Berbera, and it is apparently rethinking the future of its base at Assab in Eritrea, where it built up extensive air, naval, and training facilities. In August 2019, Lt. General Prince Fahd bin Turki bin Abdulaziz, commander of the Saudi-led coalition forces in Yemen, visited President Isaias. Present at the talks were Eritrea's naval commander and chief of staff and the head of Saudi Arabia's Naval Operations Authority. Future Saudi use of the UAE-constructed air and sea facilities was on the agenda, as was Eritrea's support for continued coalition activity in Yemen.

Even prior to the war in Yemen, Saudi Arabia believed it had successfully persuaded Sudan in 2014 to break ties with Iran. It provided significant amounts of aid and lobbied, if unsuccessfully, for the United States to lift sanctions on Sudan. In return, al-Bashir closed down Iranian cultural and medical facilities and expelled Iran's diplomats. A year later, Sudan quickly joined Operation Decisive Storm in Yemen and provided several thousand troops for the coalition forces. Al-Bashir, however, proved resistant to UAE demands to turn against Islamist elements in his Sudan army and government and continued to provide what the UAE saw as a safe haven in Khartoum for the Muslim Brotherhood. Then, in December 2017, he hosted a visit by Qatar's ally, President Erdogan, of Turkey, who signed a number of agreements on security, trade, and investment, including one to rebuild the former Ottoman port of Suakin as a tourist center, and a Hajj port. He also agreed to provide it with ship repair facilities for both naval and civilian vessels. Egypt, which had created a Southern Fleet Command for the Red Sea fleet earlier in the year, promptly claimed Sudan had given Turkey a naval base. While both Sudan and Turkey denied this, they had agreed to set up a Strategic Cooperation Council planning group. Sudan's official news agency also said they intended to conclude a military deal.[29]

---

28 Mohamad al-Bukhait, member of the Houthi political bureau, quoted in "Analysis: The divergent Saudi-UAE strategies in Yemen". Ali Younis. Al Jazeera. 31.8.2019.

29 Turkey and Sudan agree to boost ties in Erdogan visit". Hiba Morgan reporting for Al Jazeera News from Khartoum 24.12.2017

Egypt's concerns were reinforced when Djibouti's ambassador to Turkey announced that Djibouti was open to any kind of approach from Turkey, including the building of a military base to help secure Red Sea security. He said the international community should ensure the waterway was safe from threats, adding that any possible steps by Turkey to build a military base in Djibouti would be welcome. Djibouti's President Guelleh had visited Ankara shortly before Erdogan's visit to Khartoum, returning a visit paid by Erdogan to Djibouti two years earlier, after which Djibouti had allocated a plot of land close to Doraleh port as a Turkish economic zone.

Sudan

In fact, despite Sudan's support for the war in Yemen, both Saudi Arabia and the UAE considered al-Bashir unreliable. When demonstrations began to threaten the regime in early 2019, like Egypt, they were quick to look for a post-Bashir option. After the removal of al-Bashir, Saudi Arabia and the UAE quickly announced a $3 billion aid package to meet the Transitional Military Council's most immediate economic problems. It was clear they preferred to see a non-Islamic military takeover, providing a firm authoritarian government that would resist any excessive democratization.

Ethiopia and Abiy have, rightly, been given a lot of credit for the success in the negotiations between the Transitional Military Council (TMC) and the Forces for Freedom and Change (FFC). In a visit to Khartoum, Abiy persuaded both sides to agree to continue talks despite killings on June 3, stressing the need for both sides to "act with bravery and responsibility in taking quick steps for a democratic, reconciliatory transitional period." He also spoke of unity and inclusivity before announcing the appointment of his special envoy, Ambassador Mohamed Dirir. His failure to involve the African Union in his approach led the AU Commission chair to appoint his own special envoy. The two envoys cooperated, if uneasily, to produce an acceptable compromise; and it was a compromise, as the generals only signed the constitutional declaration under considerable pressure. The FFC remained suspicious of both envoys, concerned about what the African Union wanted and wondering why Dr. Abiy had appointed a former Ethiopian ambassador to Egypt, and a Somali, as his envoy. The FFC saw Egypt, Saudi Arabia, and the UAE as allies of the military.

They were also concerned about Eritrea's aims. Isaias had been critical of the joint AU and Ethiopian mediation initiated by Abiy, characterizing it as internationalizing an internal Sudanese crisis. *From the outset, he saw the situation in Sudan as one in which he could play a role. Within a few weeks of al-Bashir's overthrow in mid-May, he was in touch with* General Abdul Fattah al-Burhan, the chairman of the TMC, and Deputy Chairman General Mohamed Daglo, "Hemeti," commander of the Rapid Support Forces. The day after Abiy launched his mediation in Khartoum on June 7, Isaias visited Cairo for talks with President El-Sisi of Egypt, with Sudan at the top of the agenda. He invited General al-Burhan to Asmara on June 14 and sent Foreign Minister Osman Saleh and Presidential Adviser Yemane Gebreab to Khartoum ten days later to underline support for the "transitional process," applauding the Sudanese Armed Forces for its role in taking sides with the population at a crucial moment. A couple of weeks later, Hemeti was in Asmara to hear Yemane stress there was potential for a peaceful transition without the interference of external forces—by which he meant the African Union or IGAD rather than Egypt or the UAE. A few days later, Yemane was back in Khartoum for further talks with the chairman and deputy chairman of the TMC.

These visits were orchestrated by the UAE to bolster Isaias's position in the Sudanese crisis and to try to limit Ethiopia's influence over the negotiations. Neither UAE nor Eritrean officials attended the August agreement signing ceremony in Khartoum, but in September Isaias made his first visit to Sudan in five years, just a few days after returning from meeting UAE Crown Prince Mohammed bin Zaid in Abu Dhabi. During his visit, he met General Al-Burhan, the chair of the Sovereignty Council. Sudan and Eritrea agreed to cooperate in the "defense and military fields, including the ground forces, the air force, the marine forces, the defense industries, training and medical services." They also discussed security cooperation and the building up of defense capabilities to be funded by the UAE. The UAE and Eritrea are now coordinating policies on Sudan, and the UAE appears to have made Eritrea its surrogate voice on Sudan.

Turkish influence in Sudan in effect collapsed in April 2019 with the overthrow of al-Bashir, and any rebuilding of Suakin is unlikely to occur, though it retains considerable investments, as does Qatar. Qatar, indeed, may still hope to preserve some links with the new government, even though it indicated its support for al-Bashir during the protests that erupted towards the end of 2018, as it was the architect of the Doha Document for Peace in Darfur. However, steps towards bringing the Darfur armed groups into the Constitutional Agreement in October are now being orchestrated by South Sudan and IGAD rather than Qatar. A number of other armed groups in Blue Nile State and South Kordofan, and some opposition parties, including the communists, have yet to participate in the changes in Sudan. There remains a real need for inclusivity, a concept given considerable weight by Abiy and strengthened by his Nobel Peace Prize, but by the end of 2019 there appeared to be no role for Qatar in Sudan.

As part of its efforts to keep Turkey and Qatar out of the Red Sea, Saudi Arabia has also been trying to develop security cooperation among Red Sea littoral states.[30] A consultative ministerial meeting of the African and Arab States bordering the Red Sea was held in Riyadh in December 2018 with Djibouti, Egypt, Jordan, Somalia, Sudan, and Yemen. A year earlier, Egypt had hosted a ministerial meeting of Djibouti, Jordan, Saudi Arabia, Sudan, and Yemen that highlighted the need for a permanent mechanism to consider security challenges and opportunities in the Red Sea but made no further progress. European partners have signaled interest in supporting a Red Sea forum. Outsider powers have also shown an interest. Germany, after it became a nonpermanent member of the Security Council in 2018, invited Red Sea states to discuss the possibility of a Red Sea security forum during the 2018 UN General Assembly. Tellingly, there were significant disagreements over which countries should be involved, as well as objections to European involvement.

The Saudi Arabian conference reached an agreement to establish the Arab and African Coastal States of the Red Sea and the Gulf of Aden (AARSGA). Saudi Arabia made it clear it wanted to see a cooperation bloc that could provide a multilateral framework to manage regional disagreements and protect Red Sea security by "creating synergies" and reducing "negative outside influence," including that of Turkey and Qatar. This approach has been strongly supported by Egypt, a supporter of the Saudi coalition in Yemen, and which announced the setting up of Southern Fleet Command in early 2017 "to secure the eastern Egyptian coastline and ensure the safety and stability of maritime traffic at Bab el Mandeb and navigation through the Suez Canal."[31] Those attending the conference also participated in military exercises called Red Wave 1. Red Wave 2 took place in September 2019, with the same participants, as part of Saudi Arabia's efforts to continue to "unify and enhance the maritime security of the countries bordering the Red Sea, protect territorial waters and strengthen military cooperation."

Eritrea, as a littoral state, was invited but did not attend either meeting, though it did participate in the third meeting of high-level officials in April

---

30 Saudi Arabia has begun to develop its own Red Sea coast with the $500 billion Neom mega-project on the Gulf of Aqaba and the establishment of the Red Sea Development Company to execute the Red Sea Project, a major development announced in 2017.

31 The fleet included a multipurpose frigate, a Mistral-class amphibious assault ship/helicopter carrier, fast missile craft and patrol boats and a Type 209/1400-class submarine.

2019, when it stressed any functional framework required a careful approach and "continuous and serious consultations." It also called for clarity of objectives and goals, the mapping of threats, positive policies of cooperation, implementation mechanisms, respect for sovereignty, collective efforts, and cooperation with "external forces" where necessary and insistence that all littoral states build and possess their own effective defense capabilities and naval forces, without delegation to others.[32] It will, however, participate more fully in the future.

Another absentee was Ethiopia, which although not a littoral state is the major power on the African side of the Red Sea. It was Egypt that objected to any invitation to Ethiopia because of the issue of the Nile and the Grand Ethiopian Renaissance Dam. Ethiopia can, however, expect an invitation even if it is not prepared to commit itself to some of Saudi Arabia's regional activities. A country of over 110 million people and central to regional political, economic, and infrastructural development across the Horn cannot be sidelined, even if it has no coastline. Indeed, it is clear from Prime Minister Abiy's announcement that he intends to rebuild a navy that he intends Ethiopia to play a serious role in Red Sea security.

Abiy announced his intention to rebuild Ethiopia's navy in November 2018, and parliament passed the necessary legislation two months later. The minister of defense told MPs that a committee had been set up to identify the resources needed and had visited France, following Abiy's visit to Paris when President Macron promised French assistance. When Macron visited Addis Ababa in March 2019, he signed what he called an "unprecedented defense cooperation agreement" providing a framework that among other things "notably opens the way for France to assist in establishing an Ethiopian naval component." It also offered air cooperation, joint operations, and opportunities for training and equipment purchases.

The decision to rebuild a navy may be a matter of national pride, but it also makes sense within the geopolitical parameters of regional organizations and the Red Sea in line with Abiy's views on regional integration and Ethiopia's regional role. Where it is to be based is not yet clear. The most obvious options are Djibouti and Eritrea. Djibouti will certainly remain Ethiopia's major outlet to the sea for a long time, even though Abiy is exploring other possibilities in the region. Given the rapprochement with Eritrea, Massawa, the old imperial Ethiopian naval base, must be a possibility, as President Guelleh of Djibouti indicated earlier in 2019.[33] However, it seems more

32 Eritrean Ministry of Information, press release on "Eritrea's Stance on the Security of the Red Sea," 23 September 2019.

33 President Guelleh said that although France had agreed to build the Ethiopian navy,

likely that in the first instance, with France providing most of the required support, it is likely to be based in Djibouti. Ethiopia naval authorities, indeed, suggested in August 2019 that this was the latest plan. Djibouti is the port for Ethiopia's current merchant fleet.[34]

The reestablishment of a navy will underline Ethiopia's significance in the lower Red Sea and emphasize the reality of Ethiopia's regional hegemonic aspirations. It will also emphasize the importance of Ethiopia's relations with both Eritrea and Djibouti. An Ethiopian navy, together with the naval presence of Eritrea and Djibouti, will substitute for the former naval capability of Yemen in terms of strategic control of the Bab el Mandeb Strait. It will also be able to help form the basis of a new security and economic Red Sea zone, which could, in theory, include all the coastal states and even Israel.

The US Marine Corps Vision and Strategy 2025 concluded that the Indian Ocean and neighboring areas, including the Arabian Gulf, the Gulf of Aden, and the Red Sea, would be a central factor in global conflict and competition during this century. This will be underlined by full operationalization of China's Belt and Road Initiative and the Maritime Silk Road. The possibilities have already encouraged India, which regards the Indian Ocean as central to its strategic vision, to significantly expand its naval strength. Another interested party is the UAE, which is continuing its considerable efforts to establish itself all around the coasts of Arabia, the Red Sea and the Horn of Africa and East Africa, building up positions from which it will be able to guard and control its trade.

IGAD and the Red Sea

It is against this background that both the African Union and IGAD have finally begun to take note of Red Sea security, looking at strategic considerations of the challenges of peace, security, stability, and development in the Horn of Africa. The AU Peace and Security Council has underlined that the Horn historically straddled the Red Sea and Indian Ocean and that the current challenges need inclusive and comprehensive responses.

---

he believed its base would be Massawa. JeuneAfrique, 10 April 2019.

34 Despite the loss of the coastline in 1991, Ethiopia continued to operate a small merchant fleet that is now composed of eleven ships: nine new, Chinese-built, 28,000-ton multipurpose cargo ships delivered in 2012–13 and two oil tankers. It is currently based in Djibouti. There is also a civilian Ethiopian Maritime Training Institute based in Bahir Dar on the shores of Lake Tana with the capacity to turn out five hundred marine engineers and elector-technical officers a year.

In December 2018 it requested the AU High Level Implementation Panel (AUHIP) to call a conference on peace, security, stability, cooperation and development in the Horn and extend participation to the states of the Red Sea, the Arabian Peninsula, and other concerned international stakeholders, to "provide for a genuinely African perspective on the challenges of the Horn."[35]

The growth of external military interests in the region and their rivalry, potential or actual, has also finally alerted IGAD to the dangers and the need for a multilateral regional strategic response. An IGAD Council of Ministers, attended by Djibouti, Ethiopia, Somalia, and Sudan, at the end of February 2019, heard a presentation from the IGAD Special Envoy for Somalia on the geopolitical and security dynamics of the Red Sea and the Gulf of Aden. The council acknowledged the separate strategic interests of IGAD member states and of Eritrea but agreed on the need for IGAD to take a leading role on the issue of the Red Sea and the Gulf of Aden and formulate common goals and strategic coordination. It said IGAD should adopt a collective approach, "strengthening regional cooperation and establishing a regional platform for IGAD member states with a view to promote dialogue with other stakeholders including the AU and other international partners." It agreed to develop a common position to cover the region's maritime security, migration, fight against terrorism, the prevention of illegal fishing, pollution, and the dumping of toxic waste. It told the IGAD Secretariat to establish a special task force of experts to chart out a regional plan of action and build a common position and strategy to respond to the challenges and opportunities in the Red Sea and Gulf of Aden, and extended the responsibilities of the IGAD Special Envoy for Somalia to cover the Red Sea and the Gulf. The task force set up at a meeting of the IGAD Committee of Ambassadors in April was told to chart a regional plan of action with clear timelines; produce credible and inclusive dialogue on regional matters covering the Red Sea and the Gulf of Aden; and help formulate shared policies as well as common strategic goals to promote common regional objectives. It was also instructed to coordinate efforts with the AU Commission.

Almost immediately after the announcement of an IGAD task force, Somaliland put in a bid to be included, making the point that any initiative to coordinate a response to changing Red Sea concerns and priorities that did not include them in a meaningful way would lack the credibility and

---

35   Communiqué of the 811th AU PSC meeting on the activities of the AU High Level Implementation Panel for Sudan and South Sudan and the Horn of Africa, 6 December 2018.

capacity to deal with multinational cooperation in the region. A foreign ministry statement said, "Somaliland, despite being a major stakeholder in Red Sea governance, regrets the lack of consultation and inclusivity which it was afforded within the process behind the initiation and formulation of the Task Force. At the same time, it remains unclear what role, if any, the Task Force envisions for Somaliland." It further said: "Safeguarding the security and sustainability of the Red Sea and Gulf of Aden concerns all countries that share these coastal waters," adding that Somaliland would not recognize endeavours that excluded legitimate stakeholders. It also pointed out that the major scaling up and expansion of Berbera Port, being financed by the UAE and in which Ethiopia has a 19± percent stake, would make it "a key strategic hub within IGAD's integrated and maritime-facing regional trade network."

Despite the interest on both sides of the Red Sea, a fully inclusive and functional Red Sea Forum, perhaps the best-case security scenario for the Red Sea, is unlikely to be realized until several other problems are resolved, including the conflict in Yemen. States in the Horn of Africa need to advance domestic reforms and regional integration to allow them to articulate shared interests and negotiate with Gulf partners on a more equal footing. The current asymmetrical nature of relations between the two sides of the Red Sea needs to be minimized, if not resolved. One of the aspects of this asymmetry lies in the Horn's supply of cheap labor to the Gulf States, with the ill treatment of workers and periodic expulsions of migrant workers straining relations. Ethiopia, with an estimated five hundred thousand workers in Saudi Arabia alone, has been most affected. Saudi Arabia and the UAE in the past have used the threat of mass expulsion to try to persuade states to cut ties with Qatar. Abiy has been working to regularize the position of Ethiopian workers across the Middle East and sign labor agreements with some success, but the issue will remain live.

Medemer

Abiy has made bilateral and tripartite meetings a central element in his series of consultations on issues of common interest across the region as part of his strong belief in the value of face-to-face meetings, of dialogue and discussion, of *medemer*. While focusing on creating or (re)-establishing strategic partnerships, Abiy has also made frequent reference to regional economic integration, which he has described as one of the three pillars of Ethiopia's renaissance. He has spoken of the shared cultural values of people in the region and how social and intellectual capital can be harnessed, arguing that "history has demonstrated time and again that neighbors with intimate, rule-based, and diverse trade and economic relations are unlikely to resort to conflict." "That," he says, "is why we believe that integration must be viewed not just as an economic project but also as crucial to securing peace and reconciliation in the Horn of Africa."

A central element of Abiy's vision for the Horn is informed by *medemer*, a philosophy of collaboration including peaceful coexistence, equal partnership, and equitable sharing of benefits and burdens. It is often translated as synergy, involving the idea of cooperation, interaction, dialogue, and negotiation. He gave one version of the concept during a speech at a dinner in honour of President Isaias, during his first visit to Addis Ababa in July 2018: "*Tender love instead of abject cruelty, peace instead of conflict, love over hate, forgiveness over holding grudge, pulling instead of pushing. Peace to be the mother of prosperity, one will stay a pipe dream without the other. . . . If two individuals agree on all things then the need for the second one becomes irrelevant since he is not adding anything new. Handled wisely our differences are our assets. What medemer does not like is conflict instead of cooperation, banning instead of accommodation, polemics instead of discussion, and acquiring fame through war by killing each other instead of resolution through a healthy debate.*"[36]

In launching his book Medemer *in October in Addis Ababa, Dr. Abiy* said that the idea of *medemer* also included scaling up best practices, rectifying past mistakes, and creating a better future. He spoke of *medemer* helping to meet three goals: to keep and expand on all political achievements that have been achieved so far; to rectify mistakes committed in the past; and to satisfy the needs for freedom and dignity aside from the economic and social rights we have as human beings. The book emphasizes bringing prosperity through the creation of a free market platform and generating more employment opportunities. It calls for keeping economic gains made in the past, addressing macroeconomic imbalances, economic diversification, and reforming legal frameworks to meet future demands. It notes that *medemer* gives priority to neighboring countries, noting Ethiopia cannot be peaceful if the region isn't peaceful. It also targets expanding identified values and maintaining national pride through regional cooperation.

An editorial in the *Ethiopian Herald* in February 2019 emphasized that *medemer* could have a massive impact on political and economic integration

---

36 Medemer and the related concept of yiqirta (forgiveness) have underpinned the reform process in Ethiopia, most obviously demonstrated in the various agreements that brought home previously banned political groups. The government has created independent commissions on reconciliation and administrative boundaries. The prime minister published Medemer in Amharic and Afar Oromo in October 2019. An English version was due in early 2020.

in the Horn of Africa and beyond. It said Prime Minister Abiy had shown his determination to integrate East Africa through railway and road links. The end of the deadlock between Ethiopia and Eritrea was a sign of *medemer*, and diplomatic relations among East African countries could pave the way for political and economic integration: "When we interrelate this with the *medemer* concept, we understand that the cooperation among East African nations is immense in ensuring peace, stability and prosperity. We can understand that the Premier has an unshakable stand in realizing regional and continental goals." It suggested if countries came together under *medemer*, made peace and built foundations for peaceful relations, then the rest of Africa could follow, adding that for lasting and durable peace, there must be vital economic ties and interdependence between Horn countries.[37]

The Prime Minister's Office has cited as an example of *medemer* in action his "whirlwind of shuttle diplomacy" at the beginning of March 2019, when he hosted President Kenyatta of Kenya, who brought with him a large delegation of government officials and corporate and business community representatives to discuss a range of economic and investment issues on March 1. Two days later, Abiy and Kenyatta flew to Asmara to meet President Isaias for trilateral discussions on regional economic integration. Kenyatta returned to Nairobi, but Abiy and Isaias flew on to Juba, South Sudan, on March 4 to discuss "regional peace, economic ties, and infrastructure development" with President Kiir. A day later, Farmaajo arrived in Ethiopia for bilateral talks, and on March 6 Abiy accompanied the Somali president to Nairobi to encourage discussion with Kenyatta on the Kenya-Somalia maritime border issue. It was an impressive range of visits, but it remained unclear how much of an effect, beyond the immediacy of a handshake and public references to warm and friendly relations, they had.

Official definitions of *medemer* emphasize that all in the Horn of Africa are tied together "in a single garment of destiny, caught in an inescapable network of mutuality." So, whatever affects one state directly, affects all indirectly. The Horn of Africa faces grinding poverty, disease, ignorance, large-scale population displacements, conflict, and "war in one country threatens peace in the other; peace and democracy in one country becomes an example of good governance for others." Regional integration is essentially another phrase for *medemer*, and the tripartite discussions in March between Kenya, Eritrea, and Ethiopia; between Eritrea, Ethiopia, and South Sudan; and between Ethiopia, Kenya, and Somalia, as well as the

---

37 Ethiopian Herald, 17 February 2019.

earlier Ethiopia, Eritrea, Somalia meetings have all "focused on the need to advance the cause of regional integration" with agreements to "work out common projects that will facilitate the attainment of the goal of regional economic integration and shared prosperity."

One example of this was the first meeting between the leaders of Eritrea, Ethiopia, and Somalia in Asmara in September 2018, specifically setting up an Eritrea, Ethiopia, Somalia axis. The second tripartite meeting between Abiy, Isaias, and Farmaajo was held in November in Bahir Dar, Ethiopia. The Bahir Dar summit was billed as a meeting to "cement the outcome of the Horn of Africa economic integration agreement signed in Asmara," though no details of that agreement were released then or subsequently. A statement in Bahir Dar, however, did refer to the "tangible and positive outcomes already registered, and agreed to consolidate the mutual solidarity and support [of the three countries] in addressing challenges that they face individually and collectively." It also stressed the sovereignty, territorial integrity, and political independence of Somalia, welcomed the "impending lifting of all sanctions against Eritrea, and underscored their conviction that this act of justice would contribute to enhancing peace, development and cooperation in the region." Commitments to inclusive regional peace and cooperation were made. Another tripartite link appeared to be set up when President al-Bashir of Sudan and President Guelleh of Djibouti visited Ethiopia together in December 2018, meeting Abiy in Jimma in southwest Ethiopia. He had invited them earlier, when visiting Djibouti in August and Khartoum in September and discussing the need to elevate their already-existing "all-round, multi-dimensional relations to give impetus to the realization of fast economic integration in the Horn of Africa." The discussions between al-Bashir, Guelleh and Abiy, apart from strengthening existing friendly relations, also considered wider implications of regional peace and development. The official statements referred to the peoples of Sudan, Ethiopia, and Djibouti sharing a common heritage, languages, cultures, and traditions, to interconnectedness underlined by their joint march towards "an economic union blessed with permanent fraternal links and the strong bonds of people naturally and historically linked, and with relations based on trust and a win-win approach." Offering a model for others in the region, it should pave the way for a greater contribution towards regional stabilization through integration in various bilateral and regional sectors.

Although from Abiy's perspective the removal of al-Bashir from power has had no effect on the Ethiopia-Sudan relationship, not least because Abiy's other major foreign policy success has been Ethiopia's mediation in Sudan, it has not led to any progress towards another economic axis. The

Ethiopia-Eritrea agreement itself has had no effect on Ethiopia's relations with Sudan. Eritrea's relations with Sudan, however, deteriorated sharply again in January 2019. After being accused of supporting Sudan's opposition attacks, Isaias closed the Eritrea-Sudan border; three months later, he accused Sudan, Turkey, and Qatar of trying to destabilize Eritrea: Turkey of conducting "acts of subversion," Qatar of collaboration by providing funding and operational services, and Sudan of allowing its territories to be used for "nefarious aims." Eritrea now appears to favor the military element within the new Sudanese government.

Certainly, since taking office in April 2018, Abiy has consistently conveyed the message of reconciliation, including forgiveness, togetherness, love, and tolerance in most of his encounters with most political elements in Ethiopia. It has firmly underpinned the same approach in his foreign policy calculations, producing the paradigm change in relations between Ethiopia and Eritrea and in the Horn of Africa. The creation of a significant reservoir of regional and international goodwill has undoubtedly improved prospects for lasting peace in the Horn. For Abiy, personal style and foreign policy are inextricably linked, and he has made much of *medemer* to support this, even though translating it into foreign policy and the detailed minutiae of integration is never going to be easy.

In January, addressing a meeting of Ethiopian ambassadors and senior officials of the Ministry of Foreign Affairs, Dr. Abiy called diplomacy one pillar of economic development and a vital bedrock for socioeconomic progress. "Ambassadors and diplomats are the face and soul of Ethiopia abroad. An ambassador should relentlessly promote Ethiopia abroad for national gain, stimulate a positive country image, mobilize investment, tourism and better engage the Diaspora for national dialogue." He said he wanted the Foreign Ministry to become a catalyst for economic development, to maintain the country's positive image and, most importantly, trigger citizen-centered diplomacy in its bilateral, regional, and multilateral diplomatic activity nexus. He called on the embassies to play a much more active role in promoting investment and informing and updating potential investors on investment opportunities, trade, and tourism sectors. This should also focus on safeguarding the rights and interests of Ethiopian nationals abroad and concentrate on relations with immediate neighbors and on the promotion of integration within the Horn of Africa. The prime minister has made it clear he believes there are still huge possibilities available to explore new venues of cooperation and partnership between Ethiopia and Eritrea as well as facilitating the process of economic integration in the region, and it is through *medemer*, "coming together," that he believes previously intractable national and regional challenges must be addressed.

A central element in this approach has also been the belief in one-to-one mediation and discussion in support of integration, drawing on the reservoir of international goodwill available after June 2018, and boosted significantly in October 2019 by the Nobel Peace Prize. In the past, the Nobel Committee has rewarded aspiration over achievement. This would appear to be the case with Abiy. Ethiopian-Eritrean rapprochement has yet to see any of the necessary institutionalization of the process embraced by either leader; as of late 2019, attempts to mediate between Eritrea and Djibouti, or between Kenya and Somalia, have made no progress. Sudan demonstrated success in August 2019, but the transitional process has three years to run. South Sudan, an IGAD operation, may be on course, but there are still major concerns.

The Nobel Peace Prize has given Abiy momentum to consolidate his approach to regional diplomacy; it could, and should, inspire regional leaders to work towards economic integration, peace, and sustainable development. The Nobel Committee specified that it acknowledged all stakeholders working for peace and reconciliation and that the award recognized and rewarded reconciliation and nonviolent dispute resolution over conflict and dispute. However, not everyone appears to have been impressed; Eritrea made no effort to congratulate Abiy. Indeed, the award to Abiy alone appears to have been seen in Asmara as yet another example of the world's anti-Eritrean bias, not least because Saudi Arabia and the UAE recognized both Isaias and Abiy when they awarded the medals to the two protagonists in 2018. Abiy's major foreign policy success may have been the rapprochement with Eritrea after twenty years of discord, but the subsequent delay in any normalization of relations has given rise to concerns about sustainability. The abruptness of the change also left traditional allies, including Djibouti, Sudan, and Kenya unsighted and affected the changes needed to make IGAD an effective regional organization, as Eritrea has yet to agree to rejoin it.

While Ethiopia certainly benefited from Saudi and UAE largesse over the rapprochement with Eritrea, Abiy was careful to keep options open. Ethiopia broke relations with Qatar in 2008 over Al Jazeera's coverage of Ethiopia's Somali Regional State, but they were restored in 2012. Since then, Ethiopia has continued to look to Qatar for investment as well as to other members of the GCC. In April 2019, an Ethiopian Foreign Ministry spokesperson confirmed Ethiopia supported the efforts of the Emir of Kuwait to resolve the Gulf crisis and called for dialogue and diplomacy. A month earlier, for example, Abiy had visited both Dubai and Abu Dhabi in back-to-back visits and appears to have made an effort to mediate. Unlike Isaias, he has been careful to avoid involvement in the Saudi coalition in Yemen. Ethiopia's closest link to the Arab world historically has been Yemen, and it has no desire to get pulled into the conflict. Abiy did, however, address a statement to the people of Yemen in December 2018. It began, "To the people of the Land of Goodness, as described in the Holy Quran," before calling on Yemenis to apply wisdom and use reason. It asked the warring parties, "Why do you turn your children into orphans?" and denounced the tragedy of war but made no specific reference to the bombing campaign, neither endorsing nor criticizing it. This was not an endorsement of the activities of the coalition, but Ethiopia did vote with coalition members against a UK proposal to create humanitarian corridors into the closely besieged Houthi-controlled city of Hodeidah.

Eritrean Diplomacy

In some respects, the most immediately obvious beneficiary of the Ethiopia-Eritrea rapprochement has been Isaias. He was able to claim that Abiy's move acknowledged the legality and legitimacy of Eritrea's post 2002 policies and that it validated all Eritrea's polices, completing the collapse of an already faltering Ethiopian-driven policy of isolating Eritrea and provided the Security Council with an excuse to lift its sanctions against the country, contradicting evidence of persistent Eritrean regional destabilization. Eritrea's rehabilitation has been underlined by the subsequent upsurge in Isaias's regional diplomatic activity over the following year, some in conjunction with Abiy and some on his own. The two have not always been synchronized, despite the comments of Isaias in Ethiopia in July 2018: "I have given him all responsibility of leadership and power; from now on, anyone who says Eritrea and Ethiopia are two people is out of reality"; and to Abiy: "You are our leader." Abiy made similar remarks at the World Economic Forum at Davos in January 2019, saying, for example, he saw no need for Ethiopia, Eritrea, and Djibouti to have separate armies or embassies. A few weeks later, Abiy, apparently referring to Eritrea and underlining that Ethiopia would not disintegrate, emphasized that "it is a matter of time that those who have left will return." Such remarks have alarmed Eritreans and given rise to fears, as Bereket Habte Selassie, a leading critic of Isaias, put it, that "Eritrea has been offered to Ethiopia on a silver platter."

Of course, despite the hyperbole, Ethiopia and Eritrea are two separate states with different national interests, different administrative capacities, and very different levels of power. Their relationship, whatever Isaias believes, is highly unequal. Their respective diasporas have different interests and aims. The peace process needs structure, to be institutionalized, as did not happen in the brief euphoria of the post-Eritrean independence years; and effective institutionalization requires a clear understanding of the details of the peace agreement and realistic appreciation of the aims and intentions of both parties. Their different interests have always been clear in their respective approaches to both Sudan and the Gulf States, over Yemen, and indeed over Somalia. They have now been underlined by Isaias's own visits around the region and the role he has taken in regional diplomacy since July 2018 and the lifting of sanctions in November. Eritrea was never as isolated as Ethiopia tried to ensure after 2002, but the president's visits were fairly circumscribed, except to Egypt (almost yearly since independence) and the Gulf. Since July 2018, however, he has been able once again to treat regional presidents and leaders to the advice of one of the longest-serving leaders of the Horn; only President Museveni of Uganda has now held power longer.

One of Isaias's assumptions has always been that the region would follow his prescriptions and his interpretations of policy, not least over IGAD and regional development. One of his first moves after the agreement with Ethiopia was to build up a relationship with Somalia, which for Eritrea has always offered a counterbalance to the strength of Ethiopia. The first visitor invited to Asmara after the rapprochement was Farmaajo. Isaias has been enthusiastic over the Eritrea, Ethiopia, Somalia axis, and he underlined this in his visit to Mogadishu in December 2018, described as "part and parcel of the consultative Tripartite Summits of the Heads of State and Government of Eritrea, Ethiopia and Somalia." It was his fourth meeting with Farmaajo, and they agreed to build up trade and regional partnership for "common development, progress and prosperity." Isaias welcomed and supported the Somali government's efforts to establish Somali-led security institutions, and the two presidents agreed on the need for a "comprehensive and coordinated approach to tackle terrorism and poverty," speaking of forging a strong partnership.[38] They also agreed to work together to address the challenges they faced individually and collectively and underlined that effective regional cooperation was crucial for overcoming the common obstacles of insecurity, terrorism, poverty, and environmental degradation. Isaias included Foreign Minister Saleh and Presidential Adviser Yemane Gebreab in his delegation and a few months

---

38   There were reports in late 2019 that Somalia favored an even closer relationship and that Farmaajo had suggested that Eritrea might like to provide troops for Somalia after AMISOM leaves in 2021. If so, it would be the first time Eritrea has considered deploying its troops on a peacekeeping mission. Another possible source of troops might be Ethiopia, but that would be unpopular. The presidential election will be held in February 2021 and be preceded by a parliamentary election towards the end of 2020.

later sent them to encourage talks between Somaliland and Somalia. They made a three-day visit to Hargeisa in March 2019 and held talks with Bihi and then three weeks later made a working visit to Mogadishu for talks with Farmaajo. Somalia welcomed the effort, but prospects for successful talks between the two remain as small as ever.

It appears that the Eritrea, Ethiopia, Somalia axis is also trying to expand. In Washington for the World Bank/IMF annual meetings in October 2019, Somali Finance Minister Abdirahman Duale Beileh mentioned Somalia was working with Kenya, Eritrea, Ethiopia, and Djibouti on a five-year, $15 billion project backed by the European Union, the AfDB, and the World Bank to establish ports and transportation corridors and integrate infrastructure and energy networks. This also appears to relate back to Abiy's controversial statement in 2018 about Ethiopia helping to develop four ports in Somalia. Beileh suggested Somalia would get the lion's share of the funding and that it would be the biggest single investment in its history.

Isaias went from Somalia to Kenya to explore expanding bilateral relations and the potential opportunities of cooperation with President Kenyatta. They agreed to develop a partnership in trade, investment, and building peace and stability in the region. They also agreed to work jointly to lend support to the federal government of Somalia to promote peace and stability there and coordinate efforts for consolidation of the new positive climate ushered into the Horn of Africa. High on the agenda in both countries was the future of IGAD. Isaias immediately followed these visits with a visit to Abu Dhabi, where he had consultations with Sheikh Mohamed bin Zayed Al Nahya, crown prince of Abu Dhabi and deputy supreme commander of the UAE Armed Forces.

Isaias was also quick to resurrect Eritrean links with South Sudan, inviting President Kiir to Asmara in August 2018, referring to the distinct and special bond between the peoples of South Sudan and Eritrea that had been "nurtured through vigorous solidarity in a common struggle for justice and liberation; a colossal task that exacted precious sacrifices of heroes and heroines; the government and people of Eritrea are proud for their participation in this endeavour in a gesture of brotherly solidarity." President Isaias spoke of the "onerous struggle" for justice and liberation but added that the struggle and challenges of national building were far heavier. He said the people of South Sudan had "asserted their liberation through precious sacrifices, but due to external subversion and internal discord, they were embroiled in a relentless spiral of strife and crisis soon after independence as they embarked on the heavy task of national building. This is extremely distressing. As it happens the mission of liberation has yet to be fulfilled."

Nevertheless, he assured Kiir the people of Eritrea would stand, as ever, at their side, "until and beyond the achievement of the mission of liberation." Isaias also made a short, one-day, visit to Juba, along with Abiy in March 2019, when reference was made to another tripartite axis, this time of Eritrea, Ethiopia, and South Sudan.

Despite hopes in 2018 that the agreement with Ethiopia would lead to internal changes in Eritrea, nothing materialized, nor are they likely, as Isaias underlined in the speech at the twenty-sixth anniversary of independence in May 2019, which harked back to earlier thoughts on foreign policy. He spoke of the continued need for "reliance for higher progress," referring to the efforts to confront and vanquish the machinations of enemies to secure independence and sovereignty. But he also stressed that even after independence, the Eritrean people had faced relentless hostilities designed to subdue and weaken them while they embarked on reconstruction and rehabilitation. He said there were senseless border disputes, unwarranted sanctions, naked military attacks, economic subversion, human trafficking, psychological warfare, and demonization aimed to isolate Eritrea. "Thwarting all these wrongs would have been unimaginable without the resilience of the Eritrean people." Resilience, he said, had been driven by such values as: "not to yield to force and intimidation; not to surrender to machinations; not to compromise dignity and values for cheap inducements; not to be disheartened by overwhelming challenges; not to tire of hard work; not to spare toil and blood, including one's life; not to relent until objectives were achieved." And these were the defining characteristics of the heritage of the Eritrean people. In other words, although current events and realities might be "as the beginnings of a new era," this must not lead to any underestimating of the challenges of the new era. In this new era, the president insisted, "our cardinal objectives consist of creating and augmenting national wealth through hard work and efficient productivity and ensuring equitable distribution of resources and opportunities." In fact, he appeared to be offering nothing more than a bleak, hard-working and dangerous future with little more than promises to show for twenty-six years of continuous struggle.

There have been no indications of any internal Eritrean developments to bring its governance into line with other countries or indeed with Abiy's reforms in Ethiopia. From Isaias's perspective, there has been no need. For him, the agreement with Ethiopia meant the lifting of UN sanctions, which he had always labeled as illegal, and the refurbishing of his role as an international statesman, along with restoration of Eritrea's international position. The agreement certainly encouraged the sudden upsurge in Eritrean diplomatic activity, with Isaias, like Abiy, projecting himself as a regional mediator, with Saleh and Yemane shuttling around the region. In late March and early April 2019, for example, these two envoys visited six capitals in the space of two weeks, including Riyadh, Cairo, and Tokyo, as well as regional capitals. There were new deals in the mineral sector, notably for Dankalia potash, and financial deals with the AfDB. Eritrea was even elected to the UN Human Rights Council, much to the surprise and concern of most human rights organizations.

Although, as noted, Isaias did make some surprisingly effusive statements about Abiy: "You are our leader" and "I have given him all responsibility of leadership and power," relations appear to have cooled slightly. For a year after the agreement, the two leaders were meeting at least once a month but rather less frequently after mid-2019. It was noticeable that neither the Eritrean government nor Isaias issued any statement to congratulate Abiy on his Nobel Peace Prize. A revealing spin was put on the relationship by Yemane in April 2019, speaking privately to Eritreans in Riyadh. He said the agreement had been the result of the failed attempt to isolate Eritrea. It demonstrated that Eritrea had defeated the TPLF's Ethiopia, and it underlined Eritrea's military, economic, diplomatic, and psychological capacity. He said the present peace should not be considered final; it was necessary to work to make it last and this needed time and effort. Eritrea had opened up relations with Somalia to encourage regional integration, with Eritrea taking a leading role, not for bilateral reasons.

It is far from clear if either country considered either the internal or external ramifications of their rapprochement in advance. Certainly, Abiy doesn't seem to have considered the implications of the tripartite deal with Somalia or their different approaches to the Gulf or Yemen or the consequences for such bodies as IGAD or the African Union. IGAD is another area in which there has been no visible progress. Eritrea's failure to rejoin the organization remains a disappointment and a problem for any proposed change in the organization. Underlining the need to further expand ties with neighboring countries, Abiy has frequently referred to the close cross-cultural and intercultural linkages among all the peoples of the Horn of Africa. Ethiopia is an emblem of Pan-Africanism, a founder of the OAU, seat of the African Union, member of many important international organizations, and plays a notable role in regional, continental, and global issues. Abiy says the government will further reinforce and continue its relations withal "our African brothers." Very little of this appears to appeal to Eritrea under Isaias.

Integration

There's no doubting the reality of the momentum for discussion and peace in the region launched in July 2018 by the Ethiopia-Eritrea agreement. It provided a catalyst to encourage a spread of diplomatic activity: within a matter of weeks Eritrea, Ethiopia, and Somalia held a Trilateral Summit in Asmara, and their foreign ministers visited Djibouti, working to open a new phase in relations between Djibouti and Eritrea; Abiy and Isaias signed a further cooperation agreement in Jeddah; the presidents of Eritrea and Djibouti met; the South Sudanese parties signed the Revitalized Peace Agreement for South Sudan; UN sanctions on Eritrea were lifted. . . .

The agreement also influenced directly or indirectly other conflicts, opening up prospects and possibilities, some new, some certainly suggested earlier, but fitting into what was billed as the beginning of a major restructuring of foreign policy strategy not just for Ethiopia but for the region. Indeed, the Ethiopian-Eritrean peace deal can be likened to the breaking of a logjam in a river. The removal of the logs (including the intransigence of both parties), which obstructed a river of peace, regional diplomacy, and development, allowed a sudden flow of new possibilities to surge across the region, a flood of new ideas and possibilities previously unable to gain attention because of continued concentration on past stubbornness.

Abiy, displaying personal enthusiasm, energy, and vigor, brought major changes to Ethiopia's foreign policy in 2018, effectively resetting priorities. The rapprochement with Eritrea (despite Eritrea's failure to respond effectively), as well as bringing Eritrea back onto the regional stage, allowed Ethiopia further opportunities to play an active and constructive regional role. Abiy set up a committee to redraft Ethiopia's Foreign Policy and National Strategy Document and to (re)define Ethiopia's foreign policy priorities and goals. This was of particular importance to avoid continued ad hoc foreign policy initiatives, and to re-involve the foreign ministry's capacities and professionalism effectively in policy implementation. The committee was due to finalize its work in late 2019. In the meantime, Abiy continued to formulate foreign policy on a personal and fast-moving basis. As a result, questions were raised about his approach both to mediation and integration, underlining the need for "serious consultations and institutionalized efforts to build interstate trust and end historic animosities." More than short meetings between leaders, however charismatic they might be, are required to sustain peace processes.[39]

---

39 Mehari Taddele Maru, "Is Political Integration in the Horn of Africa possible?" Al Jazeera, 6 April 2019.

Abiy's diplomacy, receiving widespread praise, admiration, and positive media coverage both in the region and across the world, was given the final accolade of the Nobel Peace Prize for 2019. While this was appropriate in terms of Asmara and Khartoum, perhaps, his diplomacy has failed to produce practical results in a number of other areas. Unsurprisingly, diplomacy and a belief in *medemer*, however defined, have not proved sufficient to resolve issues. They may encourage dialogue and negotiation, but these also need the support of realistic and defined policies, structures, and actions.

Similarly, Abiy's often-expressed interest in regional integration, economic or political, may be an admirable concept and a worthwhile aim, but it faces a number of serious difficulties. These include distrust between and indeed within states; long-term unresolved disputes, numerous border uncertainties and conflicts, and cross-border disagreements over resources; the region has millions of refugees and internally displaced people; there are four peace missions currently in operation: UNAMID in Darfur; UNISFA on the Sudan-South Sudan border; UNMISS in South Sudan, and AMISOM in Somalia, incorporating a total of over fifty thousand UN and AU peacekeeping troops; there are ongoing border disputes between South Sudan and Sudan over Abyei and between Eritrea and Ethiopia (ostensibly settled but still unimplemented) as well as border problems between Ethiopia and Sudan, Ethiopia and Kenya, Ethiopia and Somalia, Kenya and Somalia, and Kenya and Uganda. A related issue are the ethnic and/or clan disputes to be found within the federal states of Ethiopia, Somalia, Sudan, and South Sudan, driving internal border disputes between subnational units. Foreign interests are still taking different sides in various internal problems, as in Somalia, where the efforts of Qatar and the UAE have certainly encouraged the disputes between the federal government and federal member states. In Sudan, where outside powers certainly made their interests known, neighbours also had different views on the possible government to succeed al-Bashir.

Issues affecting the region also spill outside the IGAD region, as with the Grand Ethiopian Renaissance Dam (GERD), which has significant implications for IGAD as well as the Nile basin. While tripartite talks between Egypt, Ethiopia, and Sudan have continued intermittently, Egypt has also been involved in a concerted effort to improve its diplomatic relations with Nile basin states, cultivating a close relationship with Uganda and South Sudan, supporting its request to join the Arab League and offering troops for the Rapid Deployment Force in Juba. In October, Egypt, arguing that GERD negotiations had reached a deadlock, called upon the United States to play an active mediating role to overcome the impasse. Ethiopia, while seeing this as "an unwarranted denial of the progress of negotiations," was prepared to participate in any discussions to resolve the problem. It had hoped Ethiopia, Egypt, and Sudan could resolve the dispute by themselves. Egyptian President El-Sisi and Abiy met at the Russia-Africa Forum in Sochi in October, and they agreed "to resume talks." As long as talks are confined to technicalities, it will be possible to reach an agreement. If Egypt tries to insist on the quotas under the earlier colonial era agreements that Ethiopia refuses to accept, then the most Ethiopia offers will certainly be less than anything Egypt can accept; agreement will become extremely difficult whether or not both sides accept the 2015 Declaration of Principles.

Another long-term trend IGAD must take into consideration is the international competition for influence in the Horn of Africa and Red Sea, particularly now that the two must be seen as inseparable, making up a single geopolitical area. At one level, this involves issues outside the control or competence of IGAD, including the necessity for a de-escalation of tensions with Iran, resolution of the Middle Eastern struggle for hegemony between Saudi Arabia and Iran, or the rivalry between Gulf States. However, even if Qatar and the UAE patch up their current dispute, they will remain rivals for access in the Horn to minerals, energy, control of ports and trade, land, and food. Parallel to this are the long-term geopolitical interests of China and the United States in the Red Sea. Given the continuing regional conflicts and political uncertainties, there remains a real possibility of increased tension and potential conflict. The region remains highly vulnerable, as events in 2019 in Sudan, South Sudan, and Yemen have demonstrated. It is no coincidence that both the United Nations and United Kingdom appointed special envoys for the Horn of Africa and Red Sea in 2019, as did IGAD.

IGAD is, of course, an institution that could provide the basis for integration, but its recent history underlines the difficulties that attend even the most minimal levels of cooperative activity. At a very basic level, progress in IGAD requires some minimal agreement among member states, their aims, interests, and ambitions. Disagreements over the holding of positions within IGAD do not augur well. Kenya has held the position of executive secretary since 2008; Ethiopia has been chair for the same period. Djibouti has complained this has allowed Ethiopia and Kenya to direct decisions; Eritrea, which walked out in 2007, would agree. The last ordinary IGAD summit to discuss appointments was in June 2008. Since then all summits have been extraordinary meetings that cannot discuss appointments or indeed the return of member states that have withdrawn. Both Djibouti and Somalia would like to see some changes, but the planned switch between Ethiopia's and Kenya's monopoly of the top positions in 2019 hardly qualified as real change. Abiy said after he took office in 2018 that he would hand over the chair, but he was slow to take any action. By September 2019, there were indications that Ethiopia would give Kenya the chair, while taking the position of executive secretary currently held by a Kenyan. Kenya originally indicated it would support a Djiboutian for executive secretary until the two countries fell out over the refusal of Djibouti to withdraw its application for a nonpermanent Security Council seat. Djibouti was still lobbying strongly at the Non-Aligned Summit in Azerbaijan in October 2019, despite the AU endorsement of Kenya's bid. Somalia, also at odds with Kenya, would like to see a Somali holding one of IGAD's senior positions.

These disagreements have meant IGAD has not been as effective as it might have been in pushing for the implementation of the September 2018 South Sudan peace agreement, its most recent, and substantial peace effort. It has been closely involved in South Sudan since the outbreak of civil war between President Kiir and Riek Machar in December 2013 and responsible for various peace efforts, providing the driving force behind the signing of the Revitalized Agreement for the Resolution of the Conflict in South Sudan (R-ARCSS) in September 2018. Abiy, as chair of IGAD, held talks with Kiir and Machar in June 2018 but then turned the peace process over to Sudan, which oversaw the agreement in September 2018 under which the two sides decided to set up a Transitional Government of National Unity. Throughout the entire ARCSS process, there have been concerns with the way the interests of member states, particularly Ethiopia, Uganda, Kenya, and Sudan have affected its role. There were claims that "South Sudan is on its way to becoming an informal protectorate of Sudan and Uganda. By formally acknowledging them as guarantors, the agreement recognized their strategic role in determining the future of South Sudan: Ugandan troops are physically present to support Kiir's faction, and Sudan provides critical support to opposition groups, including those led by Machar."[40]

Although the United Nations, African Union, European Union, the Troika, and IGAD are all convinced of the need to press ahead with the formation of the transitional government, due on November 12, 2019, several critical pre-transitional tasks were outstanding: security arrangements, the number and boundary of states, the allocation of ministerial portfolios, and some non-signatories to the agreement. For IGAD, South Sudan remains unfinished business, difficult to fit into any integration scenario despite its membership of the organization.

A starting point for regional integration must be the revitalization and reorganization of IGAD, allowing it to break away from a decade of Ethiopian

---

40 Professor Mahmood Mamdani writing in the New York Times, quoted in whispereye. com, 3 October 2018.

chairmanship and produce a realistic regional security architecture. It needs to be based on a foundation of serious discussion and careful consideration and followed by the creation of a framework of institutionalized structure to create trust and end disputes. It is, by definition, a lengthy process; it cannot result from brief summits and bilateral or trilateral agreements, even if they involve a shared vision and shared interests. Integration needs investment in infrastructure, cross-border economic developments, and ways to deal with ethnic conflict, poor governance, unresolved borders, and resource deficits. It needs to be able to respond to differences in national and regional interests and their peculiarities. It needs an organization properly supported by its member states and to which those states in turn are prepared to give up some of their functions.

Any process of economic integration, for example, requires different levels of commitment from member states, working through several stages, beginning with a free trade area, a customs union, a common market followed by economic union, and culminating in total economic integration involving the creation of an independent authority whose decisions are binding on member states. Indeed, once the stage of a customs union is reached there is a need for joint institutions to negotiate and administer agreed policies. Subsequent developments need considerably more negotiations and agreements on any limits for national sovereignty. Within IGAD there has been little or no indication of any interest in allowing any authority to be delegated to the organization. Given the current insistence, shared by Ethiopia as well as within the region, that states should retain total control of the processes, it is difficult to see how IGAD is going to make any change towards realistic economic integration in the near future.

The question of a revitalized IGAD also raises the issue of membership. IGAD currently involves Ethiopia, Sudan, South Sudan, Djibouti, Somalia, Kenya, and Uganda, with Eritrea a lapsed member. IGAD welcomed Eritrea's increased regional engagement after July 2018, but Eritrea indicated it would like to see major, if largely undefined, demands for change in the organization before it re-joined. Isaias has shown little interest in any realistic regional integration, but further consolidation or even regional stabilization requires active Eritrean membership. The question of which other countries might consider joining a revitalized regional body is also of some interest. Several IGAD members belong to the East African Community, and there have been discussions on the possibility of merging IGAD and the EAC in keeping with greater economic integration, as designated by the Abuja Treaty. Other possibilities for expansion might include the members of the Nile Basin Initiative or the Northern Corridor as well as states on the Red Sea littoral. An appropriate first step in this direction for a Nobel Peace

Prize winner might be the creation of a regional forum to address economic, peace, and security issues for states on both sides of the Red Sea.

National interests all too often remain mutually incompatible, whether in the region or more widely. The aims and interests of leaders are as frequently irreconcilable. A critical component is the creation of institutional and financial structures to support the lengthy processes necessary to develop common interests. This needs more than assertions of intent. It needs serious cross-border development to build socioeconomic links sufficiently strong to break down existing interests, suspicions, and conflicts. Then, and only then, will it be possible to make any realistic progress towards political integration. Equally, without real progress, the increasingly militarized and crowded Horn of Africa/Red Sea will remain a dangerously fragile geopolitical and strategic region, a potential battleground for influence between regional and global powers in an increasingly fragile multipolar world. Time is running out.

7

ETHIOPIA AND ERITREA
Making Sense of the "Deal"

Medhane Tadesse

Introduction: Imagining a Peace Deal on the Edge of Global and Local Politics.

The recent deal between the leaders of Eritrea and Ethiopia has been celebrated as a success by the international, mainly Western, media so much so that it served as the largest input for conferring the Nobel Peace Prize to Prime Minister Abiy Ahmed of Ethiopia. No doubt, Abiy played the most important role in the making of the deal, and his character and extraordinary speed have also been central to the rising appeal to peace between the two countries, cultivating closer relations with the Eritrean president and giving further impetus and an extended ridge to the peace gambit. Political and military conflicts between Eritrea and Ethiopia have scarred the citizens of both countries and have proved equally costly in terms of lives lost, economic development foregone, never-ending instability, and wider destabilization of the sub-region.[1] Arguably a peace deal between Ethiopia and Eritrea promises to transform not just the two countries but also the prospects for the entire region.

---

1   MedhaneTadesse. "Intergenerational Dialogue on Ethiopia-Eritrea Relations." Proposal for Academic Dialogue between Ethiopia and Eritrea, October 2017.

Are we now seeing a change in relations between the two countries? Should we expect closer contacts beyond the two leaders? And, is the deal bringing something new? On the one hand, it is clear that the deal represents a new development. It has the potential to de-escalate decades-long tensions and, beyond that, provide an entry point for peace building. In addition, the continued relationship between the two leaders could have the inevitable effect of further accentuating the need to do more at the level of government-to-government relations with a potential for amultiplier effect on other stakeholders. This might look very speculative, but the possibilities are out there,though this very much depends on the readiness of the signatories to give meaningful peace a chance. The recent deal, on the other hand, is intimately connected to a global geopolitical shift; hence, it cannot be understood without recognizing the intertwined relationships between local politics, power relations at the center, and regional dynamics. Equally important is that the relevance of each of these dimensions needs to be carefully examined to evaluate the likelihood of success or failure.

We often isolate processes as discrete entities with clear boundaries while we relegate the outcome to sheer luck or the absence of institutional and policy mechanisms. To date, outsider analysis has had little to say about contemporary competitive local politics in the deal, while existing commentaries by domestic observers have tended to overlook its geopolitical dimensions. Often, as is the case with this deal, the most important ones are less visible. On close examination, many of the more talked about issues of process and outcome are only tenuously linked to the necessities for peace. This is evident in the exclusionary nature of the deal and the emphasis placed on curbing the role of the most interested parties, and the paradox is that the involvement of the these actorscould becritical for the smooth implementation of the deal. A key implication of this is that the deal becomes more of a political agreement between two actors and a host of internationalplayers. Still,peace is being mentioned quite randomly and sporadically or designed and implemented and arguments are taking place based more on general norms and assumptions than on research findings or a basic understanding of what has been happening locally. This is partly the reason why open debateand national consultations have been discouraged, which in turn increases the propensity to consider the matter as being outside of public domain, effectively suppressing the need to learn from the experiences of past failures.

In this context, the call for such a paper represents an important step forward and potentially provides the basis to shift the debate to broader political and regional issues requiring a thorough political economy analysis, by extension a nuanced recognition of the multidimensional nature of the deal.How this might be related to the ongoing political turmoil in Ethiopia and the budding alliance of political forces in the last year and half requires particular attention. Most of these have been of an ideological character, often related to contestations over the constitution, claims about whether ethnicity continues to be the basis for political organization, the desecration of the multiethnic federation and the developmental state, and conflicts related to land and resources among the regions and between the center and its federal units.

The deal is, at the same time, a reflection of the broader global trend away from the normative framework and the evolving impact on Africa's international relations in general and the agility of Africa's regional security organizations in particular, which in itself is not totally delinked from the swings in Ethiopia's political landscape over the last several months.A full understanding of the origin, current status, and prospect of the deal can thus only be achieved through an examination of these intertwined dynamics. Therefore, this paper attempts to treat with equal facility economics, geopolitics, and security, along with enough history for needed background, official thinking, and public attitudes. Hence, the paper will interrogate what can be described as the *three pieces of the peace deal*: global, regional, and national.

***

The analysis is based on close follow-up of the subject for over two decades, association to global security debates and processes, and on a recently much-publicized role the author had on thedevelopment of people-to-people relations between Ethiopia and Eritrea.[2]A close examination of international engagement in the deal in general, and in particular those undertaken by Gulf countries, leads us to describe it as "top down, externally and supply driven, and elitist."[3]While it cannot be described as a peace between two countries—let alone theirrespective peoples—the conclusion that the deal typically marginalizes critically aggrieved parties, gives short shrift to the

---

2   I happen to lead the academic dialogue on people-to-people relations between the two countries and developed the concept notes for it and a similar initiative by Ethiopian artists. The debates can claim with justifiable pride to helping put peace between the two countries on the regional agenda, including the follow-up decisions of the EPPRDF to make a peace overture to Eritrea, beginning with several workshops that resulted in extensive media coverage in late 2017 and early 2018.

3   This argument very much coincides with Working Paper #7 by IDR on What Kind of Peace is Being Built? Reflections on the State of Peace building Ten Years after the Agenda for Peace..

concerns of people along the border, projects a narrow conception of peace, and is designed to contain and suppress a common adversary rather than give due attention to the underlying causes of the conflict, characterizes the deal the leaders of Eritrea and Ethiopia have delivered up to the people of both countries. To the extent that it leads to face-to-face talks between the leaders of two formerly hostile countries, it is characterized as a peace agreement, but in practice it ignores and even complicates the search for durable peace and stability in the region. And neither during the series of ceremonies in the Asmara, Abu Dhabi, and Riyadh Agreements, nor in the subsequent period, have the peace mediators or the signatories given their full attention to the root causes of the conflict.

Thus, this analysis will follow in assuming that "peace is more than an interludeto a hostile posture, and more than simple political accord. Peace is the taking of visible steps to implement its terms on a long-term basis which entails addressing factors and forces that stand as impediments to its realization, and likewise failure could be defined as the opposite— ranging from digression from the terms of the agreement to emphatic noncompliance by the signatory parties."[4] Hence, success entails the presence of several factors, and two critical issues figure prominently: inclusiveness and addressing structural causes.[5]Indeed, not only is the deal not meeting the minimum standards laid down in theories of peace, but in the case of Ethiopia it may not be even meeting the notions of promoting national security. And as far as Eritrea is concerned, it tends to solidify, if not embolden, the statusquo that has been the cause of crisis at home and instability abroad.

This analysis begins by uncovering the lack of importance given to the requirements for real peace, such as dealing with the causes of the conflict and the ever-pivotal participation of relevant stakeholders. It also reveals the weaknesses related to transparency and popular participation in the process. The excluded even included key players on the ground. This is compounded by the lack of attention given to the opening of a new chapter, permissive political climate, and demilitarization in Eritrea.

---

4   Grace Maina and Erik Melander, *Peace Agreements and Durable Peace in Africa*(Pietermaritzburg, SA: University of KwaZulu-Natal Press, 2016).

5   .I have deliberated on this subject for many years.See Medhane Tadesse, "Towards a Framework of Conflict Resolution Best Practices in the Horn of Africa." *Towards Conflict Resolution Best Practices: Report of the 2008 Tswalu Dialogue.* The Royal United Services Institute, May 2008; Medhane Tadesse, "UN Peacekeeping in the Horn of Africa,"in*From Global Apartheid to Global Village: Africa and the United Nations*(Pietermaritzburg, SA: University of KwaZulu-Natal Press, 2009).

The marking of the deal would appear to confirm the validity of the political and geopolitical agendas behind it than the prospect of giving peace a chance. And it will be argued here that the peculiar nature of the deal and its failure to improve, let alone transform, the relationships between the two countries and their peoples seriously undermines the objective of a viable peace. In addition, the opaque nature of external influence and foreign dominance of the deal will be examined, and it will be seen that this engagement has served to encourage the exclusionarythrust of the peace process and the scant attention given to the resolution of the problems on the ground[6]and places the interests of ordinary Eritreans and Ethiopians secondary to those of the geopolitical advances of foreign powers, and the individual self-interest and beliefs of national leaders.

Against this record of skepticism, there would appear to be a pressing need to seriously reappraise the deal, particularly external engagement and its geopolitical considerations, as well as assess domestic political undertones, but this is not happening. Indeed, virtually none of the main global and regional players are demonstrating any signs of introspection and at best are trying to offer a positive vibe aboutthe deal. This paper will first outline the major drivers behind the deal; second, on the basis of this analysis it will offer a critique of external, and in particular, Gulf engagement; third, it will focus on the political underpinnings—which are the main failures—of the deal, where there is an absence of even negative peace; and lastly, it will provide some concluding thoughts. Since these objectives are very ambitious and the time available to prepare this paper was limited, the result will be far from comprehensive. The author, however, will conclude that this effort has not completely failed if it is able to provide a framework of analysis and put across hard questions to stimulate broader debate.

The Precursor

The Eritrean Factor

By way of background, suffice it to say that several attempts have been made to resolve the crisis in the lead-up to the unfortunate war and its aftermath. Fast forward to 2018 the readiness of the ruling EPRDF to accept the Algiers Agreement without preconditions presented the first real opportunity for the possibility of talks. However, it was the extraordinary willingness and enthusiasm of Abiy that played the most critical role in bringing about

---

6   This aspect is also detailed in Medhane Tadesse, "Peace Agreements in the Horn of Africa: An Appraisal of the Literature,"Issue Paper. Interafrica Group, June 2010.

the compromise between the leaders of the two countries. Expressing his gratitude for the PM's olive branch, Isaias reciprocated positively, reiterating that Ethiopia and Eritrea share lots of commonalities that run the gamut from culture and languages to politics and the economy. Almost immediately an Eritrean delegation traveled to Addis Ababa for two days of sensitive talks with the new Ethiopian prime minister, among them the second-highest-ranking official in the PFDJ in an effort to determine if the Ethiopian leadership was serious about its newly proclaimed peace initiative.[7]

It is more than mere happenstance that the Eritrean leader decided to engage at the time he did. In recent years the TPLF-led EPRDF has been making several overtures, which have been consistently rebuffed by Asmara. The official explanation has always been that Eritrea will not engage in talks before Ethiopia evacuates from the areas awarded to it by the Boundary Commission.[8] For almost two decades, the Eritrean government used the threat this presented to the sovereignty of Eritrea to justify invasive but also outward-looking policies. When the deal was struck in 2018, there was thereforemuch optimism that change may be coming. Yet a year on, those hopes have been dashed and the border has re-closed, leading many to assume there must be something mysterious about this conflict. Soon after the end of the war I arguedthat the conflict has turned into "perhaps the greatest blood feud of regional politics,"[9] maybe a reflection of how Isaias learned to live with the misfortunes of the last war and its aftermath as much as it is a lack of understanding of where the true national interests of Eritrea lie vis-à-vis Ethiopia.

While not doubting that many genuinely believed the TPLF has always been supportive of Eritrean independence, without which the recognition of Eritrea as an independent country will not have been foreseen—or at least it could have been a protracted and messy affair similar to that of Somaliland—most particularly pro-regime Eritreans did not, and hence there is reason for approaching the real attitudes of Isaias towards the TPLF and Tigray

---

7   Aaron Maasho, "Eritrea Welcomes Ethiopia's Olive Branch, Raising Hopes of Breakthrough,"*Reuters*, June 19, 2018. It is not accidental that Yemane Gebreab is widely considered as the most influential next to Isaias, partly because he is in charge of Ethiopian affairs and handled the anti-EPRDF file. It is not totally out of context, therefore, to assume that the main objective of the visit was to determine if the new leadership in Addis Ababa could be trusted.

8   Decision of the EEBC, October 2012.

9   MedhaneTadesse, "On the Feud Between Eritrea and Ethiopia","The Current Analyst, July 2010. https://medium.com/@currentanalyst/on-the-feud-between-eritrea-and-ethiopia-ae065d37b77b?source=your_stories_page

that I will pick up later. From a close assessment of the political economy of post-independent Eritrea, it appears thatthis never-ending rancor has less to do with the TPLF becoming an obstacle to good relations than with reversing the PFDJs game of involvement in Ethiopia by proving that the Eritrean leadership can be confronted and defeated, hence weakened.As a deployment of hard and soft power to squeeze and constrain an adversary, the tactic was very effective but contributed to the longevity of the grudge.

It is thus less ironic that the narrative and the whole trajectory of the new state as envisaged by its leaders has been debased by the TPLF, which mainly explains why the leadership in Asmara finds it easy to portray the group and its leadership as a permanent enemy of Eritrea and cannot be considered as partner for peace. The fact that the PFDJ will not be inclined to enter into negotiations with a TPLF-dominated Ethiopia but had to quickly drop all sorts of pretexts to enter into discussions with Abiy is thus more than just an excuse or an umbrella of semanticsand is linked to the historicity of the conflict, the political economy underpinning it,and how this has played out in the last decade or so.Another reasonnot to engage has been the charge that the international community, particularly the United States, is behind the trouble, by extension the isolation of Eritrea. The United States has probably been the second in the list of "axis of enemies"[10]to Eritrea: TPLF-United States-IGAD-African Union, in that order, and the new security environment hasaltered that, which will be discussed later.

The call for dialogue only made headway whenregime change in Addis Ababa ledthe Eritrean leader to assume that the new developing situation will undoubtedly improve his lot at home and recover his regional standing. The fact that the precondition of "withdrawal from Eritrean lands first" was quickly dropped showed the issue was less about land and Eritrean sovereignty and more about the nature of the group in power in Addis and its import to the relationship between the two.Similarly, the fact that this time around US engagement was not invoked as inimical to peace tells a lot about the recent geopolitical shift or probably loosening of the rope. Both inside Ethiopia and the region, several things must have happened that helped convince Asmara that there will be zero risk to its policy at home and abroad if and when it engages in a course akin to a peace process. Thus it should be clear that the rapprochement became easier and deal making became possible in part because of a series of developments in global, regional, and national politics that preceded it.

---

10 This has been the dominant theme of the official media in Eritrea since 2000, and almost all speeches by Isaias marking the New Year and Martyrs' Day emphasized the point that the TPLF, with the help of the US, were bent on undermining Eritrea.

Besides, the Eritrean leadership seems to have concluded that it can strike a deal with Ethiopia and come out of isolation without paying a price for it in political terms. Unlike other processes in which the international community attaches issues such as good governance, demilitarization, human rights, or elections as useful variables,a process sanctioned and financed by Gulf monarchies will not include normative principles abhorred by the Eritrean president. This approach was made easier by the absence of Western, global, and African regional organizations from the whole show. The only way to guarantee peace with Ethiopia without conceding anything on the domestic political front is through the Gulf monarchies, who themselves show a disregard for democracy and elections. It would appear that the mediators, reportedly at the request of Isaias, feared including normative principles such as reform would unduly complicate the deal, and with the request of the Eritrean president reached an understanding to largely avoid the subject.[11]Besides, unlike the open documents of other peace processes led by regional and international organizations, the one led by Gulf countries will ensure secrecy of the contents. This largely follows the pattern of behavior of the Eritrean government in which all previous agreements it has been a party to such as the deal with Djibouti or the peace agreement in eastern Sudan have been inherently secretive and exclusionary.And experience has largely reinforced this assessment, and underpinned Eritrean attitudes and approaches to negotiations.[12]

The background to the recent deal therefore lies in two pivotal events: the geopolitical shift that helped Gulf powers assert policies in the Horn and the political change in Ethiopia that provided an opportunity to external players and by extension the decision of Isaias to engage with Ethiopian political and security affairs from a new standing. This is very much linked to the historicity of relations and deep hostility with the TPLF. Clearly, real peace with Eritrea requiressome form of engagement with the TPLF and Tigray, the most interested and vital party to any serious deal. Not only

---

11 These are like bottom-line positions for the Eritrean president to achieve some progress in any deal, such as on migration with the EU or Qatar-led peace with Djibouti, and particularly the two Gulf powersthe KSA and UAE have proved to be highly sensitive to these objectives.

12 John Young, "Eastern Sudan: Local Conflict, Marginalization and the Threat to Regional Security,"Policy Paper, CPRD/ISS, 2007. All deals with other neighbors followed the same pattern. For more details on the Djibouti aspect, one can also refer to Medhane Tadesse, "The Djibouti-Eritrea Conflict," Briefing,IAG, March 2008 and "Change and Continuity in the Djiboutian Foreign Policy Making Process," in *Globalization and Emerging Trends in African Foreign Policy. Volume II. (University Press of America. 2007).*

did that not happen, but instead Abiy and Isaiaschose to marginalize it and fight some of what they consider as the remnants of the group around the region, such as in Somalia, many of whom remained friends for many years on issues they thought were shared interests between them and Ethiopian national security.[13] Indeed,the emerging alliance of the two leaders with Mogadishu began to antagonize former friends, such as Kenya and Djibouti, but it also sort of trappedIGAD as an organization in which most of the regional resources of soft power of Ethiopia reside, and weakening a regional bargaining power at the time of aggressive expansion by Arab States into the region. The underlying motives of President Isaias are crystal clear as he had understandable complaints on IGAD but what Abiy will get out of this is yet to be discovered, particularly because Ethiopian foreign policy makes little sense without IGAD and the African Union.[14]

External Engagement: The Priority ofGeopolitics.

For any keen observer on geopolitics there was a series of events since around 2015. The first is a slight change in the European Union's normative actorness. The second refers to the competition in the Middle East, particularly the inter-Sunni rivalry and its possible spillover to the Horn. This will be augmented by the dispute within the Gulf centered on Qatar. And thirdly, the broader geopolitical shift in which the United States short-shrifted the War on Terror with superpower competition.Thus, this section will be devoted to looking at the nature of global geopolitical waves, their impact on the Middle East and the Greater Horn, and their import to the impending deal between the leaders of Ethiopia and Eritrea.The new global system is producing a reordering of priorities and, in some instances, a redefinition of national interests throughout the region. These have included some early signs that the war on terror loses its primacy to great power rivalry as the top US global security agenda, but it has also the European Union backpedaling on its normative commitments, privileging its own security,

---

13 Both made a tour mockingly implying the previous government in Addis Ababa was the source of instability in the region and should expect different, hence an opening for a new peace in the Horn. Compounding this was the tripartite alliance system created between Abiy, Isaias, and Farmaajo, which not only created chaos on Ethiopia's regional policy but also the collective security principles of IGAD and the common defense and security treaties Ethiopia has entered over the years.

14 .This is discussed in detail by other publications of the author, such as"Making Sense of Ethiopian Regional Influence" in *Understanding Contemporary Ethiopia: Monarchy, Revolution and the Legacy of MelesZenawi*, ed. Gérard Prunier and Éloi Ficquet(London: Hurst, 2015), 333–56.

neighborhood, and hard power over democratization.[15]Before 2016, security engagement was more normative, based on what ought to be. In recent years, it has become more strategic and pragmatic, based on what exists.

The starting point for the eventual coming out of the cold for Eritrea was the shift in European security thinking, which involved a critical trade-off between democracy, human rights, and development and a security deal to fend off migration to Europe.[16]The new mission goals of strengthening the internal security forces' capacity in the fight against terrorism and organized crime, support for managing migration flows, and border management reflected a privileging of EU security interests,[17]which is at odds with the liberal norms and madethe process of isolating Eritrea much easier.[18]While ignoring Western values of democracy and human rights as a foreign policy tool has never been officially justified, informally the rational has alternatively been first that immediate security concerns take precedence mainly due to pressure from populist parties and second that the European Union moves to define its overall approach to security and foreign affairsbased on "principled pragmatism."[19] To the extent that the European Union's goal ishumane, it sort of assumes pragmatic engagement with Asmara—by extension

---

15 S. Biscop, 'The EU Global Strategy: Realpolitik with European Characteristics' in Might and Right in World Politics, International Security: a European – South American Dialogue 2016, Konrad-Adenauer-Stiftung, Rio de Janeiro (2016) attests to the changing paradigm.

16 The so-called Rabat and Khartoum processes were designed to lure all types of regimes in Africa cooperate on blocking the flow of migrants to Europe, which has become the principal concern of the EU since 2015.

17 Use of the EU's new Partnership Framework with Third Countries (EC, 2016) is an alarming development where pragmatism is looming larger over the normative in EU policy and practice. This framework is also currently used to strike one-on-one deals with a number of rough regimes, such as in Ethiopia, Turkey, Sudan, and Libya to address the EU migration crisis. Although the EU has been able to significantly reduce the number of migrants arriving at their borders, the deal has come under heavy criticism for sacrificing international norms and principles in achieving these results.

18 A major aspect of this was the tendency to short-shrift human security issues such as governance and security sector reform in the training and equipping of African security forces. The author attended the EU-wide Strategic Framework for Security Sector Reform: Consultation workshop with civil society organizations in Brussels, December 4, 2015.

19 "Shared Vision, Common Action: A Stronger Europe—A Global Strategy for the European Union's Foreign and Security Policy"(Brussels 2016).EU External Action Service (EEAS GSFSP).

accommodating Isaias's totalitarian impulses—will lead to improvement in the daily lives of the masses and stem the outflow of refugees to Europe. The lack of capacity or willingnesson the part of the West and lately the leadership in Addis Ababa to comprehend the true nature of the regime in Eritrea is incomprehensible, and it goes without saying that there is little sign of opening up or genuine relaxation of government policies of any kind.

A major contributing factor is, however, the impending global crisis in the normative framework, which allowed the European Union to turn a blind eye to human security issuesand Middle Eastern countries to take advantage of the situation and pursue unrestrained expansionist agendas in the Horn of Africa.[20] As modern security threats come into sharper focus on the international community's agenda along with defections from the Western camp, the return of realpolitik, and the realist security dilemma in international politics, the propensity towards a unilateral and transactional foreign policy has only increased.This is partly related to what can be described as the end of international liberalism, which had necessarily lost neither its applicability nor even its appeal, but by 2016 there was no longer much political will behind it. This is also manifest in the election of Donald Trump and the proliferation of right-wing parties in Europe.The striking geopolitical reality of the past decade has been the parallel growth of nationalism and globalization. Since superpower competition took center stage in US foreign and security policy, everything became subservient to tactical geopolitical gains.[21]

The peace process must have been viewed as the best geopolitical weapon by the United States to alteror slow down Chinese expansion into the Horn, and Africa in general, mainly at the time of the increasing importance of the Red Sea in the global volume of trade, now worth $600 billion, and the proximity of the Horn, which is less than ninety kilometers away from landlocked Ethiopia.[22] However, Western attention cannot be conceived

---

20 On June 20, 2016, I made a presentation to the joint CivCom and CODEV Committees of the European Union on the practicalities of Capacity Building for Security and Development (CBSD) or Train and Equip in Africa, an informal discussion organized by and held at the headquarters of the Netherlands EU Presidency.The author has attended most of the policy discussions in Brussels and Amsterdam. Indeed, he presented the African view challenging the tendency of the European Union to adopt Train and Equip as new SSR when the Netherlands EU Presidency organized an exclusive policy deliberation on the subject.

21 Maria Danilova and Cara Anna,"Trump's New Africa Strategy Takes Sharp Aim at China, Russia,"Associated Press, December 13, 2018.

22 Alex de Waal, "Beyond the Red Sea: A New Driving Force in the Politics of the Horn,"*African Arguments*, July 11, 2018.

without the Belt and Road policy of Beijing. While One Belt, One Road (OBOR), first proposed in late 2013, provides new opportunities for African countries, many also raise concerns it expands the arc of Chinese influence and counters the anti-Chinese measures of the United States.[23]The emergence of China as the dominant economic actor in the Horn, its closer relations with Ethiopia, and massive investments in Djibouti (with which the United Arab Emirates had entered into a spat due to port services),have long been considered a threat by both Washington and its Gulf allies. This is not only about economicsbut also geopolitics as, the case of Ethiopiaclearly shows, abating leftist-leaning governments and political forces with progressive agendas has become a major contemplation. Insofar as economic rivalry requires political alliances grappling with governments willing and able to exercise policy, sovereigntybecomes a major consideration.The image of the most successful social and economic transformation in Africa in recent years, Ethiopia's Grand Experiment, was already reverberating across the continent and has been willingly so devalued, even in the eyes of the national political elite, that it makes the exertions of Western interests far easier.

Apprehension reached its height in the wake of aggressive Chinese port expansion in Djibouti, the Doraleh terminal, and fast rail link with Ethiopia. Support for peace between Ethiopia and Eritrea seemed the best approach to try a geopolitical coup and alter the rise of Djibouti as the main transshipment hub in the region by diverting the axis of Ethiopian trade to Eritrean ports.Convincing Ethiopia to abandon its antagonistic position towards Eritrea was the only way to bring the loner state,with which Gulf allies of the United States would like to cooperate on critical regional security matters, first the war in Yemen and second the encirclement of Qatar,out of the cold. Reshuffling alliances was therefore considered the best guarantee for both the United States and its friends in the region, providing a sense of security for US foreign service and military to reenter a territory they had unceremoniously been forced to leave two decades earlier and gain the PFDJ the international legitimacy that would justify US congressional support for the United Nations revoking its embargo against Eritrea. The first and most significant indication of a growing US interest in resolving the standoff between the two countries was the flurry of visits in early 2018 by top US diplomats to the region, including Eritrea.[24] The fact that this visit

---

23   Wenxian Zhang, Ilan Alon, and Christoph Lattemann, eds.,*China's Belt and Road Initiative: Changing the Rules of Globalization* (New York: Palgrave Macmillan, 2018).

24   "Yamamoto Heads to Djibouti after Rare Eritrea Visit,"*Africa Times*, April 23, 2018. Donald Yamamoto was busy touring the region, and reportedly there were several meetings between US diplomats and Ethiopian officials (mainly US ambassador

was made weeks after the election of a new prime minister in Ethiopia has led some to believe that there must have been close scrutiny by US diplomats on the political turmoil and elite rivalry within the Ethiopian ruling party.

While the change in the economic infrastructure of the region was central to the calculations of external players, Isaias's focus was almost exclusively on regime survival,and the result is that very quickly all hopes will be dashed. That, with the deal, bothnormal trade and economic relations, development, or regional integration could be achievedis a bad joke for anyone familiar with the politically, and above all demographically, restraining conditions in Eritrea.[25] Some would like to explain this failure as due to the inexperience of the new leadership in Ethiopia and its unambiguous speed to improve relations with the Eritrean leader—so much for the rehabilitating missions undertaken by Abiy—but this argument ignores the fact that foreign and security policies in the Horn are for the most part linked todomestic political considerations to which I will come back later.

However, it will be the Kingdom of Saudi Arabia (KSA) and UAE who provided the key external impetusto the making of the deal, but their motives for engagement have never been strictly confined to achieving a sustainable peace and even less to peace and stability in the region. Instead, they were a response to security and geopolitical interests, the search for allies and manpower for the war in Yemen, and the demographic underpinnings of the long game with Iran. One of the driving forces of international relations over the last several years has been a rivalry between Arab states.Particularly the UAEhas become more apprehensive about the continued primacy of its strategic assets, such as its ports and airlines, in its quest to create a Gulf hub, mainly due to recent developments in the port of Djibouti, which became glued to the Chinese OBOR initiative.[26]There is another factor at play. Checking the emergence of rival ports, probably co-opting them, in the region stretching from Libya to southern Somalia—not to mention the

---

to Ethiopia Mike Raynor and Prime Minister Hailemariam Desalegn), including EPRDF leaders sympathetic to the protests leading up to the election of Abiy as prime minister, which continued unabated and got closer each passing day. Short of endorsing the "evangelical state capture" argument, the analysis here gives credibility to the multidimensional dimensions of intimacy between the two.

25 It is interesting that this analysis about the peculiar nature of Eritrean political economy is increasingly shared by Eritreans who are close observers of the regime, if one reads the discussions in "Eritrea: Part II—Deciphering the Peace Accord between Eritrea and Ethiopia—an Interview with Yosief Ghebrehiwet," Asmarino. com, August 19, 2019is notable in this regard.

26 Asteris Huliaras and Sophia Kalantzakos, "The Gulf States and the Horn of Africa: A New Hinterland?"*Middle East Policy* 24, no. 4 (Winter 2017).

likelihood that Djibouti's elite may well reach their ambitions of becoming Africa's Dubai.

While their relations with the Horn have had a long history, the renewed focus on the area is of a far deeper and wider nature than ever before, mainly after the Arab Springand the Gulf States (especially the KSA and UAE) have increasingly widened their sphere of influence in the Horn of Africa, which also shows the political-ideological nature of the conflict.[27] A critical component of regional politics is thus the inter-Sunni rivalry between Saudi Arabia and the UAE on one side and Qatar and Turkey on the other in which the support provided by Qatar and Turkey to Muslim Brotherhood movements during and after the Arab Spring in the Greater Middle East and Horn of Africa has long remained a major source of anxiety to the royal families in Riyadh and Abu Dhabi. Most Gulf State diplomatic and military activity has had the effect of playing one African country against another, often with the promise of large amounts of money. As such, the year 2015, when the Eritrean president left Qatar and Iran and jumped into the Saudi camp, is critical.No doubt, the intervention in Yemen, launched by Saudi Arabia and its allies in 2015, has increasingly drawn in East African countries.

Today, their proactive role in this part of Africa extends beyond the cultivation and strengthening of commercial and investment ties to include important security aspects.This explains the reason why the two Gulf powers with clear interests in the deal between Ethiopia and Eritrea privilege short-term stability imposed by strong security states.And in this game, any regime, no matter how petty and monstrous, can find a protector. This paper will not aim to dwell on the questionsofwhether or not new spaces of geopolitical significance are emerging around access to ports, manpower, allies, or other resources and to what extent the Horn is a meaningful geopolitical construct and how that construct relates to other geopolitical constructs.[28]Rather, it is to emphasize that Middle Eastern powers felt compelled to adopt a more muscular posture abroad as US influence in their backyard has waned. And they don't seem fully obliged to fully cooperate with the United States or do

27 Medhane Tedasse, "Qatar and the Horn,"*The Current Analyst*, December 12, 2010,https://medium.com/the-current-analyst/qatar-and-the-horn-39010ab1777c. It was only after almost more than a decade that other pieces on the same subject started to appear at the regional and global levels.

28 There is much broader debate on this in "How Are Geopolitical Shifts Influencing Peace and Stability?"in *Understanding the Changing Planet: Strategic Directions for the Geographical Sciences* (Washington: National Academies Press, 2010), 91–96.

the bidding of the West. At best they will apply hedging as a tool. Between total defection and full cooperation, the Gulf powers are ready to project power freely. While the concept of hedging is not completely foreign to international relations (IR) theory, it has yet to be sufficiently developed.[29]

Devoid of normative values and principles, the ultrarealist foreign policy of the new US administration meansthe transactional and militarist approach to foreign policy is tolerated,[30] expediting a nineteenth-century type of rivalry in the Red Sea, partly because the power hierarchy has become destabilized. As US engagement in the region intensified, alteringEthiopia's economic trajectory, its contagion effect on the continent required slowly pulling Ethiopia into the US orbit, which can be seen in the swarming of the policy space of the country by US advisors in the months ahead.On the one hand, the strange coalitions now being formed underline the absurdity of trying to apply ideological criteria imported from the West to the countries of Africa. On the other, the détente seems, at least temporarily, to have stabilized ideological frontiers and reinforced within each satellite country the power of the national party leaders.The fact that the United States and the West quickly endorsed the deal suggests that broader ideological and geopolitical concerns, and not peacemaking endeavors, were also apparent in the international community's approach to the deal.

In practice, this meant that additional players could be tacked on to the process to provide the necessary legitimacy when they were no longer in a position to have any influence on the outcome of the deal. Major global players such as the United Nations were waiting for a green light from the aggrieved party, Ethiopia, to acquiesce to the lifting of UN sanctions.Indeed, the Eritrean leader explicitly stated that he bestows his Ethiopian counterpart the role of facilitating and empowering Eritrean foreign relations, a role Abiy happily played with astonishing enthusiasm.[31]It was a matter of time before Eritrea will be normalized in the face of Western, particularly US, policy makers,

---

29   Yoel Guzansky, "The Foreign-Policy Tools of Small Powers: Strategic Hedging in the Persian Gulf," *Middle East Policy Council* 22,no. 1(2018).

30   This has in fact been widely debated, both in media and academic circles, including Maurizio Geri,"The End of Pax Americana or a New Realignment?"*E-International Relations*, February 26, 2017.

31   This was stated during the celebrations in Addis Ababa, which both leaders attended; in fact, some argue that Isaias successfully lobbied Abiy to rehabilitate his regime among the society of nations and hopes to do the same to get an economic lifeline from outside, all without undergoing any reform, be it political or economic, on its side.

partly through the good offices of the two Gulf allies.[32]While sometimes not recognized as a critical component, the global erosion of principles, values, and norms was critical in Gulf State expansion to the Horn.

Common and collective security is being replaced by transactional, mercantilist, and (probably an extension of the neo-mercantilist policies across Asia) bilateral bargaining, signaling the beginning of the end of internationalism, or international liberalism. State security and military projection are being valued at the expense of poverty reduction, development, and human security. This is threatening the very foundation of the post-Cold War paradigm shift accompanying regional peace and security,including multilateralism, on which the conduct of foreign policy in Africa and Ethiopia is largely based.The problem is not limited to ideas but also approaches. Gulf, and even international, policy will obviously emphasize a case-by-case approach to the Horn, dealing with each specific country as a separate issue, and is happening at a time of great danger to the region, when a regional approach is sorely needed.It is against this background that the continued assault on IGAD as an organization needs to be understood. Both the secrecy surrounding the deal and its potential to empower Eritrea's regional engagement bringing back memories of Eritrean behavior in the 1990s is transposing internal rivalries in a fragile transition in Ethiopia.To the extent that Isaias became interested to engage with Ethiopia, he had to first bring with him newfound but resourceful allies from the Gulf and validate that a group other than the TPLF occupies power in Addis Ababa.

The Ethiopian Agency

As indicated earlier,Eritrea instantly dropped all preconditions when it became clear that TPLFites are not the occupants of the palace in Addis Ababa. In practice this meant the conflict had, at least in the views of the Eritrean leadership, less to do with border or territorial sovereignty and more to do with the nature of the political leadership in Ethiopia and its policies towards Eritrea. And this speaks to the political aspect of the dispute, which

---

32   Eritrea abandoned Qatar and joined the Saudi-led alliance thinking it would give it leverage financially and leeway to circumvent regional and international isolation. Some of us sensed this particular development and its potential for rapprochement between Eritrea and Ethiopia through the two Gulf allies with the blessing of the US. It was clear that the road to Washington, particularly during the Trump presidency, passed through Riyadh and Abu Dhabi. It was to prepare for this eventuality that some of us started the Ethiopia-Eritrea people-to-people dialogue to collate opinions of major stakeholders and inform the impending policy process before the actual time arrives.

in the case of Eritrea has led to investing more in anti-EPRDF media outlets and insurgency movements for more than a decade, and although the TPLF reciprocated by supporting Eritrean opposition movements, it didn't apply a relentless media war comparable tothat of the PFDJ.[33]Thus it seems clear that the Eritrean government worked hard, and often claims exclusive responsibility, to undermine the EPRDF-led government in Ethiopia.[34]By now it should come as no surprise that this adds new complications to the controversies surrounding the character of the Ethiopian agency in the post-2018 political dispensation.

The question of who is the most important force behind the recent change within the EPRDF has been a very live one for the last year and a half, at least, in the political discourse, and, given the attempt by Eritrea to get the lion's share, it is a question that will have important implications for the course of the political transition and peace and stability of the country.Indeed, there has been remarkably little effort at covering up the specific political nature of the argument, as the driving motto of continued Eritrean engagement in talks with Abiy has been the infamous "Game Over, TPLF," epithet, an adage never contested by the new leadership in Ethiopia presumably because once they accepted the saying, the logic became one of ensuring its relevance. This effectively put Abiy in the curious position of fulfilling the needs of his Eritrean counterpart and sidelining the TPLF from the talks. But the domestic political dimensions do not stop there; it also includesother Ethiopian political forces. All Ethiopian opposition and armed groups parachuted from Eritrea call for unity and democratic transition in their own ways, but they seem to be doing little or nothing about their policy towards Eritrea. If experience is any guide, security agreements relating to armed groups are made between the hosts, in this case Eritrea, and the government of a neighboring country.[35] And while demanding support from

---

33 One had to do more than assume that the trouble with Ethiopia in handling the Eritrean file is a problem of implementation on the ground. Other factors, such as interparty relations, relative openness, particularly the existence of social media and a public space in Ethiopia, and the principle of proportional response, must have had a constraining impact in pursuing a full-fledged strategy of destabilization.

34 The Eritrean narrative is that they persisted through and survived the Ethiopian onslaught and finally got what they wanted in the form of political change in Ethiopia in their favor. A related and largely unchallenged commentary on the part of the Eritrean leadership is that they are the sole owners of the change in Ethiopia. Almost all media commentaries inside, and town hall meetings outside, of Eritrea seem to follow this argument.

35 36. Young, J. 2007. Beja- Local Conflict, Marginalization and the Threat to Regional Security. Center for Policy Research and Dialogue, Institute for Security Studies.

an enemy country in the struggle for freedom, several liberation movements have compromised their own freedom by entering dependent relations with neighboring states and foreign powers.[36]

In part, this is a function of the typical ways the Eritrean government organizes itself in managing neighboring countries' armed groups.[37] This is designed to ensure control and influence in the event they enter normal politics or share power by precipitating its arrival, but it creates a context of mistrust and antagonism among the political forces, particularly during transition. Whether this is the main reason behind the lack of a clearly defined security arrangement between Abiy and the returnees from Eritrea is doubtful. However, given the closer relations between him and some of the leaders of recently returned armed groups, who in turn claim to have special relationships with the Eritrean president and his security apparatus, it would appear there are political considerations that keep the regional axis in motion. It is not the aim of this paper to discuss this particular issue in detail, except to stress that often external factors compromise healthy transitions and a foreign policy based in strategic thinking and motivated by national interest.Such a situation, for whatever it is worth, also makes other national players increasingly suspicious of even a relatively fairly negotiated deal. As a result, the delays in the implementation of the deal are now less attributable to a lack of transparency and inclusiveness than the nature of political alliances in Ethiopia, the problem posed by bringing some actors based in Eritrea into corridors of decision making, and the TPLF's concerns that power holders and domestic actors are aligning with a foreign enemy power against a specific domestic social base.

The TPLF is only one, although probably the biggest, threat to the continued survival of the regime in Eritrea and "change forces" and their allies in Ethiopia. While it might be overlapping with Tigray, there is a great deal of apprehension among the people in the Ethiopian Afar region with which the Eritrean government have had unsympathetic relationships. Similarly, the Eritrean government's continued security relationships with political players and regional structures in Ethiopia, the reinforcement of its presence in the capital, andongoing frustration among the people in the Tigray and Afar regions at the lack of progress and transparency in the peace

---

Online. http://www.iss.co.za/uploads/CPRDPAPERBEJA.PDF (25/09/2011) [Horn of Africa Case Study].

36 *Ibid.*

37 Examples include the Eastern Sudan Peace Agreement, which ended up being a peace agreement between the Eritrean and Sudanese governments, rather than between Khartoum and eastern Sudan rebel leaders.

process, all suggest the likelihood of continued suspicion and increased tensions among Ethiopian political players. The problems of mistrust have already found expression in the multitude of visits to Asmara by officials from the Amhara region.[38] While overseeing the smooth operationalization of federal highways is the responsibility of the Ethiopian Defense Forces, while the border between the Amhara and Tigray regions has been closed for more than a year, the Abiy government's exclusive focus has been on peace conferences between other regions, including the closer relations between him, officials in Amhara, and the Eritrean leadership, and the result is that relations with the TPLF have remained sticky.

Abiy had less than excellent relationships with the TPLF in the weeks leading upto as well as in the aftermath of his election as chairman of the EPRDF. This became more acute when the TPLF accused him of drifting from the EPRDF's institutional and ideological basis, for whatever it is worth, while making decisions. Another set of disagreements arose when Abiy started implying the group isa threat to his power in several official statements and public gatherings. Besides, TPLF leaders gave somewhat rhetorical support to Abiy's approach to the deal with Eritrea while many shudder in dismay at its scale, scope, and speed. Simply put, this means that the desired speed exceeds the desired outcome, which certainly got bad press, partly because of themutual habit of dropping sticky leaves on politicalpronouncements. Compounding this, the statements by the Eritrean leader,whose "Game Over, TPLF" rhetoric, premature as it may seem, followed by lack of engagement with Tigray and the continued negative propaganda campaign by official media outlets and their supporters in the Eritrean diaspora against the Weyane, all indicate the lack of commitment to mend fences, although the sincerity of that commitment has always been in doubt.Indeed,like so many ofhis intimate announcements on the border and sovereignty, Isaias's emphasis on the "stability of Ethiopia first"comes from acknowledging that there is a group that is a threat to both Eritrea and the new powers in Addis that requires more attention than say conflict transformation.[39]The first and most significant suggestion of this is that the implementation of the deal is probably conditioned on the further weakening or containment of Tigray and the TPLF.

---

38 Some claim there were eight visits between June 2018 and June 2019, some of which, such as on August 15, 2018, focused on Amhara armed groups as the Somali, Oromiya, and Amhara regional governments, were in some instances able to directly negotiate political and security issues with Eritrea.

39 This has been communicated in several ways; it is also mentioned in an article titled "Ethiopian Election 2020 and the Implementation of the Algiers Agreement," Awate.com, August 13, 2018.

What is most striking about the early handling of the rapprochement was that Abiy's claim to be pursuing a peace agenda in the interests of Ethiopian security flew in the face of the demands of the most interested actors and constituents for peace with Eritrea.A major aspect of state and peace building in the Horn is the politics of mutual destabilization.[40]Hence, the argument developed in the following pages is that central to the problemsof the signatories of the deal has been the quest to reshape regional alliance systemsand their inability to dissociate themselves from partisan political agendas and by extension programs and initiatives that win the support of all their citizens to the peace process.

Either out of a desire for a quick deal or the simplistic characterisation of the problem, Abiy moved rapidly without involving his party leadership, which can be explained in one or all of the following. First, he thought that once he had the blank check, following the excruciating party evaluation and decision making through the EPRDF Executive Committee would not allow him to get quick results.[41] Second, involving the TPLF might have required collegial relations between the two that are largely absent. Third, since both Abiy and Isaias considered the group as the biggest obstacle to political consolidation on their respective turfs, the process ended up being Abiy's, which sealed the fate of the peace deal.[42]This is also related to the odd situation in which majority Tigrigna speakers on both sides of the border have found themselves charging, a rarity and probably for contradictory reasons, that Abiy is making peace with Isaias and not with the Eritrean people. Hence, it should be clear that the speed with which the deal progressed—irrespective of the complexity of the issue requiring careful and thoughtful hands—became possible in part because of the political change in Ethiopia and the way both leaders thought about its intended results. Absent these changes, that is up until mid-2018, the very

---

40 Lionel Cliffe, "Regional Dimensions of Conflicts in the Horn of Africa," *Third World Quarterly* 20, no. 1 (2010). This is a time-tested strategy in the region, although Abiy could not command the same level of knowledge and attention as that of Isaias, who since assuming leadership of the Eritrean insurgency movement until the present seems to have perfected it into a major tool of his foreign and security policy.

41 Though the beginning of the peace overture by Ethiopia that led to an extraordinarily fast deal could be traced back to the EPRDF decision, actual responsibility lies in the stealth manner of the Ethiopian prime minister.

42 One of the syndicate analysts of the Eritrean government in the West, Bronwyn Bruton, was bold enough to entitle the TPLF as a mutual opponent in "Ethiopia and Eritrea Have a Common Enemy,"*Foreign Policy*, July 12, 2018.

idea of a "peace deal" between Eritrean and Ethiopian leaders made very little sense.

The Deal and Its Failure to Bring Peace.

The Bigger Picture

It can be argued that peace with Eritrea is good in and of itself and the PM was following through the decision passed by his party to negotiate with Asmara. The speed with which he made the deal with Eritrea should only be appreciated, and the commitment he has shown to engage is valuable, except for the lack of clarity on process and outcome.[43] This is partly because whatever happened between the two leaders is hidden from the public;the Ethiopian parliament is not reasonably engaged in the matter. Indeed, Abiy ensured that even his close aids and foreign policy officials were only given the most cursory overview of the course of the engagement, and interested parties were kept away from the talks in Asmara, Addis Ababa, or Arab capitals. This will not only harm the future prospects of the deal, assuming the deal was meant to be materialized, but it also negatively impacted the nature of relations within the EPRDF, widening a wedge among social groups and further complicating the political transition in Ethiopia. The exclusion of the TPLFin particular posed a major threat to the potential viability of the deal, not only because it controls a significant amount of the territory, including the major routes connecting both countries, and its membership and constituency is largely made up of ethnic Tigrayans, which brings a cultural and demographic dimension into the picture.

Not surprisingly, neither the course of engagement nor its culmination in the Riyadh Agreement or even the successive meetings between the two leaders has served to improve the state of peace and stability between the two countries. Moreover, quenching all instruments of pressure early on by Ethiopia and the handover of its leverage to the Eritrean president created an environment in which the situation in Eritrea will not show any improvement. To the extent that there is a connection between the domestic situation in Eritrea and the regional conflict system, the inability of the deal to positively influence the behavior of the Eritrean regime to abandon its policy of destabilization and seek regional and global relevancemeansthe fundamentals of the relationship between Eritrea and Ethiopia will remain as they are at least in the short term. From its inception as a liberation

---

43 President Isaias Afwerki and Prime Minister Abiy Ahmed signed the Joint Declaration of Peace and Friendship between Eritrea and Ethiopia on July 9, 2018. To date, the agreement is neither detailed nor official.

movement to assuming power in an independent state, the EPLF (now PFDJ) has been focusing on the creation of wealth and influenceas a spoiler in the Horn's international system.[44] The EPLF believed its neighborsto be inherently fragile and adopted a strategy of bullying—and perfected what I called the political economy of destabilization—and involving them in their internal affairs in return for wealth extraction. This explains the reason why the only growing industry in Eritrea has been the manufacturing and hosting of armed groups, as can be seen with a sizable number of them, almost one for each major ethnic group, recently returning to Ethiopia.

From Yemen to Djibouti, Sudan, and Ethiopia this policy, which is intimately linked to internal dislocation, has led to violent interstate disputes, and it has been proved winning in Sudan. By hosting and helping Sudanese armed groups, Eritrean leadershave created a niche inside its big neighbor, indirectly controlling the smuggling route in eastern Sudan through its allies. This particular strategy faced its firstobstacle when the TPLF-led EPRDF government decided to strike back, which remains the source of the long running feud between the ruling parties. The fact that Eritrea wanted an advantage on trade and monetary policies and used the Badme issue as an excuse to attack Ethiopia is well documented and need not be explained here. The only thing that needs to be highlighted here is that Eritrean leaders were always nagging TPLF leaders in all informal sessions that "Ethiopia is enough for both of us [read: leaders of Tigrigna speakers], and TPLF leaders should not stand in their way."

When the response was negative they began to threaten armed conflict, leading to the entry of an Eritrean force into Ethiopian territory in May 1998.[45]The deeper cause of the conflict is the nature of Eritrean political economy and how it has been conceptualized and articulated. The fact that TPLF leaders refused to cooperate in the grand scheme of the EPLF in Ethiopia might have been less problematic, as the level of grievance exponentially grew when the Ethiopian government dealt a heavy blow to the Eritrean military, an institution that has been an embodiment of the

---

44 Many agree on this, including Alex deWaal in "Eritrea: The Sawa Parade. What is the Meaning of Eritrea's Decision to Stage a Major Military Parade at This Precise Moment?"Asmarino.com, August 6, 2019. A similar argument is made by Yosief in "Eritrea: Part II," cited earlier.

45 Personal recollections; weeks before the attack the author found himself in Asmara. As far as the Eritrean leadership is concerned, TPLF leaders as leaders of Ethiopia were expected to prioritize shared ethnic affinities and interests and cooperate in the exploitation of their country by a neighboring ruling class. By attacking Ethiopia, Eritrean leaders were indeed proving what they have been warning about all along: "Either we eat together or die together."

sense of Eritrean invincibility. Insofar as the EPLF planned to play a regional security role in the Horn and decided to make the military an instrument of nation branding,the way in which the war ended was quite alarming, to say the least, from which it has found it very difficult to recover, an affair whichwill not be forgotten or forgiven. Quite understandably, the Eritrean leadership will change strategy and continue the politics of destabilization, supporting armed groups and anti-Ethiopian media outlets and working hard to demonize the TPLF and create a critical mass against the regime in Ethiopia. This strategy must have contributed to the upheavals seen in the country in recent years, though the real cause remains internal political problems and the fracture within the ruling elite.

The fact that the Eritrean leadership claims it has played the most important role in the recent change of leadership in Ethiopiacan be another facet of looking at group perceptions,expectations,or profit harvesting surrounding the deal.While overlapping with thepolicyof getting back at its main adversary,the real strategy is to further the dislocation of Ethiopia, create multiple centers of power, and position itself as an arbiter, a strategy which has in the past succeeded in Sudan but failed in Ethiopia. Eritrea wants to have as many allies as possible, and the number of armed groups it succeeded in parachutinglast year is a clear testimony. The main problem of the recent agreement is that this aspect of the conflict is barely addressed. For instance, what will happen if other Ethiopian actors are unable to perform the role the TPLF refused to play?

As indicated earlier, two or maybe three overlapping agendas drive President Isaias of Eritrea. One is the desperate need to come out of isolation without losing face. Second is his long-standing rivalry with the TPLF, and third refers to sharing the political space within Ethiopia and a policy space regionally.With the newfound freedom and resources, mainly due to the lifting of sanctions, the Eritrean leader sees a chance to reactivate old policy instruments (the recent large-scale Sawa military parade being one) and adjust the future economic and political landscape of the subregion and the Red Sea basin in his favor. He has already started to expand, with the help of the Ethiopian prime minister, his physical and political presence to forge new partnerships and ring-fence his enemies inside and outside of its borders. The disproportionate focus given to a regional tour covering South Sudan and Somalia, while ignoring adjacent border areas and regions, points to the level of emphasis or primacy given to geopolitics and political alliances than peace with immediate neighbors.[46]

---

46   Top Eritrean delegates visited Somaliland (March 18, 2019); South Sudan (September 17, 2019); Somalia (August 14, 2018 and April 6, 2019). The disproportionate

Towards a Political Economy Analysis

The balance shift shows Eritrea benefited from the deal, not least from the lifting of sanctions in both economic and military terms, while its regional profile has continued to grow.The return of opposition groups from Eritrea could be listed as one outcome for Ethiopia, but this could have been achieved by opening up the political space alone or declaring an amnesty, and many would have returned or risked becoming irrelevant. In fact, if this was a major reason, it should have allowed for a rigorous process of negotiation and detailed security arrangements, as happens elsewhere.Corresponding to the lack of clarity on the relations between Ethiopian opposition and Eritrean leaders has been the shared political formulas surrounding the change in Ethiopia. No wonder, both scorning the ethnic federal system for personal political reasons and Abiy's dislike of the organizing principles of the EPRDF and his ongoing attempts to remodel power relations or establish a new party need no further explanation.

Since its inception the EPLF, now PFDJ, has been consistently apprehensive about the TPLF's political program of ethnic empowerment, and the Ethiopian experiment stands contrary to the nation-building and totalitarian project in Eritrea. This becomes even more alarming when one looks at the religious-ethnic fault line in Eritrea.[47] But it is also intimately linked to political contestation in Ethiopia. That Eritrean leaders would not favor the currentEPRDF structure and federal arrangement in Ethiopia is hardly surprising, as it allowsthe TPLF to be part of the policy process in Addis, andin fact, unless the current mechanism is changed, it could help it project federal power again, as the EPRDF system is rotational. Nor is it to be expected that they would applaud the fact that managing diversity through multinational federation will make Ethiopia—which they consider as the trapped giant—less combustible and by extension a harder nut to crack.[48]Clearly, President Isaias and most of the Ethiopiangroups he has been supporting, and are now part of the close circle of the prime minister,

---

focus given to Horn of Africa countries not immediate neighbors, particularly the successive tours to Somalia, indicate where the real focus of the deal's dividends lie. However, given Eritrean leaders' long-held antagonism towards Somaliland (mainly due to its relations with Ethiopia), it is the visit to Hargeisa that probably catches more attention.

47　Unlike Eritrean, and to some extent other Ethiopian demographics, the TPLF is not vulnerable to a societal fault line, which partly explains the group's decades of strength as a political organization.

48　This should be seen against the overarching agenda of the policy of destabilization discussed earlier.

seem to have a shared understanding that tempering with the political structure and ethnic federal system is a priority. It is fairly clear on which side of the debate Abiy Ahmed's sympathies will lie.

While not doubting that Abiy and formerly Asmara-based groupsmight genuinely believe in a formula devoted to achieving a united country, some did not, and hence there is reason for approaching the real objectives of this vast and amorphous regional coalition with considerable skepticism.[49] Isaias is probably acting half out of malice and half out of paranoia when he positions himself against the TPLF and Tigray. After all, the long game of determining which part of the border will become the center of gravity for the Tigrigna-speaking political community very much depends on the place of Tigray in Ethiopian politics. More difficult to justify, however, is why leading political players in Ethiopia continue to be satisfied with the developing situation. Some note that the changes they believe in cannot be realized without dealing a crushing blow to the group considered to be not only a harbinger but also the last frontier of the political model in Ethiopia, which essentially unites not only pan-Ethiopian forces, the PM with few allies in Oromo Democratic Party, leaders of the Amhara region, and the Eritrean leadership. And in this aspect alone, Abiy has an unarguable claim to a central status; no doubt he has hinted he would like to introduce an elected presidency.[50]

Their vision was not limited to Ethiopia, but regional, as they saw themselves playing a role in Somalia supporting the Mogadishu-based government against the regions and their perceived allies in the Horn.[51]Further evidence of this trend towards centralized power can be seen in the nature of deployments by Ethiopian forces in Somalia, with a blowback impact on domestic politics, probably pointing to an otherwise puzzling aspect of the country's foreign policy.From a strictly partisan perspective, this appears to make good sense, as it would give a regional aspect to internal power

---

49 Apart from Ginbot 7, now Ezema, groups such as the ONLF, OLF, and many others, subscribe to the ethnic formula.

50 The prime minister's office and pro-regime analysts have long been hinting that identity politics is the cause of all the problems and doing away with them could be part of the solution, a position challenged by most identity-based political organizations, aka federalists; not least, the main resistance to it is being offered by the TPLF, although the significant threat to the PM's position comes from Oromo nationalists. See Tom Gardner, "Abiy Ahmed and the Struggle to Keep Ethiopia Together" *The Africa Report*, October 11, 2019.

51 Several incidents from Baidoa to the Gedeo region attest to this trend. The recent incident in Jubaland in which the Ethiopian military failed to land at Kismayo airport in support of Farmaajo is a prominent case in point.

consolidation. One would like to argue, however,that it is a matter of strong foreign policy, even of national security, that involving border peoples in the conversations is worthwhile, without which Ethiopian influence and security will not only lack a coherent rationale but could become, itself, an obstacle to its success. Perhaps because they seem so secondary to the TPLF-led EPRDF government's grandiose plans for modernization and economic expansion and integration, it had much less time for them, and it threatens to lead to a situation where the border is alarmed, the center is complacent.[52]The contention here is that should this same approach be applied—as appears to already be the case in handlingthe Ogaden element on the Somalia file and the Tigrigna factor on Eritrea—it can safely be predicted that it will aggravate the internal situation.

To the extent that both leaders currently deride the existence of a strong regional challenge in Tigray, their level of tolerance to a weak center and strong federal states previously supported by the TPLF-EPRDF in Somalia is nonexistent. While difficult to gauge, there is reason to think that managing the threat from the TPLF has become a major consideration. This approach was made easier by the perception that it is still strong enough to make a comeback—and drying up any potential allies across borders in the region has become a key consideration—though whether the group has the intent is highly debatable.No doubt, the political and rhetorical missteps of Abiy antagonized many Tigrayans, which allowed the group to mobilize and bounce back. Ever since that acknowledgement, the strategy has been for both Isaias and Abiy to bide their time until such an opportunity arrives, leading to its submissionto the parade or its replacement by friendly actors, with both taking the role of expediting that arrival.Achieving this will be more about coordinating diplomatic, political, and economic resources and less about pure military contestation.More difficult to justify, however, is the level of coordination—and how much cold calculation went into this plan—between Eritrea, Abiy, and the closure of the roads from Amhara to Tigray.But why Abiy failed to lend his good offices and open the road, not to say that there were not some shots, particularly in informal discussions; but why it was not of paramount importance to him in the face of his hands-on approachtosimilar issues[53] is hard to understand.

---

52 Former Ethiopian prime minister Meles Zenawi came to realize the importance of engaging with the ONLF, though a militarily defeated group, when he started to negotiate with it in Kenya through the good offices of the Kenyan government, and this was already ongoing around late 2017 with the former president of Ethiopia's Somali region involved.

53 Some of these include the Sidama or Somali-Afar cases.

It cannot be lost on observers that while the anti-TPLF axis must have negotiated long and hard on a whole series of political and security issues ranging from power sharing to wealth sharing, internal borders, the status of the TPLF and Tigray, there is no denying the factthat, so argue some,one of the main reasons for the latest move of Isaias to close the border is the appreciation that the encirclement of Tigray—parallel to the efforts of the Amhara region—could only be achieved through economic means but also because the brief opening started to loosen the total strangulation of the country on which his political survival depends.[54] While the presence of such a strategy cannot be authenticated, its enforcement seems to have lost in the ongoing crisis in the country, which has sapped the oxygen out of the major players.And it also speaks to the lack of credible threat assessment and conflict dynamics,which have effectively put most political players in the curious position of placing themselves against the TPLF at a time when it was leading a standing policy of disengagement from politics at the center.

Internal deliberations within the top leadership of the TPLF show the group does not have any interest to play kingpins at the federal level, instead focusing on Tigray,[55] and yet the fears are reminiscent of the group's outsized role during the war against the Derg, including the Eritrean liberation struggle, and its slide to politico-military dominance for decades. As a result, the real intent of the TPLF in Ethiopian politics, on which the projections and alliances of political players is largely based, has to date not been seriously considered. Indeed, there is not even any strategic debate underway on what many consider the most critical component of any future peace process with Eritrea. The fact that the TPLF factor remains critical to the complications surrounding the delay and eventual fate of the deal is

---

54 "Eritra: Part II."That this argument is widely shared by many in Tigray is beside the point.

55 Even the decision of the thirty-five-day-long evaluation of the front in Mekelle, held months before Abiy was elected and the deal was conceptualized, which resolved in favor of focusing on the Tigray region, which has been proved by the follow-up trajectory, is not able to fend off the fear of the Eritrean president and Ethiopian political forces inside and outside the EPRDF.There is an almost unanimous position on the resolve to focus at the regional level, with a strong sense of remorse shared by the public and Tigrayan political elite at large. TPLF leaders have neglected the region in favor of developing Ethiopia, and it is payback time. Paradoxically, many pro-PFDJ Eritreans allege that the TPLF developed Ethiopia at the expense of Eritrea, impoverishing it using sanctions, although in fact, the root cause of the problem is the PFDJ leadership itself, which is commonly underappreciated in the narrative. Discussion with TPLF leaders, and several written sources, such as Gardner, "Abiy Ahmed and the Struggle," share this assertion.

not secret, but the real challenge lies somewhere else, in other words in the survival instinct of the Eritrean regime. This is the aspect that the external players, including the current Ethiopian leadership, fail to understand.

I have been arguing as early as 1998 that the post-independent Eritrean state is not a conventional type of state, and it is structurally constrained to provide sustenance to formal relations.[56]Even a cursory reading of the regime would bring to light the fact that it is not even a normal dictatorship,resulting in it undermining a normal life. Abnormality is to be found not only in the fact that economic activity is conspicuously, perhaps shockingly, unable to serve the basic needs of the people or has metamorphosed into a rustlingbusiness controlled by a handful of party bosses or "smuggling generals," higher education is run by the military, where desperate and hungry youth leave in droves, risking their lives to sneak as refugees into neighboring countries, mainly Ethiopia, in search, literally, of survival. It is also because it has got a siege mentality and a fear of the outside world that allows the regime to keep power within the country, and it feeds on that fear by "standing up" to enemies such as the United States or the Weyane, which gives all its actions its precise content, namely the idea of a concrete enemy whose elimination must be the first circumscribed goal of the action;there is no publicspace or legal rehearsal whatsoever, and yes, one would just say there is some legal practice even in an absolute monarchy.[57]

Moreover, as anyone would learn through acquaintance with the nature of political power in Eritrea, expecting state behavior will be a big exception, and problems are likely to arise when others are forced to return to principles, because exceptional cases and states of exception cannot be resolved by the everyday routine of conventional engagement.To repeat, the external, mainly Ethiopian players', approach to the peace process and their endorsement of the PFDJ as a partnerfor peace, development, or regional integration only suggests the plausibility of extreme forecasts. To the extent that one expects a potential trans-border trade, it should be defensible to visualise an exclusive route through Asab with small corridors doled out to non-Tigrigna speakerswith a transaction tightly controlled by pro-state forces that are squeezing private enterprise and the movement of people. Not only are a group of players' political concerns reflected in the means by which the peace process was pursued, but they also figure in the lack of priority given to people-to-people relations and the balance of power, as

---

56 Medhane Tadesse, *The Eritrean-Ethiopian War: Retrospect and Prospects: Reflections on the Making of Conflicts in the Horn of Africa, 1991–1998*(1999).This was written barely one month after the Badme debacle.

57 The seminal work of CarlSchmitt:*Dictatorship*(Cambridge: Polity Press, 2014).

seen in the outcomes of the process. This coming together has never been anything more than a tactical alliancewithout any hope of achieving a shared long-term vision. The argument developed here is that the dispute between Eritrean leaders and the TPLF is not totally delinked from the wider rivalry among Ethiopian political actors and external allies and by extension regional politics.

By Way of Conclusion: Crisis of Intention or Implementation

It was said, and widely believed, that thestrong-minded sense of Abiy Ahmed has been central to the "peace" deal betweenEthiopia and Eritrea. The facts are perhaps more complicated.Yet while it has been frequently invoked in the media and security reports, the deal is understood on the surface, mentioned in general terms, and has remained outside the reach of targeted and rigorous analysis.[58]Besides, both the parties and their external funders can be critiqued for inadequate attention as well as their tokenistic approach to issues of peace.But while the deal between the two leaders is to date holding, it is largely perceived by people on both sides of the border as being exclusionary and not addressing their concerns. Intentionally or not, the label obscures an extraordinary story—of a leader who dramatically discovers himself spurred to action in one of the deep-seated rivalries that were tearing apart Eritrea and its neighbors and stood his ground as resolutely as he did when he started it one year ago. The importance of this paper is thus evident in three cases. First, the impacts of the deal are a considerable factor in the ongoing political contestation in Ethiopia, particularly the struggle for supremacy within the ruling party. Second, the lack of consensus among national stakeholders impedes the smooth implementation of the deal or broadening it to a peace agreement between the two countries and their peoples. Lastly, the deal is an interesting case where peace processes can serve as a regional geopolitical weapon.

However, while global military and ideological considerations figured highly in setting the overarching framework, there is little doubt that the immediate security interests of the two Gulf states predominated. Instead of helping the search for peace, the deal is serving as a blueprint for new alliances, and the domestic political agendas have posed a major barrier to reaching agreements elsewhere in the country, and the parties, with external support, very deliberately denied popular access of both Ethiopians and

---

58 Partly this is related to the war on knowledge and intellectual curiosity, which is spreading to Africa as well.

Eritreans to what must be considered *their* peace process. What is more, as the paper argues, these phenomena were not confined to the burned-out cases of local contestation in Ethiopia: they are also detectable in southern Somalia, Sudan, Somaliland, and elsewhere. The PFDJ is at the forefront of the players that brought about the decades-long crisis between Ethiopia and Eritrea and cannot be expected to play a leading role in its resolution in an amicable and comprehensive manner.The impact of this on the operationalization of the deal and regional insecurity cannot be overstated.

In the end, the biggest threat to the deal between President Isaias of Eritrea and Prime Minister Abiy of Ethiopia is posed by the nature of the deal itself and the process that gave rise to it.Ethiopian history is awash with stories of renegade groups looking for tactical support from outsiders to fight the powers that be, particularly when they are threatened with annihilation and, when that threat is minimizedor when more significant national issues emerge (as was the case after 2018 when democratic transition becomes a priority), then their interest in having closer relations with external players significantly drops.[59] However, a new element seems to have entered the country in which those in mainstream politics know no rules and continue to align with a neighboring power to corner a domestic actor. What is most striking about this development is that these forces' claim to be fighting for a united Ethiopia flies in the face of demands by an empowered enemy country or the concerns of domestic constituencies.

Nonetheless, it probably says more about the exaggerated fear of the TPLF or its increasing value as a rallying point to stay relevant in a highly charged partisan politics. At no time has a national political elite demonstrated any sympathy, much less support, for a neighboring regime. It is not the intention here to carry out a critique of Ethiopian politics vis-à-vis Asmara, only to state thatdelinking the two is a major requirement for a workable peace with Eritrea. Ultimately, all political forces must become convinced—whether through honest discussion or their own experience—that while competition and rivalry may serve their immediate political and commercial goals, it is just as likely to harm the long-term stability of the country.There is always a need, particularly in such ambiguous times,for political leaders who are strategic in their thinking and motivated by national interest and should avoid being unaware, impulsive, vulnerable to conspiracy theories, and motivated by their own personal grievances and grudges.

The question will be asked as to what the international community can do to assist the transformation of the deal into a genuine and accountable

---

59 Almost all contemporary Ethiopian leaders have been involved in this bargain in one way or the other.

peace agreement. And the answer for this analyst is not much. Their leverages have been spent quickly—too late to redeem their lost illusions. The deal has become totally beholden to the Eritrean leader. That is why the fate of what is left to be fulfilled very much depends on what is going on inside Ethiopia. An agreed framework among Ethiopian political players and a government that has made peace with its peripheries (especially with Tigray) would be a requirement to the viability of a peace process with Eritrea. There has been less appreciation at all of the critical connection between the two, which has been exacerbated in recent years—though there may well be a touch of deliberate parody at such moments—by the spiteful conversation prevailing in the country.

Indeed, it would appear that for the parties and guarantors of the deal, public goods such as peace and good neighborly relations and approaches and policy processes that should guide them are not highly valued, and little thought has gone into developing them. And the result can be seen in the lack of attention given to the immediate security concerns of the people on the ground and the political concerns of the broader citizenry, the overwhelming focus on partisan political aspects of the deal, the centrality of personal interests, the willingness to trade off actual peace for foreign support, the lack of attention to common existential threats such as the environment, demography, or vividly menacing foreign military intervention, and the focus on short-term rather than long-term objectives. Indeed, beyond a few basic beliefs, the signatories often do not have clearly thought out shared positions and as a result typically respond to issues that come up on an ad hoc basis and not necessarily with the view to ensuring that the decisions reached are consistent with the spirit of the deal, as can be seen in the closure of the border without further notice.

The same is true with the guarantors of the deal, the Gulf States, in which there is an orientation that puts the personal chemistry in the forefront rather than well-defined national interest set the engagement and national security considerations, as can be seen in Somalia with the beefing up of a Qatari-supported government in Mogadishu with which the KSA and UAE have serious problems. In addition, the lack of clearly defined national interests, policy processes, and instruments will leave both leaders subject to the interests of their benefactors the more so because the region is becoming a focal point for global and Middle Eastern competition. The absence of the different national stakeholders in both countries and the exclusion of key constituents along the border in the process from the outset made clear the lack of concern with supporting peacemaking efforts between the two countries.

The deal's guarantee of the dominance of the two leaders and their external benefactors in turn reduces the need for its leaders to bring other parties and their constituents into the process and broaden the basis for peace. This is not entirely surprising given the nature of the parties and the self-proclaimed guarantors of the deal. Mainly Gulf States have perfected patronage and transactional foreign policy, which short-shrifts peace, democracy, or development with military projection, and for its part the Eritrean government has always had a military orientation and failed to recognize the existence of, much less engage with, the people it considers subjects under its jurisdiction, compromised their survival, andgiven scant attention to national interest and the peace and security of the region. Far too many Eritreans are still desperate to emigrate to Tigray, Ethiopia, for a better life.

The analysis in this paper suggests that peace processes can be used as geopolitical weapons, can be confused with political agreements between individual leaders, and might serve the sole purpose of remaking regional political and economic interests at the expense of regional security.Indeed, the study is less concerned with weighing the deal in terms of internal concerns than with elaborating on the broader regional dimensions, and as a cascading effect perhaps some light is cast on the contradictions between the appearance and the reality of the peace deal and argues peace processes that focus on party-political agendas and are readily manipulated for personal or group interests cannot contribute to the peace, unity, and democracy that all the actors claim they are committed to. In the words of a prominent Eritrean politician,"The agreement is not for something but against something."Obvious though this perspective may be a new addition to the research on peace agreements in Africa, it is either not understood or rejected by the dominant elements of the international media and global players, including the political elite in both countries, who continue to believe that the conflict can be contained and resolved by the same elitist and exclusionary approaches and parochial domestic political agendas.

Milestones
Ethiopia-Eritrea Relations in the Post-1991 Period

1991

24 May: EPLF controls Asmara.

28 May: EPRDF forces occupy Addis Ababa, forcing Mengistu to flee the country.

29 May: EPLF establishes Provisional Government of Eritrea (PGE).

1–5 July: Representatives of twenty-four political parties and ethnic groups meet in Addis Ababa at national conference to discuss country's future. Participants recognize that Eritrea cannot be forced to remain part of Ethiopia and accept plan for Eritrean referendum on self-determination.

3 July: Ethiopia signs agreement with Eritrea to allow it access to port of Assab.

5 July: Eritrea announces de facto independence and organization of referendum on self-determination for 1993. New administration expels thousands of civilians—mostly Amharas and Tigrayans—long living in Eritrea.

23 July: Meles Zenawi, EPRDF leader and interim president of Ethiopia since takeover of Addis Ababa by his supporters, elected unanimously as head of state by Council of Representatives, the new parliament.

Early August: Army officers repatriated from Sudan accuse EPLF of massacring thousands of former Ethiopian government officials during takeover of Asmara in May 1991. EPLF categorically denies accusations, claiming it always applied Geneva Convention with regard to prisoners of war.

7 October: PGE creates ten administrative regions (awrajas).

7 December: Council of Representatives announces division of country into fourteen new autonomous regional administrations. According to national radio, within the framework of establishing a federal system along ethnic lines, administrations will create "regional laws, ensure internal security, and choose the official language for the region."

6 November: EPLF announces programs for national service by law.

1992

February: EPLF establishes Provisional National Assembly composed of Central Committee and sixty-four appointed members.

6 April: Provisional Government of Eritrea decrees that persons of Eritrean descent or those adopted by an Eritrean, those born on national territory, and those who lived there between 1934 and 1974 without committing "crimes against the people" are entitled to Eritrean nationality.

7 April: Referendum Commission created.

22 May: Provisional National Assembly made part of PGE constituted officially by Proclamation No. 23/1992.

28 October: In Rome, ELF-RC (Revolutionary Council), ELF-UO (United Organization), ELF-NC (National Council) and EDLM (Eritrean Democratic Liberation Movement) brought together in Eritrean National Pact Alliance (ENPA), denounce monopolization of power by EPLF, which they deem to be dictatorial.

4 November: Representative of PGE in Addis Ababa announces no political party will be considered legal before referendum planned for following year and that Eritreans living abroad do not have the right to vote.

1993

23–25 April: Eritrea votes to secede from Ethiopia by 99.8 percent in referendum vote.

24 May: Eritrea officially gains independence; Provisional National Assembly appoints Isaias Afwerki president.

28 May: Eritrea takes seat at UN.

1994

10–17 February: EPLF third congress transforms itself into PFDJ and approves a National Charter for future constitutional government.

15 March: President Isaias appoints fifty-member Constitutional Commission headed by Bereket Habte Selassie.

16 May: PFDJ promulgates National Service Law; SAWA Defence Training Center becomes operational in August. (First National Service Law was issued in November 1991, and its amendments followed in March 1995 and October 1995.)

November: Ethiopia adopts new federal constitution, with many powers devolved to ethnically based regions created by new constitution.

December: Ethiopia rejects Eritrea's request to arrest and extradite Eritrean opposition group members.

1995

August 1995: Federal Democratic Republic of Ethiopia is proclaimed. EPRDF sweeps to power in elections.

22 August: Meles Zenawi elected prime minister of Ethiopia.

15–18 December: Eritrea and Yemen battle over Hanish Islands.

1996

15 April: Eritrea restructured into six regions (zobas), greater Asmara being one region.

21 June: Eritrea and Yemen send Hanish issue to arbitration.

1997

23 May: Constituent Assembly ratifies constitution, but Isaias postpones implementation.

8 November: Eritrea introduces national currency, the nakfa, and seeks to make it directly exchangeable with Ethiopian birr in cross-border transactions.

1998

6 May: Border skirmish between Ethiopia and Eritrea over 150-square-mile town of Badme begins.

May–June: US-Rwanda mediation fails; Ethiopia starts mass expulsion of Eritreans, accusing them of being "fifth columnists."

8 June: Eritrea appeals for direct talks with Ethiopia to end border war.

9 June: Heavy fighting erupts on the Ethiopian-Eritrean frontier in latest stage of their undeclared war.

14 June: Ethiopia and Eritrea agree to halt use of air strikes in border war.

9 October: International arbitration panel awards Yemen the Greater Hanish Islands and divides smaller islands between the two nations.

1999

February–March: Second round of border war; Ethiopia recaptures Badme and refuses to negotiate with Eritrea; Ethiopia continues expulsion of Eritreans.

6 February: Ethiopia and Eritrea resume their clash after an eight-month lull. Heavy casualties are reported.

27 February: Following Ethiopia's military breakthrough at Badme, Eritrea agrees to accept an African-sponsored proposal to end border dispute with Ethiopia.

26 July: Eritrea and Ethiopia agree to send delegates to Algeria to finalize arrangements to end fourteen-month war.

7 August: In meeting with Algerian President and OAU Chairman Abdelaziz Bouteflika, Isaias makes unconditional offer to cooperate with OAU to end war with Ethiopia.

12 August: Ethiopia claims to have nearly eliminated three Somalia-based rebel groups it says are supported by Eritrea. Most of the 1,103 killed or captured rebels are of the Oromo Liberation Front (OLF).

4 September: Ethiopia claims that the proposed outline for the implementation of a peace plan contradicts original agreement regarding withdrawal of Eritrea's forces. Eritrea denounces statement as "tantamount to a declaration of war."

2000

January: Isaias turns down PFDJ's call to hold elections.

12 May: Third round of border war erupts after Ethiopian troops leave trenches and attack Eritrean defenses. Six hundred thousand troops are dug in along six-hundred-mile border.

14 May: Ethiopia claims major victory against Eritrea, says eight divisions destroyed over previous two days. Eritrea says twenty-five thousand Ethiopian soldiers killed or wounded.

17 May: Ethiopian forces push into Eritrean territory, and UN Security Council approves embargoes against both countries.

18 May: Ethiopian troops capture Barentu and Barka lowlands in Eritrea; some 250–550,000 refugees reported displaced by fighting.

24 May: Eritrea withdraws from land seized in 1998 following twelve-day offensive by Ethiopia.

26 May: Eritrea and Ethiopia agree to resume peace talks even as Ethiopia continues to push into Eritrean territory.

28 May: Ethiopian warplanes bomb nearly completed power plant in Massawa, Eritrea, as thousands of refugees flee north.

29 May: Ethiopian planes launch air raids on a military airstrip near Asmara, Eritrea, as foreign ministers prepare for talks in Algeria.

30 May: Ethiopia and Eritrea open peace talks in Algeria.

31 May: Ethiopia declares victory over Eritrea as peace talks continue in Algeria.

9 June: Eritrea accepts OAU plan to end conflict.

10 June: Ethiopian troops storm Eritrean positions on all three fronts of disputed border in break of cease-fire. Ethiopian government accepts cease-fire terms brokered in Algeria but asks for "brief delay."

15 June: Ethiopia accepts preliminary cease-fire plan and together with Eritrea plans to sign documents in Algeria.

16 June: Ethiopian election board announces that four-party EPRDF coalition has won landslide victory in four key regions in May 14 elections.

18 June: In Algeria, foreign ministers of Ethiopia and Eritrea sign accord to cease hostilities immediately. Agreement calls for international peacekeeping force in buffer zone reaching fifteen miles into Eritrea.

July: UNMEE deployed to uphold ceasefire.

September: Eritrean National Assembly debates president's handling of war and political transition and sets up commission to define rules for multiparty elections.

10 October: Meles reelected by acclamation in Ethiopian parliament to another five-year term.

12 December: Ethiopia and Eritrea sign Algiers Agreement, turning border dispute over to international commission for final decision. Boundary commission given task of defining 620-mile border, overseeing exchange of prisoners, returning displaced people, and hearing claims for war damages.

December: "Berlin Manifesto," by thirteen Eritrean academics and professionals protesting undemocratic practices of Isaias government, issued.

2001

6 February: Ethiopia and Eritrea agree to set up sixteen-mile-wide, UN-patrolled security zone effective February 12.

February: UNMEE deploys along common border; Eritrean elections postponed; Isaias rejects petitions by nineteen PFDJ leaders for emergency Central Committee meeting on stalled democratization process.

May: Fifteen of the February petitioners (G-15) publish open letter to PFDJ members on Internet.

18–19 September: Eleven members of G-15 (including Haile Woldetensa'e and Petros Solomon) and ten journalists arrested as government bans dissent and closes private press.

2002

January: Eritrea's National Assembly, meeting after eighteen months, denounces dissidents, affirms president's agenda, and promises elections.

13 April: EEBC, established to determine new border, releases report. UN panel rules in favor of Ethiopia on all territory contested with Eritrea. Ruling states that town of Engal is in fact Eritrean. Decision divides minority ethnic Irob community, one of few centers of Ethiopian Catholicism. Ethiopia's rejection of UN ruling on demarcation of border throws Addis Ababa's relations with Asmara into deadlock, prompting Eritrea to seal its borders. EEBC decision awards Badme to Eritrea. Ethiopia rejects ruling.

7 September: UNSC decides to keep UN peacekeepers in Ethiopia and Eritrea six more months to give countries time to mark border.

October: Fourteen Eritrean opposition groups meet in Addis Ababa and reorganize Alliance of Eritrean National Forces (AENF, established in Sudan, 1999) as Eritrean National Alliance (ENA) and pledge to overthrow Isaias government.

2003

August: Eritrea introduces petrol rationing.

2004

July: African Commission on Human and Peoples' Rights denounces illegal detention of G-15.

September: Hundreds of banned church members arrested (in May 2002 Eritrea banned all religious groups except Eritrean Orthodox, Catholic, Lutheran, and traditional Islam).

25 November: Ethiopia accepts, in principle, EEBC's ruling designed to resolve border dispute with Eritrea that sparked war.

2005

January: Sixteen ENA members reorganize as Eritrean Democratic Alliance (EDA).

15 May: Ethiopians vote in what is touted as country's first truly democratic election, shadowed by fraud allegations and deadly violence. Disputed multiparty elections lead to months of violent protests.

4 October: UNSC warns Ethiopia and Eritrea against reigniting their border war and urges Eritrea to immediately reverse ban on all helicopter flights by UN peacekeepers.

21 December: International commission, based in The Hague, and panel, formed to resolve disputes between Eritrea and Ethiopia, rules that Eritrea violated international law when it invaded Ethiopia in May 1998.

2006

February: Islamic Courts Union (ICU), consisting of eleven Shari'a law courts in Somalia, is established and, with Eritrean support, controls southern region of Somalia.

10 March: Legal experts from Ethiopia and Eritrea fly to London for talks with international mediators to discuss demarcating common border.

31 May: UNSC cuts number of peacekeepers deployed in Eritrea and Ethiopia by at least one-third while extending UN mission's mandate for another four months.

June: Eritrea mediates peace between Sudanese government and Eastern Front rebels.

1 July: About one hundred Ethiopian troops enter Somali border town of Beled-Hawo in eight military vehicles, the latest sign that Ethiopia might try to bolster Somalia's weak interim government as Islamic militia gains increasing power.

21 July: Islamic militia leader calls for holy war against Ethiopian troops protecting Somalia's UN-backed government.

22 July: Ethiopian troops sent to bolster Somalia's government move into second Somali town and seize strategic airport.

8 August: Eritrea announces that Kemal Gelchu, dissident Ethiopian general, has defected to Eritrea and plans to join OLF to fight for his Oromo people's rights.

25 September: Somalia's interim prime minister calls on UN to partially lift arms embargo on his country to allow for deployment of African peacekeepers, which he calls necessary to stop advance of Islamic radicals. Ethiopian troops arrive in Somalia to support internationally recognized government in faceoff with radicals. Islamic militia in seaport of Kismayo opens fire on thousands protesting fundamentalists' takeover of southern town.

29 September: UNSC extends mandate of peacekeepers in Eritrea and Ethiopia by four months and threatens to overhaul mission if two sides don't make progress toward demarcating border.

9 October: Islamic militia that seized much of southern Somalia declares holy war against Ethiopia, accusing it of deploying thousands of troops to prop up UN-backed government.

October: With fourteen reporters in prison, Eritrea called "one of world's worst jailers of journalists" by Committee to Protect Journalists and rated world's third-worst violator of free expression by Reporters Without Borders.

16 October: UN accuses Eritrea of moving 1,500 troops and 14 tanks into buffer zone in "major breach" of 2000 cease-fire agreement.

November: Ethiopian troops enter Somalia and engage in fierce fighting with Islamists controlling large parts of country and capital. Islamists disperse.

7 November: Independent commission says it will demarcate contested Ethiopian-Eritrean border on maps and leave rival nations to establish physical boundary. Both Ethiopian and Eritrean officials invited to November 20 meeting in The Hague to discuss procedure.

15 November: Isaias calls border row between Eritrea and Ethiopia a "solved problem."

20 November: Eritrea and Ethiopia both reject plans by UN-appointed border panel to demarcate contentious border on paper.

24 December: Ethiopia admits sending troops into Somalia in "self-defensive" move to oust hardline Islamic Courts Union, which controls much of country. Eritrean-backed ICU had declared jihad on Ethiopia.

28 December: ICU abandon Somali capital after Ethiopia invades country, triggering proxy war between Eritrea and Ethiopia.

2007

January: Eleven-member EDA coalition splits into two blocs at second congress.

June: Eritrea establishes diplomatic relations with Iran.

14 June: UN spokesman states that Ethiopia has accepted UN commission's ruling to turn over disputed town of Badme to Eritrea. In letter the previous week to UN Security Council, Ethiopian government gave unconditional acceptance of commission's decision announced five years prior.

28 June: Meles says he has accepted 2002 border ruling with Eritrea but insists on new talks on how to implement it.

September: Somali opposition forces establish Alliance for the Re-Liberation of Somalia in Asmara.

November: EEBC dissolves itself.

December: Eritrea declares "virtual demarcation" by EEBC sufficient, announces dispute is settled, and embargoes food and fuel for UNMEE peacekeepers, forcing latter's withdrawal from border.

2008

30 January: UNSC renews mandate of struggling UN peace force on Eritrea-Ethiopia border for six months, despite request from Secretary-General Ban Ki-moon for one month.

March: EDA coalition convenes third congress in Addis Ababa.

April: UNMEE formally dissolves after troop withdrawal from contested border.

May–June: Eritrea engages in armed confrontation with Djibouti over border issues.

July: UN Security Council votes unanimously to end UN peacekeeping mission monitoring disputed border between Ethiopia and Eritrea; UNMEE completes withdrawal of all peacekeeping forces along border and terminates mission.

2009

13–15 January: Ethiopian troops withdraw from Somalia. Ethiopia hands over security duties in neighboring Somalia to joint force of Somali government security forces and Islamic militiamen.

June: Two EDA ethnic factions, Democratic Movement for the Liberation of the Eritrean Kunama and Red Sea Afar Democratic Organization form alliance: Democratic Front of Eritrean Nationalities.

June: Ethiopia admits to "reconnaissance missions" in Somalia despite formal withdrawal of troops in January but denies redeploying troops.

18 August: International claims commission in The Hague awards Ethiopia slightly more than Eritrea as it settles mutual claims worth hundreds of millions of dollars for death, injury, rape, looting, and destruction during border conflict; concludes complex arbitration part of 2000 peace agreement.

10 October: Meles accuses Eritrea of sowing havoc in region as Addis Ababa reiterates calls for sanctions over Asmara's alleged support for Somalia's rebels.

December: Rebels of Ogaden National Liberation Front (ONLF) claim capture of several towns in east in month of heavy fighting.

23 December: UNSC imposes sanctions on Eritrea for support of armed Islamist groups in Somalia.

2010

January: Eritrean Democratic Party, Eritrean People's Movement, and Eritrean People's Party merge into Eritrean People's Democratic Party.

May: EPRDF wins huge majority in parliamentary elections, handing Meles fourth term. International observers highlight shortcomings.

August: Eritrean National Council for Democratic Change (ENCDC) convenes founding conference in Addis Ababa to launch organized drive for National Council.

2011

5 April: Meles tells lawmakers Ethiopia is ready to help people of Eritrea topple Isaias regime, ruling out military invasion.

July: UN Monitoring Mission on Eritrea and Somalia charge Eritrea with
             facilitating foiled plot by opposition OLF to bomb January African
             Union Summit in Addis Ababa.

November: ENCDC creates 127-member National Council at conference in
          Hawassa, Ethiopia, as precursor for government-in-exile; effort later
          collapses.

2012

January: Five European tourists killed in Ethiopia's eastern Afar region by
           antigovernment rebels based in Eritrea, causing tensions between two
           states to rise and Ethiopia to threaten retaliatory action.

March: Ethiopia carries out air strikes on training camps for Ethiopian opposition
           groups in Eritrea.

12 March: Ethiopian forces enter Eritrea and carry out what government spokesman
          describes as "successful attack" against military posts.

16 March: Eritrean government admits attack on military outposts by Ethiopia
          carried out with help of United States and meant to divert attention from
          border dispute.

20 August: Meles dies, succeeded by Foreign Minister Hailemariam Desalegn.

2013

21 January: "Forto" mutiny in Asmara, as small military unit briefly seizes
            information ministry to broadcast demands for reforms.

2014

6 March: Eritrean Defense Forces chief of staff Major General Gebregziabher
          Andemariam (Wuchu) dies and is replaced by Major General Filipos
          Woldeyohannes; General Sebhat Ephrem reassigned from Ministry of
          Defense to Ministry of Energy and Mines in cabinet shake-up, with post
          of defense minister left unfilled.

2015

September: Eritrea leases port of Assab to UAE for latter to base air and naval
           facilities to support Saudi-led coalition in Yemen's civil war.

May: Ruling EPRDF scores another victory (100 percent) in general elections
           widely criticized by opposition.

June: Commission of Inquiry established by UNHRC finds systematic,
           widespread, and gross human rights violations had been and are being
           committed by Eritrea.

November: Eritrean government announces that over next six weeks all paper currency must be exchanged for new bills deposited in banks; withdrawals limited to five thousand nafka per month.

2016

January: European Union signs €200 million cooperation agreement with Eritrea, mainly for energy sector; Eritrea's information minister quashes notion that national service will be scaled back before conflict with Ethiopia ends; outflow of refugees to Ethiopia tops three thousand per month.

March: Ethiopian Prime Minister Hailemariam floats idea of new peace initiative with Eritrea.

12 June: Eritrea's Information Ministry says Ethiopia unleashed attack on Tsorona Central Front.

October: Ethiopia declares six-month state of emergency following violent antigovernment protests in Oromia and Amhara regions; estimated eleven thousand people arrested in first month alone.

2017

February: Ethiopia releases half of twenty-two thousand people arrested in aftermath of antigovernment protests.

March: Ethiopian parliament extends state of emergency by four months.

August: Ethiopia lifts state of emergency after ten months, releasing all but high-level prisoners.

October: Hajji Mussa Mohammed Nur, board chair of Asmara's Al-Dia'a Islamic School, arrested after denouncing government moves to nationalize school; hundreds of Asmarinos take to streets in first such demonstration since 2001; shots fired and hundreds arrested.

2018

February: As antigovernment protests continue, Hailemariam resigns; government declares second state of emergency.

March: Hajji Mussa dies in prison, sparking second round of protests and arrests during public funeral.

April: Abiy Ahmed, an ethnic Oromo, defeats challengers to become leader of ruling EPRDF and prime minister; launches comprehensive program of political reform at home and diplomatic bridge building abroad; calls for peace with Eritrea.

May: Abiy lifts state of emergency, invites exiles and opponents to return to Ethiopia.

5 June: Abiy announces unconditional acceptance of 2000 Algiers Agreement and 2002 EEBC border decision, handing back occupied frontier town of Badme.

20 June: Isaias announces he is sending rare delegation to Ethiopia for peace talks, days after Abiy takes major step toward calming deadly tensions with rival.

26 June: Delegation of top officials from Eritrea arrives in Ethiopia for first peace talks in twenty years.

8 July: Isaias meets Abiy in Asmara for first Eritrea-Ethiopia summit in two decades.

9 July: Eritrean and Ethiopian leaders formally restore relations. Abiy and Isaias sign agreements in Asmara to open embassies in their respective capitals, restore flight services, and use port facilities in Eritrea.

14 July: Isaias pledges to resolve dispute with Ethiopia in historic visit to Addis Ababa aimed at cementing peace less than a week after nations declare end to conflict.

16 July: Isaias reopens his country's embassy in Ethiopia.

18 July: Eritrea and Ethiopia resume commercial flights for first time in two decades.

24 July: UAE hosts leaders of Ethiopia and Eritrea, lauding "bold and historic" rapprochement as enhancing prospects for peace and prosperity.

August: Somalia renews relations with Eritrea.

7 August: Ethiopia signs agreement to end hostilities with OLF, which it had previously declared a terrorist movement.

5 September: Ethiopian, Eritrean, and Somali leaders meet in Asmara, furthering diplomatic thaw in Horn of Africa.

6 September: Ethiopia reopens embassy in Eritrean capital, latest step in restoring ties between two nations.

11 September: Leaders of Ethiopia and Eritrea reopen crossing points on border, cementing reconciliation and giving Addis Ababa direct route to Red Sea ports.

September: Eritrea makes peace with Djibouti.

16 September: Isaias and Abiy sign peace agreement during summit in Saudi Arabia and open borders to unrestricted trade and visa-less travel. African Union Commission Chairperson Mussa Faki and AU Chairman Paul Kagame of Rwanda are first invited to ceremony and later disinvited. UN Secretary-General António Guterres attends.

12 October: According to UNHCR, Ethiopian authorities have registered more than 6,700 new arrivals from Eritrea since border's opening. Eritrean refugee arrivals to Ethiopia jump to about 390 per day from around 53.

October: Ethiopia's government signs peace deal with Eritrea-based separatist group ONLF, ending 34-year armed rebellion.

9 November: Leaders of Somalia, Eritrea, and Ethiopia meet in Gondar, Ethiopia, to cement regional economic ties as relations warm.

14 November: UNSC adopts UK resolution lifting arms embargo and all targeted sanctions on Eritrean officials.

2019

7 January: Abiy and Isaias reopen western border crossing between their countries as part of ongoing reconciliation.

June: Army chief Seare Mekonnen and Amhara State Governor Ambachew Mekonnen, together with their colleagues, killed in alleged coup attempt against federal government.

11 October: Norwegian Nobel Institute awards Abiy the 2019 Nobel Peace Prize, mainly for making peace with Eritrea.

Contributors

Bahru Zewde (Ph.D.), currently Emeritus Professor of History at Addis Ababa University, is Founding Fellow of the Ethiopian Academy of Sciences and Fellow of the African Academy of Sciences. He was formerly Chair of the Department of History and Director of the Institute of Ethiopian Studies at Addis Ababa University and Executive Director of the Forum for Social Studies, a think tank based in Addis Ababa, and Principal Vice President of the Ethiopian Academy of Sciences. His major publications in English include: *A History of Modern Ethiopia 1855-1991* (2001); *Pioneers of Change in Ethiopia: The Reformist Intellectuals of the Early Twentieth Century* (2002); *Society, State and History: Selected Essays* (2008); and *The Quest for Socialist Utopia: The Ethiopian Student Movement c. 1960-1974* (2014).

Belete Belachew Yihun (Ph.D.) specializes in Ethiopia's foreign policy and international relations, with an emphasis on the Horn of Africa, the Middle East, and the African continent at large. The author of several articles and two books, including *Black Ethiopia A Glimpse into African Diplomacy, 1956-1991* (TSEHAI Publishers, 2014), he currently serves as senior researcher at the Center for Dialogue, Research and Cooperation (CDRC), an Ethiopia-based think tank dealing with the Horn of Africa and the wider region.

Daniel R. Mekonnen (Ph.D.) is director of the Eritrean Law Society (ELS) and a fellow of the African Studies Centre (ASC) at Leiden University in the Netherlands. He has served as judge of the Central Provincial Court in Eritrea and as senior legal advisor with the Oslo-based International Law and Policy Institute (ILPI). He brings a rich and diverse background in human rights activism, teaching, adjudication, leadership in civil society and grassroots movements, and consulting with intergovernmental organizations, including leading development agencies and ministries of foreign affairs in Europe. He is formally trained as a human rights lawyer, and in the context of a cumulative work experience of more than two decades he has amassed a wealth of experience in matters related to international human rights law, transitional justice, forced migration, and global peace and security.

Medhane Tadesse (Ph.D.) is a visiting professor at the African Leadership Centre, King's College London. He is an academic specialist on peace and security issues in Africa who has researched extensively on civil wars, the governance of security, political Islam, and interstate conflicts. A veteran political analyst in the Horn of Africa, he has written widely on a variety of issues and assumed a high-profile advisory position, at a young age, on one of the most complicated and intractable conflicts in Africa, Somalia. An early student of Somali Islamists and the threat of radicalization in Africa, Medhane has taught at various universities in Ethiopia and abroad and has written extensively on African security and related topics, spawning four books and over 160 briefing papers, articles, commentaries, and policy memos. He has served as an advisor to governments and political and armed groups and sits on the board of directors of several peace- and security-related institutions, including the African Security Sector Network (ASSN) and the African Leadership Centre (ALC) and is a senior SSR advisor to the African Union.

Senai W. Andemariam (a Ph.D. candidate at Maastricht University) is a former judge and now an assistant professor at the School of Law in Asmara, Eritrea. He earned his LLB from the University of Asmara, his LLM from Georgetown University as a Fulbright Scholar. He is a member of the editorial team of the *Journal of Eritrean Studies*. He has published with reputable journals at Oxford University Press, Cambridge University Press, Brill, De Gruyter, Aethiopica, and others. He has recently presented parts of this chapter at the African Studies centers at the Universities of Oxford and Cambridge.

Tekeste Negash (Ph.D.) is professor emeritus of modern history at Uppsala University in Sweden. He has written on Eritrean and Ethiopian social and political history and on educational policies. He is the author of several books and articles, including *No Medicine for the Bite of a White Serpent: Notes on Nationalism and Resistance in Eritrea, 1890–1940*; *Italian Colonialism in Eritrea: Policies, Praxis and Impact*; *Eritrea and Ethiopia: The Federal Experience*; and *Brothers at War: Making Sense of the Eritrean-Ethiopian War*, with Kjetil Tronvoll. Tekeste Negash was born in Asmara, Ethiopia, on December 19, 1947. He has lived and worked in Eritrea, Ethiopia, Italy, Great Britain, Norway, the United States, and Sweden. He currently lives in Sweden.

Wegahtabrhan (Wegi) Sereke (a Ph.D. candidate at the Institute for Public Communication, Università della Svizzera Italiana in Switzerland) most recently worked as a consultant for the Belgian think tank Europe External Programme with Africa (EEPA), a center of expertise on EU foreign policy towards Africa. Formerly, she was a staff attorney at the Legal Advisor's Office to the Eritrean State President. She obtained LLMs in international law and in international dispute settlement from the Graduate Institute of International and Development Studies in Geneva and from the University of Geneva (MIDS), respectively. She is a member of the Eritrean Law Society (ELS).

Wondemagegn Tadesse (LL.B, School of Law, Addis Ababa University), LLM University of Oslo (International Law), and Dr. jur. University of Graz) was judge assistant at Federal High Court, Legal Expert at the Ministry of Foreign Affairs of Ethiopia, and currently teaches at Addis Ababa University, College of Law and Governance Studies; he is also currently the Director of Center for Human Rights of Addis Ababa University. His publications include on various topics, particularly on human rights, constitutional law, and international relations.

Appendix A

AGREEMENT OF FRIENDSHIP AND CO-OPERATION
BETWEEN
THE TRANSITIONAL GOVERNMENT OF ETHIOPIA
AND
THE GOVERNMENT OF THE STATE OF ERITREA

The Transitional Government of Ethiopia and the Government of the State of Eritrea, hereafter referred to as the "Two Parties",

Taking into consideration the historical links and the bonds of friendship, solidarity and fraternity which exist between their two peoples,

Cognizant of the mutual goodwill and desire for cooperation of both peoples and the strategic interests that bind them;

Urged by the desire to foster cooperation between their peoples based on the principles of sovereignty and mutual advantage;

Determined to revive and strengthen the economies of their countries and improve the standard of living of their peoples;

Committed to promoting collective security and resolving all differences and disputes through dialogue and peaceful means;

Determined further to cooperate to establish viable competitive economies within the framework of the global economic situation,

Intent on contributing their share towards achieving regional peace and stability as well as all-round cooperation;

Have agreed as follows:

Article 1

The two parties shall cooperate in the economic, social (health education etc.), agricultural, energy, tourism, environmental, monetary and financial, technical and scientific areas through such activities as undertaking joint projects and ventures and through the adoption of common policies which are mutually advantageous and which will serve to promote the gradual evolution of the two economies and societies into a higher level of integration in accord with the underlying bonds of brotherhood between the two peoples and in compliance with the commitment of both countries to bring about regional economic integration and political cooperation.

Article 2

The two parties shall foster cultural exchange, including cooperation in the field of education.

Article 3

The two parties shall cooperate to upgrade their transportation and communication links and accordingly work jointly to maintain, expand and modernize the transportation network linking their countries. Moreover, they shall explore possibilities of joint ventures in land, sea and air transport and promote technical cooperation in transport and communications.

Article 4

The two parties agree to cooperate in the field of trade and commerce. They shall gradually eliminate all trade barriers between them and will work to harmonize their customs policies. The two parties further agree that the ports of Assab and Massawa are free ports for Ethiopia. In this connection, both parties shall strive to muster joint resources to expand and develop the two ports.

Article 5

The two parties shall allow the free movement of their citizens and shall in this regard harmonize their immigration laws.

Article 6

The two parties shall cooperate in the field 'of energy' and explore possibilities of jointly exploiting energy resources.

Article 7

The two parties shall cooperate in the utilization of transboundary rivers and other waters and shall also cooperate in the field of agriculture.

Article 8

The two parties shall cooperate in combating environmental degradation and conserving the ecosystem as well as to promote environmentally sustainable development.

Article 9

The two parties shall cooperate in the financial and monetary fields. In this regard they shall consult each other on the use of the Birr taking into account the mutual interest of the two parties while at the same time exploring the possibilities of adopting a common currency.

Article 10

The two parties agree to coordinate their position and carry our regular consultations on foreign policy with a view to:

a) realizing their common objectives

b) contributing to regional peace and stability as well as economic, social and political cooperation

c) promoting world peace.

Article 11

The two parties agree to cooperate in the area of security and to work closely on mutual defense interests.

Article 12

The two parties agree to promote cooperation between border regions and provinces in the two countries. To this end, they shall develop contacts and necessary relations in the border areas through local agreements between border regions and provinces within the spirit of this agreement.

Article 13

The two parties agree to set up a Joint Ministerial Commission which will be entrusted with the task of ensuring the implementation of the provisions contained in this Agreement and with identifying further areas of cooperation. The terms of reference and working modalities of the joint commission shall be defined by the commission, and the commission may establish as necessary, sub-committees of counter-part ministries as well as expert bodies.

Article 14

This Agreement shall enter into force on the date of notification of approval or ratification of the agreement by both Governments in accordance with the legal procedures of their respective countries.

Article 15

This Agreement:

a) shall remain in force for an indefinite period, provided, however, that either party may terminate it by giving twelve months notice to the other party;

b) may be modified upon the request by either party subject to mutual consent of the two parties.

Done at Addis Ababa on the 30th day of July in the year one thousand nine hundred and ninety-three in two originals, in the English language, both texts, being equally authentic.

For the Transitional
Government of Ethiopia

For the Government of
the State of Eritrea

MELES ZENAWI
President of The
Transitional Government
of Ethiopia & Chairman of
The Council of Representatives

ISAISA AFWERKI
President of The State of
Eritrea and Chairman of
The National Council

Appendix B

AGREEMENT BETWEEN
THE GOVERNMENT OF THE STATE OF ERITREA
AND
THE TRANSITIONAL GOVERNMENT OF ETHIOPIA
ON THE
ESTABLISHMENT OF THE JOINT HIGH
MINISTERIAL COMMISSION

Article 1
Establishment

There is hereby established a Joint Eritrean and Ethiopian High Ministerial Commission (herein after referred to as the "High Commission") pursuant to Article 13 of the Agreement of Friendship and Co-operation signed between the Heads of state of both countries of July 30, 1993.

Article 2
Composition of the High Commission

The High Commission shall be constituted by the prime Minister of the Transition Government of Ethiopia and the Minister of Local Government of Ethiopia and the Minister of Local Government of the Government of Eritrea as co-chairmen, the Foreign Ministers of the two Governments and the Ambassadors of the two countries to each other as members.

Article 3
Purposes for establishment

The High Commission is established for the following purposes:

3.1 To preserve and build upon the achievements already made between the two countries on co-operation and friendship;

3.2 To ensure the implementation of the provisions of the Agreement of Friendship and Co-operation signed between the Heads of State of both countries;

3.3. To identify and promote areas of co-operation; and

3.4 To set up a framework of co-operation within the spirit of the Agreement of Friendship and Co-operation and to determine policy issues.

Article 4
Powers and Duties of the High Commission

Without being limited by the generalities of the foregoing, the High Commission shall have the following powers and duties:

4.1 To establish committees, authorities, commissions and offices, as well as expert bodies as may be necessary;

4.2 To follow up the works and progress reports of said committees and other bodies in their mission of implementing the Agreements and devising ways and means of co-operation in their respective or assigned areas;

4.3 To give directives regarding policy issues referred to it for resolution by said committees or bodies;

4.4 To direct and to supervise the implementation of the provisions contained in the Agreement of Friendship and Co-operation signed between the Heads of state of the two countries;

4.5 To refer matters, on which there may be disagreement to the Heads of State of both countries for final disposition;

4.6 To establish a secretariat, in the Ethiopian prime Minister's Office and the Eritrean Ministry of local Government, entrusted with the task of keeping records of all documents, agreements and correspondence as well as of assisting in making studies and collecting information and data for making decisions and issuing directives to the said committees and other bodies;

4.7 To delegate its powers to the committees or bodies as may be necessary;

4.8 To carry on and promote such other activities as may be necessary for the realization of the objectives of the Agreement on Friendship and Co-operation between the two countries;

4.9 To submit reports on its activities periodically to the Heads of State of both countries; and

4.10 To work out additional terms of reference and working modalities for itself as well as the committees and bodies as the need arises.

Article 5
Joint Committees

There shall be three Joint committees formed to follow-up and co-ordinate the implementation of agreements in the political, economic and social fields:

5.1 The Joint Political committee to be co-chaired by the Ministers of Foreign Affairs of the two Governments and to cover the following fields:

- Foreign Affairs
- Defence
- Internal Affairs
- Information
- Justice

5.2 The Joint Economic Committee to be co-chaired by the Minister of Planning and Economic Development on the Ethiopian side and the Director of Macro Economic Planning and International Cooperation on the Eritrean side and cover the following fields:

- Economic Planning and Development
- Finance
- Transport and Communication
- Trade
- Industry
- Mining, Energy and Water Resources
- Agriculture
- Investment
- Environmental Protection and Natural Resources Development
- Tourism
- etc.

5.3 The joint Social Committee to be co-chaired by the Minister for Social Affairs in the prime Minister's Office on the Ethiopian side and the Minister of Health on the Eritrean side and cover the following fields:

- Health
- Education
- Social Affairs and Labour
- Sports and Culture
- etc.

Article 6

Duties and Responsibilities of the Joint Committees

6.1   The Joint Committees shall be accountable to the High Commission for the performance of their duties in their respective areas;

6.2   The Joint Committees shall submit regular reports on their activities to the High Commission;

6.3   The Joint Committees shall refer all matters of disagreement and issues which require clarification of directives to the High Commission for final disposition;

6.4   The Joint Committees shall, in their task of implementing the provisions contained in the Agreement of friendship and Co-operation between the two countries, preserve and build upon agreements previously concluded and shall also explore other additional areas of co-operation;

6.5   The Joint Committees shall ensure that all agreements made previously as well as new ones on the various areas of co-operation are all documented and that copies of same are submitted to the Secretariats of the High Commission at Addis Ababa and Asmara;

6.6   The Joint Committees shall form counterpart committees and may form sub-committees when deemed necessary.

Article 7

Meetings and Reports

7.1   The High Commission shall have regular meetings every three months and shall present comprehensive reports to the Heads of state of the two countries every six months;

7.2   The Joint Committees shall meet and present reports to the High Commission every six months;

7.3   There shall be a General Joint Ministerial meeting every year.

Article 8

Duty to co-operate

The public authorities of both countries shall have the obligation to co-operate with the High Commission as well as the Committees in the latters' effort to implement agreements and promote friendship and co-operation.

Article 9
Entry into Force

This Agreement shall come into force upon signature and remain in force for an indefinite period of time.

Done at Asmara this 23rd day of September 1993 in two originals in the English language both texts being equally authentic.

For the Government
of the State of Eritrea

For the Transitional Government
of Ethiopia

H.E. Mr Romodan Mohamednur
Minister of Local Government of
the Government of the State of
Eritrea

H.E. Mr. Tamrat Layne
Prime Minister of the
Transitional Government of Ethiopia

Appendix C

ALGIERS AGREEMENT
BETWEEN ETHIOPIA AND ERITREA[1]

The Government of the State of Eritrea and the Government of the Federal Democratic Republic of Ethiopia (the "Parties"),

Reaffirming their acceptance of the Organization of African Unity ("OAU") Framework Agreement and the Modalities for its implementation, which have been endorsed by the 35th ordinary session of the Assembly of Heads of State and Government, held in Algiers, Algeria, from 12 to 14 July 1999,

Recommitting themselves to the Agreement on Cessation of Hostilities, signed in Algiers on 18 June 2000,

Welcoming the commitment of the OAU and the United Nations, through their endorsement of the Framework Agreement and the Agreement on Cessation of Hostilities, to work closely with the international community to mobilize resources for the resettlement of displaced persons, as well as rehabilitation and peace building in both countries, have agreed as follows:

Article 1

1. The Parties shall permanently terminate hostilities between themselves. Each Party shall refrain from the threat or use of force against the other.
2. The Parties shall respect and fully implement the provisions of the Agreement on Cessation of Hostilities.

Article 2

1. In fulfilling their obligations under international humanitarian law, including the 1949 Geneva Conventions relative to the protection of victims of armed conflict ("1949 Geneva Conventions"), and in

---

1   The Algiers Agreement, signed on 12 December 2000, marked the formal end of the 1998-2000 Border War between Ethiopia and Eritrea; it was witnessed by representatives of the United Nations, the European Union, the African Union, and the United States, as well as Algeria.

cooperation with the International Committee of the Red Cross, the Parties shall without delay, release and repatriate all prisoners of war.

2. In fulfilling their obligations under international humanitarian law, including the 1949Geneva Conventions, and in cooperation with the International Committee of the Red Cross, the Parties shall without delay, release and repatriate or return to their last place of residence all other persons detained as a result of the armed conflict.

3. The Parties shall afford humane treatment to each other's nationals and persons of each other's national origin within their respective territories.

Article 3

1. In order to determine the origins of the conflict, an investigation will be carried out on the incidents of 6 May 1998 and on any other incident prior to that date which could have contributed to a misunderstanding between the Parties regarding their common border, including the incidents of July and August 1997.

2. The investigation will be carried out by an independent, impartial body appointed by the Secretary-General of the OAU, in consultation with the Secretary-General of the United Nations and the two Parties.

3. The independent body will endeavor to submit its report to the Secretary-General of the OAU in a timely fashion.

4. The Parties shall cooperate fully with the independent body.

5. The Secretary-General of the OAU will communicate a copy of the report to each of the two Parties, which shall consider it in accordance with the letter and spirit of the Framework Agreement and the Modalities.

Article 4

1. Consistent with the provisions of the Framework Agreement and the Agreement on Cessation of Hostilities, the Parties reaffirm the principle of respect for the borders existing at independence as stated in resolution AHG/Res. 16(1) adopted by the OAU Summit in Cairo in 1964, and, in this regard, that they shall be determined on the basis of pertinent colonial treaties and applicable international law.

2. The Parties agree that a neutral Boundary Commission composed of five members shall be established with mandate to delimit and

demarcate the colonial treaty border based on pertinent colonial treaties (1900, 1902, and 1908) and applicable international law. The Commission shall not have the power to make decisions *ex aequo et bono*.

3. The Commission shall be located at The Hague.

4. Each Party shall, by written notice to the United Nations Secretary-General, appoint two commissions within 45 days from the effective date of this agreement, neither of whom shall be nationals of permanent residents of the Party making the appointment. In the event that a Party fails to name one or both of its party-appointed commissioners within the specified time, the Secretary General of the United Nations shall mane the appointment.

5. The president of the Commission shall be selected by the party-appointed commissioners or, failing their agreement within 30 days of the date of appointment of the latest party-appointed commissioner, by the Secretary-General of the United Nations after consultation with the Parties. The president shall be neither a national nor permanent resident of either Party.

6. In the event of the death or resignation of a commissioner in the course of the proceedings, a substitute commissioner shall be appointed or chosen pursuant to the procedure set forth in this paragraph that was applicable to the appointment or choice of the commissioner being replaced.

7. The UN Cartographer shall serve as Secretary to the Commission and undertake such tasks as assigned to him by the Commission, making use of the technical expertise of the UN Cartographic Unit. The Commission may also engage the services of additional experts as it deems necessary.

8. Within 45 days after the effective date of this Agreement, each Party shall provide to the Secretary its claims and evidence relevant to the mandate of the Commission. These shall be provided to the other Party by the Secretary.

9. After reviewing such evidence and within 45 days of its receipt, the Secretary shall subsequently transmit to the Commission and the Parties any material relevant to the mandate of the Commission as well as his findings identifying those portions of the border as to which there appears to be no dispute between the Parties. The Secretary shall also transmit to the Commission all the evidence presented by the Parties.

10. With regard to those portions of the border about which there appears to be controversy, as well as any portions of the border identified pursuant to paragraph 9 with respect to which

either party believes there to be controversy, the Parties shall present their written and oral submissions and any additional evidence directly to the Commission, in accordance with its procedures.

11. The Commission shall adopt its own rules of procedure based upon the 1992 Permanent Court of Arbitration Option Rules for Arbitrating Disputes Between Two States. Filling deadlines for the Parties' written submissions shall be simultaneous rather than consecutive. All decisions of the Commission shall be made by a majority of the commissioners.

12. The Commission shall commence its work not more than 15 days after it is constituted and shall endeavor to make its decision concerning delimitation of the border within six months of its first meeting. The Commission shall take this objective into consideration when establishing its schedule. At its discretion, the Commission may extend this deadline.

13. Upon reaching a final decision regarding delimitation of the borders, the Commission shall transmit its decision to the Parties and Secretaries General of the OAU and the United Nations for publication, and the Commission shall arrange for expeditious demarcation.

14. The Parties agree to cooperate with the Commission, its experts and other staff in all respects during the process of delimitation and demarcation, including the facilitation of access to territory they control. Each Party shall accord to the Commission and its employees the same privilege and immunities as are accorded to diplomatic agents under the Vienna Convention on Diplomatic Relations.

15. The Parties agree that the delimitation and demarcation determinations of the Commission shall be final and binding. Each Party shall respect the border so determined, as well as the territorial integrity and sovereignty of the other Party.

16. Recognizing that the results of the delimitation and demarcation process are not yet known, the Parties request the United Nations to facilitate resolution of problems which may arise due to the transfer of territorial control, including the consequences for individuals residing in previously disputed territory.

17. The expenses of the Commission shall be borne equally by the two Parties. To defray its expenses, the Commission may accept donations from the United Nations Trust Fund established under paragraph 8 of Security Council Resolution 1177 of 26 June 1998.

Article 5

1. Consistent with the Framework Agreement, in which the Parties commit themselves to addressing the negative socio-economic impact of the crisis on the civilian population, including the impact on those persons who have been deported, a neutral Claims Commission shall be established. The mandate of the Commission is to decide through binding arbitration all claims of loss, damage or injury by one Government against the other, and by nationals (including both natural and juridical persons) of one party against the Government of the other party or entities owned or controlled by the other party that are (a) related to the conflict that was the subject of the Framework Agreement, the Modalities for its Implementation and the Cessation of Hostilities Agreement, and (b) result from violations of international humanitarian law, including the 1949 Geneva Conventions, or other violations of international law. The Commission shall not hear claims arising from the cost of military operations, preparing for military operations, or the use of force, except to the extent that such claims involve violations of international humanitarian law.

2. The Commission shall consist of five arbiters. Each Party shall, by written notice to the United Nations Secretary-General, appoint two members within 45 days from the effective date of this agreement, neither of whom shall be nationals or permanent residents of the party making the appointment. In the event that a party fails to name one or both of its party-appointed arbitrators within the specified time, the Secretary-General of the United Nations shall make the appointment.

3. The president of the Commission shall be selected by the party-appointed arbiters or, failing their agreement within 30 days of the date of appointment of the latest party-appointed arbiter, by the Secretary-General of the United Nations after consultation with the parties. The president shall be neither a national nor permanent resident of either party.

4. In the event of the death or resignation of a member of the Commission in the course of the proceedings, a substitute member shall be appointed or chosen pursuant to the the procedure set forth in this paragraph that was applicable to the appointment or choice of the arbiter being replaced.

5. The Commission shall be located in The Hague. At its discretion it may hold hearings and conduct investigations in the territory of either party, or at such other location as it deems expedient.

6. The Commission shall be empowered to employ such professional, administrative and clerical staff as it deems necessary to accomplish its work, including establishment of a Registry. The Commission may also retain consultants and experts to facilitate the expeditious completion of its work.

7. The Commission shall adopt its own rules of procedure based upon the 1992 Permanent Court of Arbitration Option Rules for Arbitrating Disputed Between Two States. All decisions of the Commission shall be made by a majority of the commissioners.

8. Claims shall be submitted to the Commission by each of the Parties on its own behalf and in behalf of its nationals, including both natural and juridical persons. All claims submitted to the Commission must be filed no later than one year from the effective date of this agreement. Except for claims submitted to another mutually agreed settlement mechanism in accordance with paragraph 17 or filed in another forum prior to the effective date of this agreement, the Commission shall be the sole forum for adjudicating claims described in paragraph 1 or filed under paragraph 9 of this Article, and any such claims which could have been and not submitted by that deadline shall be extinguished, in accordance with international law.

9. In appropriate cases, each Party may file claims on behalf of persons of Eritrean and Ethiopian origin who may not be its nationals. Such claims shall be considered by the Commission on the same basis as claims submitted on behalf of that Party's nationals.

10. In order to facilitate the expeditious resolution of these disputes, the Commission shall be authorized to adopt such methods of efficient case management and mass claims processing as it deems appropriate, such as expedited procedures for processing claims and checking claims on a sample basis for further verification only of circumstances warrant.

11. Upon application of either of the Parties, the Commission may decide to consider specific claims, or categories of claims, on a priority basis.

12. The Commission shall commence its work not more than 15 days after it is constituted and shall endeavor to complete its work within three years of the date when the period for filling claims closes pursuant to paragraph 8.

13. In considering claims, the Commission shall apply relevant rules of international law. The Commission shall not have the power to make decisions *ex aequo et bono*.

14. Interest, costs and fees may be awarded.
15. The expense of the Commission shall be borne equally by the Parties. Each Party shall pay any invoice from the Commission within 30 days of its receipt.
16. The Parties may agree at any time to settle outstanding claims, individually or by categories, through direct negotiation or by reference to another mutually agreed settlement mechanism.
17. Decisions and awards of the Commission shall be final and binding. The Parties agree to honor all decisions and to pay any monetary awards rendered against them promptly.
18. Each Party shall accord to members of the Commission and its employees the privileges and immunities that are accorded to diplomatic agents under the Vienna Convention on Diplomatic Relations.

Article 6

1. This agreement shall enter into force on the date of signature.
2. The Parties authorize the Secretary-General of the OAU to register this agreement with the Secretariat of the United Nations in accordance with article 102(1) of the Charter of the United Nations.

Appendix D

Joint Declaration of Peace and
Friendship between Eritrea and Ethiopia

Conscious that the peoples of Ethiopia and Eritrea share close bonds of geography, history, culture, language and religion as well as fundamental common interests;

Recognizing that over the past decades, they were denied the opportunity to build a bright future for their peoples on the basis of their common heritage;

Determined to close this very costly chapter, which also had a detrimental role in the Horn of Africa, and to make up for lost opportunities and create even bigger golden opportunities for their peoples;

The governments of Ethiopia and Eritrea have reached the following joint agreement which reflects the desires and aspirations of their peoples:

1. The state of war between Ethiopia and Eritrea has come to an end. A new era of peace and friendship has been opened;
2. The two governments will endeavor to forge intimate political, economic, social, cultural and security cooperation that serves and advances the vital interests of their peoples;
3. Transport, trade and communications links between the two countries will resume; diplomatic ties and activities will restart;
4. The decision on the boundary between the two countries will be implemented;
5. Both countries will jointly endeavor to ensure regional peace, development and cooperation.

Both governments express their gratitude to all friends of Eritrea and Ethiopia and call upon them to redouble their solidarity and support.

Done in Asmara, July 9, 2018

For the State of Eritrea

President Isaias Afwerki

For the Federal Democratic
Republic of Ethiopia

Prime Minister Dr. Abiy Ahmed Ali

Appendix E

Agreement on Peace, Friendship and Comprehensive Cooperation between the Federal Democratic Republic of Ethiopia and the State of Eritrea[1]

The Federal Democratic Republic of Ethiopia and the State of Eritrea, hereinafter referred to as the Two Parties;

Considering the close bonds of geography, history, culture and religion between the two countries and their peoples;

Respecting each other's independence, sovereignty and territorial integrity;

Desiring to achieve lasting peace and cement their historical ties to achieve their lofty objectives;

Determined to establish comprehensive cooperation on the basis of complementarity and synergy;

Determined further to contribute actively to regional and global peace and security;

Reaffirming the Joint Declaration on Peace and Friendship that they singed on July 9, 2018 in Asmara;

Reiterating their commitment to the principles and purposes of the Charter of the United Nations;

The Two Parties agree as follows:

Article One

The state of war between the two countries has ended and a new era of peace, friendship and comprehensive cooperation has started.

---

1 The signing of the Jeddah Agrrement, as it is commonly known, was witnessed by Saudi Arabia's King Salman bin Abdelaiz, Crown Prince Mohammed bin Salman, Emirati Foreign Minister Sheikh Abdullah bin Zayed Al Nanyan, and United Nations Secretary-General Antonio Guterres, among other dignitaries. Afterwards the King awarded Eritrean President Isaias and Ethiopian Prime Minister the Order of Abdulaziz Al-Saud Medal, the kingdom's highest civilian honor.

Article Two

The two countries will promote comprehensive cooperation in the political, security, defense, economic, trade, investment, cultural and social fields on the basis of complementarity and synergy.

Article Three

The two countries will develop Joint Investment Projects, including the establishment of Joint Special Economic Zones.

Article Four

The two countries will implement the Eritrea-Ethiopia Boundary Commission decision.

Article Five

The two countries will promote regional and global peace, security and cooperation.

Article Six

The two countries will combat terrorism as well as trafficking in people, arms and drugs in accordance with international covenants and conventions.

Article Seven

The two countries will establish a High-Level Joint Committee, as well as Sub-committees as required, to guide and oversee the implementation of this Agreement.

This Agreement is made at Jeddah, Kingdom of Saudi Arabia on this day of September 16, 2018 in two original copies in Amharic, Tigrinya, Arabic and English languages; in case of discrepancy in interpretation, the English version shall prevail.

For the Federal Democratic
Republic of Ethiopia   For the State of Eritrea

Abiy Ahmed Ali   Isaias Afwerki
Prime Minister   President

Index

Abdel Fattah El-Sisi (President) 194, 212

Abdirahman Duale Beileh 207

Abdul Fattah al-Burhan (General) 194

Abdulazziz Bouteflica (President of Algeria) 95

Abdulmajid Hussein (Dr.) 24ff

Abiy Ahmed (Dr., Prime Minister of the Federal Democratic Republic of Ethiopia) 5-8, 40, 40ff, 41, 47, 78, 79, 96, 99, 99ff, 100, 101, 103, 103ff, 107ff, 109ff, 122, 145, 149, 149ff, 154, 158, 161, 167-169, 171, 173, 175, 177-183, 186-187, 193-194, 196, 199, 200-205, 207,-211, 213, 217, 221, 223, 225, 225ff, 229, 229ff, 231, 231ff, 233-237, 237ff, 240, 241, 241ff, 242, 243ff, 245, 246

Abu Dhabi Fund 168,

Abyei 211

Addis Ababa Agreement (1896) 85

Africa Union Peace and Security Council (AUPSC) 197

African Union 99, 184, 186, 193, 194, 197

Algiers Agreement (2000) 19, 20ff, 96, 99, 100, 101, 102, 103, 104, 105, 106, 115, 130ff, 136, 137, 140, 141, 141ff, 142, 168

Al-Shabaab 177, 182-184, 184ff

Amhara region 6, 235, 235ff, 241-243

AMISOM 185, 185ff, 186, 186ff, 211

Anda'ali training camp (Eritrea) 171

António Guterres (UN Secretary General) 167, 169

Arab and African Coastal States of the Red Sea and the Gulf of Aden (AARSGA) 7

Arabian Sea 191

Asfha Woldemichael (*Bitweded*) 88

Assab 27, 91, 134, 190, 192

Assab/Debay Sima-Burie border 147

Awalom Woldu (Ambassador) 28ff

Bab Al-Mandab 20ff, 42ff, 86, 92, 94, 96-97, 102, 117, 127, 238, 244ff

Badme 41-42, 42ff, 47, 86, 92, 94, 96-97, 102, 117, 12127, 166

Bahrain 171

Berbera 178ff, 188, 188ff, 189-190, 192, 199

Bin Sulayem (DP World CEO) 174

Bossaso 178ff, 189

Brava 178ff

Canada 158ff, 171

China 89, 175, 178, 190, 190ff, 191, 197, 212, 228

China Belt and Road Initiative 175, 191, 197, 228, 228ff

China EXIM Bank 175

Cuba 60, 89

Damerjock port 174

Derg (military government in Ethiopia) 6-7, 17, 39, 51, 56ff, 60ff, 61ff, 86, 89, 90

Djibouti 7, 63, 93, 169-172, 172ff, 173-176, 179, 181, 187-188, 190, 190ff, 193, 196-197, 202, 205, 207, 210, 212-213, 224, 228

Djibouti International Free Trade Zone 171, 175

Doraleh multi-purpose port 174, 193, 228

DP World 174, 188, 189

Duri Mohammed (Dr.) 27ff

Eduardo Anze Matienzo 87

EEBC: Delimitation Decision 116, 118, 124-125, 127-128

EEBC: Demarcation Decision 123

EEBC: Virtual Boundary 124-125

EEBC: Virtual Demarcation 119, 123, 125-126, 128

Egypt 51, 60, 167-168, 171, 191-196, 206, 211-112

Enzo Moaveru Milanesi (Italy's Foreign Minister) 179

EPLF/PFDJ 42, 44, 58ff, 59-62, 60ff, 62ff, 64, 68, 89-93, 104, 238-239, 222-223, 228, 243ff, 244, 246

EPRDF 5, 7, 21, 32, 42-44, 90, 99, 168, 221-222, 222ff, 229ff, 233, 235-238, 236 ff, 240, 242, 243ff

Eritrea-Ethiopia Boundary Commission (EEBC) 20ff, 96, 98-103, 114-119, 117ff, 122-124, 124ff, 125-128, 128ff, 129ff

Eritrea-Ethiopia Claims Commission (EECC) 43, 57-58, 58ff, 59-60, 60ff, 89-90

Eritrean Liberation Front (ELF) 89

Eritrean Liberation Movement (ELM) 60, 88, 89

Eritrean Shipping and Transit Agency Services (ERSTAS) 30

Ethio-Djibouti railway 173-174, 176

Ethiopia-Eritrea Agreement of Friendship and Cooperation (1993) 15, 15ff, 16-18, 21-25, 24ff, 30, 42, 45, 90-93, 143ff, 166ff

Ethiopia-Eritrea Agreement on Peace, Friendship and Comprehensive Cooperation (Jeddah Agreement) 7, 15, 15ff, 100, 106ff, 122-123, 126-127, 135, 169

Ethiopia-Eritrea Free Trade Area (FTA) 24-25, 27-28, 214

Ethiopia-Eritrea Joint Declaration of Peace and Friendship (Asmara Declaration) 100, 102, 136, 145-146, 154, 167, 169, 237ff

Ethiopia-Eritrea Joint High Ministerial Commission 10, 16, 18, 22, 25, 27-29, 166ff

Ethiopia-Eritrea War (1998-2000) 5, 19, 39, 42ff, 47, 67ff, 74, 92, 94-95, 114-115, 165, 180

Ethiopia-Eritrea-Somalia Joint Declaration on Comprehensive Cooperation 169, 178, 172, 179-181

EU 224ff, 226, 226ff, 227ff

Ex aequo et bono 119, 120 122, 122ff

Eyland 188

Fahd bin Turki bin Abdulaziz (Lt. General) 192

Federica Mogherini (High Representative and Vice President of the European Union, 2014-2019) 167

Forces of Freedom and Change (FFC, Sudan) 193

Forum for China-Africa Cooperation (FOCAC) 178

France 86, 190ff, 196-197

Gedo (Somalia) 184

Gedu Andargachew 174

Geneva Convention of 1949 130

Goubet port 174

Grand Ethiopian Renaissance Dam (GERD) 196, 211

Great Britain 51, 86

Gulf of Aden 7, 187, 190-191, 195, 197-199

Gulf of Oman 191

Haile Menkorios 42

Haile Selassie I (Emperor) 39, 50, 53, 57-58, 72-74, 79ff, 86-89

Hailemariam dessalegn (Prime Minister of Ethiopia, 2012-2018) 96, 99, 229ff

Hajj port 192

Hamed Idris Awate 89

Hanish Islands 30

Hargeisa 181-182, 185, 207, 240

Hassan Sheikh Mohamoud 189

Hizbul Islam 177

Hobbyo port 188

Horizon port 174

Horn of Africa 5-7, 13, 34, 63, 101, 146, 166-170, 172-173, 176, 179, 189, 197, 200-203, 207, 209, 212, 215, 227, 230

Ibrahim Sultan 57

IGAD 8, 16, 34, 94-95, 99, 161, 166, 169, 174-175, 177, 184, 186-187, 194, 197-199, 204, 206-207, 209, 211-214, 223, 225, 232

IGAD Task Force on the Red Sea and the Gulf of Aden 198-199

Indian Ocean 178, 182, 189-191, 197-198

International Court of Justice 170, 182

International Court of Justice (ICJ) 170, 182

Iraq 60, 89

Irob border 86

Isaias Afeworki (President of the State of Eritrea) 5-7, 12, 32, 39-42, 44-47, 62-64, 71, 76-78, 80, 91-92, 99-100, 103, 105, 122, 166-167, 169, 171-173, 176-178, 180-181, 186, 192-194, 200-209, 214, 222, 224-225, 225ff, 227, 229, 231ff, 232, 235-236, 239-243, 246

Ismail Omar Guelleh (President of Djibouti) 171-173, 172ff, 173ff, 174, 193, 196, 202

Israel 58, 135, 191, 197

Italian East Africa 51, 52ff, 53, 86

Italian-Africa Forum 179

Italy 50-51, 53ff, 74, 74ff, 85, 87, 117, 179

Izedin Ali 28

John Bolton (US National Security Adviser) 176

Jordan 195

Jubaland 178ff, 181, 184-186, 189, 241ff

Kagnew station 58-59

Kairat Umarov (Ambassador) 169

Kenfe Gebremedhin 23ff

Kenya 7, 46, 73, 149, 157, 168, 175, 179ff, 181-187, 201, 204, 207, 211-214, 225, 242ff

Kingdom of Saudi Arabia 7, 34, 100, 146, 167-168, 171, 188-189, 190ff, 191-193, 195-196, 199, 204, 212, 229-230

Kismayo 178ff, 181ff, 183-185, 184ff, 189, 241ff

Kismayo port 186

Lake Assai 174
LAPSSET Project 187
Leykun Berhanu 27ff

Mahamoud Ali Youssouf 173
Mahboub Maalim (Ambassador, IGAD
    Executive Secretary – 2008-2019)
    166
Margaret Thatcher 62
Massawa 29, 43, 60, 62, 89ff, 91, 134,
    174, 176, 196, 196ff
Medemer 149, 186, 199-201, 200ff, 203,
    211
Meles Zenawi (Prime Minister) 44-45,
    78, 91-92, 96, 103, 242ff
Menelik II (Emperor) 50, 74, 74ff, 85
Mengistu Hailemariam (Leader of
    Ethiopia, 1974-1991) 39, 60, 70
Merka 178
Mesfin Hagos 42
Mike Pompeo (UN Secretary of State)
    167
Mohamed Abdullahi 'Farmaajo' 169,
    171, 177-178, 181, 183, 185-189,
    201-202, 206-207, 225ff 241ff
Mohamed Daglo 'Hemeti' (General)
    194
Mohamed Dirir (Ambassador) 193
Mohamed Siad Doualeh (Ambassador)
    170
Mohammed bin Salman (Crown Prince
    of Saudi Arabia) 167, 191
Mohammed bin Zaid (UAE Crown
    Prince) 194
Mohammed Farah Aidid 93
Monica Juma 182

Moussa Faki Mahamat (AU
    Chairperson) 166
Musa Bihi (President of Somaliland)
    181, 189, 189ff, 207
Mussolini 86

Nairobi Manifesto 158, 158ff, 159
Nakfa 29, 45-46, 62, 92-93
National Bank of Ethiopia 25, 27, 168
Nebil Said Idris 170
Nobel Peace Prize (2019) 6 149ff, 179ff,
    194, 204, 209, 211, 214, 217

OAU 16, 94-96, 115, 120, 209
OAU Framework Agreement 94, 120
OAU: Cairo Declaration (1964) 120
Ogaden 180, 242
Omar El-Bashir (President of Sudan)
    99, 186, 192-194, 202, 211
Omhajer-Humera border 147
ONLF 180, 180ff, 184, 184ff, 241ff,
    242ff
Oromo Democratic Party (ODP) 241
Oromo Peoples' Democratic
    Organization (OPDO) 41
Osman Salih Sabbe 57, 89ff, 100, 166ff,
    172, 181ff, 194

Paul Kagame (President of Rwanda)
    175
Preferential Trade Area (PTA) 16
Puntland 178ff, 185, 189

Qatar 171, 182, 187-188, 191-192,
    194-195, 199, 203-204, 211-212,
    224ff, 225, 228, 230, 232ff, 247

Ras Doumeira, Doumeira Islands 170

Recep Tayyip Erdogan (President of Turkey) 188, 192, 192ff, 193

Red Sea 7, 34, 65, 75, 167, 170, 174, 178, 187-193, 195, 195ff, 196-199, 212, 214-215, 227, 231, 239

Red Sea Forum 195, 199

Riek Machar 213

Ronald Regan 62

Rwanda 94, 157, 175

Salman bin Abdulaziz Al-Saud (King of the Kingdom of Saudi Arabia) 167, 172

Salva Kiir Mayardit (President) 201, 207-208, 213

Sawa camp 238ff, 239

Shamsudin Ahmed (Ambassador) 181

Sheik Idris Mohammed Adem 89

Sheikh Abdullah bin Zayed Al Nahyan 167, 168

Sheikh Ahmed Mohamed 'Madobe' 181, 184-185

Sheikh Mohamed bin Zayed Al Nahyan 167-168, 207

Sheikh Muktar Robow 185

Shoa region 53, 72

Somalia 7, 16, 19ff, 20, 34, 46, 60-61, 86, 93, 99, 168-169, 171-173, 175, 177-181, 181ff, 182-189, 194-195, 198-199, 201-202, 204, 206-207, 210-214, 225, 229, 239, 241, 241ff, 242, 246-247

Somaliland 178, 178ff, 180-182, 181ff, 188-189, 198-199, 207, 222, 239ff, 240ff, 246

South Sudan 7, 91, 157, 169, 174-175, 187, 194, 198ff, 201, 204, 207-208, 210-214, 239

Suakin port 192, 194

Sudan 7, 16, 19ff, 51, 57, 60, 62-63, 65, 86-87, 93, 99ff, 157, 168-169, 171, 174-175, 179ff, 180, 186, 192-195, 198ff, 201-204, 206-207, 211-214, 224, 224ff, 226ff, 234ff, 238-239, 246

Suez Canal 53ff, 190, 195

Syria 60, 89

Tadjourah port 174

Tedla Bairu (*Grazmatch*) 87

Tedros Adhanom (Dr.) 184

Tekeda Alemu (Dr., Ambassador) 170

Tibor P. Nagy (Ambassador) 176

Tigray Regional State 7, 22, 26-27, 40ff, 41

TPLF 5-7, 12, 12ff, 21, 26, 41, 43-45, 47, 59, 71ff, 72, 72ff, 76ff, 77-78, 89-93, 97, 100, 104, 160, 166, 209, 222-223, 223ff, 224, 232-236, 236ff, 237-238, 238ff, 239-240, 240ff, 241, 241ff, 242-243, 243ff, 245-246

Tserona 124

Turkey 167, 186ff, 188, 191-193, 195, 203, 226ff, 230

Uganda 157, 168, 175, 186, 206, 211, 213-214

Uhuru Kenyatta (President of Kenya) 183, 187, 201, 207

UN Commission of Inquiry (COI) on Human Rights in Eritrea 148

UN Eritrea-Somalia Sanctions Committee 169

UN General Assembly 87, 169, 195

UN Security Council 94, 169, 182, 186-187

UNAMID 211

UNISFA 211

United Arab Emirates 7, 34, 41, 167-
    168, 171, 174, 182, 186ff, 187-
    195, 199, 204, 211-212, 224, 228-
    230, 247
United Kingdom 62, 86, 173, 212, 205
United States 7, 48ff, 49, 51, 62, 76,
    175-176, 191-192, 211-212, 223,
    225, 227-228, 230-231, 244
UNMEE 94-95, 116-117, 141
UNMISS 211
US Department of Defense 176
US-Rwanda peace proposal 94
USSR 86
Uti possidetis 115, 120ff, 121

Vienna Convention on Diplomatic
    Relations of 1961 130, 132
Villa Somalia 178

Wallega region 55
Workeneh Gebeyehu (Dr.) 41, 165,
    170ff
Wuchale Treaty (1889) 85

Yemane Gebremeskel 166
Yemen 30, 64, 91, 171, 187, 189, 189ff,
    190-193, 195, 197, 199, 204-206,
    209, 212, 228-230, 238
Yemene Gebreab 100, 166, 173, 181ff,
    194, 206, 209, 222ff
Yoweri Museveni (President) 206

Zalambesa-Adigrat border 88, 124, 147

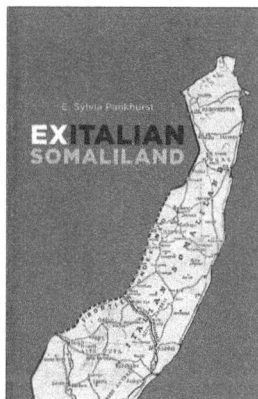

www.ingramcontent.com/pod-product-compliance
Lightning Source LLC
Chambersburg PA
CBHW022349280326
41935CB00007B/128